"GRITTY."
Newsweek

"Roemer brings the reality of organized crime home to us."

Boston Herald

"What was particularly refreshing was the author's ability to jump back and forth between a chronological narrative and discussing specific mobsters in depth without losing the pace of the story."

Chattanooga News-Free Press

"Murder, torture, mobster chases and confrontations— Bill Roemer's book on his life in the FBI has all that, and more."

The Arizona Daily Star

"Distinguishing between 'good' bad guys who could be trusted, and 'bad' bad guys, he shows that some gangland figures virtually became his friends. His intimate knowledge of them enriches the book."

Publishers Weekly

ROEMER

MAN AGAINST THE MOB

William F. Roemer, Jr.

IVY BOOKS • NEW YORK

To Jeannie—the best thing that ever happened to me!

Ivy Books
Published by Ballantine Books
Copyright © 1989 by William F. Roemer, Jr.

Library of Congress Catalog Card Number: 89-45345

ISBN 0-8041-0718-1

This edition published by arrangement with Donald I. Fine, Inc.

Printed in Canada

First Ballantine Books Edition: March 1991

Acknowledgments

I wish to acknowledge many people who have been of tremendous assistance to me in making this work possible. My agent, Jed Mattes; my editor who shaped this up before it was submitted to publishers, Tom Seligson; and the many fine people at Donald I. Fine, Inc., especially Don Fine and David Gibbons.

But without the help of many many colleagues through the years in the FBI, I couldn't have begun. Although I can't begin to name them all, I do want to acknowledge my great partners through the years: in Chicago, Marshall Rutland, Ralph Hill, and John Bassett; Ray Fox in Baltimore; Bob Puckett, Dick Cromwell, Galen Willis, Pete Durland, and Lew Whitworth in New Haven; Stan Staples, Bill Hartnett, and Darwin Thornton in New York; and in Arizona, "Bud" Gaskill, Donn Sickles, Bill Christensen, "Skip" George, Eddy Hall, and Larry Bagley. And certainly the following C-1 Squad and C-10 Squad agents in Chicago: John Roberts, Vince Inserra, Christy Malone, Denny Shanahan, Paul Frankfurt, Gus Kempff, Tom Parrish, Lloyd Nelson, Jimmy Dewhirst, Bob Cook, Elliott Anderson, Hal Johnson, Lenny Wolf, John Oitzinger, Frank Mellott, Jim Abbott, Charley Brown, Bill Meincke, Joe Shea, Bill Bailey, Ray Connelley, Harold Sell, Ros Spencer, Bob Dolan, Pete Wacks, Art Pfizenmayer, Ray Shryock, Max Fritschel, Bill Dougherty, "Sonny" Martin, Adrian Mohr, George Benigni, Burt Jensen, Mike Byrne, Gerry Buten, Curt Fitzgerald, and Bob Long, as well as Dick Held, Bill Beane, Marlin Johnson, John Otto, Jim Gale, and Buck Revell.

I can't skip paying tribute to my mom and dad; my brothers, Walt, Tom, Joe, Jim, and Chuck; my sister, Mary; my aunt, Sister Cecile Marie, C.S.C., of St. Mary's College, Notre

Dame, Indiana; and last, but far from least, my sons, Bill and Bob.

My acknowledgments would not be complete without a special show of gratitude to Professor G. Robert Blakey of the University of Notre Dame Law School, a role model for all of us in organized crime investigation. Prof. Blakey completed a thorough libel read of my manuscript before it went to press and pronounced it free of anything libelous about any of those described herein. I made every effort in writing these pages to insure that I did not treat anyone herein inappropriately, unfairly, or inaccurately. This was made possible with the most generous assistance of Professor Blakey, who checked the whole book, and of many others who helped me with my fact checking, including some within the mob and several current FBI agents. In neither category can I identify them. But I can identify the following: Bill Ouseley, Joe Yablonsky, Denny Walsh, Sandy Smith, John Bassett, Ray Shryock, Bill Duffy, Jim Mulroy, Dick Ogilvie, Tommy Parker, Art Petacque, Bill Lambie, Jerry Gladden, Jack Danahy, Nick Lori, Warren Salisbury, Tom Carrigan, Jack Barron, Chuck Thomas, Al Zimmerman, Jack Walsh, Burns Toolson, Donn Sickles, Pat Roemer, Jeff Gerth, Barry Goodenow, Bud Hall, Bill Malone, John Drummond, Welton Merry, Phil Manuel, Bob Puckett, Greg Kowalick, Ralph Salerno, Christy Malone, John O'Brien, Virgil Peterson, Walt Sheridan, Luke Michaels, Ron Koziol, Bob Slatzer, Jim Mansfield, Gino Lazzari, Ed Hagerty, Tom Foran, Mike Hawkins, Max Fritschel, Pat Healy, Bill Brashler, Jack Brickhouse and his wife, Pat, Ben Bentley, Bill Hartnett, Judge Abraham Lincoln Marovitz, Bill Fudala, Miles Cooperman, George Benigni and Jackie O'Shea. My heartfelt thanks to all of them.

Contents

Introduction

After serving in the Marine Corps during World War II and obtaining my law degree at Notre Dame in 1950, I joined the FBI as a special agent. I served for some thirty years in that capacity. From 1957 until 1980 I worked on organized crime investigations. When I retired from the FBI in 1980, I opened my own consulting agency in Tucson and have been involved ever since in investigations nationwide on behalf of clients who are having problems with organized crime figures. I have been the prime investigator for the defense team in libel actions brought against newspapers, magazines, and television networks by plaintiffs who are alleged organized crime figures or associates. I am also a special consultant on organized crime for the Chicago Crime Commission.

My career has been noteworthy mainly for the length of time I stayed on the street fighting the mob. I worked on organized crime investigations exclusively in Chicago from 1957 to 1978 and then in Arizona from 1978 to 1980. Denny Walsh, the Pulitzer Prize–winning investigative reporter, formerly with *Life* magazine, now with the *Sacramento Bee*, identified me in 1987 in a sworn statement "as the most decorated FBI agent in the history of that organization." When I called him to ask him for the source of his statement, he told me that although the FBI has never kept official records of commendations, he had contacted many FBI agents and ex-agents and that was the consensus. I have also been called "the nemesis of Chicago organized crime who dogged the footsteps of [leaders of organized crime in Chicago] for years—around the clock in a tireless effort" in a motion filed by Jackie Cerone when he was the boss of the Chicago mob in 1981.

All of this may or may not be true. If so, it was because I

resisted promotions that would take me off the streets and away from my very direct efforts against the insidious threat that organized crime presents to this country. For the work of the FBI is out on the streets of America, not behind a desk in an air-conditioned office high up in some federal building. It is in the streets, where a lawman can touch his adversary and, it's hoped, bring him down. Many law enforcement officers burn out after decades on the street. I never did.

Cerone used the word "nemesis" to describe my relationship to the mob. That really tickled me because he was confirming what had always been my secret fantasy: that I, more than any other lawman, would be the one responsible for thwarting the mob, especially in Chicago. I cast myself more in the mold of a counterintelligence officer who ferrets them out and foils their plans rather than the old Wild West sheriff who guns them down or hangs them up. I have always felt that it is important to arrest and successfully prosecute mob leaders and their associates, but that it is at least as important to neutralize them, to prevent their plans from bearing fruit. Murder and mayhem are part and parcel of the mob. They cannot enforce their edicts, they cannot extort and intimidate ("throw fear" as they call it), they cannot infiltrate legitimate enterprises or command their own empires without resorting to violence. And their illegal activity, per se, is, of course, most objectionable. But it is another area of their activity which has always commanded my special investigative interest. And that is the wealth which they accumulate, in untold billions, to corrupt our public officials, our law enforcement officers, our labor leaders, members of our judiciary, our legitimate businessmen. For it takes graft to establish, maintain and expand their domain. That is what is so insidious to me. As a result, while most of my great colleagues in the FBI spent their time attempting to establish hard evidence designed to send mobsters to prison, I spent most of my time attempting to gather the information necessary through surveillance techniques to determine who they were corrupting. My prime interest is to use this information to neutralize their efforts.

There are four basic methods the FBI uses to gather intelligence on organized crime: developing informants inside the mob; planting microphones inside mob meeting places and wiretapping their phones; physical surveillance; and undercover work. After a slow start as I stumbled and bumbled through a period of trial and error on the streets, I believe I became very accomplished in the first three areas; J. Edgar Hoover never allowed his agents to become involved in "u.c." assignments, and since most of my career was in Mr. Hoover's FBI, I never did. This book will reflect my efforts in the three other methods of investigation and, I believe, will give the reader, for the first time anywhere, a firsthand account by the lawman on the spot of how these operations against the mob are carried out. I'll take the reader behind the scenes from the beginning, in 1957, when Mr. Hoover finally brought the FBI into the fight against the mob. It was a move he had resisted for decades until shortly after the famous "peace conference" attended by some seventy hoodlums in the upstate New York hamlet of Apalachin. In 1957, like other agents in other large cities, I was assigned to the Top Hoodlum Program in Chicago. After a very slow start we finally mastered the game up to the point where today my successors see the light at the end of the tunnel (hoping it is not the proverbial oncoming train!). From the beginning, I remained in the fight on the streets, refusing promotions to a desk longer than anyone else. I am still at it today privately as I crisscross the country doing what I can to see that the mob is kept as much under control as possible. Although it ranges nationwide from the west (Arizona and California) to the east (New York) to the south (Miami), this story is primarily focused in Chicago and Las Vegas, the areas of my special assignments.

I was the first four-time university boxing champ at Notre Dame, I was the first FBI agent to install a microphone in a mob headquarters, I was the first to develop a full-fledged informant inside the Chicago mob and now I have attempted to be the first to tell the inside story of the FBI's massive attempt to fight the mob from the very first day we were finally unchained to battle them. This is it.

THE CHICAGO FAMILY

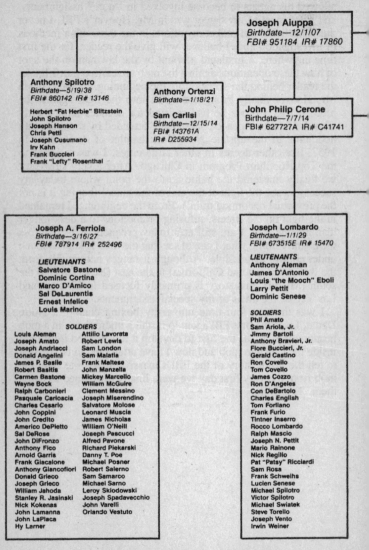

Joseph Aiuppa
Birthdate—12/1/07
FBI# 951184 IR# 17860

Anthony Spilotro
Birthdate—5/19/38
FBI# 860142 IR# 13146

Herbert "Fat Herbie" Blitzstein
John Spilotro
Joseph Hanson
Chris Petti
Joseph Cusumano
Irv Kahn
Frank Buccieri
Frank "Lefty" Rosenthal

Anthony Ortenzi
Birthdate—1/18/21

Sam Carlisi
Birthdate—12/15/14
FBI# 143761A
IR# D255934

John Philip Cerone
Birthdate—7/7/14
FBI# 627727A IR# C41741

Joseph A. Ferriola
Birthdate—3/16/27
FBI# 787914 IR# 252496

LIEUTENANTS
Salvatore Bastone
Dominic Cortina
Marco D'Amico
Sal DeLaurentis
Ernest Infelice
Louis Marino

SOLDIERS

Louis Aleman	Attilio Lavorata
Joseph Amato	Robert Lewis
Joseph Andriacci	Sam London
Donald Angelini	Sam Malatia
James P. Basile	Frank Maltese
Robert Basitis	John Manzella
Carmen Bastone	Mickey Marcello
Wayne Bock	William McGuire
Ralph Carbonieri	Clement Messino
Pasquale Carioscia	Joseph Miserendino
Charles Cesario	Salvatore Molose
John Coppini	Leonard Muscia
John Credito	James Nicholas
Americo DePietto	William O'Neill
Sal DeRose	Joseph Pascucci
John DiFronzo	Alfred Pavone
Anthony Fico	Richard Piekarski
Arnold Garris	Danny T. Poe
Frank Giacalone	Michael Posner
Anthony Giancofiori	Robert Salerno
Donald Grieco	Sam Samarco
Joseph Grieco	Michael Sarno
William Jahoda	Leroy Skiodowski
Stanley R. Jasinski	Joseph Spadavecchio
Nick Kokenas	John Varelli
John Lamanna	Orlando Vestuto
John LaPlaca	
Hy Larner	

Joseph Lombardo
Birthdate—1/1/29
FBI# 673515E IR# 15470

LIEUTENANTS
Anthony Aleman
James D'Antonio
Louis "the Mooch" Eboli
Larry Pettit
Dominic Senese

SOLDIERS
Phil Amato
Sam Ariola, Jr.
Jimmy Bartoli
Anthony Bravieri, Jr.
Flore Buccieri, Jr.
Gerald Castino
Ron Covello
Tom Covello
James Cozzo
Ron D'Angeles
Con DeBartolo
Charles English
Tom Forliano
Frank Furio
Tintner Inserro
Rocco Lombardo
Ralph Mascio
Joseph N. Pettit
Mario Rainone
Nick Regilio
Pat "Patsy" Ricciardi
Sam Rosa
Frank Schweihs
Lucien Senese
Michael Spilotro
Victor Spilotro
Michael Swiatek
Steve Torello
Joseph Vento
Irwin Weiner

Anthony Accardo
Birthdate—4/28/06
FBI# 1410106 IR# D83436

Gus Alex
Birthdate—4/1/16
FBI# 4244200

Dominic Blasi
Birthdate—9/9/11
FBI# 635770 IR# E8187

Willie Messino
Birthdate—1/7/17
FBI# 922367 IR#55433

Angelo LaPietra
Birthdate—10/30/20
FBI# 1777469 IR# D48410

LIEUTENANTS
Frank James Calabrese
Frank Caruso
John Fecarotta
James LaPietra
John Monteleone

SOLDIERS
Joseph Albano
Ernest Amodei
Frank Bruno Barbara
Sam Bills
Anthony Bova
Frank Butera
Frank Michael "Mike" Caruso
Rich Catezone
Charles DiCaro
James DiCaro
Paul DiCaro
Sam Gallo
Morton Geller
Jerome Gralla
Anthony Imperata
Angelo Imperato
Vincent Inserro
Joseph LaMantia
Richard LaMantia
Anthony Maenza
Nick Montos
Dominic Palermo
Aldo J. Piscitelli
James Quarello
Carmen Russo
Terry Scalise
Tom Scalise
Nikolic Slobodan
Michael Talarico

Vincent A. Solano
Birthdate—10/12/19
FBI# 1995437 IR# D4182

LIEUTENANTS
Joseph Arnold
Joseph DiVarco
Michael Glitta

SOLDIERS
Anthony Armieri
Dan Bartoli
Ray Caccamo
Thomas Campione
Jasper Campise
Orlando Catanese
Anthony Cipriano
Anthony Cirignani
Frank DeMonte
Sal Dodero
Sid Finzelbar
Sal Gruttaduaro
Murray Jans
Walter Micus
Joseph Morici
Daniel Morsovillo
Nick Nitti
Frank Orlando
Leonard Patrick
Mike Patrick
Frank Paula
Sam Sarcinelli
Christ Seritella
Morton Shapiro
Calvin Sirkin
George Sommer
Anthony Spadafore
Ray Spencer
Arnold Taradash
Frank Tornabene
Len Yaras

Albert Caesar Tocco
Birthdate—8/9/29
FBI# 296484

LIEUTENANTS
Joseph Barrett, Jr.
Tony "Dago Tony" Berretoni
Richard Guzzino
Chris Messino

SOLDIERS
Douglas Aldridge
Harry Ansel
Daniel Bonnets
Roy Bridges
Clarence Crockett
Frank D'Andrea
Gerry Ferraro
Sheldon Fishman
Joseph Marek
Gino Martin
Seymour Miller
Tony Pelligrino
Joseph Jerome "Jerry" Scalise
Jerry Scarpelli
Eric Schmidt
Al Troiani
William Zanon
Richard Zink

Prepared by
NEIL F. HARTIGAN,
Attorney General,
State of Illinois and
the Chicago Crime Commission

March 4, 1983

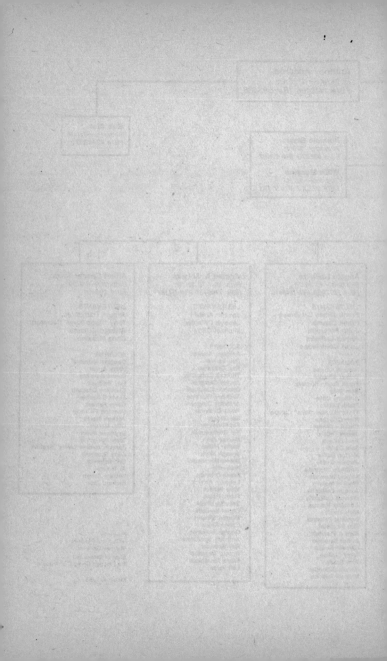

ROEMER:

Man Against the Mob

1 Chicago Ambush in California

The cactus canyons of the Sonoran Desert in Arizona are a far cry from the asphalt jungle of Chicago.

It was a typical sunny, warm September day at our home in the foothills of the Tucson Mountains. I was at work in our citrus and fruit tree grove, tending to a particularly heat-stressed fig tree.

All around me was the plant life of the desert: the stately saguaro, the cholla, the prickly pear, the desert willow, and the ocotillo.

Instead of mob chiefs like the family of Capone and his lineage of predators in Chicago, my thoughts were more of the pillaging coyotes and their haunting nocturnal howls.

My thoughts were more inclined to the tomahawks of Indian chiefs like Geronimo rather than the tommy guns of the Mafia in the Windy City by the Lake, as I gazed at their former hideouts on the mountain ranges surrounding the valley.

But I was about to be jarred out of my serenity and dragged back into the real world. My other world.

Jeannie, my wife, called from the house. "Honey! Telephone!" It turned out to be a call from Chicago.

I immediately recognized the caller as an old friend of some twenty-five years, a guy with both feet in the mob there.

Once a mob fighter, always a mob fighter!

"Bill," my caller said after the usual amenities, "I'm calling because 'the man' wants a 'sit down' with you."

Now, for the past forty years there has been only one "man" in the Chicago family of La Cosa Nostra. No matter who the boss of the day in Chicago may be, Tony Accardo is the "man." Accardo was a bodyguard for Al Capone in the twenties. In fact, he was one of the triggermen at the St. Valentine's Day Massacre in 1929 when Capone's gang wiped out the rival Bugs Moran

1

gang. He became a "capo" under Frank "The Enforcer" Nitti, when Nitti succeeded Capone in the thirties. He became the "underboss" under Paul "The Waiter" Ricca in the forties. He became the absolute boss in his own right in the mid-forties until he voluntarily stepped down in favor of Sam Giancana in 1957. At that time, he became the "consiglieri," the adviser whose sanction is necessary for every major policy decision. He holds that spot to this day. Nobody gets hit by Chicago unless Tony Accardo gives the okay.

So I did not have to ask my caller who he meant by the "man." But I had an immediate problem with meeting Accardo. I have known him pretty well since we first met in 1959. As a private consultant on organized crime, I am dependent on cooperation from many local and federal law enforcement agencies. If it became known that I was meeting with Accardo, this cooperation could abruptly end.

So I demurred. But my intermediary played his trump card. He told me he was instructed to remind me that I "had a marker out."

I needed little reminding. Some twenty years before, I had requested a "sit down" with Accardo in Chicago. At the time Johnny Bassett, my partner, and I had established a witness against Funzi Tieri, a New York capo who was later to become a boss there, and "Milwaukee Phil" Alderisio, then a Chicago capo on the rise, among others. When the mob became aware of the witness's testimony, however, a contract was put out on him. Due to the problems involved, as I will describe later, the government was no longer to use his services. His life suddenly wasn't worth a dime. I felt responsible for the witness, and I went to Accardo, who did me a "large one" by calling off the contract.

What goes around, comes around. It was obvious that I was now expected to reciprocate in some fashion, so I reluctantly agreed to the meeting.

When our mutual friend advised me to go to Palm Springs for the meeting, I protested loudly. Accardo lives there most of the year, in Indian Wells, one of the seven enclaves running down Palm Canyon Drive, Highway 111, which people consider Palm Springs. He is under regular surveillance there, and Jack Warren and Phil Altmeter, the top FBI agents in Palm Springs, are friends who know me well. In fact, the last time I was in Palm

Springs, Jack met me at the airport. I could not risk being spotted meeting with Accardo, and I explained the situation to my friend.

"I can understand why the man wants to meet close by to where he is. Tell him I'll meet him on the west side of the mountain. He can pick the place." When my friend seemed confused, I said, "Just tell him what I said. He'll understand." When conversing with mobsters, one almost always talks in riddles. They are so paranoid about being bugged they talk in circles habitually—even when it makes no difference. Therefore, it was out of habit that I referred to Los Angeles, which is west of the San Jacinto Mountains from Palm Springs, as "the other side of the mountain," and I knew Accardo would understand.

The next day my friend called me back. "He says make it Santa Monica," surprising me by naming the location so openly. "On the Municipal Pier by the Ferris wheel. Make it Thursday. At dawn. Check in at the nearby Miramar Hotel Wednesday and I'll call you at five o'clock."

The time of day didn't surprise me. The last "sit down", as we referred to these meetings, I had with Accardo was at midnight. The location sounded as good as any other at the time.

So on Wednesday, September 23, 1987, I flew to Los Angeles, checked in and then walked the mile or so to the Santa Monica Municipal Pier where I checked out the area by the Ferris wheel.

Immediately I recognized a dead end. To get to the Ferris wheel I'd have to walk out onto the pier for about 150 feet. There would be nothing around but the ocean. For a guy who has learned never to walk into harm's way with no way out, this scenario rang alarms.

Under ordinary circumstances I would relish a meeting with Accardo. In my opinion, he is the most important mobster in America today. He's been a prominent member of the Chicago mob for about sixty years. And he's always been dangerous. His nickname, "Joe Batters," was given him by Capone after he killed a rival of Capone's with a baseball bat. While I was with the FBI he had to put up with me. The mob must reconcile itself with law enforcement. After all, it's not going to go away. But when I retired from the FBI in 1980, I was no longer an official burr under his saddle but more a private nuisance. No more badge, no more gun, no more eight thousand fellow FBI agents backing me up.

In 1983, in my capacity as consultant to the Chicago Crime Commission, I testified before the U.S. Senate Permanent Subcommittee on Investigations. I outlined the history of the mob in Chicago, starting with Diamond Jim Colosimo in World War I, through Capone to the present. I helped prepare a chart with current names and photos of the Chicago outfit, and I put "Joe Batters" Accardo right at the top. As a result of my testimony, Accardo was subpoenaed to appear before the committee. When he refused to answer questions by repeatedly "taking the Fifth Amendment," the committee appealed and eventually won a ruling forcing him to answer. He then perjured himself by denying even his membership in the mob, thereby opening himself up to indictment and possible imprisonment. Though he eventually beat the rap, it was a bad scare for him, which he obviously blamed on me. There were plenty of other reasons for me to suspect that Joe was unhappy with my activities since leaving the Bureau. Just for openers would be the seven libel cases involving him and his associates that I have helped win since becoming "just plain Bill."

I was curious to hear what Accardo wanted to meet with me about, but I was not about to walk blindly into a trap.

So I scouted the immediate area. Joe wanted to meet in Santa Monica and that made sense. He was eighty-one then and not in the best of health, so he wanted to stay close to home. As I walked back to the Miramar I found I was in Palisades Park, high above the Pacific Coast Highway. I passed a statue of Saint Monica, the town's namesake. I noted that the ocean side of the statue is secluded, and a meeting could be held there with some degree of privacy.

I also noted that the area in front of the statue is pretty wide open, being at the corner of Wilshire Boulevard and Ocean Avenue, both large thoroughfares. I decided that if Accardo would agree to meet there, we could have a walking "sit down" just as we had twenty years before in Chicago.

I devised a scheme. When our friend called me that afternoon at the Miramar, our conversation went something like this:

"Are you all set?" he asked.

"Not really. I'll be in Santa Monica at dawn as you want. But not at that pier."

"Why not?" he asked, perplexed.

"Just say I'm not comfortable there. Look, about a mile north of the pier, along Palisades Park and right on the street, at the corner of Wilshire and Ocean, is a statue. He can't miss it. I'll be there."

"For Christ sake, Bill," my intermediary said, "this is getting all fucked up. First you couldn't come to Palm Springs. Then when he agreed to change that, now you can't come to the pier. This ain't fucking Mickey Mouse you're dealing with, you know. He won't like bein' waltzed around."

"Friend," I said, "this is his idea. I didn't even ask what he wants. I have agreed. But remind him he set the ground rules the last time. Just tell him I'll be at the statue. If he's there, I look forward to seeing him. If he doesn't like it, too bad."

"Bill," our friend said, "this is horse shit!"

"I'll be there at dawn. That's it." And I hung up.

I left a wake-up call for two-thirty at the Miramar. As part of my scheme, I wrinkled up my clothes and neglected to shave.

Long before dawn I walked into the park. I selected what appeared to be the best vantage point between some shrubbery but close enough to the statue and the intersection to see clearly, and I lay down between a couple of the derelicts who were sleeping on the grass.

All was quiet. Just before dawn, there were a couple of joggers. Then a little after five-thirty, two Italian-looking guys walked by. They were in their late thirties, early forties, dressed in sweaters and slacks with caps pulled down low. Were they scouting the area for Accardo? Were they looking to spot me?

I didn't see Joe. He never appeared in the park, nor did he drive by as far as I could tell. I would have noticed any car that drove slowly back and forth.

No sign of Joe. I watched the two walkers. They seemed to have no ordinary mission in the park. They were just looking around. It was a set-up! They gave me the once-over, but I pretended to be asleep, just like the other bums around me. I saw them leave the park, and well into daylight I got up and meandered back to the Miramar, entering through the parking lot rather than the front entrance.

I drove back to LAX, boarded a PSA plane in midafternoon and left the smog of Los Angeles for the bright sunshine of Tucson. Had I been overly cautious? Or had I been right to suspect a trap? If so, was this the mob's last attempt, or would the grizzly old Accardo continue his hunt, never forgiving me for what I had done to him?

Resolved to clear up my anxieties, I called my friend, the intermediary, immediately upon my return to Tucson.

"Buddy, I really got jacked around out there. You owe me an explanation!"

"Bill, I'm in a bad spot," he replied. "I can't tell you what that was about, I'm not even supposed to know. It was just my job to get you out there."

"You mean, to set me up!" I said. "You and I are supposed to be friends, and you put me in a spot like that!"

"Well, if you'll keep it to yourself, I'll tell you what I learned. But you got my ass right in your hands if you don't handle it right, you gotta know that!"

"Friend, you and I have been through these things before," I said. "You know I won't do anything to hurt you. I'll handle it without involving you.[1] But I want to know what that was all about."

"They decided to 'throw some fear' at you, Bill."

I knew immediately what he meant. The mob wasn't upset enough with me to kill me—the potential repercussions would have been counterproductive—they just wanted to intimidate me, do what they call "throw some fear" into me. To throw some fear could mean anything from a broken nose to a bullet in the kneecap but not beyond that.

My intermediary could fill me in no further. He said he was not intended to know even that. He said he had no idea as to the mob's motive.

But I did.

I have lived my whole life as a fighter—from the age of fifteen when I entered my first Golden Gloves boxing tournament as a scrawny welterweight at 147 pounds to my enlistment in the Marine Corps during World War II to my tenure of thirty years in the FBI, most of which was spent battling the Chicago mob.

There was no way that I was going to show some fear now, after all these years. As you will see, it only strengthened my resolve to carry on the battle. Throw some fear at me, huh!

---

[1] My friend has died of natural causes since this call.

2 Before the Bureau

I was born in South Bend, Indiana, in 1926.

Dad was a professor of philosophy at Notre Dame. Mom was a parochial grade-school teacher until her own kids began to arrive. There were seven of us in all.

I grew up in a warm, loving family, well protected from most of the world's vicissitudes. Not that I wasn't aware of them. Inasmuch as South Bend is located just ninety miles from Chicago, we heard our news from the radio stations there. The exploits of the Capone mobsters like Frank Nitti and Murray "The Camel" Humphreys, public enemy number one in 1932, and some of the gangsters like John Dillinger, became well known to us as I was growing up during the Depression.

In the fall of 1943, I enrolled at Notre Dame. Though I set no records as a student, I did excel as a boxer, my favorite sport.

In the spring of 1944, at the age of seventeen, I fought in the famed Bengal Bouts university boxing championships at Notre Dame as a middleweight (165 pounds). In that war year, all my opponents were older Marines who were enrolled in the officer training program at Notre Dame. One by one, I beat them and became the youngest student ever to win the Bengals.

Now, as I approached eighteen, the war beckoned me. After a short stint in the Merchant Marine, I joined the Marine Corps.

As a Marine, I distinguished myself in no way. Except one. I won the light/heavyweight championship at the Marine boot camp in Parris Island, South Carolina.

At Christmastime in 1945, after winning all nine of my bouts at Parris Island, I was shipped to Camp Pendleton in Oceanside, California, between San Diego and Los Angeles.

Actually, I was part of the group of servicemen who would have been cannon fodder if Harry Truman had not decided to drop the atomic bomb on Hiroshima and Nagasaki. As a Marine rifleman, I was surely one of those destined to storm the beaches of Japan. It had been estimated that one million American servicemen might have lost their lives in that invasion. I very well could have been one of them.

It was a lucky break to avoid that, but the luckiest break of my life occurred just before I was shipped to Pendleton. I met Jeanne Uphaus, a beautiful seventeen-year-old blonde from Cincinnati. The thunderbolt struck immediately; it was love at first sight. A love that has grown and grown since.

After a few weeks at Camp Pendleton, I was shipped to northern China, assigned to a rifle company high up in the mountains near the Great Wall. Our job was to guard the railroad tracks that the Chinese Communists were trying to take from Chiang Kai-shek's Nationalists.

I was stationed in China until September 1946. I returned just in time to enroll in the fall semester at Notre Dame. Every third weekend I hitchhiked to Cincinnati to see Jeannie, and once a month or so she made the trip to South Bend. At the end of the summer of 1947 I proposed and she said yes.

We were married on June 12, 1948. Within a month Jeannie was pregnant, and I got a job on the night shift at the Studebaker Corporation in South Bend. I attended law school during the day and worked from four in the afternoon until twelve-thirty in the morning six nights a week and sometimes seven. Studebakers were in great demand in those days!

April 2, 1949, was a big day. Bill III was born in the morning, and that night I became the first fighter ever to win four Bengal Bouts championships. This time it was the heavyweight crown, and I beat Big Gus Cifelli, Notre Dame's starting tackle on the 1949 national champion football team, who went on to a long successful NFL career with the Detroit Lions.

In June 1950, Jeannie was pregnant again, this time with Bob, and she and little Bill looked on as I received my law degree.

What would I do with the degree? I had it all planned. The great legendary Notre Dame football coach Frank Leahy was a great fight fan, and he and I had become close. Leahy obtained coaching jobs at Jesuit High School in Dallas for me and Lancaster Smith, who was a star defensive back under Leahy. Lank was my best friend in law school, and we intended to get our feet on the ground in Dallas, then practice law there. We went to Dallas and on June 20, 1950, Jeannie and I bought a house there. On June 25, the Korean War broke out.

I had already served in one war. I knew I couldn't just sit this out, not while I was still young and the country needed young men to get it through another crisis.

I soon realized there might be another way for me to serve my country. Since my youth, I had always been very much aware of the mob and its menace. I had listened to the Chicago radio stations and read the newspapers about the likes of Capone, Nitti, and Dillinger, and I had often fantasized about being a gangbuster. I imagined the excitement of investigating, chasing, and arresting these public enemies, and the great satisfaction it must be to solve a bank robbery, kidnapping, or other major criminal case.

There was only one way I could serve my country while satisfying this more personal quest: I could become a special agent of the Federal Bureau of Investigation. In those days, the FBI under J. Edgar Hoover was the zenith of law enforcement. Its motto—"Fidelity, Bravery, and Integrity"—just fit my ideal self-image.

The problem was they only accepted the very best; only one in a hundred applicants made it. The requirements were a law degree or a CPA certificate, passage of written and oral examinations, a lengthy interview with a top Bureau official, and clearance through a full-field investigation into an applicant's entire life.

I decided to try it, hoping I had what it took. I returned to South Bend, underwent the testing, and waited for the results.

In late August I received a telegram. I had been accepted. On September 24, 1950, I waved good-bye to Jeannie, who was four months pregnant, my son Bill, my mom and dad, my brothers Tom, Joe, Jim, and Chuck, and my sister, Mary, as I boarded a train to Washington. I was on my way to join the FBI.

3 Early Days in the FBI

On September 25, 1950, I reported to the FBI headquarters in the Justice Department Building at Ninth and Pennsylvania NW in Washington, D.C. I was assigned to New Agents Class #9 consisting of twenty-five new agents, all of whom were law school graduates, CPAs, or former Bureau clerks. After spending the first couple nights at the Harrington Hotel, where most FBI agents have resided at one time or another, I rented a bedroom in a private home in Washington. I was staying there on the day I was issued my .38, the standard FBI weapon. I remember practicing my quick draw all evening long in that room before the mirror.

For the first couple weeks we remained in the classroom. We learned all the rules and regulations of J. Edgar Hoover's FBI, as well as the hundreds of laws that the Bureau enforced. We were tested almost daily.

Next we moved to the FBI Academy in Quantico, Virginia, located on the Marine Corps base. Unless you are a beer drinker, there is not much to do there. There was a small gym in the basement, however, and every evening I would break the tedium and loneliness brought on by separation from Jeannie and Bill by banging the speed bag.

There was so much to learn in training. We were schooled in all the techniques of investigation. We underwent firearms training for hours and hours, mainly with the standard issue .38 police special, either a Colt or a Smith and Wesson, but also with machine guns, rifles, and shotguns. I finished first in my class with the rifle, having been a Marine sharpshooter, but way down with the pistol. Defensive tactics was also high on the list, another area in which I excelled in view of my boxing background.

But there were several skills I was not taught at Quantico,

skills that would be crucial to my occupation thereafter. First of all, we were not taught surveillance in those days. I would have to learn how to tail a suspect out in the field, on my own, by trial and error. And, as you will see, there was a lot of error! Today, I understand, a great deal of time is spent teaching physical surveillance at Quantico, but this was not the case in 1950.

The other skill I was not taught then but which is the subject of long hours of schooling in the current FBI is investigation of organized crime. The reason it was not in the curriculum in 1950 is that the FBI exercised no jurisdiction whatsoever over the affairs of organized crime. The Hobbs Act was on the books then, but Mr. Hoover saw fit to use it only to investigate labor racketeering and then only in very selective situations; later it was to be the cornerstone of early FBI investigations of the mobs. If they were known, the names of the mob kingpins, like Accardo, Frank Costello, Meyer Lansky, and the others were never mentioned. The word Mafia was never mentioned. The words organized crime were never mentioned. There simply was no reason in the FBI in 1950 to discuss such nebulous topics.

Another skill we weren't taught back then that was to become very important to us in the years to come was how to install a microphone. That would come later to those agents qualified to become ''sound men,'' technicians (for those experienced agents who demonstrated the ability for such proclivity). As you will see, although I was to become the foremost planter of such bugs, if it was up to me to design them, or to actually understand the scientific aspect of wiretapping and eavesdropping, it never would have gotten done.

All of the above is not to say that our training was lacking anything essential in terms of how far law enforcement had progressed in 1950. It was not. It was the most thorough regimen any law enforcement officer could be put through. It just did not address some of the problems some of us would encounter in tracking down the mobsters. There was no way to know in 1950 that several years later organized crime investigations would become not only significant to the FBI but, in fact, its number one priority.

On November 11, I reported to my first field office, Baltimore. Jeannie joined me there but only for a few days, because almost as soon as we found an apartment in the Belvedere Avenue section near Towson, I was assigned to investigations on the Eastern Shore in Salisbury, Easton, and other nearby towns.

I almost didn't make it during the first two weeks on the Eastern Shore. First, while working late one night, I sped through a herd of cattle out on the highway. Not only did I kill the prize bull of the Eastern Shore but I totaled the Bureau car. A week later, with a new car, I tried to catch a Korean War deserter working as a crab catcher in low-lying waters of Chesapeake Bay. He fled by car, approached a ditch, and hung a left. I drove right up to that ditch, slammed on my brakes, and discovered what I hadn't been taught at Quantico. Brakes don't hold when they are wet.

In two weeks, I had wrecked two cars and one prize bull. What a start to my Bureau career! It could well have been over even before it started.

But my supervisor Jack Lentz, although a tough guy, had a good heart. He brought me in from the Eastern Shore and assigned me to minor criminal violations in Baltimore. One of my first cases was a doozy. Pennsylvania Avenue in Baltimore is a black neighborhood of nightclubs, rib joints, taverns, and bars. One evening the personnel at a bank on Pennsylvania Avenue went home without closing the vault. Hundreds of thousands of dollars were there for the taking. When the cross-eyed janitor arrived for work that night, what he saw almost uncrossed his eyes! He didn't clean up the bank that night. He cleaned it out!

This janitor was some piece of work. After stuffing thousands of dollars into his pockets, he set out for a popular local night spot where he picked up literally at least fifty prostitutes. His taste in sex was most unusual. He took them into the alley next to the club, where he lay down in the dust. He then had the prostitutes whip down their pants and urinate into his face! All fifty of them.

It was my job to track down each of those whores and convince her that she should return the money. That's because, even though we'd caught the janitor, a bank robbery is not considered solved in the eyes of the Bureau unless all the loot is retrieved. Though I had been in the Marine Corps, been a boxing champion and knocked around a little, nothing had prepared this young man from a deeply religious home, whose father had even studied to be a Jesuit, for this kind of investigation. It proved to be quite an education for a young FBI agent. I'd recommend it to anyone.

After that off-the-wall case, I was fully prepared for what became my one claim to fame during my days in Baltimore. Since I could now find my way down Pennsylvania Avenue, I was assigned to work on a string of bank robberies that had taken place in the neighborhood. Walt Chantry and Oliver Kelley, new agents like myself, but with great experience as former police officers, had also been assigned to the cases. They had some leads suggesting that a notorious local bank robber named Joe Lucky might be the culprit. In a series of raids on homes and bars we found the evidence we needed to arrest and convict Lucky. His luck ran out; we effectively solved more than a dozen bank robberies, quite a feat for young agents like us. Although Chantry and Kelley received the bulk of the credit, some rubbed off on me. Just as I had gained some needed confidence when at fifteen I successfully fought Johnny Rucano, the defending Golden Gloves welterweight champ in South Bend, now as a twenty-four-year-old FBI agent, I came to believe that I could do the job after all.

In early August 1951, I received a new assignment to New Haven. In those days a new agent was expected to serve nine months in one office and then move to a second office where he could be entrusted with bigger and better things. I'm sure the Bureau supervisor in Washington knew that I still had a lot to learn, such as the difference between a cow and a bull or how to drive a car. Nevertheless, after nine months it was time for advancement.

On August 16, 1951, I reported to Galen Willis, the special agent in charge of the New Haven office. He told me I had been assigned as the primary agent working security and loyalty cases at Yale.

"I was hoping to be assigned to criminal cases, Mr. Willis," I said. "That is the kind of work I enjoy the most and the work I thought I did pretty well in Baltimore."

"Yes, your file reflects that. But we have a buildup of cases at Yale involving Communist infiltration of education and also a number of loyalty investigations. Also, you come from a college family. You should be able to fit right into the ambience at Yale."

Though I tried to plead my case, I could see that my assign-

ment was cast in stone. It was 1951 and Senator Joe McCarthy
of Wisconsin was just about to begin the "McCarthy Era" with
his congressional investigations of the Communist party–USA.
Whittaker Chambers and Elizabeth Bentley had testified about
Communist infiltration of our government; Alger Hiss had been
convicted. The Communist party–USA was at the height of its
influence in the United States. The Smith Act of 1940, making
it a crime to advocate the violent overthrow of the United States
Government, was being implemented to ferret out Communists
all over the country. William F. Buckley, Jr., had written his
book, *God and Man at Yale*, and alluded to Communist influence at Yale. It was obvious, therefore, that I had joined the
Bureau at precisely the wrong time if I was hoping to be a
gangbuster.

I went about my work at Yale. Most of it consisted of loyalty
investigations of applicants for promotions within the federal
government. Since there were many Yale professors and graduates among these applicants and the investigations all had short
deadlines, I had to keep my nose to the grindstone.

Jeannie and I found a very nice apartment in East Haven, but
were to remain in New Haven for a very short time. After I was
elected president of the FBI Recreation Association, a social
committee for agents and their families, I began to have differ-
ences of opinion with the new special agent in charge (SAC),
Joe Casper. First it was because I went to bat for some agents
he discovered having a cup of coffee during working hours. Then
Jeannie's parents gave me a yellow shirt. Wearing a yellow shirt
on duty in Mr. Hoover's FBI was considered a serious breach
of discipline. When I argued with Casper's order to take it off,
he and I had reached the end of the line. I was soon transferred
to New York.

Compounding my problems in the early stages of my new assignments, I had trouble even finding the office in New York. I
was told it was at 290 Broadway, that when I got off the New
Haven Railroad at Grand Central Station I should take the subway to Chambers Street and then walk the three or four blocks
to 290 Broadway. But when I got off the subway, I found I was
on West Broadway. Not knowing that in lower Manhattan there
is a street called Broadway and an entirely different street called
West Broadway, I walked up and down West Broadway for a

long time trying to find 290 Broadway. I finally called the FBI office and explained my dilemma. As the switchboard operator gave me directions I could almost hear her thinking: "Boy, what rubes they send us as new agents!"

In the New York office (NYO), I was immediately assigned to the Major Case Security Squad, Section 7, which was charged with investigation of the Communist party–USA and its top functionaries. Although I had again requested assignment to criminal matters, my top priority by far, it was actually a pretty choice assignment. It was better than Section 12, which was charged with investigating ordinary members of the CP–USA, where most new agents were assigned. And much better than an assignment to the Applicant Squad, which investigated the backgrounds of applicants for government jobs, a routine and unexciting job. A New York assignment in the FBI in 1952 represented a real financial strain. In order to afford the high cost of living in the Big Apple, a young agent on a salary of roughly $5,500 found that he had to house his family, if he had one, way out in New Jersey or on Long Island, a commute of at least an hour and a half each way. Jeannie and I found a nice two-bedroom expandable home in Levittown, way out on the Island, for $75 a month. Bill and Bob would have fresh air, sunshine, and a nice big yard to play in. I rode in a car pool. My good friend and fellow agent, Stan Staples, drove when it was my turn since Jeannie and I had no car at that point, our fourth and fifth years of marriage. We drove into Brooklyn, caught the subway there to my old nemesis, Chambers Street, and then walked from there. I was up before five and home after seven.

Today things are different for NYO agents. When an agent is assigned to New York he immediately receives a $25,000 bonus, and a 25 percent pay differential, with the promise that after five years every attempt will be made to assign him to his office of preference. Now agents can afford to live close in.

One of the high points of my tenure in New York was the capture of Sid Taylor. Taylor was the head of the Communist party of Connecticut, so it was a continuation of my work in New Haven. I had written the five-hundred-page prosecutive summary of his activity on behalf of the party while in New Haven that led to his indictment for violation of the Smith Act. But he fled before we could arrest him in New Haven.

When I transferred to New York we found him in the Pelham Parkway section of the Bronx. I participated in his arrest.

The other high point in my New York years was my involvement in capturing the members of the Nationalist party of Puerto Rico, the NPPR. On March 1, 1954, they shot five congressmen from the gallery of the House of Representatives. They were all captured in Washington but interrogations determined that they were part of a group that conspired to assassinate President Truman at Blair House in Washington in 1950 and were plotting to kill President Eisenhower and other top officials. Their fellow conspirators were located in Spanish Harlem. I was relieved of all other duties and assigned to a special investigation (referred to as a "special"), a handpicked group of agents assigned for a limited period of time to a particularly sensitive or urgent case, this time the capture of the NPPR conspirators. It took us almost six weeks, seven days a week, working in Spanish Harlem, not a particularly hospitable place for law enforcement agents, but I never had to use my gun or blackjack and we got them in the end.

But my specialty was Communist party infiltration of education, and it was this specialty that eventually led to my transfer from New York. These days I love it when business takes me there, but only knowing I don't have to commute three hours each day. Now I stay at the Plaza, the Pierre, or the Waldorf, all on an expense account, while earning much more than even the present day New York FBI agent. But that was hardly the case in 1954.

Because of my specialty, I was offered a job by the New York City Board of Education at twice my Bureau salary. I turned it down and so informed J. Edgar Hoover. I still have a copy of the letter he wrote in response. It reads: "I have received your letter of February 11, 1954, advising me of your refusal of another position, and I wanted to thank you in this manner for your outstanding loyalty to the Bureau. The fact that you received such an offer reflects that you have represented the Bureau in a most favorable manner in your contacts with outside agencies and that your competence and skill has been impressive. The splendid attitude you have manifested is truly gratifying to me and merits special recognition."

When the special agent in charge called me in to hand me that letter, he told me: "I have never seen a letter so laudatory from

Mr. Hoover except for truly outstanding performance. You'll probably be back in the Seat of Government [SOG] as a supervisor in six months.''

But this is exactly what I didn't want. I wanted out of the NYO, but I wanted very much to get to Chicago and go head-to-head with gangsters like Dillinger. I never wanted to put my feet up on a desk and shuffle papers, living vicariously on the work of the street agent, the brick agent, the action agent, who is the backbone of the FBI—not then, not ever.

When I told the SAC, Jim Kelly, that my career goals did not include supervisory duties, he told me that if I truly wanted continuous and perpetual street action, I should write a ''hardship letter,'' requesting a transfer to Chicago. When I told him I didn't have a ''hardship,'' he asked me about my mother's health in her advancing age. We then agreed I had a hardship.

It didn't happen immediately but on my second try. I got my hardship transfer to my office of preference: Chicago. I was finally on my way to fight the Dillingers, the Capones, the Nittis—those bad guys who I fantasized about when I was feeling particularly tough growing up in nearby South Bend, Indiana. Now maybe I could jump into the action I truly craved.

But when I arrived in Chicago I was assigned to the Communist Underground Squad, S-1. In those days, the late summer of 1954, the CP-USA sent particularly dangerous members to ''colonize,'' to go underground. A special ''hard case'' member in New York, for instance, would be assigned to change his identity and move to another city, say Chicago, to lay low for years in a particularly strategic industry or agency. It was the job of S-1 to locate those colonizers and keep them under surveillance. They were committing no crime but they had to be watched. We had to monitor their activities to determine who their associates were and make sure they were available in case of a national emergency when they would be rounded up.

This was obviously not the assignment I asked for. I told the SAC, Guy Bannister, ''Mr. Bannister, I've fought the commy battle for four years now, and I really hoped you would assign me to C-1.'' In 1954, Criminal Squad Number One in Chicago was arguably the top squad in the whole FBI. All of the major criminal cases were assigned to C-1, and its agents were the most experienced, the best the FBI had. The C-1 was responsible for investigating bank robberies, kidnappings, extortions,

fugitives, and other major federal crimes. It had none of the
lesser investigations, the car thefts and accounting and fraud
cases.

"Bill, I think you know," Bannister said, "you're not going
to get C-1." He explained that it took years to work your way
onto that squad. Only our "cigar smokers" (the top veterans)
got assigned there. The supervisor, Ross Spencer, was perhaps
the most respected in the whole FBI. I had established myself
as a fine Communist investigator, and I was going to the most
desirable security squad in the Bureau. I was supposed to consider myself lucky.

The work proved to be enjoyable if not fascinating. I received
my first "incentive award" for my work on S-1. There are several primary ways the Bureau recognizes superior performance.
The lowest is a letter of commendation from an immediate superior or SAC in the office where the recipient is assigned. Next
is a letter of commendation from the director or from the attorney general. A step above that is the incentive award, a one-
time cash award. One step further is a quality raise, a cash award
that repeats itself annually for as long as the agent remains in
the Bureau; ordinarily an agent can qualify for just one quality
raise in his career. The next step up is advancement. Obviously,
promotions are awarded only to those agents who prove worthy.
As a practical matter, however, advancement is not as difficult
as might be expected for the reason that many agents, like myself, join the Bureau to enjoy the excitement of working on the
street and don't want to be promoted and put behind a desk.

I quote from my first award for my work on S-1: "I am writing
to advise you that a cash award has been approved for you in
view of your splendid participation in the development of a number of highly ₃onfidential sources of information pertaining to
the nation's security. I consider the high degree of investigative
skill and discretion manifested by you to be in accordance with
the finest standards of the Bureau. I want you to know of my
appreciation and commendation for your exemplary efforts." It
was signed by J. Edgar Hoover. (I had conducted a number of
"black bag jobs," surreptitiously entering the homes and offices
of important members of the Communist party–USA.)

I received scores of commendations and cash awards, even a
quality raise (the first one in the Chicago Division), but I will
always treasure that first one. Awards were especially meaning-

ful during the directorship of Mr. Hoover because they were so scarce. He was not an easy man to please.

On the other hand, as hard as awards and commendations were to win under Mr. Hoover, the other side of the coin, the letter of censure, was easy. It was an axiom in the Hoover FBI that no agent worth his salt failed to receive several letters of censure during a career. If you hit the street and worked at the job, you made mistakes and you got letters of censure from Mr. Hoover. I am almost ashamed to say, since under those conditions it was almost a badge of honor, that I never received a letter of censure during my thirty years as an FBI agent.

During my tenure on S-1, I was assigned to one "special," a short-lived but intense investigation noted for an infusion of many agents that concentrated on a particular crime or sensitive matter. It was the case we code-named "GREENAP." A young boy named Bobby Greenlease had been kidnapped in the early 1950s in St. Louis. Ransom money was paid, and in about 1957 it began showing up in Chicago. Fred Evans, the financial wizard of the Chicago mob, although we literally knew nothing about him in 1957, deposited some in a bank. I recall we had evidence of some Teamsters Union involvement. I was designated as the agent from S-1 who would serve on the "GREENAP Special." It was some of the most enjoyable work I had done in the Bureau to that point. I was doing what I truly desired, working on a real live criminal investigation of major importance. Not only that, I was partnered with Curt Hester, a boyhood hero of mine when he was captain of the Notre Dame track team in the early forties. We turned over a lot of rocks in Chicago, although we didn't uncover the kidnappers. But I had come to the attention of Ross Spencer, the great boss of the great C-1.

When the special was completed, I returned to S-1. But events were coming together in my old stomping ground, New York, that would change my life.

While I was attempting to chase down Communist colonizers in Chicago, Albert Anastasia, the New York boss of a family of La Cosa Nostra, was having his problems.

On October 25, 1957, "Double A," as he was called, left the office he maintained on 57th Street off Seventh Avenue and walked with his bodyguard to the barber shop of the Park Sheraton Hotel on the corner of Seventh Avenue and 55th Street. It was his daily ritual, and two gunmen were ready to spring an ambush. Anastasia settled into the chair, his favorite barber laid a hot towel over his face in preparation for his morning shave, and the gunmen burst in and pumped Albert full of lead.

They then dropped their guns, headed out through the lobby to the 55th Street entrance of the hotel, ran down the subway steps on 55th Street and were not seen again.

I have since surveyed the whole scene, from the barber shop to the subway. And it seems to me they could have run north to 57th Street and emerged from the subway at Carnegie Hall, hastened north two more blocks to Central Park and disappeared into the trees . . . who knows? They were never identified or apprehended, although there are several theories as to who they were.

None of this grabbed my attention back in Chicago. I may have read about the killing in the paper, but I quickly forgot about it. I never suspected it would affect my entire life.

4 The Top Hoodlum Program

The killing of Albert Anastasia in New York may have escaped my notice at the time, but it caused repercussions that would keenly embarrass J. Edgar Hoover and the FBI.

I had decided to leave the Bureau. Although I liked the other people I worked with, I just couldn't be satisfied with the work. In 1956, Nikita Khrushchev had denounced Stalin and Stalinism, causing an uproar in the Communist party that led to hundreds of defections. And the Soviets put down the uprising in Hungary, causing more sheep to leave the fold. No longer did I perceive the CP-USA as an imminent threat to the security of our country; whereas before I thought I had been serving a worthy purpose, I now failed to see the challenge.

My brother, Tom, was practicing law in South Bend. My brother, Chuck, would be graduating from the Notre Dame Law School in June of 1958. They decided they wanted to practice together and that I would be welcome to join their firm, making it Roemer, Roemer, and Roemer. I would just have to pass the Indiana Bar examination, which I never took when I was in such a hurry to join the FBI. It wouldn't be easy eight years after graduating law school, but I decided to give it a try and I told my brothers I planned to join them.

I would study law four hours each weeknight and eight hours each Saturday and Sunday, starting during my annual leave at Christmas 1957 and until the exam was given in July 1958.

But circumstances conspired against my plan. The Anastasia gangland slaying caused a ripple effect. Ripple effect, hell, it was more like a tidal wave.

It seems the mob chiefs around the country were concerned about internecine warfare that seemed to be raging, as evidenced by the murder of Anastasia. They decided to hold a sit down to prevent its spread. The site they chose was Joe Barbara's estate in Apalachin, a small village in upstate New York.

Some seventy top mob leaders from across the country met at Barbara's place on November 14, 1957. Up to the estate rode Sergeant Edgar Croswell, of the New York State Police, and several of his troopers. Croswell's territory encompassed Barbara's estate and he had seen suspicious characters there in the past, leading him to believe that it might be the scene of regular gatherings. On November 13, he observed a number of cars in the immediate vicinity and his interest was piqued. On November 14, when a great crowd descended on the small community and then headed for Barbara's, Croswell gathered a small detail of his men and swooped down. They rounded up many of the conferees, many others escaped by fleeing through the back woods. Those they were able to detain were identified from their driver's licenses.

When the story broke in the papers that this meeting had turned into a roundup, Edgar Croswell suddenly became the number one Edgar in the annals of law enforcement, whereas the other prominent law enforcement official named Edgar had never joined the fight against the mob. In fact, the other Edgar (Hoover), espoused the theory that there was no such thing as a national crime organization and specifically no such thing as the Mafia!

The press came knocking at Mr. Hoover's door. ''Who are these guys? How are they affiliated with each other? What is the nature of their business? Why were they meeting? Does this prove there is in fact such a thing as the Mafia?'' Mr. Hoover could answer none of these questions. Another Edgar had stolen the limelight, another Edgar knew more about organized crime than he did, and if you know anything about J. Edgar Hoover, you know that he was furious. No upstart upstate New York cop could upstage him.

Mr. Hoover had no knowledge of organized crime in the United States because except for a "special" such as CAPGA (code name for "reactivation of the Capone gang") in Chicago, which lasted just a few months in 1946, the Bureau had never investigated organized crime. Up until the Apalachin meeting, we only investigated such things as bank robberies, interstate theft, car theft, kidnapping, or military desertion. Since no serious member of the mob would do such things, we had never locked horns with them.

But, on November 27, 1957, a furious Hoover declared war on the mob. If the mob was the heavyweight champ of law violators and the FBI the heavyweight champ of law enforcement, then it was, at long last, time for a title fight. Hoover sent out a tough, no-holds-barred edict in a letter to all field offices entitled "The Top Hoodlum Program: Anti-Racketeering." Until then, he had not found a statute on the federal books on which to peg an intelligence gathering mission against the mob. Now, anticipating a congressional investigation into the meaning of Apalachin for which he would have to save face by providing some answers or forever be known as "Edgar Number Two" in the fight against organized crime, Mr. Hoover found the Hobbs Act. The Hobbs Act, which was passed in the early forties, made racketeering a federal crime. It had been applied mainly to labor racketeering, almost never to organized crime, but that was about to change.

November 27, 1957, found me, as I say, with little to excite me in the way of my profession. Bill and Bob were eight and six, respectively. Jeannie was involved as a volunteer at St. Jude the Apostle School, which the boys attended close by our home in suburban South Holland. We had finally scraped together enough for a down payment, $900, on a $16,950 house. Jeannie was also a Cub Scout den mother, and I was coaching a Little League team. We had good neighbors, were active in the parish, and life was good at home. Very good. But I wasn't finding much of a challenge at work.

Shortly after Thanksgiving in 1957, I was called into the S-1 supervisor's office. He told me that the Bureau would begin investigating organized crime per se for the very first time and asked me, in view of my experience on the GREENAP special, whether I would be interested in volunteering for this new program. He warned me that it would be the focus of J. Edgar Hoover's scrutiny and that there would be extreme pressure to produce results.

This posed a dilemma for me. By now I was pretty well committed to join my brothers' law firm. But the Top Hoodlum Program, being a major criminal investigation, would be handled by C-1, the premier squad in the Bureau, the squad I had wanted to join so badly ever since I arrived in Chicago. Here was a chance to do what I had always wanted to do, jump in the arena against the heirs of Capone. I volunteered and was told to report to the famed Ross Spencer, chief of C-1. It was obvious when I walked into the C-1 squad area that Spencer had little idea who I was, which of course was not surprising. He looked me over and said, "Kid [I was thirty-one at the time], we got a new thing here. We don't know what it is going to entail. But we do know that Mr. Hoover is going to put all the pressure on to make sure we do a job. I'm told that he expects New York and Chicago to carry the ball on this program. When he says he is going to give it his utmost personal attention, you can believe that. You guys are gonna be under the gun. He'll put the whip to the Bureau supervisors, they'll put the whip to me, and I'll put the whip to you. There will be nothing hotter in the Bureau, at least until we make some sense of this and accomplish something; nothing will hit you harder if you don't produce. Now that you understand that, do you still want to be here? If not, I'll get somebody else."

"I want it," I told him. I was impressed with this guy. He was not big or strong, but he looked you in the eye. Aware of his achievement over the years, I decided right then and there that working for him was right up my alley. Now, maybe, I could take some real pride in my work. Now, from the perspective of my boyhood fantasies, I would be a real G-man! I would carry my gun. Maybe I wouldn't smoke cigars like many of the old-

timers, but if I swaggered a little, what the hell, I was on C-1—
The hottest squad in the Bureau and it had just gotten hotter!

There were ten agents assigned to the fledgling program, to
be assigned one target each. The target, we hoped, would be a
leader of what they called, in Chicago, the outfit. Call it anything
you want—the outfit, the mob, the Mafia, the syndicate, organized crime, the wise guys, or as the hoods themselves designated it, "La Cosa Nostra," (Italian for "our thing")—it was
all the same thing.

I say we hoped the target would be a mob leader because we
had no way of knowing who the leaders were. In fact, no one
did. The Chicago Police Department had a unit they called
"Scotland Yard" in the early fifties. But when Mayor Richard J.
Daley discovered they were bugging a bookmaker in the Morrison Hotel, the headquarters of the Cook County Democratic
Organization, which he chaired, that was a little too close to
home, and he had "Scotland Yard" disbanded.

Obviously, the FBI's knowledge of the Chicago mob was
sketchy to say the least. We were plowing into unchartered waters without even a compass. We had so little for background to
guide us. About all we knew about the mob was what we had
seen in the old Edward G. Robinson and James Cagney movies.
Over the years we filled in the gaps, and I was able to offer a
pretty good summary of the history of organized crime, particularly in Chicago prior to the beginning of the Top Hoodlum
Program (THP) in 1957, in my testimony before the U.S. Senate
Permanent Subcommittee on Investigations on March 4, 1983
as a special consultant on organized crime for the Chicago Crime
Commission. What follows is a summary of that testimony,
which should help to illuminate many of the characters and actions in this book.

The origin of what has become known as organized crime can
be traced to Chicago during World War I when Jim Colosimo,
in order to eliminate competition for his night spots and houses
of prostitution, put together a very loose, poorly disciplined
group of thugs and thieves of Italian and Sicilian extraction.

There was little formal organization until Johnny Torrio, who
joined Colosimo in 1910 and who made some efforts to organize
along the lines of the Sicilian organization known as the Mafia,
to which many of his underlings belonged, brought in a young
New Yorker named Al "Scarface" Capone. Capone had done

some "heavy work" for the mob in New York and had a reputation there for being a resourceful, aggressive young gunman with a future.

Torrio had come to the conclusion that Colosimo did not realize the potential of the organization and was an overly cautious leader whose lack of aggressiveness was wasting the opportunity that Torrio and the others had in Chicago. He, therefore, commissioned Capone to execute Colosimo, which Capone did with quick dispatch in 1920.

Torrio then succeeded to the leadership of the motley crew left him by Colosimo and, with the aid of Capone, began to pursue two basic strategies. First, he began to enforce a tight discipline, and secondly, he enlarged the membership. Sometimes, the distinctions between actual members of the Torrio mob and those who were on the fringes were so blurred that it made no difference.

With the advent of prohibition, Torrio and Capone, with the counsel of their old associates in New York, were made aware of the enormous potential for gain from bootlegging and speak-easies.

At this point organized crime in Chicago became big business, as it did all over the country. The membership was greatly enlarged and although, strictly speaking, Italian or Sicilian descent was a requirement for a "made" member of the group, many individuals who worked on the fringes of the organization and many who belonged to groups who made agreements with the Torrio group to operate in its territory were not of such descent. As a result of this history, many of the people who actually became upper-echelon leaders of organized crime in Chicago were not Italians or Sicilians, a situation that is almost unique to Chicago.

During the early 1920s, Capone got greedy. Mainly for the same reason that Torrio wanted Colosimo out of the way, Capone, seeing even more wealth available, had an attempt made on Torrio's life. Although not successful in killing Torrio, it caused Torrio to decide he had enough, and he turned over the leadership of the mob to Capone as soon as he was able to leave the hospital.

Under Capone, the Chicago mob became perhaps the most disciplined and the most wealthy group of organized criminals in the country. Capone and his successors maintained alliances with groups of organized criminals elsewhere. It should be understood up front, however, that there is no national organization where a leader, say in New York, can issue an order to the leader of the Chicago group as to how he should run his outfit. There is a grouping of the heads of "the families" in the major sections of the country, who have formed what in effect is a "board of directors" of organized crime that they call "the Commission." Capone, as top boss in Chicago, represented Chicago. The leaders of the five New York City families, the Buffalo family, the New England family, the Pittsburgh and Philadelphia families, the Detroit and the Cleveland families, have traditionally had membership on the Commission. Membership has varied from nine to twelve throughout the years, and the Commission continues to be a highly structured, tightly disciplined group to date.

Actually, the primary purpose of the Commission is to enforce the boundaries of organized crime. It is the current consensus of knowledgeable sources and informants that the Chicago family of organized crime controls all areas west of Chicago as of 1983. This would include the Kansas City, Milwaukee, St. Louis, Denver, Los Angeles, San Diego, and San Francisco (actually San Jose) areas where organized crime is controlled by established groups inasmuch as these groups are actually subservient to the ultimate authority of the Chicago mob. As a matter of fact, the Chicago family has made a substantial drive in recent years to solidify its hold on the West Coast and the Mountain States. Certain areas such as Las Vegas and Miami are "open territories" where families from all over the country are allowed to make investments. For instance, for years The Stardust in Las Vegas was a Chicago investment while the Sands was a New York operation.

Returning to the Capone era, the membership of organized crime mushroomed during the Prohibition era, and almost the entire membership reaped tremendous profits from the mob's various enterprises.

These enterprises included illegal whiskey and beer, the speakeasies in which it was sold, night spots where prostitution flourished, gambling, "juice" (the extortionate lending of money at usurious rates, which is known as "loan sharking" and "shylocking" elsewhere), and labor racketeering.

At about the same time the Prohibition amendment was repealed, Capone was convicted in federal court in Chicago of income tax evasion. This ended his reign, as it turned out, since he was never to return to Chicago except to be buried there.

Taking over for Capone was his top lieutenant, Frank Nitti. Nitti, known as "The Enforcer," was Capone's muscle man and the obvious choice to succeed him.

Nitti, however, encountered an overwhelming problem immediately.

The proceeds from Prohibition-related activities were staggering. But Prohibition was over. How could organized crime make up the loss? In fact, there was no way it could. Nitti was very fortunate that a man named Jake "Greasy Thumb" Guzik was part of the organization. During the reign of Al Capone, Guzik was the finance chief of the mob. They called him "Greasy Thumb" Guzik because he got his thumbs greasy counting all that green stuff. After Guzik was kidnapped by a rival mob and survived, he hired a bodyguard. Although he was a Greek, Gus Alex filled that position; Alex eventually became Guzik's top lieutenant, then his confidant. Gussie knew where all the bodies were buried in Chicago. Under Nitti, Guzik became a mastermind who showed the mob how to invest the millions garnered from Prohibition and trickling in from gambling. Gambling became the lifeblood of the outfit, but investments in legitimate businesses, primarily through front men, not only multiplied the profits but also gave the mobsters a method by which they could evade the efforts of the government to do with them what it had done with Capone.

Parenthetically, it is of interest to note that Guzik, a Jew, was the forerunner of several high echelon non-Italian criminals. Murray "The Camel" Humphreys succeeded Guzik when Guzik died in the 1950s and promptly enlarged the functions of this faction of organized crime to become "the fixers" who built and maintained contacts with public officials, law enforcement officers, labor leaders, the judiciary, and businessmen who could be influenced or controlled to provide favorable treatment to organized crime. As a matter of fact, to show how this nonethnic feature progressed through the years, when Humphreys, a Welshman, died in November 1965, his functions were taken over by Alex, who in turn, in the mid-1970s, became one of the members of the triumvirate that ruled Chicago organized crime. (Much more on that later . . .)

Aided by the expertise of Guzik, Nitti rebuilt organized crime in Chicago to the point where, although it was not producing the income available during the Capone era, it remained a viable, tightly structured organization able to support its members.

In the early 1940s, Nitti, along with several other top leaders of the mob in Chicago, including Paul Ricca, Louis Campagna, Ralph Pierce and others, was indicted for extortion of the Hollywood movie studios through the use of labor unions controlled by the Chicago mob along the guidelines set up by Guzik, now assisted materially by Humphreys. Shortly following the indictment, Nitti committed suicide in 1943.

Succeeding Nitti was Ricca, also known as Paul "The Waiter" DeLucia. Ricca, a very capable leader, had his own troubles. He was soon to be convicted in the Hollywood Extortion Case. And he had a son who was a drug addict, so he had the chance to observe firsthand what drug addiction can do to society. During his reign, he decreed that no member of Chicago organized crime could have anything to do with narcotics traffic. Actually, his decision was not strictly humanitarian, but it allowed for the fact that drug traffic alienated the contracts set up by the Guzik-Humphreys-Alex faction. The influence of the mob would wane, according to the Ricca theory, if the heinous crime of narcotics was associated with it. According to his reasoning, as long as victimless crimes such as gambling were the mob's sole means of support, their contracts outside the organization could be maintained.

Ricca continued as the boss even while he spent three years or so in federal prison after his conviction: Anthony J. Accardo was his caretaker chieftain. Ricca was paroled in the late 1940s, in a scandal that engulfed the Truman administration, since he was turned loose long before his sentence expired.

Following Ricca as boss, and as the Chicago representative on the Commission, was Accardo, another in the long line of capable leaders. Accardo has been, perhaps, the most capable leader in the history of the Chicago group. With the aid of the Guzik-Humphreys faction, which was able to expand the number of contacts providing favorable treatment to the mob, Accardo had a very successful reign. The membership expanded and income flourished, primarily from the wide-open gambling then allowed by the Guzik-Humphreys contracts in Chicago and its environs.

By 1957, Accardo had had enough and handed over the reins to Sam "Mooney" Giancana (his other more frequently used nickname was "Momo" or "Mo"). Giancana, a tough, swaggering, flamboyant murderer who had long served Accardo, was a natural for the spot.

Which brings us back to a young agent who had just received his plum assignment. I looked around me to see who else was a member of the Top Hoodlum Squad in C-1. I knew none of them, although I had seen them around the office. Five were the younger members of C-1, those agents taken off the other violations the squad was responsible for and put on the Top Hoodlum Program, the THP. The other five guys were agents like myself, volunteers, more or less, who had been taken off other squads, some criminal and some security. From C-1 came Frank Matthys, who I was to find was a Notre Dame man. Ray Stoelting, a former All Big Ten tackle from Purdue. Vince Inserra, serving his second tour of duty in Chicago and a Boston College man, a former Army Air Force officer in World War II. Frank Mellott, who was to leave shortly to become an agent in Rome. Les Esarey, who I had seen around both in the NYO and in Chicago.

From other squads came Ralph Hill, a University of Miami grad who had made a fine reputation for himself on the "pussy posse," the prostitution squad. John Roberts, a fine halfback both at the University of Illinois and at Georgia Tech. Paul Frankfurt, a former second baseman in college and a former pro baseball player.

As our targets we picked Tony Accardo, who we suspected was the boss; Sam Giancana, who turned out to be the boss, having just succeeded Accardo; Murray "The Camel" Humphreys, the master fixer and successor to Guzik, who had died the year before; Ralph Pierce, the boss of the South Side; Gussie Alex; Paul Ricca, aka DeLucia; Rocco Fischetti, the cousin of Capone, who turned out not to be appropriately targeted in this company; Lenny Patrick, the boss of gambling in the Jewish neighborhoods of Lawndale and Rogers Park; Eddy Vogel, the slot machine king, likewise over his head in this company; and Jimmy "Monk" Allegretti, the boss of the Rush Street nightclub area on the near North Side of Chicago, also out of his league here.

My target was Gussie Alex and what a target he proved to be

for most of the next two decades! As it turned out, we soon
dropped Fischetti, Patrick, Vogel, and Allegretti and quickly
added Marshall Caifano and Johnny Roselli, the outfit reps in
Las Vegas and on the West Coast; Felix "Milwaukee Phil"
Alderisio and Chuckie Nicoletti, the mob hit men; and Ross
Prio, the boss of the North Side of Chicago.

Properly identified, they now became the enemy. It was our
job to destroy them.

5 To Grips with Gussie Alex

I started my assignment on the Top Hoodlum Program
by researching our closed files for information on what the Chi-
cago office had done twelve years before with the short-lived
CAPGA investigation. Just the title of that investigation gives a
clue to the mentality of the Bureau up until Apalachin roundup.
"Reactivation?" As if the Capone gang had dried up and blown
away. How little the Bureau knew about Jake Guzik, Frank "The
Enforcer" Nitti, Murray "The Camel" Humphreys, Tony "Joe
Batters" Accardo, Paul "The Waiter" Ricca, Louis "Little New
York" Campagna, Ralph "Bottles" Capone, Ralph Pierce,
Jimmy "The Bomber" Belcastro, Dandy Phil D'Andrea, "Ma-
chine Gun" Jack McGurn, "Two Gun" Louie Alterie, "Tough
Tony" Capezio, "Three Finger" Jack White, and the many
others who had continued the affairs of the Capone mob after
his 1931 conviction for income tax evasion.

I received very little instruction as to any specific goals vis-
à-vis my target, Gussie Alex. Who would give me any? Nobody
in the FBI knew enough to set any goals. This was virgin territory. Ross Spencer gave us all our heads and told us, "Go out
and find out whatever you can. Find out where your target lives,
who he associates with, where he meets them. From there we'll
see what's next." He had assigned Gussie to me because he was
the last target on the list, and I was the last agent to arrive on

C-1. The reason Gussie was picked last was that he was more or less the mystery man of the bunch. Very little was known about him, and, looking back, I wondered why Spencer even picked him at all. As it turned out it was a very wise choice, but that was far from evident on November 27, 1957, when the THP got under way.

While my target seemed to be a mystery, I found the CAPGA files, about forty volumes as I recall, to be highly illuminating. Much of the information was mere gossip, but some of it contained the transcripts of wiretaps on some of the very mobsters we were targeting, including Accardo, Ricca, Humphreys, and even, to my pleasant surprise, Gussie Alex, in his role as the top aide to "Greasy Thumb" Guzik. The best information came from the tap on the phone at the Morrison Hotel barber shop, which had obviously been a prime mob hangout in 1946.

It was extremely helpful for me to learn, for instance, that Gussie Alex had a wife named Margaret Reilly. In 1946 they apparently lived at the Stevens Hotel, which later became the Conrad Hilton and is now the Chicago Hilton and Towers. Actually, Margaret Reilly is a pseudonym I'll use for Gussie's wife, who is a decent person now living away from the shadow of the mob: I also learned that Gussie was code-named "Slim" by his associates. Most of the mobsters use code names so as to make identification difficult for outsiders. For instance, the press always referred to Murray Humphreys as "The Camel," but his mob associates code-named him "Curley" for his fine head of hair in his youth.

I must have spent my first two or three weeks on the squad perusing the CAPGA files. The other guys paired up into twosomes and started beating the bushes. But I couldn't even start, since I knew so little about my target—not even where to look for him.

It so happened that Ed Neafsey, a veteran agent on the Labor and Accounting Squad, C-4, had a wife who was a prominent Chicago fashion model. Ed's wife knew Gus Alex's wife Margaret Reilly, who was herself one of Chicago's top models. She was a very popular girl and was at the height of her profession. Ed and his wife were reluctant to help me too much. It seemed that Margaret had a great reputation among her peers. (A visit from an FBI agent asking questions about her husband's reputed

underworld connections certainly wouldn't help her standing.)
But Ed gave me a tip. "Go see Lulu Levitus, the director of
modeling at Marshall Field's. She can help you out."

So off I went to Marshall Field and Co., the flagship Chicago
department store located in the heart of the Loop.

I found Louise "Lulu" Levitus to be very accommodating as
far as telling me the story of Gussie and Margaret. It seems that
at a very early age Margaret Reilly's mother recognized her
daughter's exceptional beauty. Mrs. Reilly raised her daughter
in a midsize midwestern town in a strict Catholic environment.
Margaret started modeling early on so by her midteens it became apparent she was outgrowing local opportunities.

Upon Margaret's graduation from high school in 1942, her
mother brought her to Chicago and took her to Lulu at Marshall
Field's. When Lulu agreed that she had all the attributes to become a successful model, Mrs. Reilly expressed misgivings
about allowing her seventeen-year-old daughter to live in the
wicked city of Chicago without parental supervision. It was
agreed that Lulu would be Margaret's surrogate mother.

Margaret's career rocketed. She became one of the most
sought-after models in Chicago. In addition, she was a model
young lady.

Unbeknown to Lulu, Margaret was moonlighting at the College Inn, the famous showroom at the Sherman Hotel where the
big bands like Glenn Miller, Benny Goodman, the Dorsey
brothers, Woody Herman, Chicago's own Al Morgan, Sammy
Kaye, Guy Lombardo, and Kay Kaiser held sway.

One evening while Margaret was modeling at the College Inn,
Gussie Alex showed up, taking an evening off from his duties
as the chief bodyguard for "Greasy Thumb" Guzik. The
nineteen-year-old, five-foot-seven, 121-pound copper blonde
beauty, Margaret Reilly, caught Gussie's eye, and he sent one
of his associates to ask her if she would join him after the show.
The other models twittered that Gussie was a "gangster, one
of the Capones!" But this was an added attraction in the eyes of
the young, impressionable Irish girl.

It wasn't long before the two fell deeply in love, Gussie with
the virginal young princess of Chicago models, Margaret with
the handsome, debonair gangster. The fact that he was a rising
young star in the Chicago underworld added a certain cachet.

When Lulu became aware of the liaison, she had it out with

Margaret. It was in direct contradiction to the agreement she had made with Margaret's mother. She felt she had no choice but to fire Margaret. Understandably distraught, Margaret turned to Gussie, who offered her an ace in hole, which was Gussie's blossoming association with a Chicago attorney named Sidney R. Korshak.

In the infamous Hollywood Extortion Case of 1944, wherein several of the top leaders of the Chicago mob, including Paul Ricca, were convicted of extorting all of Hollywood's movie studios, Korshak was identified as being closely associated with the Chicago mob. Willie Bioff, who was blown away as a result of his testimony, testified that Charley "Cherry Nose" Gioe, a top Chicago hoodlum, told him at a meeting at the Bismarck Hotel in Chicago in 1940 that any message that Korshak might ever deliver to Bioff "is a message from us." Years later I heard Murray Humphreys telling Gussie that he had reminded Korshak "who he belongs to," meaning the Chicago mob, when Korshak angered Humphreys by negotiating a contract for his client, Dinah Shore, at a Las Vegas hotel not controlled by Chicago.

It turned out that Sid Korshak's wife, Bernice, was also a highly regarded fashion model. Since Guzik was the liaison between the Chicago underworld and Korshak, Gussie had gotten to know Korshak pretty well. He now turned to him for a favor. It was a simple matter to hook up the veteran model with the rising young star. They became partners and presented fashion shows for the upper crust throughout Chicago and its most fashionable suburbs.

Lulu told me that one of the locations where Margaret and Bernice performed was a well-known restaurant on the near North Side. It was called the Kungsholm, and featured a great Scandinavian smorgasbord.

It was this lead that allowed me to locate Gussie. In early March 1958, I dined at the restaurant and caught Margaret's act. Margaret was everything I had been led to believe. Absolutely gorgeous! I waited for her outside and followed her to the Murray Hill Apartments at 4300 Marine Drive, a very posh apartment building located along the lakefront at Montrose Avenue. I waited outside for several hours. Since she never left, I assumed she lived there.

The next day I approached the building manager, A. C. Jaworek. I didn't even have a photo of Gussie, that's how bereft of clues we were in 1958. But I did have a fairly good description, and Lulu had given me a very nice photo of Margaret. I showed the photo to Mr. Jaworek. "That's Mrs. Reilly," he said. "She lives in 1001 with her husband."

"What's her husband's name?" I inquired.

"Why, Mr. Reilly, of course. Michael Reilly."

It looked like I might be off base. But when I questioned Mr. Jaworek about the physical description of Michael Reilly, I felt sure that Mr. Reilly and Mr. Alex were one and the same.

I should say here that of the four basic techniques for investigating organized crime, there was just one available to me at the time. First, in 1958, Mr. Hoover would not authorize undercover work. Second, I was in no position even to consider a microphone or telephone tap (eavesdropping or wiretapping, respectively) at this point. Third, development of a source or informant, terms that I'll use interchangeably, was just as unlikely for me at this stage. The distant fourth technique, however, a physical surveillance or tail, was within my ability. Although I learned almost nothing about tails at Quantico, I had participated in scores of them while on the Communist party Underground Squad, S-1, and I considered myself a pretty good tail man.

On March 17, 1958, St. Patrick's Day, I decided to determine whether Mr. Reilly and Mr. Alex were, indeed, one and the same. So I got up about five in the morning, drove to the Illinois Central Railroad Station, caught the I.C. into the Loop, walked the seven blocks or so from the I.C. Station at Randolph and Michigan (the same spot where Capone had had Chicago newspaper reporter Jake Lingle murdered), signed in, walked two blocks to the garage where we kept Bureau cars, got into car thirty-nine, a 1956 Ford, which was assigned to me, and drove up to the Murray Hill Apartments. I arrived at about seven-fifteen in the morning and parked on Marine Drive just south of Montrose Avenue.

Now remember that Gus Alex, although he was arrested on several occasions, at least once for suspicion of murder after he shotgunned Vince Bozic, a rival gambler, on Bozic's front steps on August 2, 1947, and was identified by Bozic on his deathbed, had perhaps never before been tailed. I asked Bill Duffy, a veteran of "Scotland Yard," the Chicago PD mob intelligence section in the early fifties, and he said to the best of his recollection they had never followed Gussie.

Gussie left the underground garage entrance on the north side of his building. When he got to the street he sat in his car for at least a minute, looking around the area. He then turned south, away from me. I let him go for a couple of blocks. He was moving very slowly, and although I had no idea he would be at all suspicious there was no reason to speed up to him. He continued south to Irving Park where he turned west. Out of my sight. I slowly drove to Irving Park, arriving perhaps forty-five seconds after he did. As I turned the corner, there he was. In his blue Thunderbird. Parked on the corner, watching for whoever might turn from Marine Drive onto Irving Park. I moved past him, continued down a block or two and when I could see in my rearview mirror that he wasn't moving, I parked. After a minute or more, Gussie started up again.

When he got to my car, he pulled in right behind me. He made a big point of copying down my license number. The first time I ever had attempted to tail him and he made me in six blocks! I felt quite embarrassed and frustrated, especially when I had to report on it later. But it didn't dampen my resolve.

I pulled away and discontinued the surveillance. Now, it wasn't even eight o'clock yet, the office hadn't even opened officially for business. You will remember that I was studying for the Indiana Bar exam. Contrary to Bureau rules, but feeling morally justified, because I had started so early in the day, I decided I would spend an hour or two studying my Forrest Cool handbook on torts. So I drove to Meigs Field, the small municipal airport located on the lakefront near Soldier Field. There I remained in contact with my car radio, but put my mind to Forrest Cool, not Gussie Alex.

About ten o'clock the radio blared. "KSC 210 to Car thirty-nine."

"Car thirty-nine," I replied.

"Car thirty-nine, call the SAC immediately."

Wow, I had never met this SAC, Dick Auerbach. He didn't know me from a hole in the wall, only my name on the agent roster. But I hustled into the airport terminal and called him right away. Wait a minute, I told myself. You better make up a good alibi. Maybe somebody has spotted you here reading and has reported you. What's your excuse?

I reminded myself of the agent's adage. "Don't cop out. Make them prove it."

I called the office and was put through to Mr. Auerbach. "Where are you, Roemer?" he asked. His tone was not the least bit friendly.

"On the near South Side," I responded.

"Get in here right away, and come right to my office. I'll expect you in fifteen minutes."

I was thrown for a loss. He was obviously angry about something. It was very unusual for a young agent to be summoned from the streets directly into the SAC's office. Occasionally to the supervisor's office, but not bypassing him right to the boss.

When I arrived and Olga Ciesa, the secretary, motioned me in glumly, I knew I was in hot water.

"Roemer, what's your story!"

"What story?" I said, respectfully. "I don't know what you mean." I could have copped out. I could have told him I felt justified copping an hour or two because I had gotten on the job so early. But I didn't. Thank God.

"Well, let me tell you a story, okay? I just got a call from the SAC in Springfield, where they keep the motor vehicle records. He tells me that about an hour or so ago, DMV got a call from the Cook County Sheriff's Office. They were checking the registration on a license number for hit-and-run driving! License number 1106-238, which is car thirty-nine. Now what's your story!"

Wow, was I relieved! It wasn't my misfeasance at Meigs Field at all. It was Gussie's doing. Gussie took down my license number and called a deputy sheriff's officer, one he undoubtedly had on the pad, to find out who I was or at least who I was working for. In order to obtain the registration information expeditiously from the Department of Motor Vehicles, the deputy had to allege that the car was involved in a major offense such as hit-and-run driving. As I offered this logical explanation to the SAC, demonstrating perhaps that I wasn't the best surveillance agent around but on the other hand exonerating myself from any violation of the law or of Bureau regulations, I thought to myself, Thank God I didn't cop out!

The incident got my blood pumping. I realized that for the first time, I had come to grips with the mob . . . not yet exactly face-to-face, but close to it, and that it would be like a chess game, with continual moves and countermoves, each player constantly trying to fake and outguess his opponent.

My next move was to check with the Passport Agency at the State Department. Had Gussie ever traveled abroad? Yes, he had, and he had a passport, and the passport application said that he was employed by the Atlas Brewing Company of Chicago.

When I found out that Gussie was employed by Atlas, it immediately struck a chord. While plowing through the old CAPGA files, I found out Atlas had been controlled by mobsters. So I hustled over to the office of the Alcohol and Tobacco Tax Unit (ATU), which is responsible for supervision of the alcoholic beverage industry, to check their records on Atlas. I discovered that Atlas was an outgrowth of the Manhattan Brewing Company, which was controlled in the 1920s by Al Capone, Johnny Torrio, Dion O'Banion, and Hymie Weiss! What a bunch of thugs! It was practically a Who's Who of Public Enemies in the 1920s. The records also reflected that Alex Louis Greenberg, financial adviser to the mob, took over the company in 1943. Joining him as investors were Joe Fusco, another highly placed Capone mobster I was to get to know personally, Jake Guzik and Frank Nitti. A Who's Who of Public Enemies in the 1940s! My interest was piqued. What did Gussie do at Atlas Brewing? I went to their offices and inquired. The answer was nothing. We reviewed his sales records, and they revealed that he didn't sell anything; we interviewed some honest employees there, and they confirmed that he didn't do anything. He didn't really have much of a cover and he didn't really need one; until the THP came along, no one had ever bothered him.

What he did was shake down the sales manager, a guy named Stanley Stupner. For every barrel of Atlas beer sold to the many mob joints on Rush Street and throughout the Chicago area, Gussie received a kickback. For instance, if the Tradewinds, a mob joint on Rush Street, bought five hundred barrels of beer during the next six months, Gussie would receive two bucks for each barrel delivered. Not a bad tribute to a guy who did nothing!

There was no particular secret as to how Gussie enforced this incursion into Atlas. They had been under control of mobsters since time immemorial, and it was Gussie's turn to dip into the till. Atlas simply built Gussie's kickback into the price of their beer and then paid him for what was essentially a no-show job. Meanwhile, it was made known by Gussie or one of his associates to the tavern owners that "Gussie Alex says you should buy from Atlas." And there was no doubt about who Alex was and that if necessary he could enforce his edicts.

Atlas was an important concession, and it demonstrated to me that Gussie's services to the outfit were of great value. It obviously would not be awarded to just any low-level mobster.

Ralph Hill and I convinced the Atlas comptroller, after a couple months of making ourselves a nuisance in his office, that such an arrangement was not really a good idea. It violated several federal and state beverage acts we could think of. Gussie's hefty Atlas paychecks, which he used to justify to the IRS how he could live in the Murray Hill Apartments, drive new Thunderbirds, belong to private clubs like the exclusive Whitehall Club, and otherwise maintain a high standard of living, soon dried up.

Then I found out Gussie had a nice arrangement as an "at-large" salesman with the Blatz Brewing Company of Milwaukee, then a subsidiary of Schenley Industries, both legitimate companies with no hoodlum investors (unlike Atlas and Manhattan). I paid a visit to the management there, and soon Gussie was short another check each month. Though I knew we weren't putting a serious dent in his income, we were certainly introducing ourselves. And, the formal meeting had yet to come.

6
Face-to-Face with Gussie Alex

When the THP commenced it was obvious we were going to need a lot of help. We were greenhorns, and we couldn't just go out and introduce ourselves to the mobsters and hope that an ape would become a canary. It took more than that. So Ralph Hill devised a plan of attack to "turn" Marshall Caifano,

the Chicago mob's representative in Las Vegas. With his experience on the "pussy posse" Hill had become quite adept at
talking to the ladies. The more fallen the angel, the better from
Ralph's perspective. He was not a real handsome guy, but he
had a way about him. I have never known a guy who could
extract more information from women than he could.

It was Ralph's plan to compromise Caifano's wife. Ralph investigated Caifano thoroughly and determined that Caifano was
the Chicago mob's representative on the West Coast and in Las
Vegas. He succeeded Johnny Roselli and was the predecessor
of Tony "The Ant" Spilotro. The Chicago boys always have
guys in Las Vegas looking after their many interests, and those
three guys have been the top reps through the years. Roselli
operated in Hollywood in the late 1930s and added Las Vegas
to his domain in 1947 when Bugsy Siegel opened the Flamingo;
Caifano was the man there from the mid-fifties to 1971, and
Spilotro had the job until he was murdered by orders of Chicago
in June 1986.

In any event, Caifano's wife was named Darlene. She was a
Kentucky hillbilly who had adapted to the good life after she
met Caifano in Chicago.

Whatever Hill had planned, it turned out like this. We followed Darlene and discovered that every Friday night she had a
date with Sam Giancana. They would spend the evening dining
and then retire to a hotel. Now this was promising. The absolute
boss stealing the favors of the wife of one of his top subordinates! Ralph thought he could really use this to drive a wedge
between them.

He intercepted Caifano going into his apartment on the near
North Side. "Marshall, I think you ought to know that Darlene
is shacking up every Friday night with Giancana," he said.
Obviously, Ralph had naively expected Caifano to come back
with something like, "That fucking Giancana! Let me tell you
some things about him!"

Imagine Ralph's surprise when Caifano gleefully exploded:
"Really! My God, Sam's got the hots for Darlene? Hey, that's
great!" Caifano was proud that the boss went for his wife! We
were learning that we were moving into a different world. Most
of these guys had mistresses or girlfriends, but many also had
wives and stable family situations and they kept these aspects of
their lives separate.

* * *

In May 1958 the Senate Rackets Committee requested the assistance of the FBI in compiling information and subpoenaing witnesses for its upcoming hearings on organized crime. The Rackets Committee was chaired by Senator John L. McClellan, the sponsor of the great laws to follow, Title III of the 1968 Crime Act and RICO. These hearings were largely inspired by Apalachin. This time, since the THP had been in effect for six months or so now, the FBI could be of help. Senator John Kennedy was a committee member, and his brother Bobby was the committee's chief counsel.

One of the hoodlums they keenly desired to hear from was our friend Gussie Alex. But when I was assigned to locate Gussie for the committee, I discovered that he and Margaret had fled. They hadn't been seen anywhere near the Murray Hill Apartments for weeks. The building manager, Mr. Jaworek, told me that at some point in the past "Mike" had shown interest in moving to an apartment on Lake Shore Drive, the poshest address in Chicago.

So I canvassed the big apartment buildings on Lake Shore Drive. I finally came to one managed by the highly regarded Lake Shore Management Company. I found that Gus and Margaret Alex, under their true names, had applied to rent an apartment there in the spring of 1957. Gus listed his employer as Senator Marshall Korshak, the brother of "any message is our message" Sidney R. Korshak, and there were letters from both Korshaks contained in the files. Sidney's was dated April 25, 1957, and recommended Alex as a man of "excellent financial responsibility" whom he could recommend as an "excellent tenant."

As I mentioned, Willie Bioff, the government witness in the Hollywood Extortion Case, testified that Charley "Cherry Nose" Gioe told him that Korshak was "our man." Also present in the Bismarck Hotel conclave in 1940, according to Bioff, were Frank Nitti, Paul Ricca, and Louis Campagna. This accounted for three of the top four bosses in the Chicago mob at the time. Only Tony Accardo apparently was missing. We were advised by a labor informant that the person to watch to keep tabs on the mob leaders was Sidney Korshak. This informant also identified Gussie Alex as very close to Korshak.

First I went to see Korshak's brother, state Senator Marshall Korshak. "Where is Gus Alex?" I asked.

"How should I know? I only met the man once and that was on the street," he replied.

Then I mentioned the letters in the file at Lake Shore Management. I did not receive a cogent reply or any leads to the whereabouts of Alex.

So, on July 14, 1958, I went to see Sidney Korshak in his law offices at 134 LaSalle. He patiently explained that although he knew Gussie, it was only due to the fact that Margaret and Bernice were friends and associates in the modeling business and that he had absolutely no professional connection with the man. Korshak added that about a month earlier, Margaret mentioned that she and Gussie were going to Los Angeles. Since Korshak always kept a spare car at the Beverly Hills Hotel, he contacted the hotel and authorized Margaret Alex the use of the car, a 1958 white Lincoln Continental Mark III. We found out later that Korshak also let the Alexes use his villa at the Ocotillo Lodge in Palm Springs.

"Mr. Korshak," I said, "if the reason you're so close to the Alexes is because of your wife, then I should probably be talking to her."

"Roemer," Korshak said, "you leave my wife out of this. You have embarrassed my brother with this nonsense, now you're embarrassing me. Leave my wife alone!"

"Why don't we come to an understanding," I said, very calmly. "Obviously if I can find Mr. Alex in the next few days, I won't need to bother your wife. So if Mr. Alex could somehow get the word that he should surrender for purposes of receiving a subpoena, it might just save the Korshak family any more embarrassment. Why don't I just hold off until Friday and see if I hear from him."

I assumed we understood each other.

But when Friday afternoon came around and I still had not found Gussie, I called Korshak. "Mr. Korshak, we still haven't served that subpoena on Mr. Alex."

"Well, Mr. Roemer, I guess you will have to talk to Bernice then. I'll tell you where you can reach her this evening. She will be at the Mocambo on Sunset Boulevard in Los Angeles having dinner with Peter Lawford and his wife."

When I said nothing, Korshak added, "I think you know who Mrs. Lawford is, don't you?"

I did. Patricia Kennedy, the sister of John and Bobby. That didn't faze me, and I politely thanked Korshak and hung up. I then called the Bureau in Washington and told Johnny Leggett, who supervised the Chicago THP, that Bea Korshak would be at the Mocambo with the Peter Lawfords and that the Rackets Committee investigators could talk to her there about her relationship with Alex.

"Are you kidding, Roemer? They wouldn't touch that with a ten-foot pole!"

Korshak had pulled a fast one on me, but I wasn't giving up. I was determined to get Alex yet.

On July 22, at six in the evening, while I was watching the Murray Hill Apartments, Margaret arrived. I called Dick Sinclair, the Rackets Committee investigator who had the subpoena and radioed for assistance from any available agents. At 6:48, I spotted Gussie driving a 1958 black Mercedes-Benz convertible with the top down on Montrose Avenue nearby. I ducked down. After pulling over and checking the building for several minutes, Gus drove into the circular driveway up front. I immediately radioed Ralph Hill, who had responded to my call, and asked him to pull up in front of Gussie's car, blocking his exit. I pulled up right behind, preventing him from backing up. Sinclair and I moved in on Gus. Sinclair asked him if he was Gus Alex. Gussie said no.

"He's a liar, that's Gus Alex," I snapped. Sinclair handed him the subpoena.

As we moved away, I made a big deal of copying his license number just as he had done to me weeks before. Alex jeered at me: "Write it down, that's a good policy number to play!"

On July 30, Gus appeared before the committee in Washington. He took the Fifth Amendment some fifty times. As reported in the Chicago *Sun-Times*, "He cowered in his chair like a man about to get a belt from a rubber hose." I don't think Gussie enjoyed that day, which pleased me no end. And at last, we had come face-to-face.

7 Stumbling and Bumbling

Now that I had served Gussie with the subpoena, I concentrated on my final preparations for the Indiana Bar exam. Seven months of studying thirty-six hours a week were coming to a close. I traveled down to South Bend, picked up my brother Chuck, and together we drove to Indianapolis where the two-day exam was given. I could see that Chuck was much better prepared than I was, but that was to be expected since he had just graduated from the Notre Dame Law School, whereas it had been over eight years for me. At the end of the two days I was confident that I had passed the exam. On August 20, 1958, I received a letter from the State Board of Law Examiners for the state of Indiana confirming my success. I was told to present myself for admission before the Bar on September 24, 1958. Eight years to the day after I had said good-bye to Jeannie and Bill and left for Washington to join the FBI, I was leaving for Indianapolis to be admitted to the Bar—only this time it was with the family, including Bob.

Now that I had finally come face-to-face with the successors to Capone, Nitti, and Dillinger, I was not so sure that I wanted to stop. I explained my doubts to my brothers. They decided they would start the practice without me, saving me a spot if and when I wanted it.

As I mentioned before, when we started the THP we needed help. And there was one guy in Chicago who was in a position to help us a lot. His name was Sandy Smith, the ace of the investigative reporters in Chicago. Sandy had been with the *Chicago Tribune* for a decade or so. He knew the hoodlums by sight, having covered their weddings and wakes and having studied the few mug shots the Chicago PD had gathered. We were grateful for his help, and we took him along on surveillance missions,

43

asking him to identify the likes of Joey Aiuppa, the boss in
Cicero; "Milwaukee Phil" Alderisio and Chuckie Nicoletti, the
two mob hit men; Ross Prio, the boss up on the North Side;
Caesar DiVarco, the Rush Street boss; and Dominic "Butch"
Blasi, the bodyguard, appointment secretary, driver, and con-
fidant of the boss, Sam Giancana.

In the summer of 1958, about the same time as I was working
to serve the subpoena to Gussie Alex, Screwy Moore died.
Moore, whose true name was Claude Maddox, was a hoodlum
since Capone days, never of major importance but an old-timer
who had worked with just about every mobster of any consequence. So we figured his wake and funeral would provide a
great opportunity to photograph many of the current hoods. We
asked Sandy Smith to accompany us and help us identify them.
On the night of the wake, we must have photographed fifty or
sixty of the most prominent guys in the mob. But toward the
end of the evening it became quite obvious to them what we
were doing. The next day, when the mob assembled at the funeral parlor on the far West Side of Chicago, they were in an
ugly mood. Sandy had decided to bring his own photographer
from the *Tribune* to augment his coverage of the funeral. Lo and
behold, as soon as the photographer stepped out of his car and
set up his camera, he was attacked and chased down the street
by the mob. Fortunately, Frank Mellott, who was completing
his stint with C-1 before his transfer to Rome, immediately spotted the problem and waded into the attackers, dispersing them
and saving the photographer's neck.

I remember another such incident involving Sandy. This time
we were covering a wake of a bookmaker in "the Patch," the
Italian enclave on the near South Side of Chicago.

Ralph Hill, Sandy, and I set up in a third floor apartment
across the street from the funeral parlor. But, as Sandy makes
sure to repeat whenever he recounts this incident, Ralph "stuck
his big nose out the window too far once too often" and the
hoods noticed us. Very shortly, we heard the shrill of sirens.
The Chicago Police Department arrived in force, several squad
cars full. They leaped from the cars, guns drawn, and ran into
our building and up the stairs. "Open this door or it's coming
down!" they shouted. We opened it quickly to find a dozen cops
with guns pointed in our faces. Of course, we quickly identified
ourselves, and when the commotion subsided, we learned that

one of the hoods at the wake called his friend, the 19th police district commander, and told him that "shots were being fired" from the apartment where we had set up.

The worst ignominy was yet to come. When we emerged from the building in the company of the police, we were greeted by a loud jeering crowd of hoods. I kept my head down, and got out of there as quickly as possible.

In general, Sandy's help was invaluable. Whenever we possessed information that we could not use to make a case or to assist in gathering further intelligence, we fed that info to Sandy for publication in the *Tribune* and later, when he left the *Trib*, in the *Sun-Times*. (Sandy later left the *Sun-Times* for *Life* magazine and eventually *Time*, where he cemented his reputation as the top crime reporter in the country. In 1986, he retired to Annapolis where he still writes but finds plenty of time to enjoy hunting and fishing. We will stay in close touch.)

Public exposure of the mob after the Apalachin roundup in November 1957 and the Senate Rackets Committee hearings in July 1958 caused the FBI to join the war against organized crime for the first time and in general created a heightened awareness of the problem. But by late 1958 the pressure eased. Mr. Hoover seemed to lose some interest. Organized crime was no longer his top priority. As a result the THP in Chicago, manned by ten agents for a year, now was reduced to five. And those of us who remained received other assignments in addition to our top hood cases.

One of the most interesting of these cases, at least from my perspective, was the Chicago Transit Authority (CTA) Extortion Case. Frankly, I was surprised Ross Spencer assigned it to me because I was not one of the cigar smokers, the long-time criminal agents on C-1 who would be expected to handle such a major local case. The chairman of the CTA, Virgil Gunlock, received a letter threatening to blow up an El train or a city bus if he didn't hand over $50,000. It was designated a special investigation and I was assigned as "case agent" under the direction of my supervisor, Spencer. As with all specials, agents from most of the squads in the office were delegated to me. One of these was a new agent recently arrived in Chicago from Los Angeles, working on a security squad. His name was Marshall

E. Rutland. Better known as Maz, he was big, handsome, twenty-nine years old, with prematurely graying hair.

The extortionist called and gave Mr. Gunlock instructions: he was to follow a prescribed route in his car with a laundry bag containing $50,000. As soon as he heard a whistle, he was to throw the bag out the window. I assigned Maz to a remote spot along the route at Ogdon and Halsted. Sure enough, that's where Mr. Gunlock heard the whistle. He tossed the bag as instructed, the extortionist grabbed it and started to run. But Big Maz Rutland grabbed him and made the collar.

When I congratulated Maz for this fine piece of work, he informed me that what he really wanted was to get off the Security Squad where he was assigned and join us on the THP. I could identify with that! The next day, when SAC Dick Auerbach called me in to offer congratulations, I told him that the real hero was Maz Rutland and that Maz wanted to be transferred to the THP on C-1. "Tell him to report there today," Auerbach said. When Maz did, it was in no time at all that he became my primary partner. We worked in tandem for the next seven years.

The THP continued more or less to languish. I went back to In-Service Training, which is refresher training required every two years in an agent's area of specialization. It turned out that C-1 had to designate one agent as the office expert on arsons and bombings, crimes that the Bureau expected would require special attention in the upcoming era of civil rights violations. Spencer summoned the three agents who were scheduled for In-Service Training at the time: Vince Inserra, Lenny Wolf, and me. "I don't care who goes, you guys decide," he said. We flipped a coin, and I lost. I was thereafter the "arson and bomb expert" of the Chicago office, as inept in that job as any agent could be.

In any event, when I got back to the Seat of Government (SOG) for the training, I went immediately to Johnny Leggett, supervisor of the Chicago THP. "John," I said, "I am really concerned about the Top Hoodlum Program. I think it deserves more attention. The mob is the most dangerous threat to this country, and you guys are losing interest. We have half the squad we had several months ago, and those of us still left are working half the time on other assignments. I don't know what to suggest, but I just want you people back here to know that in Chicago we're afraid it's going down the tubes.''

Leggett was sympathetic. He said he would pass my comments on to the higher authorities at SOG, but that he didn't know what good it would do.

Back to Chicago I went in the summer of 1959, hoping I would never be called on to head an arson or bomb investigation.

About this time I met Richard B. Ogilvie. He was chief of the Attorney General's Midwest Office on Organized Crime. He went on to become sheriff of Cook County, the first Republican to be so elected to that post in decades; president of the Cook County Board of Commissioners, the so-called mayor of Cook County, and governor of Illinois. He is the public official I came to respect more than any other I have known.

At that time, Dick Ogilvie was initiating an investigation of Tony Accardo and his top lieutenant, Jackie Cerone, who were on the payroll of Premium Beer, the distributor of Foxhead 400, a beer brewed in Waukesha, Wisconsin. It was Ogilvie's theory that Accardo and Cerone had probably muscled into the job by putting the arm on Dominick Volpe, the owner of Premium Beer, and that they probably sold their beer by putting similar muscle, probably through lesser members of the mob, on the restaurants, bars, and retail liquor stores in the Chicago area that sold Foxhead 400. We had no direct evidence of such mob control. It was strictly a theory. We simply felt that this was the type of activity that was typical of the Chicago mob. It seemed obvious to us that they had enforced their extortion of labor unions, bookmakers, and legitimate businessmen of all sorts for years in Chicago. So why not bars, taverns, and restaurants? John Roberts was assigned as the case agent, and I was assigned to work with him more or less under the direction of Dick Ogilvie.

I should explain that when I say "more or less under the direction of Dick Ogilvie," I refer to the working relationship that existed in the Hoover FBI among the Department of Justice, the United States attorney's offices, and the offices of the Justice Department Strike Forces. The dog wagged the tail in those days. We had a pleasant relationship with most of the department lawyers. They were not our bosses; we worked together as a team, none of us more important than the other. Today the

tail wags the dog. When Justice Department types snap their
fingers, the FBI jumps. I'm not saying which way is better.
That's the way it was, that's the way it is now. When Hoover
left, the Justice Department took command.

In any event, John Roberts, myself, and other agents went out
and talked to every bar owner, restaurant owner, and retail liquor store owner who sold Foxhead 400 in Chicago and its
suburbs. We struck out. We couldn't find one who would admit
he had even met Accardo or Cerone. With our tail between our
legs, we reported our lack of findings to Ogilvie.

But, as I said, Dick Ogilvie was as sharp a guy as I have
known.

"Let's see here," he said. "If Accardo and Cerone haven't
ever been seen by their customers selling beer, how can they
claim expenses? I see here on Accardo's income tax return he
charges the cost of his Mercedes-Benz as a business expense.
This is the only business he claims he's in. That's income tax
fraud. You guys have actually nailed it down. You've got all these
statements from his customers saying they have never seen him,
don't deal with him in any way. We'll bring these guys in as
witnesses to that effect and, by God, I think we'll nail him!"

And we did. Or I should say Dick did. He reversed his original
strategy and proved that Accardo was guilty of income tax fraud,
as was his old boss, Al Capone. We could never get Accardo for
anything else; he never spent a night in jail even for anything
stretching back before his involvement in the St. Valentine's Day
Massacre in 1929 when he was Capone's bodyguard. But we did
get him for income tax fraud.

Our victory didn't last long. The United States Seventh Circuit Court of Appeals reversed the conviction, citing prejudicial
publicity, and ordered a retrial without use of the W-2. That,
plus the fact that Dick Ogilvie had moved on by that time, resulted in an acquittal on the retrial.

About this time, I was also assigned to look after Murray "The
Camel" Humphreys. Like Gussie, we didn't know even where
"The Camel" lived. "Hump," as he was called by many of his
associates, although his mob name was "Curley," was named
Public Enemy Number One by the Chicago Crime Commission
in 1932, following the incarceration of Al Capone. He was the
consummate mobster. He had performed contract killings for

Capone in the 1920s, when, even though he was a Welshman—
not Sicilian or even Italian—he became one of the top Capone
mob members. During Frank Nitti's regime he became more
and more important, particularly as a "fixer." Obviously, Hump
was of extreme importance as a Chicago mobster in 1959. We
heard from the Chicago Police Department that he was an old
man, retired, and living in Arizona. He supposedly never came
to Chicago anymore. But one day we saw him, and we followed
him most of that day and night. Ralph Hill, Vince Inserra, Maz
Rutland, and I followed him to St. Hubert's Grill, one of the
very finest restaurants in Chicago. The owner, a guy named
Tommy Kelley, was a pal of Humphreys, and, as we later found
out, it was Humphreys' money behind the place. In fact, the old
St. Hubert's Grill, located on Federal Street in the Loop, was
the place where Jake "Greasy Thumb" Guzik had died of a
heart attack in 1956. That's a funny story. When Guzik died,
Humphreys didn't want the body found in his place. So he had
his guys cart the corpse to Guzik's home in South Shore on the
South Side of Chicago and dump it before his shocked wife with
instructions that she was to tell the authorities the old man had
died at home.

In 1959 we followed Humphreys to the new St. Hubert's Grill
on East Lake Shore Drive, where he was greeted like the owner,
which he was. Soon we saw Lester "Killer Kane" Kruse, a guy
we didn't know much about then, but who was the boss of Lake
County, Illinois.

They sat down and it seemed they were waiting for someone
else. So the four of us approached the maitre d' and took a table
about fifteen feet away. Soon the party Humphreys and Kruse
were waiting for arrived. We didn't recognize him, but from the
conversation we were able to learn he was Johnny Drew, the
Chicago mob's man at The Stardust in Las Vegas.

Now the waiter approached us. Ralph ordered. "I'll have
the Waldorf salad," he said. "And I'll have Thousand Island
dressing on it."

"No, no, no, you don't have Thousand Island on Waldorf
salad," the waiter snorted.

"I do," Ralph said. Humphreys lifted his eyebrows as he
overheard this bit of conversation.

The waiter looked at me. "I'll have the lionized potatoes."

"No, no, no, you mean the potatoes lyonnaise."

"Whatever."

Now Humphreys took a longer look. We obviously weren't the type of clients usually attracted to a first-class restaurant like St. Hubert's.

What cooked our goose was when I had to go to the john. Just as the waiter was arriving behind me, I jumped up and bumped him. Ralph's Waldorf salad with Thousand Island dressing and my lionized potatoes fell right off the tray and landed with a crash. For a party attempting to be discreet, we had hardly succeeded. Any further attempts to overhear the conversation at the nearby table were futile. We were to learn our way around the very best places in Chicago as the years went by, but when we first started we had a long way to go.

8 The Family Pact (Mistresses Don't Count)

About this time I began to have some trouble at home. It started to bother Jeannie when I would call from the office to say I'd be late. This was very unusual. Jeannie is nobody's patsy: she knew that evening work was part of the job. When I pressed her on it she told me she had been receiving telephone calls on the evenings when I worked on Rush Street, the nightclub section. The caller would ask in very vulgar and obscene terms whom I might be sleeping with that night. On other occasions, the caller would ask Jeannie if she had kissed me well when I left home because she was never going to see me again . . . they would get me that night!

Then she noticed that two men in a car were parking down the street just as Bill and Bob left the house to walk to school. One day she noticed that the car followed the boys. With a coat over her pajamas and robe, she dashed out and placed herself between the car and the boys. Bill and Bob were surprised and embarrassed. When they asked what she was doing, she tried to be nonchalant, which wasn't easy under those circumstances.

When she described the men to me that evening, I realized that they fit the description of mobsters.

And that was just the beginning. Shortly thereafter, a man came to the house and told Jeannie that I had sent him because I was changing our household insurance policy and he had to evaluate all our belongings. Jeannie is nobody's fool and this one was especially phony because she handles all family business matters like insurance, and my brother, Joe, was an agent with Travelers and she knew I would never take our business away from him. So she slammed the door quickly and called the office. I wasn't in, so she spoke to Maz Rutland who agreed with her that something was wrong.

When I heard the story I decided I had had enough. From her description, I immediately suspected Carl Hildebrand, who was a business agent for the Hotel, Restaurant, and Bartenders Union and doubled as the bodyguard-chauffeur for Murray "The Camel." I went out the next morning and photographed him as he emerged from his home. But when I showed the photos to Jeannie she didn't recognize him.

Murray Humphreys was at that time the master fixer of the mob. He was in charge of the self-titled "connection guys." Humphreys, Gussie Alex, Ralph Pierce, Les Kruse, and Frank "Strongy" Ferraro fixed the politicians, judges, public officials, law enforcement officers, labor leaders, and businessmen who provided favorable treatment to the mob. They were all strong guys in other areas as well. Gussie controlled mob operations in the Loop. Pierce had the South Side. Kruse had Lake County, Illinois. Ferraro was the underboss, and Humphreys was in charge.

So I picked out Humphreys as the guy who could solve my problems at home. I had just located his residence, at 4200 Marine Drive, just a block from Gussie. I waited for him one morning as he left his building. He was white-haired and hatless. I later found out he never wore a hat, even on the worst Chicago winter days, due to a case of shingles—an affliction that caused his forehead to be extremely sensitive. I also discovered that the shingles had blinded him in one eye. "Mr. Humphreys," I said, as I showed him my credentials, "my name is Bill Roemer."

"Yes, Mr. Roemer, I know who you are. What can I do for you?"

"I believe you are in position to do a lot for me." I told him my problem. "Mr. Humphreys, I'm sure you realize that the FBI is much better equipped to harass your family and those of your associates. We have the authority to go to their schools, their jobs, even visit their neighbors. I know for instance that Llewella, your daughter, has had health problems and is living on your farm in Oklahoma with Billie, your first wife. I haven't gone near her, nor do I plan to and never would. But if that's the way you guys want to play, harassing my family, then as far as I'm concerned, Mr. Humphreys, your family is also fair game."

"Mr. Roemer," Humphreys said. "I understand your situation. I'll look into it."

"Let me make a suggestion," I said, leaning close to him. "Talk to your people. And if you want to set some guidelines, some ground rules, let's do it. You stay away from our families and we'll stay away from yours."

"That sounds good to me," the white-haired Humphreys said. "You meet me right here at this time a week from today. I'll have something to tell you then."

Now I suppose that making any kind of an agreement with our arch foes, the mob, was per se a violation of Bureau guidelines. But I had discussed it with my fellow THP agents and we were all for it. It was one thing for us to be in the line of fire but something entirely different for our families to be there. God knows, the wives and children of FBI agents go through enough without being subjected to the harassment Jeannie, Bill, and Bob were receiving. And if we let them get away with it, the mob could conceivably turn their efforts to the families of the other agents. They had picked my family first, I guess, because I was known to them; it wouldn't be long before the other agents, particularly Hill and Rutland, would be at least as well known. So it was agreed that as long as we made no concession that might hamper our investigation of the mobster himself, as long as we could continue to train our guns on the target, it was a good idea. As a matter of principle, we had no reason to want to harass mob families; it was against our principles. We felt that we should strive to refrain from visiting the sins of the father on the kids. And so what we came to refer to as the "family pact" was a sound idea from our viewpoint.

A week later I met again with Humphreys. "Bill," he said,

assuming we were now on a first-name basis, which didn't disturb me, "this was the work of a misguided individual. I have spoken to him and you can rest assured your family will have no more problems. Now, as far as guidelines are concerned, we would be very happy to set some standards. We will never again bother your families. In return, you don't bother ours. Is that a deal?"

"That's a deal," I said. "We have never had any intention of visiting the sins of the father on the family. I'll shake hands on that."

The FBI and the mob had a pact. I went back to the office and explained the situation to my colleagues. They all agreed.

I'm getting ahead of myself here, but a couple years later I got a call from a mutual friend of Hump and mine, Morrie Norman, who owned a very nice restaurant in the Loop.

I frequently lunched there and would often run into the likes of Ralph Pierce, who used it as his message drop; Bill McGuire, a former Chicago cop, then involved in gambling operations; Les "Killer" Kruse, the Lake County, Illinois boss; their bodyguard and courier, Hy Godrey; and occasionally Alex and Hump.

Morrie asked if I could make sure I would come to lunch that day. "A mutual friend wants a word with you."

When I got there, Morrie escorted me into a private dining room off the restaurant. There was "The Camel."

"Bill," he said, "I thought we had a deal."

"About the families? Sure we do."

"Well, you guys broke it."

"Not that I'm aware of," I said, very surprised.

"You guys gave the story on Frankie's girl to Sandy Smith."

"Whoa," I said. I knew immediately what he was talking about. Maz Rutland found out that Frankie Ferraro had a mistress he kept in an apartment in the South Shore area. He gave that info to Sandy since it was of no strategic value to us, and Sandy did a story in the *Tribune*. "Whoa, wait a minute here, Hump. That had nothing to do with families. That girl isn't *family*."

"You tell that to Frankie, Bill. And I agree with him, she's family."

"Hump, mistresses don't count. I had no idea you would include mistresses in your definition of 'family'."

"Well, they should be. From now on, they count."

"I'll tell you what," I said, "I'll take it up with my guys and get back to you on it. But you know my feelings, mistresses don't count."

"Bill, there might come a day when you regret this. You might not always be so righteous."

"Hump, I think I see what you're saying. But if you think you'll find me screwing around, then you might wait a long time. I don't even have a girlfriend, let alone a mistress."

I took it up with Maz, Ralph, John Roberts, Vince Inserra, and the rest. We agreed. Mistresses don't count.

Years later the pact would again come into play. Again Morrie Norman called me. Another guy wanted a sit down. This time it was Lenny Patrick. Lenny for years was the crime boss of the Lawndale Jewish section of Chicago on the West Side, near Independence Boulevard. In the sixties, when the area became predominantly black, Lenny moved with most of his Jewish gambler clientele to Rogers Park way up on the North Side.

Lenny started the conversation by telling me he knew I regularly played handball at the Austin YMCA. That was no surprise to me as mob guys like Johnny "Bananas" DiBaise were also members there, and I occasionally played alongside them. I always thought if the mob wanted to take me out, that would be a good place to find me. But at least I'd be in shape to handle it.

Then he got serious. Real serious. Tears came to his eyes, and I knew something was very wrong. "Bill," he said. "I got a beautiful daughter. She was engaged to a society guy, a first-class legit family. One of your people goes to the mother and says 'Don't you know that your son is gonna marry the daughter of one of the worst thugs in Chicago? He is the guy who murdered Ragen.' " James Ragen was the owner of the Continental Wire Service, an essential element of any bookmaking operation in those days in that it provided immediate horseracing results. The mob wanted to take it over, he resisted, and in 1946, Lenny Patrick, Davey Yaras, and Willie Block shot him. (Lenny became somewhat notorious nationally in 1963 when our investigation in Chicago determined that Jack Ruby, Oswald's killer, had been an associate of his before Ruby left Chicago, where he

lived in Lawndale, to settle in Dallas. This info was furnished
to the Warren Commission and became public knowledge.)

I was flabbergasted. I knew of Lenny's two daughters, who
were both beautiful blonde girls, but I was completely unaware
of this situation. I expressed my apologies to Lenny and went
back to the office. I knew who was assigned as the case agent
on Lenny, and sure enough when I talked to him about it he
admitted he had done just what Lenny said. The agent was very
young, and had just come on the squad. He thought it was a
good technique. And in many circles of law enforcement it would
have been. But not in the Chicago FBI, where we had a pact
with the mob concerning families. There was nothing I could
do, however; the damage was already done.

Speaking of restaurateurs, we had a great one in Chicago named
Jim Saine. He owned and operated Jim Saine's Restaurant at
871 Rush Street. Right next door to Jim's prestigious restaurant
was the notorious Tradewinds, owned by the mob. Felix "Milwaukee Phil" Alderisio had the biggest piece of the place. Ralph
Hill staked out the Tradewinds. He soon got to know Jim Saine
next door and introduced Jim to me.

You've heard of "police buffs." Well, there are also "FBI
buffs." Very legitimate, civic-minded, public-spirited people
who enjoy the company of FBI agents and will do anything, so
long as it's ethical and lawful, for them. Jim Saine was that kind
of guy. He and I immediately hit it off, especially since we were
both Cincinnati Reds fans.

Probably the most embarrassing night of my life involved Jim
and Jim Saine's. Maz, Ralph, and I took off in the midafternoon
and joined Jim at the Boyar Club. I enjoyed Stingers in those
days, but three of them was my limit. That afternoon I had four.
Now Jim proposed that we go over to the Barclay Club and have
dinner. I was woozy and protested that I had had enough. Jim
persisted and then suggested that I go back to his restaurant and
go up to the second floor to his office where he had a cot. I could
take a nap and join them when I felt like it. I went up to his
office, took off all but my tee shirt and shorts and lay down. But
as I did, the room started spinning. I had to hit the men's room
and fast. Without even thinking that it was downstairs, through
the restaurant and down in the basement, I took off. No problem. After a few minutes in the men's room, it hit me. There I

was in my undershorts! To get back I had to go right back through the fairly crowded restaurant. "My God," I said to myself, "how did I get down here!" I guess I went back as fast as I had come down. Later, Maria, the hostess, told me she was shocked out of her wits when she saw this big, burly guy in his undershorts flying down the stairs, through the restaurant, and into the men's room. I probably cost them some customers that night.

One afternoon Jim told me he had a real problem that he didn't know how to handle. It seems that the mob guys from the Tradewinds felt they couldn't use the phones there because they were afraid the phones were tapped. So they would come over to Jim's place next door, have a drink or two at the bar, and then use one of the three public phones in the foyer. As a result, when Jim's customers entered his restaurant the first thing they saw was a hood on the phone. Jim Saine's was getting a very poor reputation, especially because the hoods brought their girls with them, many of them hookers. I knew exactly how to handle it.

A couple days later, Jim called the office, and said it was urgent that I reach him. I got there in about fifteen minutes. There was Marshall Caifano at the bar with a sleazy-looking young thing.

Like most of the hoods in those early days, Caifano didn't know me by sight but by name. I introduced myself.

"Marshall, this is our place. Your place is next door. Let's make a deal. You stay on your side of the wall, we'll stay on our side, okay?"

He agreed.

So the FBI had another pact with the mob. Neither of those treaties, so to speak, would cause us to back off our investigations or hinder our operation in any way. But they made it more comfortable for all of us—mobsters and agents.

Mad Sam

About this time I got to know Mad Sam DeStefano, the worst torture-murderer in the history of Chicago. He was a sadistic, arrogant, swaggering thug of the worst order, responsible for scores of killings, almost all by his own hands. I had a long series of confrontations with this beast, and looking back I must admit I enjoyed every one.

One day in the spring of 1959, the thaw finally set in after a long, tough Chicago winter. A sewer out on the far West Side near Sayre and Harlem avenues was backed up. The neighbors called the Streets and Sanitation Department.

What was clogging the sewer was the nude, frozen and completely preserved body of Artie Adler, a local restaurant owner. He had been missing for several months. I was the case agent. We would not ordinarily be responsible for a missing person investigation, but Artie had been a witness before the Dick Ogilvie grand jury.

After some weeks, we learned that Adler had been "on juice." In the parlance of the mob that means he had borrowed money at exorbitant rates of interest. It's usually six for five, meaning that for every five bucks you borrow you owe six. And until you pay off the whole five you pay the six weekly. If you borrow $1,000 and pay off $999, you still better come up with your weekly $200 or else. Or else means broken legs, the rape of your wife, or just about anything else including death. Most juice victims are burglars, thieves, and gamblers who are down on their luck waiting for a score. But many are legitimate businessmen who have exhausted their line of credit at legitimate lending institutions and have nowhere else to go for a loan.

Artie Adler was, in my opinion, one of the latter. And he had the great misfortune to go to the very worst juice man in Chicago—Mad Sam. He was demented. He would prefer that you didn't pay him, because then he could torture you. He lived in the vicinity of Harlem Avenue on Sayre in one of the nicest homes in a lovely neighborhood. And in the basement of this lovely home he had a torture chamber!

That is where he had Adler brought. His wife Anita, his twin daughters, and his son who was home from college were upstairs. It didn't matter because Artie couldn't pay. Off came his clothes, and out came Sam's ice pick. A few preparatory jabs here and there, like in the testicles and in the throat. Bingo! Artie had a heart attack and dropped dead in Sam's basement.

I could imagine Mad Sam laughing. "Ha, ha. Did you see that fat cocksucker fall? Boys, just go dump him in a sewer somewhere. Nobody will ever connect him here."

And that's where Artie's body lay for a couple of months. Until the spring thaw.

I told Ray Connelley, the relief supervisor, that I intended to go out and confront Mad Sam with my theory, not expecting Sam to confess but hoping that he would maybe slip up and inadvertently give me some evidence I could use against him. I had no direct evidence of my supposition, but after having spent days on the investigation, it was my hypothesis. We had come to an impasse, and I had no other leads. Connelley agreed but ordered me not to go alone. Too many guys never came out of that basement.

As he did on the occasions of many future visits, Sam DeStefano met us at the door in his pajamas, fly open, his dingus hanging out. I suppose I was surprised but not really shocked because I knew he had a reputation for strange behavior.

He ushered us into his living room, which had mirrors from floor to ceiling on all four walls. "What brings you guys out here?" he asked after we had identified ourselves. "I never heard of you two before, are you rookies?" As he talked he walked around the room with his thing in his hand, examining it in the mirror. I guess he admired it; I sure didn't.

"You killed Artie Adler!" I said, getting right down to business.

At least I had gotten his attention away from the mirrors. "Anita! Children!" he shouted. His wife, son, daughters, and two or three of their friends came running into the room. "These two gentlemen are FBI agents," he cried. "They have come out here to accuse me of killing Arthur Adler! I cry out to God up above! If I am guilty of killing Arthur Adler may God come down, right now, and put cancer in the eyeballs—of you, and you, and you!'' He marched in front of each of his family and their friends pointing his finger at them.

I guess he was trying to impress us with his innocence. All I knew was that I had deep pity for the man's wife, children, and especially their friends. How would you like to be a visitor in that house? Even if you didn't go near the basement?

Ray and I drove back to the office. I don't think either of us said a word. Sam's bizarre behavior pretty much spoke for itself.

Sometime after my first visit with Mad Sam, I decided I had had so much fun the first time, I'd go back again. Actually, my purpose was to attempt to turn him into an informant. He was very close to many of the most prominent guys in the outfit and especially Paul Ricca, the old boss who had recently been released from the federal prison at Terre Haute, Indiana, where he had been confined on a tax charge during the late 1950s and very early 1960s.

I arrived by myself at about nine in the morning. Sam was still sleeping but Anita, his wife, let me in and went to wake up Sam.

While Sam was awakening but not dressing—he seemed always to be in his pajamas with his fly open—Anita offered to fix me breakfast. When Sam came downstairs, we got into a discussion of just how nice a man he really was.

Anita told me a story to demonstrate. When they were engaged to be married, she said, ''Sam promised me he would take communion at our wedding Mass. But he had not been in the state of grace for many years, and so I knew if he really loved me he would go to confession and prove his love.''

''My Lord,'' I said, ''that must have been really tough, going to confession after the life you had lived.'' I knew that his rap sheet showed arrest for rape, assaults, and burglaries, and that he had been a member of the ''42 Gang,'' a bunch of young toughs from the Patch, the Italian section that spawned much of the top leadership of the Chicago mob including Giancana and Sam Battaglia, who was to succeed Giancana as mob boss.

''Naw,'' Sam came back, ''I just told the priest I had gone to confession the day before and hadn't committed no sins since yesterday.''

"Well your confession the day before must have been the tough one then," I said, quite naively.

"Who the hell went to confession the day before!" he replied.

Anita beamed brightly: "Isn't he a nice man!" I muttered something about perhaps it is not so easy to outwit God, then just shook my head and didn't get into an argument about it.

After breakfast, Sam took me into the living room, still mirrored from wall to ceiling. While he walked around the room admiring himself, we talked in generalities, my purpose being not to pin him down on his crimes, but to warm him up so that some time in the future I might be able to obtain some valuable information from him. We got into a discussion of just how tough a guy he was. He told me that he was not actually a "made" guy because he would never submit to the discipline of the outfit, but that they were always after him to join up. "One time they come to me and sat down two trunks of money, one over here and one over there," he said. "If I would join them, they were mine. But I said 'Are you trying to buy Sam DeStefano?' I told them just to prove what kind of a man I am they could get the toughest man they had in the outfit and we would go belly-to-belly, gun-to-gun and see who the best man in Chicago is!"

On my next visit, Anita again served us breakfast and on this occasion I used a pretext, telling Sam that I had a little problem I hoped he could help me with. Sam said, "Mr. Roemer, I ain't no stool pigeon. But here's what I'll do for you. I'll answer your questions by giving you a parable."

"Giving me a parable? I don't understand, Sam."

"Here's an example. Coppers came into me a couple weeks ago and said, 'You killed them two burglars they found in a trunk.' I said the hell I did, they committed suicide. They said how could they commit suicide, they was both shot in the back of the head. I said they committed suicide when they fucked with Sam DeStefano! That's what I mean by a parable!"

Our relationship thereafter consisted of me asking him questions about his mob associates and him answering me in parables.

There is one story, however, I never did get a chance to ask Sam for a parable about. A black man had come into the police district in a great state of agitation. He said that he was at Sixty-third and Ashland on the South Side waiting for a bus when this wild-eyed white guy in a big Caddy pulled up, jumped out of the car, and shoved a big gun in his face. He forced him into the car and then drove him to a large, very expensive house on the West Side, where he was forced out of the car, and with the gun at his head forced into the house. There was a pretty white lady in the house. At gunpoint, the man forced the pretty white lady and the black guy to engage in oral sex. He then shoved the black man out of the house and told him to get lost. The black man felt that he might be charged with rape, and he therefore went to the police with his story. The police could not believe such a story and asked the man to take them to the house. He did. When the police still did not believe the story, the man told them that he was sure that if they looked into the Cadillac they would find his lunch pail, which he had been carrying when abducted. Sure enough, they found the lunch pail and now they believed his story. It turned out that Sam and Anita had had an argument, and this was Sam's way of disciplining his wife. Such a nice man!

Sam had a number of underling juice collectors working for him—Tony Spilotro, a guy named Leo Foreman, and another guy who we'll call Patsy Colletti. (I found out later he was a nice guy and I don't want to embarrass him). Patsy absconded with some of his collections, and Sam caught him in Milwaukee and brought him back to Chicago. Sam took Patsy to Mario's Restaurant in Cicero, owned by Sam's brother, Mario. In an upstairs room, Sam had Spilotro strip Patsy and then handcuff him with his wrists around a radiator that was going full blast in the Chicago winter. Then Sam very politely called Patsy's mother, father, wife, and children. "Patsy has returned to us," he told them, "and in celebration we are going to have a dinner honoring him Saturday night in the private dining room at Mario's Restaurant. You are invited." Patsy's relatives were relieved that he had returned and assured Sam they would be at the dinner.

On Saturday night, the dinner was held as scheduled. It was a feast consisting of many fine Italian specialties. Patsy wasn't there, but Sam told the assembled to be patient, that he would be down shortly.

When dinner was over, Patsy was down all right. He was dragged in naked, giving off a powerful odor of burned flesh, right at the feet of his mother, father, wife, and children. Sam then forced each of them to urinate on Patsy. That would teach him.

Based on this story, I felt that Patsy had the potential to be a good source of information on Sam. He certainly had the motivation! So one morning I went out to his apartment. His wife was there, but Patsy had already started on his collection rounds. I identified myself by showing my credentials, the usual practice; she told me that she expected him home the next morning about nine. I told her I would probably be back.

The next morning, however, we had a squad conference in the office and I had to postpone my planned visit with Patsy. Ordinarily, the squad secretary will not disturb agents in conference with a phone call. But on this occasion, our secretary hurried into the squad room and said, "Excuse me, Mr. Roemer, but there is a man on the phone who insists on talking to you and he's very upset. Could you take the call? I don't know how to handle him."

When I took the phone, this is what I heard: "You are a dirty coward, Mr. Roemer! You've got no guts, Mr. Roemer!" I recognized Sam DeStefano's voice. Patsy must have just turned around and told Sam about my visit to his (Patsy's) house, which got Sam all riled up.

"What are you talking about, Sam?" I asked.

"You were supposed to come out to Patsy Colletti's place today weren't you, Mr. Roemer, but you didn't show up, did you, Mr. Roemer? You got no guts, Mr. Roemer! You knew I'd be here, didn't you, Mr. Roemer? And I was and I had Tony Spilotro and Leo Foreman with me, Mr. Roemer. We were waiting for you, Mr. Roemer, but you chickened out, didn't you Mr. Roemer? You're a dirty coward, Mr. Roemer!"

"Sam," I said quite calmly, well aware I was dealing with a very demented individual, a guy who had probably killed dozens. "Sam, where will you be in an hour? I'll meet you wherever you say, you come alone and I'll come alone. And then we'll see who is a coward."

"Fuck you. I fuck your mother, you dirty cocksucker you! I'll be at my house in an hour! If you come out there I'll shoot you as soon as you step on my sidewalk, you dirty motherfucker you! I'll whack you, I'll get you if it's the last thing I do!''

"Be ready in one hour, Sam, I'll be there." Then I threw his words back at him at the last moment, just as I was about to hang up. "Sam, Sam, you still there? Sam, then we'll find out who the best man in Chicago is!"

The last words I heard were, "Fuck you, you dirty cock-sucker! I'll whack you and stick my big finger up your ass!''

Now, this happened right in the middle of our squad confer-ence. All the guys heard my side of the conversation. They all looked perplexed. "What the hell was that all about?" I told them, then I stood up, checked my gun, and prepared to head for Sam's house.

"Wait a minute," they said, "you can't go out there. That guy is bonkers. He means it. He'll kill you."

"He'll get the first shot," I replied. "I have to give him that. But he's no sharpshooter, he shoots people in the back from a distance of a few inches." I fully intended to go. I was hot and I sure wasn't going to back down. Not to anybody, but certainly not to Sam DeStefano, the self-acclaimed "best man in Chi-cago."

Before I could clear out of the office, the secretary came run-ning again. "Mr. Roemer, now there's another call. It's a woman this time and she says it's life or death that she talk to you. Those are the words she used."

It was Anita. "Mr. Roemer, please don't come out here. Please. Sam means it when he says he'll kill you, and if he does he'll be in big trouble. Please, Mr. Roemer, for my sake. Please."

"Anita," I said, "okay, I won't. But promise me one thing. Tell Sam what I said. Okay? Tell him I said if he wants to hide behind his wife's skirts, that's okay with me. Will you tell him that?"

She said she would. I don't know if she ever did, it would have further infuriated Sam. I breathed a quiet sigh of relief. I couldn't have backed down, because the story would have been repeated all over Chicago, embellished by Sam. But I *was* re-lieved. I truly believed that Sam would have missed that first shot because I had no reason to think that he was any kind of sharpshooter. My monthly firearms training sessions going all the way back to my Marine Corps days would have made me the heavy favorite. Unless he had waited until I was inside the house. Then, at close range, in the presence of at least one witness, Anita, and in his own dwelling, which is a man's castle in the eyes of the law, it would have been different. In any event, I was very happy that Anita resolved the situation the way she did.

There was another reason, however, why I was unhappy with Anita. The reason I decided to attempt to turn Patsy into an informant on Sam was that I had quit going out to Sayre Avenue for breakfast. I got a phone call from Bill Duffy, a very close friend, who was head of the Intelligence Division of the Chicago Police Department. "Bill," he said, "have you been going out to Sam DeStefano's house?"

Now I don't tell anybody about my informants, not even as close a friend as Bill. "Why do you ask, Bill?"

"Because, you dumb ass, he's been pissing in your coffee!" Sam had been telling his pals and Duffy doubtless had heard from one of his detectives on the street, "This guy Roemer, from the G, he comes out to my house and I piss in his coffee, that dumb ass!" I don't know if it was true; I *had* noticed a strange taste to the coffee Anita had served me, but ascribed the taste to the "Italian" coffee beans she used. Italian all right! It may have been, however, that Sam was protecting himself from the likes of "The Ant," making up an alibi for why I might have been seen coming to his house. In any event I did two things: I quit drinking coffee, even to this day, and I decided to take a shot at turning Patsy Colletti. The former has been good for me. The latter . . . well, it turned out all right in the long run.

None of the three guys who were there at the "ambush" fared very well thereafter. We know what happened to Spilotro. Foreman was killed by DeStefano, Spilotro, and another DeStefano henchman, Chuckie Crimaldi. John Bassett, who was to become my partner, successfully recruited Crimaldi as a witness against DeStefano. He testified in court that in November 1963 they lured Foreman to Mario DeStefano's house and then knocked him down. They then took turns cutting hunks out of his fully conscious body. They broke his kneecaps. They shot him in the buttocks. All the time he was pleading with Sam DeStefano who was called "Uncle" at his insistence by his underlings: "Please,

Unc, please, kill me, kill me, please kill me now!'' Eventually, after watching Foreman suffer for an hour or so, "Uncle" did.

As Chuckie Crimaldi told us later, when DeStefano went into a rage, he went into some kind of rage. "He would smash his fists against the floor. The drool would pour from his mouth in streams. His gravelly voice would become so guttural that his words were barely comprehensible. He would pray to the devil, 'I'm your fucking disciple. You put me where I am. How can you do this thing and cause me all this Goddamn heat—all this agitation? What do you want me to do? Kill somebody?' ''

That was the Mad Sam DeStefano I grew to know but not to love.

My last experience with Sam came much later, in 1970. I spent almost every early evening of almost every summer day in the sixties coaching baseball teams. Sometimes two teams at a time. Baseball was a family affair since Bill and Bob played on the teams and Jeannie came to all the games. Bill cut his hand when he was thirteen and severed all the nerves and tendons in his throwing hand and shortly thereafter had to give up the game. But Bob became one of the very best players in the Chicago area. He was named All State in high school and drafted out of high school by the Atlanta Braves even though by that time he had already accepted a football scholarship to Notre Dame. In any event, in 1970 I was managing the Berkeley Braves, a team of college All-Stars from all over the south suburban area, Frankie LaPorte's territory.

In July we went to Stateville, the Illinois State Prison at Joliet to play against their team. I coached third base. All of a sudden I hear this very loud chant go up: "Fuck J. Edgar Hoover! Fuck Mr. Roemer! Fuck the FBI!" It was Sam DeStefano. As a prisoner there he had recognized me in my baseball uniform. Soon he had the whole inmate population chanting, "Fuck the FBI!" They had to stop the game and quiet down the crowd. It was my last sighting of Mad Sam DeStefano.

After he got out, he went back to his usual game—juice. One Saturday morning in 1973 he was out in his garage. Two guys walked in, pulled out shotguns, and blasted him so hard they severed one of his arms and killed him instantly. He was no longer "the best man in Chicago."

We suspected that it was Tony Spilotro who got rid of Mad Sam. Spilotro was scheduled to go on trial with Mad Sam, and, as Spilotro well knew, Mad Sam had in the past made a complete mockery of the system with his courtroom antics while acting as his own attorney. At one well-publicized trail, Mad Sam had carried on with a wheelchair and a bullhorn, haranguing the judge and everyone else in the courtroom with long, rambling speeches. Spilotro, we felt, wanted to avoid this kind of spectacle and the ensuing probability that he would be convicted with Mad Sam, and decided to eliminate Mad Sam to avoid the problem.

10 Penetration!

Throughout the early days of the THP, J. Edgar Hoover put extreme pressure on us to locate the prime headquarters of the mobs and to install hidden microphones, enabling us to overhear their plans.

Mr. Hoover felt that electronic bugging, along with the development of informants inside the mob, would be a devastating one-two punch against organized crime.

None of us had any problems with the theory, but putting it into practice was another matter.

It was now well into the second year of the program and we still hadn't installed a bug. Not in Chicago or anywhere else in the country. Nor did we have any well-placed informants.

The first year of the program was rewarding primarily because we learned so much. But we also had so much to learn. We engaged in physical surveillance, but simply tailing your subjects generally accomplishes very little. If you get lucky you might see Tony Accardo meeting with Sam Giancana. Now when you know nothing about the mob hierarchy, that meeting might tell you something. But other than establishing that Accardo and Giancana are associates, you don't have much else. But, if you

can hear what Accardo and Giancana are discussing, it becomes
an entirely different ball game! In order to hear what they're
saying, you've either got to make one of them act as your ears
by turning them into a full-fledged informant or to install a microphone (a telephone tap isn't good enough because hoodlums
are so guarded on the phone). Difficult? You bet your bippy!

Still, Mr. Hoover kept up the pressure. All across the country
we gave lip service to his orders. "Sure, we're trying, but do
you realize what you're asking?" There had never been a microphone installed in a mob hangout, and it seemed as though
every FBI field division was waiting for someone to show the
way.

The challenge was twofold. First, you had to find a really
strategic spot. There would be no sense planting a mike in a
place where the conversations overheard were not of importance. You had to find a spot where important members of the
mob met to discuss topics of major concern to them and therefore to us. Second, you had to figure out a method of penetrating
the spot without being apprehended either by the mobsters or
by the police for breaking and entering. It was such a hazardous
endeavor to break and enter even a mob meeting place. Who
could dispute them if they shot you in their belief that you were
burglars? And wasn't it reasonable to believe that the mob must
take every precaution to guard their meeting places? After cop-
ing with that, you had to figure out exactly where in the meeting
place the microphone could be placed to its greatest advantage
and then how to secrete the mike so it couldn't be located. The
wires to the mike had to be secreted in the premises and then
strung to a location away from the meeting place where the mike
could be monitored and transcribed. Obviously, it was not a
task for a weak-minded or weak-kneed FBI agent.

In spite of all this, I decided I would be the first guy to plant
a mike. I had been the first and only guy to win four Notre
Dame boxing championships. It wouldn't be my first first.

So I went to Ross Spencer, our supervisor, and volunteered.
"Let me see what I can do," I said. He was happy to give me
the assignment. The pressure from Mr. Hoover was mounting.

Here's what had been happening. Many of us, Hill, Roberts,
Inserra, and now Rutland, had been tailing our targets onto the
near North Side. We were following them to the corner of Rush
and Ontario, into an office building that housed the Black Orchid

nightclub on the ground floor. Since the place was owned by
two guys suspected of being mob fronts, we thought that's where
they were going. But then Ralph Hill recruited one of the owners
as an informant and he told Ralph, pretty convincingly, that the
boys weren't using his place for a hangout.

So now we had to figure out exactly where these guys were
going. Ralph had Giancana assigned to him, Roberts had Accardo, Inserra had Ross Prio, Rutland had Ferraro, and I had
Gussie and Hump. As winter turned into spring we all had seen
our targets disappear into the building at Rush and Ontario.

We checked out all the offices in the building, but we still
couldn't figure it out. Since Hump seemed to be the guy we had
tailed there most often and he was my subject, I elected myself
to set up a fixed surveillance. In other words, I would anticipate
that he was going to show up at a certain location and wait for
him there.

Hump came in one April day, stood inside the doorway to see
whether anybody was following him, and then apparently satisfied he was "clean," walked deep into the building and into
a corridor that led through the building into another building,
this one fronting on Michigan Avenue. It seems the guys weren't
meeting in the building at Rush and Ontario at all. They were
meeting at a building a block away!

So far so good. Where in that building? It was an office building right on Chicago's Magnificent Mile, with shops on the lower
floors, a large shoe store, a well-known restaurant, and a couple
of art galleries.

I hadn't been able to tail Hump down the corridor leading to
the building. Remember, he knew me now after our two meetings to negotiate the "family pact." And it was the consensus
of the other agents, after I reported what I had discovered, that
no self-respecting hoodlum would be caught leading a stranger
down that corridor and then into the office where they met.

So Ralph and I went across the street to the east side of Michigan Avenue.

We canvassed that building and discovered an artist's studio
on the third floor. We approached the artist and asked him if we
could use his studio as an observation post for a few days. He
agreed.

We peered through binoculars into the window of each of the
shops and offices across the street. Nothing. Then Ralph got the

bright idea to have Vinny, Maz, and John watch the doorway of the building at Rush and Ontario. They did, and when they spotted Ferraro entering the building they radioed Ralph and me in the artist's studio. Finally, we spotted Ferraro entering a custom tailor's shop on the second floor!

We watched that tailor shop, Celano's Custom Tailors at 620 North Michigan, for the next several days. Sure enough, almost like clockwork at about ten each morning, Humphreys, Alex, and Ferraro appeared. Giancana appeared about twice a week, Accardo and Cerone about once a week, Prio every once in a while, and the other connection guys, Ralph Pierce and Les Kruse almost every day. One day John D'Arco and his First Ward associate, Pat Marcy, turned up with Mike Brodkin, the mob attorney. In other words, we had located the headquarters of the entire upper echelon leadership of the Chicago mob!

Now that we'd found the headquarters, our real job was just about to begin.

Mr. Hoover believed he had the authority to install bugs since more than one attorney general had authorized him to use wiretaps to preserve the national security. He believed that top hoodlum matters affected the national security. I personally had no problem with what I was being asked to do. I equated this form of eavesdropping with what was done in World War II to break the Japanese code or what the British did with "Operation Ultra" when they decoded the German code. In the field of clandestine operations, the British Y-2 group is legendary. They learned where General Rommel was to attack in North Africa, and that Hitler had fallen for the deception of the Allies that we were to land at Calais rather than Normandy. How many lives were saved by the agents who broke the Japanese and German codes? I wanted to emulate their work. I might not save lives with my eavesdropping, but then again I might.

The first thing we had to do was request authority from Mr. Hoover for a survey that would establish 1) that this was truly a strategic location, 2) that we had a plan of attack that the Bureau could see was logical and potentially successful and 3) that it could be done without any "embarrassment to the Bureau." The latter was always Mr. Hoover's greatest concern. "Do the job, by God, but don't ever let anything happen that might embarrass the Bureau."

The Bureau's policy on all operations of this type, the so-

called black bag jobs, was that if we got caught, we were not to
identify ourselves as FBI agents, and we were to attempt to
escape without being identified. We were to carry no badge or
credentials, no gun, nothing to connect us with the FBI. But,
heaven help us if we were apprehended and it eventually came
out that we were employed by the FBI; then the Bureau would
denounce us. We were "rogues," carrying out an unauthorized
operation.

In the past two years, I've been following the Iran-Contra
affair in the news, and I think in many ways our situation back
then was similar to that of Ollie North. North followed orders
from his superiors basically without question, and when the time
came when his superiors could have come forward to extricate
him from his situation, they did not. I could very well have found
myself in the same quandary in 1959 as we were bugging the
tailor shop on Michigan Avenue. Had my colleagues and I been
caught either by the mob or by the authorities, we would have
been thrown to the wolves. The major difference, perhaps, between our situation and Ollie North's is that we were made very
much aware going into the operation that such would be our
fate.

In the event that I was apprehended by the Chicago Police
Department and I was identified as an FBI agent, I was not to
refute the Bureau's portrayal of me as a rogue agent. I would
certainly be fired from the Bureau, probably convicted of at least
breaking and entering, disbarred from the legal profession, perhaps serve time in prison, certainly be very much disgraced,
and in the future be seriously impaired from earning a living at
my chosen profession—law enforcement. Of course, if I was
apprehended by the mobsters or by anybody they had guarding
the tailor shop, they would have shot first and asked questions
later!

Under the circumstances, it is no wonder that many agents
didn't want to be involved in this type of covert activity. I don't
blame them. Those of us who were, were so shot through with
our mission of penetrating the mob, and so convinced that our
mission was right and honorable, that we accepted Mr. Hoover's
dictate and went right ahead full steam with our "voluntary"
mission. I thank God to this day that I had competent associates
and that the good faith of my objective allowed me to succeed
with the mission. If it hadn't, I hate to think where I might be

today . . . or where the FBI would be in the crusade against the
mob.

Our infiltration of the tailor shop was much more serious business than when I made a comeback against a pro fighter at Parris
Island or went up against Gus Cifelli at Notre Dame. But, all of
that was good training. Those building blocks would support
me. Or so I hoped.

The first thing I did was canvass the occupants of the other
offices in the building to find out who would help. We needed
keys to the building and a spot inside from which to operate. I
finally found someone.

Most citizens are more than ready to assist in law enforcement, especially if they can do so anonymously. Some will help
even if there is physical or financial risk. This man gave me all
the assistance he could. I talked to him seven or eight times
before I actually asked him. I had to know I could trust him.
After all, I was planning to lead six or seven guys into that tailor
shop. If the mob had been forewarned we'd be in big trouble.
And if they blew us away, they could always justifiably claim
they thought we were burglars.

Finally, I got the keys to the front door of the building and
the right to use my new friend's office as both a staging point
and a safe house to which we could retreat if necessary.

I included all of this in my report to the Bureau. What I didn't
put in was the fact that we found out that the hoods may have
had a guard with a shotgun in the tailor shop all night, and the
Chicago Police Department had a detail of riflemen on the roof,
not only of the building we were targeting but also of several
others in the vicinity, on guard against a rash of burglaries of
jewelry and fur stores on the Magnificent Mile. We obtained
this information through our routine contacts with the CPD.

I should say here that we would never have considered contacting the CPD in this or any area where the mob was concerned. Many of the officers of the CPD are the most honest
guys in the world. But the mob also has many contacts in the
department, and if they found out that the FBI requested the
cops in the vicinity of Michigan and Ontario be removed, we
could conceivably be facing not just one, but six or seven guys
with shotguns inside the tailor shop.

Just after Memorial Day the authorization came through. Go
ahead, but be careful and don't embarrass the Bureau. The au-

thorization letter was just that blunt. We better not get caught.
And it better be worth the effort.

We felt that the best time for the penetration was in the wee
hours of Sunday morning. There was no business on Sunday:
even the restaurant was closed. So we would meet at the FBI
office at midnight, then take a leisurely drive up to the Magnificent Mile. I'm not going to identify the agents who participated
in this operation with me except for Maz Rutland and Ralph
Hill. I know at least a couple who prefer it that way. Ralph and
Maz were always there whenever needed for whatever it took.
They were the greatest partners a guy could ever have.

It took about eight entries to get the job done. I was always
the lead scout. I would take the key I had obtained from my
friend and enter the building through the front entrance on
Michigan Avenue. On the first entry, since we didn't have a key
to the tailor shop itself, I just scouted the building to make sure
we were alone and then radioed the all-clear. Ralph, Maz, and
the other guys then followed. Other agents were posted in Bureau cars outside as lookouts. We all carried walkie-talkies.

The first entry in early June was the most harrowing. There
were so many unanswered questions. Was there in fact a guard
with a shotgun inside? Did my earlier excursion, while I was
attempting to determine if there was a burglar alarm, miss something? Had the police observed us entering the building and
would they now investigate? Was there someone in another office who would hear or see us and call the police? Was there a
janitor on duty I didn't know about? Would someone across the
street see our flashlights and call the police, which is what happened at the Watergate? Remember, the police were almost as
much our "enemy" on this job as the hoods themselves.

With our hearts in our mouths, we picked the lock to the tailor
shop. I remember my hands were clammy. Fortunately there
was nobody inside. I was the first one in and we checked every
nook and cranny. We weren't home free but it was one great
relief, let me tell you!

We had observed from the artist's studio across the street that
when the hoods entered the tailor shop, which was probably
about 150 feet along the front and 100 feet deep, they always
went directly to the owner's private office. He would greet them
and then leave, closing the door behind them. Now in that private office we found a telephone, a couch, a desk, a television

set, a small bar, a desk chair, and two large soft chairs. Also an adding machine. Where to put the mike?

The decision was made, not by me but by others with much more expertise in these matters, that the best place to conceal it would be behind the radiator on the Michigan Avenue side of the room. I'll be the first to admit that I am a clumsy ox when it comes to doing anything mechanical. Jeannie knows more about cars and machines than I do. If it had been up to me to do the actual installation we'd never have done it. It was my role to plan the entry, get the keys, make the survey, be the lead scout, provide security while the work was being done and, if successful, monitor the mike, transcribe the conversations, analyze the information, report it to the Bureau, and cover any logical leads developed.

We had a vintage World War II microphone. It was almost the size of a pineapple, and it had to be connected by wires to someplace away from the premises where it could be monitored on headsets.

We had some interesting moments. Once, while stringing the wires, one of the guys fell through the crawl space between the tailor shop and the first floor restaurant, O'Connell's. He went right through the ceiling. Thank God the restaurant was closed on Sundays! We had to stop what we were doing, go back to the office for some plaster and paint, and then break into the restaurant in order to patch up the ceiling! It was almost as risky entering the restaurant because it was on the first floor and wide open to any passerby on Michigan Avenue.

After eight Sundays, we were finally done! We tested the old mike and found that it worked just fine. We later discovered that in the winter when that old radiator was going full tilt, much of the conversation was drowned out. I guess it was just one of the lessons to be learned in the infancy of our operations against the mob. We had to go back and install new mikes in the baseboards of the other walls, thereby giving us stereo reception.

We had accomplished what no other field office had done; we were the first! And our fears that it would not prove worthwhile were completely unfounded. As Notre Dame law professor Bob Blakey and author Dick Billings, the organized crime experts on many Justice Department and congressional investigations, agreed many years later in their book *The Plot to Kill the Pres-*

ident: "It was to be the biggest, most reliable source of information on the Chicago syndicate anywhere at any time."

We decided to code-name the source. We found out that the mob also code-named the location—and for the same reason we did, that is in the event anyone ever slipped and named it as the source of some information in the course of a discussion. The mob code name was "Schneider's." German for tailor shop. Ours was "Little Al." After all, weren't these the successors to Al Capone?

Our first eavesdrop was on July 29, 1959. Little Al was operated for six years, until July 1965.

My job was to monitor the conversations with the help of Ralph Hill and Maz Rutland, then to analyze them, interpret the information, and report it in a "daily summary airtel" to the Bureau. (In Bureau terminology, an "airtel" is nothing but a letter that is typed on blue paper and captioned "airtel." It receives priority handling and priority investigative attention and is sent airmail to its destination.) We maintained this routine day in and day out. The stuff was so intriguing that Mr. Hoover wanted it without fail every day. If you don't think that was a job, you don't grasp the problem. Anyone could sit there and record the conversation. But it took time and patience to learn the voices of the different hoodlums. Hump was easy; he was stentorian. Gussie was hard, being very soft spoken. And the rest were somewhere in between. In time, Ralph, Maz, and I mastered their inflections and accents. Once we understood the conversations, it was vital to provide analysis.

For instance, Mike Brodkin, the mob mouthpiece, would arrive at the tailor shop and announce:

"Curley, I'm having trouble with that judge on that kid's case from Bridgeport. He's an asshole."

"Judge," Hump would say, "he may be an asshole but remember, he's our asshole."

Now who were they describing? What judge? What kid from Bridgeport? Why did Humphreys consider him "our asshole"? Was he on the mob pad? Is that what Humphreys indicated? Just ten seconds of conversation and if you didn't know what they were discussing, as hardly any outsider would, it wasn't worth recording. And if you didn't know who Curley and Judge were, or recognize their voices, you couldn't start.

I spent countless hours monitoring Little Al in the tech room of the FBI office, first at 536 South Clark and then when we moved at the Everett McKinley Dirksen Building at 219 South Dearborn. The tech room is located in a special soundproof suite of rooms, one of which served as my office although I also retained my desk in the C-1 squad room. Since we were able to string the wires to reach our office, it made monitoring much more convenient than having an office outside the FBI site. Having access to stenographers on a moment's notice was just one such advantage. I spent the bulk of my time in the years to follow listening, transcribing, analyzing, and preparing a complete daily report to the Bureau on a daily basis on what we called a "daily summary airtel."

I remember the summer of 1960 when Jeannie, the boys, and I went to Cincinnati for three weeks, and for some reason Maz and Ralph were tied up on something else. Another agent was assigned to prepare the daily summary airtel and it suddenly became the "semimonthly" summary airtel. I was not a better agent than my substitute, just a lot more experienced.

Now that Chicago had broken the ground, the Bureau was all over the other field offices to do likewise. We were used as the example of hard work and dedication. I was called back to an in-service class to lecture my peers on the techniques of electronic surveillance. As pressure on the other offices mounted, I was not the most popular guy in the Bureau. "Why did that smartass out there in Chicago get the Bureau all heated up," they would lament.

Although the other offices never quite caught up to Chicago—we made several other equally successful installations—some of them did come close, namely New York, Philadelphia, Newark, Los Angeles, Boston, and in recent years, Kansas City. But the Chicago FBI, I am proud to say, still leads the pack in the installation of microphones. Only today they are court-ordered and the tapes admissible as evidence, which was not the case in our day. Today, the importance of bugs and phone taps, at least from a prosecutorial perspective, outshines our old Little Al's, which was strictly used for intelligence.

Our goal was to learn of the innermost secrets of the mob and then use that information in an attempt to thwart its operations. Since we had entered the premises to plant the bugs without benefit of a search warrant, none of the evidence we obtained was admissible in court. But if, for instance, we learned that the commander of a police district was on Gussie Alex's pad, we could make certain to avoid placing any trust or establishing any kind of working relationship with that commander. Likewise, if we learned that a particular judge was one of "Pat's guys," i.e., Marcy of the First Ward, we knew to avoid him. Or, as we will see later, if we found out that the mob intended to kill someone, we could take steps to ensure the safety of the intended victims. But we had to be highly discreet in handling any such information. It had to be used in deference to the source; we could not jeopardize that source or risk losing it by exposing it. In the early days of the Top Hoodlum Program, when we had so much to learn about the mob—particularly who its members were and what their methods were—any type of intelligence we could obtain was absolutely vital to us.

And from an intelligence viewpoint, when the victims were virgins as they were in the late 1950s and the early 1960s, when they were free and easy with their talk, there was never a better time to listen in. It'll never come again. The mob will never be burned as easily again. (As easily? What am I saying? Was it all that easy?)

11 Early Informants

During the summer of 1959 while we were working to install Little Al, we were also working on other projects. As I explained, Mr. Hoover followed two basic methods of intelligence gathering. One was installing bugs and the other was the developing of informants inside the mob.

Mr. Hoover never believed in a third technique, which has been pursued by the Bureau since his death: undercover assignments. It was his belief that "u.c." as it is called, was not suitable for his agents. He felt that in order to assume the lifestyle of a mobster, the u.c. agent had to make himself over into one of them. Mr. Hoover felt that his agents were above that.

He didn't want them participating in the low life, drinking, fornicating, using drugs, committing crimes, and, in general, lowering themselves to the level of the mobster. My own objection to u.c. is the inherent betrayal. I would find it extremely difficult to ingratiate myself into a group knowing all along that I was going to be disloyal in the end. That may be a weakness on my part. In any event, I have never been able to do it.

I think I did quite well, however, with the other techniques. I had a knack for planting bugs and I developed a knack for recruiting informants. The first one I really recruited was a guy named Fred Evans. Evans seemed to Ralph and me to offer considerable potential. He had been involved with Murray Humphreys and other mobsters for decades in various financial dealings. In 1940 he was indicted with Hump and Frank "The Enforcer" Nitti for conspiracy to embezzle $350,000 from the Bartenders Union. This case became a showpiece of Hump's ability to mastermind legal strategy. The principal witness against the mob was an official of the Bartenders Union, named George McLean. He had testified before the grand jury, which returned the indictments. Between the time of the indictment and the trial, however, Hump got to McLean. He convinced McLean not to inform the prosecutors that he would be changing his story on the stand. When he did, Hump and his confederates were acquitted and could not be tried again. If McLean had refused to take the stand or had told the prosecutors that he was changing his story, the prosecutors could have redevised their strategy or asked that the charges be dismissed without prejudice, meaning that Hump and the rest could have been tried whenever sufficient evidence was obtained. Once the trail started, however, double jeopardy set in and the case collapsed because of McLean's refusal to implicate the defendants, and it could not be brought again. Hump frequently bragged about his strategy in this case.

Evans was described by the *Chicago Tribune* as being the "financial brain" of the syndicate and as "the genius who guided Frank Nitti." Obviously his cooperation could be very valuable to us.

Ralph and I approached Evans in his offices on the far West Side. He ran his three laundry and linen supply companies from there, including the Industrial Garment Service. We very gently led him into his association with Humphreys and Nitti. He was a willing talker. He told us about the Humphreys youth, mentioned a couple of Hump's associates such as Abe Oslan and "Doc" Ginsburgh, and discussed his trial with Humphreys and Nitti. He also told us that Humphreys had a current financial interest in the Superior Laundry and Linen Supply Company and that a Morrie Gordon was the front for Humphreys in that venture. All this was very interesting to Ralph and me, not only because it gave us some solid intelligence concerning Humphreys but also, even more important, it indicated that Evans if properly handled might prove a fine source of information on Humphreys and the modus operandi of the mob in its infiltration of legitimate business.

Ralph and I went back to the office feeling pretty satisfied with ourselves. We had made arrangements to meet with Evans again in the near future.

About three weeks later, however, we consummated Little Al, which meant that we now had to devote the bulk of our time to monitoring, analyzing, and reporting the information. I was also scheduled for a short annual vacation in Cincinnati.

It was a Sunday morning in Cincinnati. Prior to heading off to Mass, and then to Crosley Field to catch a Reds game, I picked up the *Cincinnati Enquirer*. There on the front page was a story about the gangland slaying of Fred Evans!

On the previous day, August 22, 1959, Evans had left his offices on Lake Street, where we had interviewed him just six weeks before. As he walked toward his car in the parking lot, he was accosted by two gunmen. They threw him against the wall of his building, searched him for something, and then shot him twice in the head and twice more in the throat. The shots in the throat may well have been to ensure he would do no more talking to the FBI. Actually, we never knew how, or even if, the mob found out that we had visited Evans, except that somebody in his office might have told them. A local police investigation of the murder never identified the suspected killer or killers. I certainly didn't need any more convincing to realize what deadly adversaries I was dealing with!

About this same time I was contacted by Tom and Chuck, my brothers. "What about it?" they asked. "What do you intend to do about joining us in South Bend to practice law?"

I was really in a quandary. I enjoyed life in South Bend where

I had so many friends. And I wasn't making a great deal of money in the FBI. The salary when I joined in 1950 was $4,800 per year. While in New York I was promoted from grade GS 10 to GS 11, which paid $5,750. In 1956, I was promoted to GS 12, which paid $7,570. In 1959, I was probably making about $10,000. It would be expected that I could do much better in South Bend.

I was all caught up with the Top Hoodlum Program, however. It was proving to be the precise niche in the FBI I felt suited for. I enjoyed coming to work every day. I wondered what would happen. Giancana, Humphreys, Alex, Ferraro, Accardo, or Pierce might be up to something: planning to bribe a public official or the witnesses in a case, counting all their money from their illegal activities, even plotting murder. Each provided us with the challenge as to how to thwart them. It was too exciting to give up.

I finally had to tell my brothers that as of now I had decided to stay with the FBI. I'm sure it didn't break their hearts, although they probably would have been happy if I had decided otherwise.

I made ten or twelve such decisions during my career. Dick Ogilvie offered me three or four key positions as he progressed to sheriff of Cook County, president of the Cook County Board of Commissioners, and finally to governor of Illinois. I had chances to take a key position at the Better Government Association, the watchdog agency that monitors politics and governmental affairs in Chicago and does such a fine job. I also was offered a top spot in the Department of Revenue in Illinois. I gave careful consideration to each opportunity. But I ultimately turned each one down. The Top Hoodlum Program gave me every opportunity to meet the challenge that I had been looking for when I entered the Bureau. I had just about everything a guy could want. A great family, ideal health, a firm faith in God, and although $10,000 a year wasn't a great deal even in those days, it was enough for Jeannie and me.

About this time, I developed one of my most interesting sources ever. She was one of the most popular burlesque queens in America. She went on to win some fame in the movies. Once I followed Gussie Alex and his close buddy, auto dealer Henry Susk, when they went out on Susk's yacht with a statuesque young lady. When they came back in I tailed the girl, hoping to identify her, and lo and behold found that she was the star attraction at the Follies Burlesque Theater at State and Congress.

The owner of the Follies was Augie Circella, the brother of Nicky Circella, aka Nick Dean, a Capone mobster who had been deported to Argentina, but who was living in Mexico operating a score of shrimp boats. Without wanting to tip my hand, I conducted an interview of Circella on pretext, telling him I needed to check the personnel records of all his entertainers. As a result of this ruse, I found out where the girl was staying.

One afternoon before she was scheduled to go to work, I hit on her. After a few preliminary compliments about her accomplishments as a stripper, I explained the reason for my visit. She admitted she knew Susk but would not admit knowing Gussie. Realizing it was going to take a little finesse, I asked if I could see her again for lunch. She agreed.

At lunch she admitted knowing Alex, but just as a friend of Susk's. Another lunch and she admitted a little bit of romance with both on the yacht. Yet another lunch and she told me that Gussie used a suite at the St. Clair Hotel for meetings with his associates. She confided that Dave Gardner, manager of the hotel, was very friendly with Gussie and that if anyone came around asking questions, Gussie was immediately alerted. The suite was 14E, and consisted of a parlor, a bedroom and bath with a private phone. She told me that the suite was rented under the name of Joe Henry, and that when Gussie met there with his associates Gardner would cater a lunch so that the meetings could continue without interruption. As the years went by this information was to serve me very well.

I used to catch the young lady's movies as they came to Chicago. I thought she had considerable talent and beauty, but I also speculated that Gussie, especially with the help of his close Hollywood buddy Sid Korshak, was her guardian angel, influencing her success through his contacts in the movie industry.

12 "Little Al" Talks

On July 29, 1959, which happens to be Jeannie's birthday, we initiated the monitoring of Little Al. And on the very first day we hit pay dirt.

It was just after ten in the morning, which was the accustomed hour for the "connection guys," Hump, Gussie, Strongy Ferraro, Ralph Pierce, and Les "Killer Kane" Kruse, to arrive. After they showed up, they were soon joined by Frankie LaPorte.

"Connection guys" is what they called themselves. Their responsibility was to be "fixers" to provide a stable of politicians, judges, law enforcement officers, labor leaders, and legitimate people of all occupations who are in position to provide favorable treatment to the mob and can be influenced to do so. In the FBI we called this group the "corruption squad," because that seemed to us terminology that better explained their function.

At the time, LaPorte was a "capo," or captain, of the Chicago mob, given responsibility for southern Cook County with his headquarters in Chicago Heights, twenty-seven miles south of the Loop. LaPorte's responsibilities included Calumet City, which was wide open in 1959 before Dick Ogilvie became sheriff and cleaned it up. Gambling, prostitution, juice, just about any vice you wanted was available. In 1959 Calumet City and Cicero were the mob's two prime vice pots.

What a bombshell LaPorte laid on Little Al. Although Al was my source and I had the "ticket," making me responsible for monitoring, transcription, analysis, and reporting to the Bureau in Washington on a daily basis, all of us on the Top Hoodlum Squad at the time—Hill, Roberts, Inserra, Rutland, and I—crowded around to see what we had planted. We were not disappointed. That first day was one of the best.

LaPorte was visiting the mob headquarters in Chicago to report to the connection guys on those law enforcement officials in his territory who were "on his pad." What the connection guys did was the heart of the mob's work. The syndicate didn't worry about rival mobs—not since Capone had wiped out Hymie Weiss, Dion O'Banion, Bugs Moran, and the other gangs that gave him trouble. He eliminated them, and his successors made sure they stayed eliminated. But what still continued to bother them was the law.

In the areas around Chicago there are a number of law enforcement agencies with responsibilities vis-à-vis organized crime: the local police departments, the sheriff's offices, the Illinois State Police and, of course, the federal agencies such as the FBI, Alcohol and Tobacco Tax Units, IRS, marshal's office, Bureau of Narcotics (now the Drug Enforcement Administration), among others.

For this reason, the mob allocates a large portion of its profits to graft. A law enforcement officer in or around Chicago has always been in a position to augment his income substantially. I've often raised my eyebrows when a local candidate for sheriff raises hundreds of thousands of dollars to run for an office that pays only several thousand. Many of these officials come into office penniless and leave wealthy.

Corruption has always been my prime interest in investigating the mob. The alliance between politicians and the mob is to me the prime reason organized crime is so much a threat to this country. Many of the crimes committed by the mob are more or less victimless. I don't get all that excited if a guy wants to bet on the Super Bowl or the Hearns-Leonard fight. And if a "john" is stupid enough to have sex with prostitutes or borrow from juice guys, then that's his problem. My problem is that the millions generated by the mob as a result of these activities are what they use to corrupt our public officials.

The mob can't operate without corruption. If every public official, law enforcement officer, judge, labor leader, and legitimate businessman were completely honest and conscientious, there would be no organized crime. There are those who have a price. If we could keep the mob from obtaining great wealth, we could destroy their means of corruption. And then there would be no mob. This circular logic has always been my inspiration. It has been my motivation, the reason I have strived so hard to be "the mob nemesis."

So on the very first day that we listened to Little Al, when Frankie LaPorte reported on his success in corrupting the law enforcement officials in his territory, I got a taste of the extent of the problem confronting us. Frankie identified by name and position dozens of policemen, sheriff's deputies, and state policemen who were on his pad. Worse than that, it seemed as if all the bosses—every police chief, sheriff, lieutenant, captain, and major on the state police—were also in his pocket. The very worst was that three or four of these people were "N.A." men, graduates of the FBI's national academy at Quantico, Virginia, where they train the very best local law enforcement officers across the country. It is a great honor for a local or state law enforcement officer to be selected to attend the academy. The Bureau is very careful whom it selects, conducting a thorough background investigation on each candidate that's almost as exhaustive as its investigation of a prospective FBI agent. Even more important, when the N.A. man completes his lengthy training at Quantico and returns to duty back home, he is the trusted local authority the Bureau agents work with thereafter. For many years the FBI refused to allow Chicago police officers to become N.A. men due to the extent of corruption in the CPD. But that prohibition had not extended to law enforcement departments outside Chicago and in the dozens of other counties in Illinois.

Several N.A. men were posted in the territory controlled for the syndicate by LaPorte. And here we were, discovering that at least three of these guys, who most of us knew and regarded highly, were on LaPorte's payroll.

So much for our illusions. I don't think we were ever naive about it; we knew that there were crooked cops in Chicago and environs. But here it was, graphically spelled out to us. Who and how much. On the very first day, Little Al had already proved his worth and made all our dangerous work worthwhile. His tale that day wasn't anywhere near the best material produced for us, but just as you never forget your first girl, I'll never forget that first day with Al.

Of course now we had a real problem. I suggested to Spencer, the supervisor; Ray Connelley and Harold Sell, the coordinators; and to Hill, Inserra, Roberts, and Rutland, my fellow THP agents, that we keep whatever we might learn from Little Al strictly to ourselves. If what Al spit out lived up to just a fraction

of our expectations, it would be dynamite stuff. And, as such,
it would be the talk of the office. A loose lip anywhere would
kill Al. Not that any agent would deliberately spill the beans.
Corruption in the Bureau, especially in those years under Hoover, was unheard of. We never suspected a fellow agent and we
never, in my years, found one worthy of suspicion. But I, myself, have been guilty of a careless word when talking to mobsters. It is easy, especially in order to solicit information, to
grease the skid, steering your potential informant to a subject
you want him to talk about by letting him know you are already
somewhat knowledgeable about it. In doing so you might un-
suspectingly alert him to your source. It was not that we worried
any agent might deliberately blow Little Al, it was just that he
might do it by mistake.

Therefore, we had agreed not to disclose Al's existence or
anything that Al might tell us to anyone outside the THP.

Now here was our dilemma. Do we hold to our restrictions
as proposed? Or was there a higher duty here? Do we alert the
agents working at the Chicago Heights Resident Agency, which
was responsible for LaPorte's area, as to the identities of the
corrupt cops? At least that way they could be circumspect in
dealing with them.

We left it up to the boss, Ross Spencer. He resolved it by
calling in Kenny Groeper, the senior resident agent in the
Heights, to whom he outlined the problem and sealed his lips.
Kenny became a good friend of mine as the years passed, and
we never had any problems with a leak.

I was very surprised at how much the connection guys knew
about us and especially me. I had already firmed up the "family
pact" with Hump and I therefore knew they had substantial
knowledge about me. But I was flattered when I heard Hump
refer to me as "a rock of Gibraltar." "Rock" had been my
code name while on the Underground Squad, S-1, and was again
to be my code name when I transferred to Tucson many years
later. I remember when I transferred to Tucson I was assigned
the code name "Romeo," the designation for "R" in the military code. I heatedly protested, saying I was anything but a
romeo, and requested that I be named "Rock" (code names
were assigned primarily for car radio purposes). Some time
later an agent from Phoenix had come into Tucson and heard

radio calls to Rock. Knowing that Rock was not an official designation and speaking to a Tucson agent in front of an open radio transmitter and not knowing his conversation was being broadcast, he asked, "Who the hell is this Rock?" The Tucson agent responded, "Oh, that's Roemer, he likes to think of himself as a tough, macho son of a bitch!"

So, I guess to have Humphreys refer to me as a "rock of Gibraltar" made me proud. He also referred to me once as a "workin' bastard," in describing my dedication to the job. Another time he described me as "that poor guy," when he bragged about a dummy background he had set up for himself that I had been unable to fathom even though I had spent hours and hours attempting to do so. At least I hadn't been able to unravel it until he told Little Al.

Another conversation we overheard in the early days of Little Al was not only humorous but also demonstrated to all of us Humphreys' insight. One day in August the gray eminence of the mob was holding sway, giving several other mobsters the benefit of his experience and knowledge. His lecture was in response to a complaint by John D'Arco that the FBI had been bothering him.

"Who's been bothering you, the federals? The FBI?" Hump asked D'Arco.

"Yeah, three times," the First Ward alderman replied. Obviously he was referring to three contacts I had recently made with him.

"Oh, they won't call you before a grand jury, John. Here's what they're doing. This is the Republicans' orders. You know you've got a very straitlaced administration with this bastard in there for President. So what they're doing is building, setting up records, so that if anything ever happens they can walk right over and nail you."

Hump banged his fists on the desk. "You understand," he continued, "they got all your contacts. Why they would put you, a public official, in it I don't know. But you see with us guys they figure that if we try to lam or anything, they'd be ready to snap all our contacts and catch us quick."

Hump paused, apparently to gauge the attentiveness of his audience, and then went on. "Now, they have one other object here, to find us guilty of something and get us sentenced to jail.

Even a twenty-five-dollar fine is alright. They said get 'em, convict them of something. You get it now, Johnny? That's the way
they stand.''

D'Arco said nothing for a while and then whined, "It looks
like I'm being made a political football.''

Humphreys made another very interesting statement in late September. I had recently interviewed Frank Lee, the owner of the
Lee Brothers Trucking Company in Chicago, who we knew to
be an associate of Hump since the 1930s. Initially, Lee had lied
to me about knowing Hump, but when I pressed him and referred to specific places where he had been seen with the mobster, he admitted his association and furnished me my first
information about Hump's new wife. Hump divorced his wife,
Billie, after thirty-seven years of marriage and married a young,
blonde cocktail waitress some thirty years younger, Betty Jeanne
Neibert. Lee had obviously told Hump about my interview with
him, and this was Hump's reaction: "Frank says Roemer is a
nice guy. He says, 'Here I was lying to him but he knew every
fucking thing.' He said, 'The guy is a pretty nice guy.' I said,
'Yeah, but he just fucked you.' ''

Again in September, Hump talked about the problems the new
THP was causing him and his associates. This time his audience
was Eugene "Jimmy" James, the mob's man in the Laundry
Workers Union, and Eddy Vogel, boss of the mob's coin operated machines. When Hump complained about the FBI's investigation, Vogel said, "What the hell, they been followin' you
for forty years!" Hump said, "Yeah, but this time they got a
real tough one. Put you to bed and take you out. They don't
leave you go. Terrific drive they got on. They're on a lot of
people that way. I'm telling you, I'm having my troubles.''

Hump and his conferees frequently talked about the problems
they had with the FBI's new Top Hoodlum Program, although
they never indicated they knew that terminology. In January of
1960, exasperated, again in front of D'Arco and with underboss
Frank "Strongy" Ferraro also present, he expressed a new philosophy as follows: "Here's the only way to do this. We're not
gonna be no more patsies 'cause I'm gonna fight everybody
around from now on. If a fuckin' general is out in the field with

an army, and he's gettin' the shit beat out of him, he has to throw
caution to the wind and try stuff, he can't just stand there and
get shot down. Any time you become weak you might just as
well die. I'm gonna tell you something. When Courtney was
state's attorney and all of us guys got indicted and Nitti was
hollerin' like hell, we broke through and we got the assistant
state's attorney and we got the witness and let me tell you I had
the jury, too, just in case. That's the way we got to revert to
these days.'' Obviously, Hump was referring to 1940 when he
was indicted with Fred Evans and Frank Nitti for extortion of
the Bartenders Union. Thomas J. Courtney was the state's attorney of Cook county, the chief local prosecuting attorney at
the time of Nitti's trial.

There were reams of information from Little Al to follow in the
next six years. We had indications of Chicago police officers on
the take, details of the sources of their income. We found out
that the first of the month was payoff day. Alex and Ferraro, in
particular, would put the adding machine in the tailor shop to
great, if not expert, use. The identities of the bookmakers in
particular, who were supplying the bulk of the mob income,
became well known to us. My statement that ''gambling is the
lifeblood of the mob'' has been quoted extensively, and this was
the first indication that it is a truism.

On November 1, 1960, Gussie and Frankie Strongy, who controlled gambling in the First Ward, counted their income from
the bookmakers under their control. Al gave us this bit of conversation as Gussie counted out the stacks of bills for Strongy
to tabulate on the adding machine at Celano's: ''800, 8,100,
1,700, 3,700, 2,870. Leave a blank. 4,400, 1,200, 500, 800,
310, 1,000, 3,750, 1,000, one more thousand, 10,000, 4,000,
6,375, plus 3,750, 1,500, ah, 1,600, 2,650, 1,560, 6,060, add
it. Hold it. Now 1,650, 3,750, 2,870, 4,400, 1,200. Add it.
What's our third?'' Every month we heard a similar conversation. It appeared quite obvious to us that what Alex and Ferraro
were doing was counting up their cut from the bookmakers in
the First Ward. We also concluded that this was the 50 percent
that each street boss took from the net winnings of each of his
bookmakers. It also appeared to us that the street boss, or capo,
would take one-third of this total and send the rest ''out West''
to Giancana to fill the mob coffers. If you could surmise, and

we thought we could, that this type of scenario would be repeated every month (not only by the Alex-Ferraro faction in the
First Ward but by Ralph Pierce, who had the South Side; Fifi
Buccieri who had the West Side; Caesar DiVarco who had the
near North Side; Lenny Patrick, who had the Rogers Park area
on the far North Side; Ross Prio, who had the far Northwest
Side; Les Kruse, who had the northern suburbs; Frankie La-
Porte, who had the southern suburbs; Joe Amato, who had the
western suburbs and Frank Curry who had Will County, the far
southwestern suburbs) you could begin to get the picture of what
the Chicago mob took in on a monthly basis. Over half a million
dollars—just from bookmaking in the First Ward. Per month!

Little Al was there when Humphreys lamented about having cut
a particular CPD lieutenant off the mob Christmas list inasmuch
as he was later named chief of detectives. We learned the identity of D'Arco's informant in the Republican party, who kept
him informed of the opposite party's plans. We listened as Colonel Charles "Babe" Baron, one of several mob associates in
Las Vegas, complained about a welsher who owed thousands to
the Sands, but who, when he came to town gambled at the
Tropicana. They debated whether to "hit" the guy (he was a
well-known Chicago jeweler). Al told us about Les Kruse's plan
to set up an advertising agency in Puerto Rico because a close
source in the Nixon administration gave him inside information
that Puerto Rico would soon become a state, enhancing tourism.
   Little Al was there when they discussed what to do with Lou
Brady, a Cleveland mob associate who bilked Giancana out of
$90,000. They killed him. Upon learning of the situation we
had attempted to locate Brady in order to secure protection for
him but were unable to do so. His body was finally located in
New Orleans, as I recall. Again, there was a local investigation
that never revealed the killer(s). We also listened to Lou Lederer, another mob man in Vegas, who was assigned the task of
recovering $89,000, which had been confiscated from Rocco
Fischetti, Gus Liebe, and Les Kruse when the sheriff raided the
Viaduct Inn in Cicero.

We heard the whole story of the Chicago mob's interests in Las
Vegas on Little Al (more on that in Chapter 16). We learned
how Hump went there in 1946 to assist Bugsy Siegel in estab-

lishing the first hotel-casino on what is now known as the Strip: Las Vegas Boulevard. It was known as Highway 91 then and Hump worked with Siegel, Meyer Lansky, and others in the New York mob putting the Flamingo together. He also worked with Siegel in those days in Los Angeles where he supervised the work of another early pioneer in the virgin territory of Las Vegas, Johnny Roselli, who had been sent out to the West Coast to represent Chicago's interests. Chicago gained an early foothold in Vegas through Humphreys' work, and it was to provide Chicago with its greatest payday, with income that was unmatched by any other source and would multiply many times from those early days into the 1980s.

We overheard a conversation between Hump and Joey Glimco, president of the Taxicab Drivers Union in Chicago, Local 777 of the Teamsters, about Jimmy Hoffa, who Hump described as "the best man I ever knew." Glimco agreed. They remarked how, when Hoffa was asked to do something by the Chicago mobsters he "just goes boom, boom, boom, he gets it done." In the summer of 1975, when he disappeared never to be seen again, I thought of this and other conversations about Hoffa. I realized that while he was "boom, boom, boom" for the mob, his successor, Frank Fitzsimmons, had been more compliant and when Hoffa started making noises about returning to the presidency of the Teamsters, Chicago nixed that. You can be "boom, boom, boom," but if Chicago decides you have outlived your welcome, that's it. "Boom, boom, boom," indeed!

We made contact with Deputy Superintendent Joe Morris, one of the two officials in the Chicago Police Department whom we trusted explicitly, the other being Bill Duffy. Without specifying our source or revealing any of our information, we generally gave Morris to understand that a particular captain was not trustworthy in our opinion. Our working relationship with Morris was such that we did not have to spell it out. He knew that our information was well-founded. When we took him into our confidence, he acted on it. In this case, for instance, the mob's carefully cultivated captain was diverted to an area of the police department where he could do no further harm. This is how we made use of the intelligence we derived from our microphones;

we couldn't use it to prosecute, but it was valuable in so many other ways.

Sam "Rip" Alex, who was Gussie's older brother, had the sole function of delivering the monthly pensions to the mob widows, which was the organization's way of making sure that the widows stayed loyal and never went to the FBI.

We listened through Little Al when Ralph Pierce, the connection guy for the South Side, described how he spent weeks successfully corrupting a captain who was slated to take over the Intelligence Division of the CPD, which was charged with the responsibility of investigating organized crime. Pierce was flabbergasted when, just as this officer was to assume his duties, he was instead sidetracked to the Human Resources Division. Poor Ralph! All that time and money wasted.

Ralph Capone, Al's brother, brought in a sad story. His nephew, Al Capone, Jr., called "Sonny" by the Capone family, needed $24,000. The Chicago mob was taking care of Sonny—according him the same treatment as they did all mob widows—while he was attempting to make a go of a Miami Beach restaurant. Sonny would continue to receive his usual stipend, but he wanted an additional $24,000. Hump, Gussie, and Frankie felt it was a good cause and decided they would agree to send the money. When the boss, Giancana, was polled, however, he voted in the negative. Hump then sat down in front of the radiator, home of Little Al, and actually dictated a letter to one tailor shop employee to tell Sonny his request had been disapproved.

On September 13, 1960, we got an eye-opener. We found that the connection guys had obtained the jury panel list (the list of 150 prospective jurors from which the eventual 12, plus alternatives, are picked) for Tony Accardo's trial in federal court; he was indicted for income tax evasion and the prosecutor was Dick Ogilvie. The conversation went, verbatim, like this:

Humphreys: What's that address on Farwell? That's in Lenny's [Patrick's] district [Rogers Park on the far North Side of Chicago].

Ferraro:	Personally, I think we should wait until the jury is definitely picked and then you and I go see them.
Alex:	They'll know you. You'll expose yourself.
H:	We're gonna have to make the approach, though, by ourselves, first. Pin them down, then let the guys hit them. But we've got to be careful.
A:	The G will have a tail on all of them.
F:	You can rest assured on that. Instead of a triple X you want six X's before you approach [meaning, we determined later, that they had to have six good reasons to approach this potential juror rather than the usual three]. Fear ain't gonna stop me. But you got to be cautious.
H:	Here's what we're gonna do. After we've decided which ones, then we'll decide how to make the approach. [Shortly thereafter, the group met again.]
A:	Here's this one woman, from Wood Dale [a Chicago suburb]. That's a small little town, friend of ours has a gas station there. Cousin of Gags, Joe Gagliano [a "made" guy]. In these little towns everybody knows everybody. We can approach this fella see?
H:	Then we can decide on how to make the approach to her. You work on a plan. Be like an investigator would do. Find out if there's a connection there. Send Gags out there to talk to the gas station guy, find out how well he knows this woman. Then we'll decide.
F:	I think I got a good one in the banker here, he is the most intelligent one.
H:	Yes, he used to be the mayor. Now I got a truck driver. We have an ace there.
F:	Have Hoffa call this truck driver. I will. I'll go downstairs and call him now.

As we perused the jury panel list, we could see exactly which jurors the connection guys were highlighting because their occupations and home addresses were listed. We made use of this intelligence by ensuring that another jury panel was substituted for the original one just before selection was about to begin. We had discussed it with Dick Ogilvie, another guy we trusted implicitly, only after allowing the connection guys to spin their wheels, making all their planned moves.

In regard to Accardo's defense, Humphreys decided to work full time approaching jurors and lining up witnesses. As a result, he moved his base of operations from the tailor shop and Little Al. For a few days we were stymied. But one day Ralph and I successfully tailed Hy Godfrey until that evening when he drove to the Lake Tower Motel located at Lake Shore Drive and Ohio Street along Lake Michigan. We made a discreet inquiry after he left, two hours later. Our source there identified photos of Hump as being ''Mr. Olson,'' who was renting a suite of rooms in the hotel. By October 20 we had installed Little Al, Jr. in Hump's suite. We made sure that Ogilvie continued to be kept abreast of the connection guys' work.

As it turned out, the mob was able to make one actual approach in the Accardo case. A lady from Lyons, a western suburb, was selected. One Sunday morning there was a knock on her door as she was preparing to go to church. Her husband answered it and greeted the top city official of Lyons. Could he talk to the lady privately? The official informed her that Accardo was a good friend of his, that he was a very decent man, and that the lady should be careful not to believe everything bad she heard about him. When the lady told this story to the judge, she was questioned closely, but the ruling was that there had been no tampering. So the man thought Accardo was decent? And certainly she should be discriminating in weighing her testimony.

Gussie Alex blew his top when he learned that the owner of the tailor shop had gone out to Las Vegas and lost $20,000 gambling, necessitating that he sell some stock holdings at a loss. Alex gave the man a sermon telling him of the folly of trying to win money in Las Vegas. ''It's a sucker's game,'' he said. ''You can't win out there, you understand. We got the percentages rigged all in our favor. The longer you stay, the more you play, the more chance you got of losing. I don't let nobody around me who gambles. A couple thousand, okay, but no gambling!''

* * *

We learned a little about the extent of Hump's wealth. He informed an associate who wanted him to invest in a Chicago restaurant and who offered Hump $1,000 a month in return. "A thousand dollars, what would I do with a thousand dollars? I give that to broken-down old broads!"

We learned that respected Chicago attorney Mike Brodkin had discovered that William "The Saint" Skally, a prominent Chicago burglar, was a stool pigeon for the Bureau of Narcotics. Brodkin took this information to Sam Giancana. Brodkin told Giancana that Skally was informing on another Chicago burglar named Carl Fio Rito. Brodkin described how Giancana passed this information on to Fio Rito with the sanction for Fio Rito to kill Skally. Skally's body was found in a church parking lot in a western suburb in January 1960. So much for the ethics of respected Chicago attorneys! Actually, Brodkin never got much respect from those of us who knew he was a mouthpiece for the mob.

We also learned about a contract out on one of Denny Shanahan's informants. Denny was one of the cigar smokers on C-1, a most respected veteran criminal agent. He became one of the very best THP agents. We passed the information on to Denny in a way that wouldn't jeopardize Little Al. Denny passed on the warning to his informant. The informant, I'm told, merely shrugged his shoulders saying he would take what came. It came. He took it.

We were there with Little Al when Eddy Vogel came in with what was apparently hundreds of thousand-dollar bills as his monthly payment to the mob coffers. Vogel was the mob's man in charge of its vending machine business. He owned DeLuxe Cigarette Service, a cigarette vending machine distributor; Apex Amusement, a distributor of coin-operated games, and another vending machine company that in later years would be handled for the mob by Gus Alex. Obviously, those big bills were his profits for the period, which he was splitting with the mob. He was bawled out for not having sent those big bills to Las Vegas to be "laundered." Normally, they would be broken down into smaller bills by the cashiers at the Chicago-controlled casinos.

Then they would be brought back to town in the form of smaller bills, so no one would ever know their source.

Al was also on the job when the connection guys discussed with Alderman D'Arco that Dick Cain, the flamboyant Chicago policeman, was "their guy." This came about when Cain sent word to the boys that he was taking Jack Mabley, the Chicago newspaper columnist, for a tour of the "kinky" nightclubs in Chicago. Cain's judgment in doing this was questioned since these mob joints would have to shut down for a short time while Mabley made his tour. But it was decided that Cain's making himself a confidant of the very influential Mabley was a plus in the long run.

We were very interested when Colonel Charley "Babe" Baron made his first appearance. He had just been booted out of Havana, when Castro took over Cuba and banned all gambling. Baron, now a general in the Illinois National Guard, had been a Chicago bookmaker. After he shot a fellow bookmaker on Clark Street, he skipped town, winding up as Chicago's man at the Riviera in Havana. Subsequently, Hump and Giancana sent him out to Las Vegas to be one of their reps, first at the Sands and later at the Riviera. In 1981 he terminated an interview with me in the middle of a conversation that dealt with his appearances at the tailor shop. I knew he'd visited the tailor shop to squeal on Johnny Roselli, another Chicago rep in Vegas, and he didn't take it kindly that I was aware he was a fink.

We listened to Al as Hump and John D'Arco discussed two members of the Seventh Judicial Circuit Court of Appeals. They felt both members of the Court would be susceptible to an approach when Accardo was convicted and appealed. We never learned definitely whether these judges were bribed; but Accardo's case was reversed and sent back for retrial with the proviso that the W-2 forms, the record of income, were not to be evidentiary at the retrial. This led to Accardo's acquittal—so this "boss of all bosses" could still boast he "never spent a night in jail." We later overheard a conversation in which two guys joked that a judge—"one of our assholes"—had been roused from bed at three in the morning to set bail for Accardo just to preserve Accardo's unblemished record.

* * *

Little Al also gave us a conversation that indicated a congressman was on the take. On November 11, 1960, Gussie and Hump were discussing their relationship with Congressman Roland Libonati. It went like this, verbatim:

Alex: Curley, every time I think of Libby, it takes me back about twenty-five years. Frankie [Ferraro] and I were on the North Side, we were with two cars. Front car with Frankie had more material in it than I had in mine. We had the hardware in my car. Coppers pulled up on us. I went from my car to the front car. They grabbed me. I walked up to a big, fat cop, mentioned Libby and gave him twenty dollars. Twenty dollars is all! Twenty dollars and I walked out. Every time I see Libby brings me back to those days.

Humphreys: I had the same experience. I had two pistols. He hollers, "Pull over." So I pull over. He hollers, "Get out." So we get out. The dumb cocksucker, he lifts the seat up and we got two boxes under the seat. And two pistols fall out. So I give him a hundred and fifty and got the fuck out of there.

Another overhear concerned the problems in the faction of Sam "Teets" Battaglia. Battaglia, who was to become the successor to Giancana as the Chicago boss in 1966, headed a group of the Chicago crime syndicate that included "Milwaukee Phil" Alderisio (another in the line of Chicago bosses-to-be and then one of the two mob hit men). Battaglia had an argument with Marshall Caifano, then the mob's main man in Vegas. Ferraro, as the underboss, was selected to settle the matter.

Caifano's domestic affairs became a matter of worry for the connection guys, who were concerned that Caifano's current wife would become a stool pigeon. We learned then that this is

the reason Chicago took such good care of the widows and had
given Sam "Rip" Alex the full-time job to look out for their
welfare. By controlling the stipend that the widows received,
the mob could ensure their silence.

Of comic interest was the time we heard Hump instruct his
appointment secretary/chauffeur, Hy Godfrey, to bring him
$50,000 in small bills in a briefcase. Hump was traveling to his
Florida home in Key Biscayne the next day. At the time, we
didn't know the address on Key Biscayne where he was keeping
his new young bride. So Ralph Hill and I tailed him. We followed Hump out to O'Hare, which had just opened, and as he
walked through a deserted corridor in the airport, we joked
about this being a perfect opportunity to relieve Hump of his
$50,000 in ill-gotten goods. All we'd have to do is grab the
briefcase and walk away. What could he do about it? He certainly couldn't complain to the authorities.

On another occasion a Chicago restaurateur brought Hump a list
of all the license numbers and a description of all the cars assigned to "Disneyland," the police moniker for the Bureau of
Inspectional Services (the unit that monitored the hoodlums in
the early 1960s). This restaurant owner was a "double-breaster,"
in Hump's words a person who "butters up" both sides of the
law. I was to find this guy a good friend and sometimes very
good company. I remember when my brother, Tom, had just
been elected prosecutor in St. Joseph County, South Bend. He
and a friend came into Chicago to attend a White Sox game at
Comiskey Park one night. I met him for lunch at the double-
breaster's restaurant. While we were eating, in walked Ralph
Pierce, the South Side boss and a connection guy. The restaurateur pointed me and my brother out to Pierce and mentioned
that Tom was in town to attend a Sox game that night.
    About twenty minutes later Hy Godfrey hustled up to Pierce
and handed him an envelope. Pierce then walked over to our
table and, without identifying himself, dropped the envelope in
Tom's lap. "Two box seats for the Sox game," he said. "Enjoy
yourselves."
    I often kid Tom that after he was elected prosecutor he wasn't
in Chicago a half hour before he was corrupted! Of course, it
wasn't his fault. He didn't know Ralph Pierce from a hole in the

wall, and I'm sure Pierce didn't even know that Tom was a prosecutor, only that he was my brother.

We had a big scare in 1960 when Hump announced that he was going to have Dick Cain come to the tailor shop and check for bugs. Fortunately, it was one of the stupidest things Hump had ever done, because he let Little Al in on the secret the day before Cain's scheduled visit. We got up to the tailor shop that night, took Al from his hiding place behind the radiator and let him visit the FBI office for a week or so. Later on, we returned him to the tailor shop.

When we put him back, we decided to take a look inside the safe in the tailor shop. Now it just so happened that two of my buddies on C-1 had recently met two girls from St. Louis named Francine and Johanna. They were in town with their husbands for a convention. While their husbands were at a seminar, they went to Jim Saine's for drinks. There they had met the two FBI agents. We now tucked Al back behind the radiator and opened the safe. Since Al was operative once again, instead of making notes of the contents of the safe, I dictated them to Little Al for later transcription off the tape.

I dictated very rapidly. This is how the recording came out: "Here is a letter addressed to Murray Humphreys. It is postmarked St. Louis. It reads: Dear Hump. I'm going to be in Chicago for a convention my husband is attending, and I thought it would be nice if we got together while I'm there for old-times' sake. Maybe we could take up where we left off. Call me at the Conrad Hilton on Wednesday, November 15, if you're ready. All my love. Francine? Francine!'' I had been reading the letter hurriedly, but when I came to "Francine" I realized just who she must be—one of the two girls my buddies told me about, who just happened to be an old flame of "The Camel"! It's sure a small world.

Another very interesting conversation was about to take place. I had developed a friendship with Morrie Kaplan's brother, an associate of Murray Humphreys and Morrie Gordon. (Fred Evans had told us that Gordon was a front for Hump in the Superior Laundry and Linen Supply Company.) Morrie Kaplan was a multimillionaire attorney, who owned with Gordon the entire block of the Magnificent Mile across Michigan Avenue from the Drake Hotel. In addition, Morrie Kaplan was the president of the Chicago Linen Supply Association, the association of all companies supplying linen to the hundreds of hotels, hospitals, and restaurants in Chicago.

One day Hump asked an unidentified party: "Do you think he would go for that?" There was a pause, and then Hump went on. "That would be a great spot for him. It'd get him out of our hair and it would be a spot where he could never hurt us. It's a perfect setup. What do you suppose he makes now? Find out and offer him twice as much. Give him some perks, a pretty secretary, furnish a nice office for him, give him a car. But here's what else you do. Give him a carrot. If he keeps his nose clean, he gets a big bonus. See, offer him what he's making now. But then tell him you'll double it as a bonus at Christmas. Then that way, you don't have to say it, but if he gets any smart ideas he knows he's locked in. You keep him in line that way. You understand me? Go see what you can do with him. Get back to me on it."

About a week later, I got a call from Morrie Kaplan's brother, who said that Morrie wanted to have lunch with me. I agreed to meet him.

After lunch, Morrie Kaplan asked me to come with him back to his office, where we had another drink. "Bill, we're looking for a new man here in the Linen Association," he said. "Kind of a trouble-shooter—a guy who could give us a nice image. You could name the title, whatever you want. Now I understand you are making about twelve thousand a year now. We'll match that. And give you another twelve thousand at Christmas as a bonus if things go the way I know they'll go. What do you think?" It was an awkward situation, but I managed to decline graciously.

In July of 1960, the owner of the tailor shop complained to Hump that I was bothering his mistress, a girl named Ann Bradley, whose brother William Stabler was an escapee from San Quentin. Hump admitted he could do nothing about that one. He wished he could. "But I can't," he said. "Not with Roemer."

Hump reminisced about the time he bought off the primary witness against Paul Ricca, by purchasing the witness's home at an exorbitant price on the condition that the witness move back to Europe.

About this time, we overheard a heated discussion between Hump and Gussie wherein Hump berated his number-two man. Apparently, Gussie and his driver Hy Godfrey were under orders from Hump to check in every day with their contact in "Disneyland," the headquarters of the Intelligence Division of the Chicago Police Department. Although it was headed by the incorruptible Bill Duffy, the Intelligence Unit contained a number of corrupt officers. One of them was working with Gussie, feeding him both oral and written reports. It seems Gussie's contact had even destroyed the CPD file on a TWA pilot who Duffy suspected of being a mob courier, carrying "skim" money from Vegas to Chicago. Duffy told us about the pilot, we went over to Disneyland to take a look at the file, and sure enough as Gussie claimed in his conversation with Hump, it was gone. Here's how the conversation went:

Humphreys:	Why didn't you check today?
Alex:	Well, Curley, I . . .
H:	That's very important!
A:	I can't help it, I made a mistake!
H:	Don't get sarcastic with me! You're going too far!
A:	I'm sorry, Curley, I didn't mean to be sarcastic.
H:	Well, don't go too far with me, I don't go for that! If you're not careful, let someone else take over. If you aren't capable, we can get somebody else to check those things.
A:	I thought maybe Hy [Godfrey] looked at that date.
A:	We went over and checked through the cross files and tore them up, that's why I never brought them. There's a guy named Gipp. Pilot that lives near Joe [Accardo]. They took his license plates and they said they think he's the guy that brings stuff back and forth from California. Supposed to be a TWA pilot. Gipp. Rented a car in California, they check the credit card.

H: Listen, Gussie, if you do anything, do it thor-
                ough, don't do it halfway.
A: I'm sorry, Curley, I made a mistake. And they
                were also listening to a building in the Loop
                where they had two men detailed in the building
                . . . thinking there's an office [a handbook] there.
H: Let's check that out. Find it. I haven't heard of
                the FBI on me this week, inquiring.

Later on, I discussed the situation with Duffy, who said he'd
take appropriate action, while at the same time admitting whatever he did would be like the little Dutch boy putting his finger
in the dike. Duffy was able to identify one particularly suspicious detective and have him transferred out of the Intelligence
Unit, at which point that particular leak stopped. The incident
alerted Bill to the mob's knowledge of the operation of the Intelligence Unit in the Loop. Again, it demonstrated the use to
which we could put the intelligence information gathered by the
carload from Little Al.

Pat Marcy (as I testified before the U.S. Senate in 1983), was
then and now the "made" man in the Democratic organization
of the First Ward. The ward office was the mob conduit to politicians, judges, and other public officials. Marcy came by Little
Al one day and gave a report about the vast amounts of money
needed to pay police officials for "slots, pins, whores, gambling, and trucks." Pat explained that "there is hardly a truck
driver around who can make a profit by staying within the law
as far as loads are concerned. Any trucker with a legal limit of
ten tons will load twenty tons. Then he has to depend on the
state police." If the state police were not paid off, there would
of course be trouble. Since the mob owned trucking companies,
they saw to it that many state troopers were on the pad.

When Dan Ward was elected state's attorney, one of his first acts
was to appoint Ross Spencer to the office of chief investigator.
Incorruptible state's attorney appoints an incorruptible chief investigator. Ross had turned fifty, the minimum retirement age
for an FBI agent. To augment his pension he was glad to take
the job where he could continue to oversee investigation of the

syndicate. We were happy to see such a competent, honest guy
in that job. Ross's reputation hadn't reached Hump, however:
"We'll have to see what we can do with the G guy over there at
twenty-sixth and California. He was FBI but now he isn't. Maybe
we can do something now." How we laughed with Ross when
we passed on that bit from Little Al.

The Alderman Who Couldn't Be Embarrassed in This Town By the FBI

13

In 1959 I met John D'Arco. Rutland, Hill, and I
considered him to be the Chicago mob's man in the Chicago
City Council. He had been an Illinois state representative, was
then the Democratic ward committeeman of the First Ward and
alderman of the First Ward, which includes the Loop and the
near South and West sides.

Now Sam Giancana, who was boss of the Chicago mob in
1959, had recently traveled to Mexico to secure the mob's interest in a Mexican racetrack. When we learned of his whereabouts
we alerted U.S. Customs, and they were waiting for him when
he crossed back into the United States at Nogales. They found
in his possession a piece of paper listing the names of Accardo,
Humphreys, Ricca, Alex, Ferraro, Cerone, Prio, Frank La-
Porte, the boss of the southern suburbs, Fiore "Fifi" Buccieri,
the boss of the West Side of Chicago, John D'Arco, Pat Marcy,
and Buddy Jacobson.

The last three guys on the list were First Ward politicians.
D'Arco was the ward committeeman and alderman in 1959;
Marcy was an actual "made" member of the outfit, and Jacobson, an elderly man who had been with "Greasy Thumb" Guzik
in the thirties, was still involved in the machinations of the mob's
interests in politics.

I decided to pay a visit to D'Arco. I had never met him but

had been reading a lot about him and been hearing that he was "awful close" to the boys—Humphreys, Alex, and Ferraro in particular.

So I dropped into his office on one of the top floors at 100 North LaSalle, appropriately enough right across the street from City Hall. To give you a little flavor of the First Ward, I'll quote from an insert for a report of Ralph Hill I wrote in late 1962 on the First Ward.

"The First Ward of the city of Chicago has been said to contain the best—and the worst—of everything. The reason for this is that it contains not only the Loop—the business center of the country's second-largest city [which Chicago indeed was at the time]—but also the teeming slums that crowd in on the Loop.

"Inside and on the fringe of the Loop are some of the largest and most luxurious structures in the world, such as the Merchandise Mart, the Board of Trade Building, McCormick Place, the Civic Opera Building, the Prudential Building, City Hall, the County Building, the Chicago Public Library, and the Marshall Field Department Store, along with the finest of hotels, theaters, and restaurants.

"Outside the Loop, to the south and southwest, is a two-square-mile section of low-income housing, blending the best and worst of many ethnic groups, especially Italians, Orientals, blacks, and Puerto Ricans, which is also part of the First Ward. The ward extends from the Chicago River on the north to as far as Thirty-first Street in some areas of the south, and from Lake Michigan on the east to as far west in some locations as Damen Avenue (2000 west).

"During the heyday of Al Capone, the First Ward was 'bossed' by the infamous alderman, Michael 'Hinky Dink' Kenna and by Democratic ward committeeman John 'Bath House' Coughlin. They were followed briefly by Fred Morelli until 1947 when the old First Ward swallowed up the 'Bloody 20th,' the scene of many a vicious struggle for power. At that time, Peter Fosco of the 20th became Democratic ward committeeman and Anthony Pistilli, also of the 20th, became alderman of the First Ward. Fosco, also a Chicago labor leader, who now represents the Hod Carriers in Washington, held power until one of his henchmen was named as one of those who handled the money spent to obtain paroles for Capone mobsters, Paul Ricca (DeLucia), Louis Campagna, Charles Gioe and Phil

D'Andrea. Fosco was then dumped, and a man with an unblemished record, Frank Annunzio, was appointed acting Democratic ward committeeman and state director of labor by Governor Adlai Stevenson. In the early 1950s, John D'Arco, former secretary of Pistilli, left his post as state representative and was elected alderman of the First Ward. Shortly thereafter, D'Arco was also elected Democratic ward committeeman of the First Ward.''

This pretty well sums up the status of the First Ward at the time I first met John D'Arco in 1959. The title of that report was ''Influence of Samuel Giancana and His Organization in Activities of the First Ward Political Organization of Chicago.''

John Roberts, a fellow agent on the THP, accompanied me to that first meeting. We showed our credentials and exchanged a few pleasantries. Then I got down to business.

''Alderman D'Arco, Agent Roberts and I are here today to ask your cooperation. We feel that you, as a public official, naturally would have an interest in assisting us. We're involved in the investigation of the man who is alleged to be the head of organized crime here in Chicago.''

''Well, what's on your mind?'' D'Arco replied.

''Do you know Sam Giancana?'' Roberts asked.

''Sure, I grew up with him.''

''We recently came up with a list of names he had in his possession. You will note that your name is on the list along with your associates Mr. Marcy and Mr. Jacobson. But what concerns us most is that it was in the possession of Mr. Giancana and also named on the list are many of the major mob leaders in Chicago. Would you look at it?'' I asked.

D'Arco looked at the list for a minute or so. Then he looked up. ''So?''

''We'd like you to explain the significance of that list of names for us.''

D'Arco looked at John, then he looked at me. ''How the hell would I know?''

''Do you know Accardo, Humphreys, Alex, Ferraro, Ricca, and these others?'' John asked.

''Hell no.''

''Well, what is it all about then, explain it to us,'' I said. D'Arco drummed his fingers on his desk. He said nothing for about thirty seconds. Then he stood up. ''Fellas, I have nothing to say. I know nothin' about this list as you call it. Tell me, why do you come to me about this? What's your point?''

''Well, we could have gone elsewhere, say to your associates on the City Council. But we came directly to you as a matter of courtesy. We don't intend to embarrass you,'' I said, remaining seated and looking him in the eye.

''Roemer, is that your name? You can't embarrass me in this city. I am too big a man in this town for the FBI or anyone else. This is Chicago! As long as my constituents like the way I handle myself I don't have to worry.'' He paused. John and I just looked at him. He continued. ''Go throw your best shot at John D'Arco, I don't give a fuck!'' With that he walked out of his office.

Six months later, I had reason to talk to the alderman again. This time I was alone and the conversation went something like this:

''Mr. Roemer, come right on in. It's good to see you again.''

''Well, thank you Mr. Alderman.''

''Do you smoke cigars? Here's a good one.

''I understand you are a lawyer. Got your degree from Notre Dame.''

''Yes, alderman, that's right. But I have never practiced law,'' I said.

''Well, why not? I could set you up real good right here in the Loop.''

''But I'm not a member of the Illinois Bar, just the Indiana Bar,'' I said.

''What the hell,'' he said, ''that's no problem. Did you ever hear of reciprocity? We could have you fixed up in no time!''

''Yeah, but I've got the security of my job. Who knows what I'd make trying to get started practicing law here in Chicago where I hardly know anybody.''

''Roemer, I will guarantee that you would make twice as much money in the very first year if you leave that lousy job and set up practice.''

It was obvious what he was doing, but I wondered if it legally constituted a bribe attempt.

When I got back to the office I took it up with Spencer. ''Go see the U.S. attorney's office,'' he said. I did. It was their opinion that the bribe attempt was not specific enough. D'Arco had made no offer to set me up in return for consideration. No quid pro quo. He was just being a nice, gentlemanly benefactor and that was no crime.

I guess I should have felt flattered that D'Arco, a mouthpiece for the mob, had made me such an offer. But his earlier boast that "the FBI can't embarrass me in this town, go throw your best shot" was the thing that rankled me. That and the fact that he obviously wanted me out of the way made me all the more eager to wipe that big grin off his face. Maybe someday the FBI could embarrass him. Even in Chicago.

14 The Mob Coexists in Dick Daley's Chicago

During the early 1960s we heard that on the recommendation of John D'Arco the mob had supported Richard Daley when he initially ran for mayor of Chicago against Martin Kennelley in 1955. We heard Hump say to D'Arco in 1960, "This mayor has been good to us." D'Arco replied, "And we've been good to him. One hand washes the other."

We immediately took note of the use of the word "we" by D'Arco conferring with Murray Humphreys, who had been mob leader since the days of Al Capone. Humphreys had also been the leader of the connection guys, and it was his job to handle the corruption of D'Arco, the alderman and ward committeeman of the First Ward. Later Hump was to complain that Mayor Daley was a "weak guy—he's gotten too big for his britches," a comment that implied exactly the opposite of what Hump was saying. And, in fact, Daley progressively got stronger as the years went by, so that he did not need the support of the mob. He tried to distance himself from them.

However, the mob did all it could to help Daley. They also lent their support to the Chicago Police Department, a police department under the strict and fast control of Daley. Here's what happened. In 1959, Richard Morrison, who was to gain fame later as "the babbling burglar," was arrested by a squad of police officers from the Summerdale District in Rogers Park, on the far North Side. Instead of booking Morrison and taking him to court, they made an agreement with him. If he would lead them in burglaries in the Summerdale District they would stand guard, give him protection, and help him haul the loot out and fence it. All this protection for a partnership of fifty-fifty. What a deal for Morrison! Instead of being put in the can, he was offered a can't-lose situation. He made the deal. Dozens of Chicago cops, including at least one top police official for Evanston, the northern suburb, became his partners. It was a glorious enterprise for as long as it lasted. But just as thieves fall out, so do cops with thieves, even when they're partners. Soon Morrison was babbling to the state's attorney's office, headed by Republican Ben Adamowski. For obvious political reasons, Adamowski gobbled this story up! This could bring down the whole police department and Mayor Daley with it! Adamowski attacked this police-corruption issue with every ounce of energy he had. He received great cooperation from the media, and it became one of the biggest scandals in the history of Chicago.

The connection guys were furious. If you were uninitiated in Chicago you would expect the Chicago mob to be on the other side of the Chicago Police Department—against them. You'd think the mob would be happy that the police were in trouble, hoping that all the implicated cops be fired along with their bosses, from the sergeants and lieutenants up to the commanders and superintendent. Not in Chicago! The mob was annoyed, and Hump was especially upset. These were bosses in the Chicago PD upon whom millions of dollars, and thousands of hours of effort, had been expended. From the Capone era up to 1959, the mob had carefully nurtured a close relationship. If those guys were replaced, the mob would have to start again from scratch. Mayor Daley had not exactly cooperated as they expected. What if a blue-ribbon guy got a bug up his ass and decided to run for mayor? Say a guy like Dick Ogilvie? "Then we'd really be in a mess," according to Hump. But what could the mob do to restore the status quo?

Not much, as it turned out. But dame fortune almost cast her smile on "The Camel." One day soon after the Summerdale Scandal broke, Mike Brodkin, the mob mouthpiece, hustled into the tailor shop. "H," he shouted, "do you know who this little shit Richie Morrison really is?"

Hump said he had no idea. "Hump, you *got* to remember," Brodkin went on. Do you remember when you called me here and told me about that blonde you were dating then . . . that she had a nephew who had gotten pinched for burglary. And you wanted to help him as a favor. Remember you had me represent him? That's *Richie Morrison*, for Christ sake!''

A light exploded in Hump's mind. He was connected to the babbling burglar! And without Morrison the case against the coppers would blow up in their faces. And Morrison owes him!

On January 18, 1960, Hy Godfrey appeared before Little Al. Godfrey was the chauffeur, bodyguard, courier, and appointment secretary of the mob, a former pro middleweight. Godfrey got started on the subject of Morrison. He was addressing Humphreys and Frank "Strongy" Ferraro, the mob underboss:

Godfrey:	Curley [Humphreys], Saturday Mo [Giancana] thought somebody ought to try and reach this kid, this stool pigeon with them coppers. This kid is a bad kid. When he got grabbed once before, he lammed on his bond. So what happened now, when he got grabbed this time nobody would go on his bond. That's why he hollered copper. Now the state's attorney has got this guy in a hotel.
Humphreys:	Do you know where at?
G:	That's just it. I don't know. But Mo, I don't know what Mo has in mind. He wants to know of any way to reach this kid.
H:	Is he single?
G:	Yeah.
H:	The best way to do it would be if he had a relative or something. To bring him some food.

Again on January 18, 1960, Humphreys, Giancana, and Ferraro conferred about the matter.

H: You know who this boy is that squealed on all
                these cops? Morrison? He's the brother of a little
                blonde I used to have. The one I run away with
                that time I lammed on my income tax.

Giancana: Billie!

H: Yeah, that's right, Billie Jean! That's Morrison's
                sister! Here's what happened. He's a little cock-
                sucker evidently. Listen to this story. So he got
                in a jam and she wrote me a letter and asked me
                to help him. He was robbin' cars up on Marine
                Drive. So I got Brodkin to represent him and got
                him out of there. He helped him and got him
                out. In the meantime, my old lady finds the let-
                ter.

(Giancana and Ferraro laugh loudly.)

H: She didn't say anything to me but she gets on the
                phone and she tells the broad. She's hot! She
                says, "Listen, you son of a bitch, if I get my
                hands on you, you won't write any more let-
                ters!"

(Giancana and Ferraro continue to laugh loudly.)

H: She calls right in front of me! Then she hung up
                the phone and said "I have some more letters
                from girls, too and I'll take care of them, too."
                So I said, "Okay, but you got no business reading
                my mail, see?" This is gonna be the biggest thing
                that ever hit the mayor. This kid has got thirty
                coppers, he has them all set up.

Ferraro: There is no way we can send word to the mayor?

H: They already got recordings and everything! But
                I think you ought to send word to him not to put
                his head out too far. This will spread like wild-
                fire.

G: Our main job now is to beat this thing.

H: I got to get to this kid's sister and get her to come
                in and get him away.

G: You could say he was hypnotized.

H: But they already got six coppers who have con-
                fessed!

F: If we could find out where they're holding this
                guy. But Billie Jean could find out.

H: I don't know. When my old lady gets rough, she gets rough. I told her, "Don't you use that language around me. Be a lady," I told her. You got to control them. Well, boys, I don't see how the Democrats can win with this scandal. This will whip the hell out of this administration. What a lucky break for those bastards. We gotta get this kid out. I hate to do it but we got to watch out for this administration. But this might take some of the heat from the state's attorney off us, they'll be working so hard on this. I'll bet you anything that O'Connor [the superintendent of police] gets removed. But hell, the newspapers know he is an honest guy.

The next day, Humphreys and Ferraro conferred with Mike Brodkin, the mob attorney.

F: What a fuckin' mess! This stink will last forever! Thirteen more coppers they grabbed this morning!

Brodkin: You remember how me and Pat Marcy went to the judge for this kid? We got him a break, even had the charge changed. Covelli.

On January 26, 1960, Pat Marcy appeared at Celano's.

Marcy: Geez, the mayor is fit to be tied, Curley.

H: He's letting the pollack, Adamowski, rib him. And he shouldn't do that. Now the thing we don't want is for Joe Morris or Duffy to go in there, Pat. You suggest Phelan. Okay, let's see what we can do with Phelan.

Joe Morris and Bill Duffy were the two most incorruptible police officers in the CPD. Both friends of mine, and Duffy is one of my closest friends to this day. Kyran Phelan, at the time of the conversation, was acting superintendent of the Chicago PD.

On January 26, 1960, Humphreys was still trying to locate Morrison's sister. He told Ferraro: "We can tell her to give him five thousand dollars and tell him to claim he was hypnotized."

In the end, all the machinations of Humphreys, Ferraro, Giancana, D'Arco, and Marcy failed to bear fruit. They never did find Morrison's sister, and in fact, it turned out that Billie Jean Morrison was his aunt, not his sister. A "little birdie," the same one that flew over Chicago whenever we got a piece of intelligence that we could put to good use without jeopardizing our sources, whispered in State's Attorney Ben Adamowski's ear. "You better hide that informant of yours away in a nice secure place. The mob has an in to him. They're trying to find him to work an angle. And if they do, he'll either be rich or dead." Obviously, Adamowski knew he had a source who needed full protection in this case. However, he may not have realized that it was the mob that wanted Morrison to be quieted.

With Adamowski's protection, Morrison eventually blew the whistle on dozens of Chicago cops who were later convicted. The Summerdale Scandal engulfed the entire Daley administration, particularly the police department. Orlando W. Wilson, an honest California law professor who chaired the search committee commissioned by Daley to find a new police superintendent, was named the new superintendent in the end.

The uproar was so great, even Marcy and D'Arco in the First Ward could not put Phelan in the superintendent's spot. And as soon as Wilson was named superintendent a little birdie sang in his ear. Joe Morris was named deputy superintendent of the department and placed in charge of the Bureau of Inspectional Services with jurisdiction over the organized crime function. He immediately named Bill Duffy the commander of the Intelligence Division, which directly investigated the Chicago mob. The worst fears of the connection guys were realized.

This is a perfect example of the use of intelligence to fight the mob. We might not have been able to utilize the information we were getting from Little Al to prosecute mob figures, since that information was not valid evidence in court, but we could make excellent use of it to thwart Giancana, Humphreys, and the rest by negating their schemes for corruption.

The Summerdale Scandal was perhaps the low point in Daley's administration. It caused a complete reorganization of the police department. Humphreys continued his attempts to prevent this reorganization. On March 9, he met with Bill McFetridge, one of the police commissioners he had known for years, in a car out near O'Hare Airport, but this approach fizzled also. In the end, Daley survived the scandal and went on to serve as mayor for some sixteen more years.

In a strange twist of mob politics it wasn't long, October 1960, before the outfit was backing Adamowski, who they were working against just months earlier. Their enemy was now their favorite. Not because of anything Adamowski did or didn't do but because the connection guys concluded that as bad as he was he wouldn't be as bad for them as his opponent, Dan Ward, a law professor with an impeccable reputation. It was one of the few times the mob backed a Republican in Chicago.

Gussie Alex was the connection guy in charge of the Adamowski caper. He called Mike Brodkin to Celano's. He instructed Brodkin to meet with a close supporter of Adamowski and a top official in Adamowski's office, the Cook County state's attorney's office. Alex gave Brodkin an envelope that he told him contained $20,000. He instructed that the money be given in the presence of both contacts and that they be told: "This money is from Sam for any way he wants to use it." It would be understood by Adamowski's people that Sam was Sam Giancana, the mob boss.

The next day Brodkin returned with the $20,000. The two men had refused it. Brodkin was at a loss to explain his failure. "They wanted to talk to Sam even when I told them Sam is out of town. I think they might want an understanding of what we want for this." But they didn't take it.

As the years went by, the mob coexisted with Daley but with less and less contact. As I testified in 1983 before the U.S. Senate, Humphreys was to complain one day to John D'Arco, the man who recommended him to the connection guys, that "we can't even get our toe on the fifth floor." The fifth floor of City Hall is the location of the mayor's office.

Strange things were about to happen, though. Any problems Mayor Daley was to have with organized crime in Chicago were soon to be overshadowed by problems with the hippies and yippies who came into Chicago by the thousands during the Days of Rage in 1968.

It was one heck of a year. April 4, Martin Luther King was assassinated. And all hell broke loose in Chicago. Both the West

Side and the South Side exploded with rioting. For days all of
us, even in the FBI, stayed away from those areas except for the
most crucial business.

On June 6, Bobby Kennedy was killed in the Ambassador
Hotel in Los Angeles. Of course, he had left the Justice Department in late 1964. I have in my office in Tucson a large
Plexiglas case inscribed with the Justice Department shield, my
name, and the words: "Robert F. Kennedy, Attorney General,
1961–1964," a gift he sent me as he left the Justice Department.
I missed him a lot—a great and most capable guy.

But the real disruption in Chicago in 1968 came about, of
course, because of the Democratic Convention held at the International Amphitheater in Chicago the last week of August.
First the rioting at Lincoln Park at night; then the hippies and
yippies moved into the Loop during the day. "The whole world
is watching," they shouted as they ran roughshod over Chicago's downtown. This ended in a huge fracas at the Conrad Hilton. Johnny Bassett was assigned there, as liaison with Daley's
police.

Then on to the convention itself. I was the liaison there, at
the 13th Chicago Police District, down the block from Mayor
Daley's home at Thirty-Fifth and Lowe on the South Side, in
Bridgeport. That was the day Mayor Daley mouthed the words
that millions appeared to see on TV: "Fuck you, you Jew son
of a bitch. Go home!" These words were addressed to Senator
Abraham Ribicoff of Connecticut, who from the convention po-
dium was roundly criticizing the deplorable handling of the riot
situation.

Then came the prosecution of the Chicago Seven, the yippies
who had been involved in the riots. The finest Chicago United
States attorney I was to know, Tom Foran, personally led the
prosecution.

I remember those days well. I got into hot water with the
special agent in charge of the Chicago FBI, Marlin Johnson. It
wasn't the first time, nor would it be the last. I was the manager
of a baseball team in the Northern Illinois Collegiate Baseball
League; my son Bob was the catcher and leading hitter. We
played a weekend tournament in August in Hamilton Park.
Hamilton Park is located on the South Side of Chicago within
two miles of Marquette Park. The same weekend one of the
worst race riots in the history of Chicago occurred in Marquette

Park. We were the only white team out of eight teams in the tourney and spent the entire weekend less than two miles away, in perfect harmony, surrounded by black residences, with the park populated with blacks, with the exception of the fifteen members of our team.

I wrote a letter to the editor of the *Chicago Daily News* pleading for racial harmony in Chicago, mentioning our experience at Hamilton Park in contrast to the riots nearby at Marquette Park. I wrote as a concerned private citizen and did not identify myself as an FBI agent.

A couple days later, however, I was called on the carpet. The SAC, Marlin Johnson, was quite upset. He felt that I had no position to take upon myself the duties of an FBI spokesman in such a delicate matter. When I protested that I felt that I had my own rights as a private citizen to write such a letter and that nowhere therein had I identified myself with the FBI, he advised that many people who saw the letter would know of my affiliation. I shot back that I hoped he realized that I was on the right side of the issue and that it was time for healing. Nevertheless, he again called me "impetuous" as he had once before after he had been cited for contempt in a mob-related lawsuit. He warned me to keep a low profile thereafter.

In my opinion, Dick Daley was a good Chicago mayor. He had his weak points, as do all men, and I fault him for not dumping D'Arco. He always said that the people of the First Ward control their own destiny and if they wanted D'Arco and his ilk, that was their choice. He professed he could do nothing about it. As powerful a political boss as he was, however, I'm sure he could have exercised some leadership qualities and taken the bit in his mouth. But he never did. When Joe Valachi testified before the Senate in the sixties, he said that the mob had good relations with politicians in Chicago and that Chicago was politically corrupt. In response, Daley railed at Valachi rather than addressing the problem. In my opinion, Daley was not the best politician Chicago ever knew—that honor belonged to Governor Dick Ogilvie—but he was not the worst either. He certainly could have been a lot worse.

My point is that with the clout the Chicago mob had during the reign of Daley from the mid-fifties to the mid-seventies, it took a strong chief executive of the city to resist them. And Daley resisted them in most regards.

Eight years after the Days of Rage in Chicago, Jeannie and I were returning from Tucson after having spent three weeks visiting our son Bill. (It was December 1976, and Bill was the sports director of the CBS-TV affiliate in Tucson, KOLD-TV.) Early that afternoon we heard the news on our car radio that Daley had died of a heart attack! Another Chicago dinosaur was dead; a sad day . . . the end of an era.

Now Daley's son, Richard M. Daley, who's known as Rich, not Dick like his dad, is mayor of Chicago. May the mob find him, like his father, ''too weak'' to be corrupted. I'm sure that will be the case.

15 The Commission

One of the biggest bombshells Little Al dropped on us was on September 8, 1959, within just five weeks after we activated him. On that date Tony Accardo and Sam Giancana had a lengthy conference. Accardo had been the Chicago mob boss in the 1940s and until 1957 when he had had enough—enough power, enough money, enough headaches. So he had voluntarily stepped down as the top man at which point he selected Giancana to succeed him. But Accardo remained in a most powerful position of consiglieri (counselor and adviser). Consiglieri is an extremely powerful spot, in many ways more important than that of the boss himself. Of course, the importance of the post depends on the stature and influence of the man who holds the title of consiglieri. Accardo, a prominent member and/or leader of the Chicago outfit for parts of seven decades—since his beginnings with Al Capone in the mid-1920s—has been the most powerful member of the Chicago mob since 1946. As such Giancana did not hesitate to confide in him.

The first item on their agenda was the upcoming elections—
who they could support, who they should fight. They then
discussed a local prosecutor who they agreed was unduly influenced by the FBI in making gambling raids.

Giancana then discussed the problems Joe Bonanno was causing. Bonanno has been a mob boss longer than any other but
had become quite independent in dealing with his colleagues,
the bosses of the four other organized crime families in New
York City. He had compounded the problem by moving to Tucson and "planting a flag" there.

"Whoever goes for a vacation or lives there, they gotta go to
him now," said Giancana.

Accardo became quite upset with that. "That cocksucker!"
he said. "That's open territory. Who is he to put a fuckin' flag
up there and claim squatter's rights."

This led into what was to be, for us, and for all law enforcement, virgin territory. Never before had anybody outside the
mob been privy to the kind of conversation that followed.

It became obvious from the statements made by these two
most powerful mob leaders that there was, in fact, a national
ruling body of the mob! There was what Accardo and Giancana
referred to repeatedly as the Commission, a group of the most
powerful mob bosses in the country, which apparently varied in
size from nine to twelve. This commission ruled over the affairs
of organized crime nationwide. We discovered several years
later, when Joe Valachi, a member of the Genovese family in
New York, testified before the Senate, that they called their organization "La Cosa Nostra." In Italian La Cosa Nostra means
"our thing," but we hadn't adopted that terminology as of the
date of this conversation.

Up to that day in 1959, we were not aware that they had an
official name for the organization and we equated all of the
names in common usage as meaning organized crime—the Mafia, the mob, the outfit, the crime syndicate. In fact, I don't
recall that I ever heard any of the Chicago mobsters refer to their
organization as La Cosa Nostra or Our Thing. That was used in
the East and became the official nomenclature used by the FBI
in referring to what is known as "traditional organized crime."

We used it, I believe, much more often than the mob did in
referring to traditional organized crime as opposed to street,
prison, or ethnic gangs. Those gangs were the responsibility of

local law enforcement. (The FBI in my day had no investigative interest in street gangs. Today the Bureau spends a great deal of time investigating them due to their deep involvement in narcotics. In my day [1950-1980] the FBI had no responsibility for drug investigation; but today the FBI works closely with the Drug Enforcement Administration [DEA] and local police in that area.)

As if that wasn't enough to put on our plate, Giancana and Accardo went on to cut us in on the identities of the then current members of the Commission.

There was Joe Zerelli from Detroit; Joe Ida in Philadelphia; Bonanno, Carlo Gambino, Joe Profaci (Accardo referred to him as Joe Profach), Vito Genovese and Tommy "Three Fingers Brown" Lucchese from the five New York families; Raymond Patriarca from Boston; Giancana from Chicago; John La Rocca from Pittsburgh; and Steve Maggadino from Buffalo. It appeared there was also one other on the Commission, making a total of twelve at the time of the conversation, but we could not be certain of the identity or location of the twelfth member. It may have been John Scalish in Cleveland.

When I monitored, transcribed, and analyzed that conversation and sent it off in the daily summary airtel to the Bureau, it caused an overnight sensation. Because of the obvious importance that was attached to the information, we called the Bureau on the day we heard it. The supervisors at the time were inclined to be skeptical. This was too much! Hadn't Mr. Hoover been saying for years that there was no national body of organized crime? Our evidence amounted to heresy!

I knew this would be the reaction at the Bureau. As a result, I was very careful in transcribing the tape of the conversation. I wanted to make no mistakes. If the tape was unclear at any point, I resolved the interpretation by being very conservative.

When the Bureau received our airtel, they burned up the wires to Chicago. "Are you sure you heard this? Are you sure you mean that?"

I told them I was sure.

A copy of the airtel went to each of the offices that had a commission member. New York, Buffalo, Detroit, Boston all had no problems with the information. Of course they hadn't known about a commission that acted as a national ruling body.

But they readily accepted the information and the identification of the members in their divisions.

Not so Philadelphia and, to a lesser extent, Pittsburgh.

The Philadelphia office had closed its investigation of its member, Joe Ida. That office told the Bureau that Ida was "an old man, he's retired, he doesn't amount to anything anymore." Obviously, they now had egg on their face. The Bureau immediately plastered them, telling them they obviously weren't making much of their THP program. Why couldn't they be more like those guys out there in Chicago? the Bureau demanded. They were told to get on the ball, and do it pronto!

Pittsburgh was in similar shape. They had been telling the Bureau that John La Rocca (or La Rock, as Accardo called him) was of diminished importance in the Steel City. As a result they were not putting much effort into investigating him. The Bureau saw fit to chide them more than a little.

In order to save face, Philadelphia protested to the Bureau that we couldn't have heard right or that we hadn't interpreted the conversation properly, that Ida couldn't possibly be important enough to be a member of something called the Commission. If he was, then the Commission couldn't be what we interpreted it to be, a national ruling body of the mob.

With that, the Bureau instructed us to send them the tape of the Accardo-Giancana conference. They would listen to it with the more sophisticated equipment available in Washington. They would enhance the conversation, and they would interpret it.

Now I was a little anxious. If the Bureau came up with a different understanding—if they heard the Accardo-Giancana conversation differently and put a different spin on the analysis— I would be discredited. I held my breath, although I was confident that I was right.

When the Bureau returned the copy of their transcription, it completely vindicated me. I had heard what Little Al had given us, precisely and accurately, and my analysis was right on target. The Bureau had no quarrel with my work; indeed, they endorsed it.

The Commission has become a real lightning rod in recent years. Rudolph Giuliani, the top-flight United States attorney for the southern district of New York (Manhattan), has used the RICO Statute (Racketeer-Influenced and Corrupt Organizations Act) to attack the Commission itself, or at least its members

from the five New York families. He and his staff won that case.
The New York family bosses and many of their subordinates
have been sent to prison.

The Commission should not be confused with the gathering
of some seventy top mobsters around the country convened at
the estate of Joe Barbara in Apalachin, New York, on November
14, 1957. That was obviously intended to be a high-level meeting of top mobsters from around the country. It is believed that
each member of the Commission attended, but there were many
more mob members there than just members of the Commission. As far as I know, no one ever knew the definitive reason
for the Apalachin conference. The best theory may be that it
concerned the killing of Albert Anastasia on October 25 in the
barber shop of the Park Sheraton in New York. The conference
arose from a need to damper the internecine warfare that may
have been about to take place, especially among the five New
York families.

The Commission overheard on Little Al was a great breakthrough in our intelligence work. Coming as it did, just five
weeks after we had penetrated their headquarters, it guaranteed
our standing in the Bureau as the most highly regarded Top
Hoodlum Squad. We had already been privy to a dozen highly
significant conversations, and we were to pick up hundreds more
during the next six years. But the news about the Commission
really established our credentials. As a matter of fact, I got two
incentive awards from Mr. Hoover for the installation and development of Little Al, one award for putting him in place, and
the other for the monitoring, transcription, analysis, and reporting. I was Little Al's daddy.

As our interest in the Commission was whetted, we strained
for more news of the same. We were to learn that Buffalo was
dropped when Maggadino died and that Pittsburgh was also
eliminated from membership on the Commission. We were to
find that although it was the ruling body of the mob across the
country, it was not to involve itself in the internal workings of a
"family"—the group that controlled each area. There was the
Giancana family for Chicago, the Gambino family for one of
the five New York groups, and the Patriarca family for New
England. And as powerful as the Commission is, it cannot mess
with individual families. For instance, Giancana had no power
whatsoever to go into Detroit and tell Zerelli, the boss there,

how to handle his affairs or who to appoint. More importantly, Giancana could not become involved in an activity in Detroit without the clearance of Zerelli.

But that prohibition did not extend to open territories. Miami, for instance, has been more or less an open territory for many years. The limit of that territory was defined by Santo Traffi-cante, Jr., who was the boss down the road in Tampa. So Miami—at least during the life of Trafficante—was open but not wide.

However, there was one *wide*-open territory and it was a doozy!

16

Las Vegas— "Vegmon"

From the beginning, Al brought us the intelligence that the Chicago family had vital interests in the desert. Conversations were often spiced with mentions of Las Vegas. We learned that when Ben "Bugsy" Siegel, with his partner, Meyer Lansky, was building the Flamingo, the first hotel-casino on Las Vegas Boulevard, Murray Humphreys was there with him. More than once, Hump was to comment about his experiences with "Bugs" in Las Vegas and in Los Angeles (where the Chicago family was also solidly entrenched).

We never knew what, if any, financial interest Chicago had in the Flamingo. But as time went on, we learned that Chicago was thoroughly enmeshed in the desert gambling capital, and was en route to becoming the primary mob family in control.

In 1931, Nevada legalized all forms of gambling. Some of the early casinos—like Harold's Club, Harrah's Club and the El Rancho—did quite well in places like Reno and downtown Las Vegas. But it wasn't until Frank Costello and Meyer Lansky, the New York family bosses, sent Siegel to begin construction of the Flamingo in 1943 that organized crime became aware of the gold mine that Las Vegas gambling could become.

Then Siegel was murdered at the home of his girlfriend, Virginia Hill, in Beverly Hills. Coincidentally, Wilbur Clark began to build the Desert Inn. And in 1948 came the Thunderbird, another Lansky venture.

In 1949, although it was not to be apparent at the time, a landmark decision was made. The International Brotherhood of Teamsters started its Central States Pension Fund.

This was to become of extreme pertinence when Humphreys, with Paul "Red" Dorfman out front, became acquainted with Detroit Teamster James Riddle Hoffa. Dorfman, an old-time labor hack in Chicago who was close to Humphreys, vouched for Hoffa and told Hump that if the boys in Chicago would support Hoffa, he, "Red" Dorfman, could influence and control him.

The same year, 1949, saw the arrival in Las Vegas of Morris Barney "Moe" Dalitz. He was to become known popularly as "the godfather of Las Vegas." Although never a made member of La Cosa Nostra, Dalitz enjoyed a close association with many of the top members of the New York and Chicago mobs, to say nothing of Detroit and Cleveland. As a result of his prominence in Las Vegas, he was probably the number-one target of the Top Hoodlum Program in our Salt Lake City Division. In 1957, the Las Vegas FBI office was a resident agency reporting to its headquarters, Salt Lake City. Not until the THP got fully under way did Mr. Hoover find that there was more than enough work in the Sin Capital to justify making it a full division. Soon the Las Vegas agents like Tommy Parker, Warren Salisbury, Mike Simon, and others focused much of their attention on the investigation of Dalitz and his associates. They discovered that Dalitz had been a bootlegger in Detroit in the prohibition era. He had teamed up with members of the Purple Gang (the ruling body of organized crime in Detroit before the Italians took over) such as the Bernstein brothers, Joe and Benny. But when the Zerellis were chased out of St. Louis and invaded the territory of the Purple Gang in Detroit, Dalitz moved to Cleveland where he again became involved in bootleg alcohol on a large scale. In addition he muscled his way into the rackets—gambling, pinball machines, and slot machines. He became leader of a powerful mob in Cleveland known as the "Mayfield Road Gang." Dalitz developed strong political connections in Cleveland and soon controlled the bookmaking, policy, and numbers rackets. He then took control of the racing news service, without which horse bookmakers could not operate.

In the late 1930s, Moe Dalitz developed a close alliance with New York mobsters Louis Buchalter and Jake Shapiro and with Abe "Longy" Zwillman in New Jersey. Dalitz became especially close to Frank "the Prime Minister of Organized Crime" Costello and to Lansky, the New York mob financial genius. This led to an association with Humphreys, Nitti, and Guzik in Chicago.

In the early forties, Dalitz and his Mayfield Road Gang associates worked closely with Joe Massey in Detroit. They built a dog track in Dayton, Ohio, with the Polizzi brothers and moved into northern Kentucky, across the Ohio River from Cincinnati, where he built the Beverly Hills Country Club in Fort Thomas and the Lookout House in Newport, both sites of casino gambling. From 1942 to 1945 he was in the Army, but continued to maintain his interest with members of the Mayfield Road Gang such as Morris Kleinman, Louis Rothkopf (aka Lou Rody), Sam Tucker, and Charley Polizzi. Their headquarters was in Suite 281 at the Hollenden Hotel in Cleveland.

It was soon after Dalitz got out of the Army in 1945 that he made his move on Las Vegas. Through his alliance with Costello and Lansky he became aware of the city's potential. He made overtures indicating that he wanted to become financially involved with the Flamingo. And when Wilbur Clark had financial trouble at the Desert Inn, Dalitz and his Mayfield Road Gang moved in. In 1949 they finished construction of the D.I., as it is commonly referred to, and opened it in 1950.

Coincidentally, the same year the Kefauver Committee held its widely publicized televised hearings, Dalitz and Accardo, then the absolute boss in Chicago, were both in the spotlight.

In 1952 the Sands opened. The Strip was building up. In 1955 came the Riviera, the Dunes, and the Royal Nevada. In 1957, just before Albert Anastasia was killed, Costello was shot in the lobby of his residence opposite Central Park in New York. He survived, and when the police arrived and searched his pockets they found the records for the Tropicana in Vegas, which had just opened the day before. The records were in the handwriting of a key employee, Louie Lederer, a frequent visitor to the tailor shop in Chicago. Obviously, Lederer was fronting for Costello and the New York families in the "Trop."

Although Humphreys was closely following developments in Vegas through Chicago's rep, Johnny Roselli, we know of no financial interest up to the mid-fifties on the part of Chicago in Las Vegas. But things were about to change—and when they did, Chicago landed in Vegas with both feet.

A Los Angeles gambler named Tony Cornero had started to build the Stardust on the Strip, across the street from the Riviera and the D.I. In 1955, Cornero died and Jake "The Barber" Factor moved into the Stardust.

Factor had a long association with Hump. Hump is thought to have been behind the scenes when Factor was kidnapped in Chicago in the early 1930s. Roger Tuohy, a rival mob leader, was convicted for the crime and sent away, probably framed by Hump and Factor. When Tuohy returned from prison in 1959 he was immediately murdered on the steps of his house in front of his bodyguard, a retired Chicago cop. Although the newspapers blamed Humphreys and the police sought him for questioning, Little Al, who had taken up residence in the tailor shop a couple months before the Tuohy killing, never indicated to us that Hump was involved.

Throughout Factor's involvement in the Stardust Hump stayed close to him and in 1958 influenced him to lease the Stardust to Dalitz's United Hotels Corporation, the corporation that was running the D.I. Our friend, Johnny Drew, the guy Hump and Les Kruse were meeting at St. Hubert's Grill when Ralph Hill ordered his Waldorf salad with Thousand Island dressing and I ordered my lionized potatoes, was installed by Hump as the boss at the Stardust.

Obviously, their meeting concerned their move into Las Vegas, although it escaped us at the time. The Chicago mob had arrived. Now there would be no holding them in Las Vegas.

In 1959, another landmark development. The Central States Pension Fund of the Teamsters loaned the Stardust one million dollars. From then on, truck drivers, warehousemen, and taxi drivers from all over the country would be using a hunk of their hard-earned wages to finance the Chicago mob's moves in Las Vegas. Hump manipulated the fund through his dealings with Hoffa. He moved Red Dorfman's son, Allen, into a position with the Central States Pension Fund. Consequently very high-risk loans were made from the fund, thereby making the fund the personal bank of Hump and his fellow Chicago mobsters.

This was to be completely documented, not by me but by my fellow agents, Pete Wacks and Art Pfizenmayer, who succeeded me soon after I left Chicago in 1978, in what they code-named the "Pendorf" case—penetration of Dorfman. Wacks, Pfizenmayer, and other Chicago FBI agents planted microphones in the offices of Dorfman in the International Tower near O'Hare airport on Bryn Mawr Avenue. These mikes were planted under the authority given the FBI in the Safe Streets Act of 1968 wherein an affidavit can be presented to federal court and authority granted by the court for the installation of the microphone. Under this law, any information developed from the eavesdropping is evidentiary and can be used in court to assist in the prosecution of the subject. Like the tapes we got from Little Al and his brothers, installed throughout Chicago, the information obtained was for intelligence purposes only. Obviously, that information was of highly significant value, especially in the early stages of the Top Hoodlum Program when we were starting from scratch in our investigation of the mob. But since "Title Three's"—the FBI terminology for the court-ordered eavesdropping authority, named after the section of the act that authorizes it—are admissible in evidence, they are a big step up from our early installations.

It was in 1959 that Little Al began telling us that Hump, Paul Ricca, and Tony Accardo had made an accord with Dalitz and his Cleveland Mayfield Road Gang. What the gang had in Vegas they shared with Chicago. On January 5, 1961, Dalitz and Kleinman came into Chicago. They met in a Chicago hotel with Hump, Accardo, and Giancana. A new deal was worked out making Chicago a greater partner not only in the Stardust but also in the Desert Inn, the Riviera, and the Fremont. They discussed Giancana's idea of making a paper transaction at the Stardust so that Factor could take $11 million out and then the Chicago group would sell it for a profit of $6 million. That idea was rejected because the skim at the Stardust was worth much more over the long run.

"Skim" in Las Vegas is the raison d'être for the mob's interest. If the mob could not skim from a casino there would be little reason to be involved. The mob does not actually expect profit from the operation. Most owners and operators of the casinos hope for profit from the tables and the slots, and they earn enough to make gaming industry stocks hot. The gaming industry is big business and it's good business.

But the mob cares a lot less about showing a paper profit on its hotel-casinos than do legitimate operators. Instead, the mob wants to know how much it can skim. Quite simply, skim is the practice of taking money after it leaves the tables or the slot machines and before it is officially counted. In each casino there is a counting room. It is under twenty-four-hour camera surveillance. Periodically, the drop box under each table is picked up by security guards and taken to the counting room. There it sits until the next day when its contents are officially counted and the day's tabulation is entered on the books. The proceeds of the slot machines are handled similarly, although the coins are weighed rather than counted.

The principal method of skimming money from the casinos is by intercepting it between the tables and the counting room or in the counting room before the daily tally is taken, using pit bosses and other casino employees who are under control of the mob. It can be accomplished by shielding security cameras or in the "eye in the sky" (the peepholes in the ceiling of the casino where security employees peer down on the tables). Carl Thomas, who worked for the acknowledged master of skim, Joe Agosto, was overheard by the FBI in a conversation later used as evidence in the Strawman Case that there were "twenty-one holes in the bucket," meaning there were at least that many foolproof methods of skimming. (The Strawman Case, by the way, was a big trial in which a number of mobsters from major metropolitan areas across the country were indicted and convicted for illegal activities in Vegas; more on that later.)

However, the money from the tables and slots can be waylaid. This money never gets counted; it's never officially tabulated and recorded for income tax purposes; and it's never divided with the ostensible owners. It becomes pure gravy for the mob.

This income, couriered to Chicago, was to be the number-one source of income to the Chicago mob for more than the next two decades.

In 1963, we initiated the "Vegmon" caper—Vegas money. We traced the money as it poured out of Las Vegas. The money got to Chicago, to Miami (where Lansky was residing), and to New York, Cleveland, Detroit, Kansas City, Philadelphia, Tampa, and Milwaukee. It also reached lesser places such as

New Orleans (where Carlos Marcello had a piece), Providence, Rhode Island (where Raymond Patriarca had a hunk), and St. Louis (the home site of Morris Shenker, a court attorney who has represented many of the St. Louis and Kansas City mobsters).

The Las Vegas office bugged one of the mob-run casinos (the Fremont) and learned that Ida Devine, the wife of Irving "Niggy" Devine, owner of the New York Meat Company, which supplied the hotels in Vegas, was being used as the prime courier for skim money.

So the Bureau coordinated a nationwide surveillance of Ida. She left Las Vegas by train. On January 10, she arrived at Union Station in Chicago. There she was met by George Bieber. Bieber was the law partner of our friend Mike Brodkin. Whereas Brodkin was extremely close socially and professionally to Gussie Alex, Bieber worked hand in glove with Felix "Milwaukee Phil" Alderisio.

Bieber escorted Ida and her luggage to the Ambassador East Hotel on Goethe Street, a couple of blocks from Gussie's condominium on Lake Shore Drive. It is one of the posh Chicago hotels, next door to the Ambassador West, the home of the famous Pump Room where Gussie and Margaret dined frequently with Sidney and Bea Korshak.

Bieber and Ida spent a couple of hours at the hotel. When they reemerged, they went back to Union Station where Ida left on the 4:33 en route to Hot Springs, Arkansas.

Within a week, the skim was so heavy that Ida was back again to make her trip. This time her escort was Mike Brodkin whose law firm appeared to do a lot of business with Ida. Again they went to the Ambassador East. This time Ida stayed overnight. The next day, confirming our information that she would travel from Vegas first to the boys in Chicago and then to Lansky, she left on the train to Miami.

On subsequent trips Ida was tailed to Cleveland, confirming that John Scalish, the boss there, had interests in Vegas. However, we later learned that Scalish had his own personal courier, Georgie Gordon. He was sent from Vegas to Cleveland in September 1963 and on March 5, 1964.

We learned that Sam Giancana no longer trusted anybody else to bring his money in from Vegas. We found that he was flying regularly to Los Angeles, renting a car there and driving to Vegas. (We also learned that Giancana, the biggest playboy in

the Chicago family, had a love interest that took him to Las
Vegas. But that information will be chronicled later.)

In the late 1950s Chicago's man in Vegas, Johnny Roselli,
fell into disfavor with the mob. Roselli was perceived by the
mob bosses back home as having gotten a little too big for his
britches. He had been sent out West by Nitti, kept there by
Ricca, and when Ricca had been convicted in the Hollywood
Extortion Case, by Accardo. The Chicago mob, through their
control of labor unions, had put the squeeze on the movie industry to the tune of over a million dollars. Nitti himself had
been indicted, but in 1943, rather than face trial, the old "Enforcer," Capone's underboss who had succeeded him and run
the Chicago family for over a decade, finally lost his nerve. He
committed suicide. Ricca took over for him and held the reins
until he was convicted in the mid-forties. Then Accardo took
over. All of these bosses retained Roselli as their man on the
West Coast.

But in the late 1950s, Giancana replaced Roselli with Marshall Caifano. Roselli was to go on and find more trouble for
himself by cheating celebrities in Beverly Hills. He devised a
scheme whereby he had a peephole in the ceiling of the Friars
Club on Wilshire Boulevard, just inside the Beverly Hills city
limits. His men were able to observe the cards of the many
movie moguls who played there and to send an impulse elec-
tronically to a confederate in the game. Caught and convicted,
he was sent to prison. Roselli came out a broken man. Although
he hung on for a while, supported by friends who had known
him in the salad days, in the late seventies he moved to Florida
to live with his sister. One day his dismembered body was found
in an oil drum floating in Biscayne Bay, not far from Hump's
home at 210 Keystone Drive.

Caifano arrived in Las Vegas soon after his disagreement with
the mob hit man, "Milwaukee Phil" Alderisio, which we heard
from Little Al. But Alderisio was to find himself in hot water in
Vegas shortly thereafter. He and a gunsel named Willie "Ice-
pick" Alderman got caught by the FBI "putting the arm on"—
that is extorting—from a legitimate guy from Denver named
Robert Sunshine. They threatened his life. Alderisio was caught
and convicted.

Actually, Ralph Hill, Maz Rutland, and I had a nice little
reunion at "Milwaukee Phil's" expense. In 1963, Ralph had

been transferred to Miami where he became supervisor of the organized crime squad; in 1966, Maz had been promoted to Bureau headquarters where he became a supervisor in the Chicago organized crime program. In 1966, Alderisio appealed his extortion conviction, claiming we used an illegal wiretap to collect the evidence against him. Ralph, Maz, Christy Malone, Gus Kempff, Vince Inserra, and I were subpoenaed to testify in Denver. I broke a record at the Bratskeller, a basement restaurant in Larimar Square, the ''old town'' district, by eating nine bratwurst plates—that's bratwurst on a bun with potato salad on the side. As far as I know, I still hold that record. And, by the way, Alderisio was convicted on appeal—in part due to our testimony.

In 1962, some time after Caifano took charge as the Chicago rep in Vegas, a startling event occurred. The eccentric multimillionaire industrialist, Howard Hughes, arrived on the scene. He made contact through his right-hand man, former FBI agent Bob Maheu, with the then governor, Paul Laxalt. At the time it was against the laws of Nevada for a public company to own casinos. Laxalt, apparently hoping that he would get a job with Hughes when he left office, inveigled a change in the law. Hughes then brought his Summa Corporation into Vegas. Eventually he was to own the Desert Inn, then the Sands, the Frontier, and the Castaways, all on the Strip, and the Landmark, several blocks off it.

The next year saw another interesting development. Frank Sinatra gave up his gaming license, all because of our buddy, Sam ''Mo'' Giancana. That summer Mo shook our tail and flew from Chicago to visit the Cal-Neva Lodge. We suspected, from information furnished us by Little Al's brother, that Giancana owned an interest with Sinatra in the Cal-Neva. Sinatra was the owner of record. The Cal-Neva is a hotel-casino, half of which is located in the state of California and the other half, in Nevada. It sits high on a bluff above Lake Tahoe. Behind the high rise part of the hotel are a dozen or more villas strung out down the bluff almost to the lake. In one of those villas stayed Phyllis McGuire, one of the singing McGuire Sisters, who were entertaining at the Cal-Neva at the time. Mo and Phyllis had a thing for each other and he moved in with her.

This is against the Gaming Control Commission rules. No mobster who is listed in Nevada's ''Black Book'' can be allowed on the premises of a hotel-casino in Nevada. Violation of the

rule means disaster for management and ownership. A little
birdie sang to the chairman of the Gaming Control Commission.
That little birdie, the same one who chirps so often in Chicago,
said, "Giancana is being entertained by Sinatra at the Cal-
Neva." Sinatra was called on the phone by the Gaming Control
chairman. One word led to another, and soon Sinatra completely lost his head and shouted obscenities. As it ended up,
Sinatra had no more license. In fact his license was not restored
for many years until Ronald Reagan became president and went
to bat for him. (Reagan also gave Sinatra the Medal of Freedom,
considered—at least until the singer got it—the highest award a
civilian can win in this country.)

Meanwhile Caifano had become a problem in Las Vegas. He
was too highly visible, fighting with his wife and arguing with
his buddies. He extorted from a southern Indiana oilman, Ray
Ryan, and drew the attention of the Gaming Control Board by
provoking a situation at the Desert Inn. Enough was enough
already for Mo.

The Chicago mob selected a tough young firebrand to replace
Caifano—Tony "The Ant" Spilotro. Spilotro had been a noto-
rious Chicago burglar, but soon after he went on to bigger things.
Spilotro became a juice collector for our friend, Mad Sam
DeStefano. You'll remember that Spilotro was with DeStefano
when they attempted to ambush me at Patsy Colletti's.

Spilotro arrived in Vegas in 1971. He set up his act in the gift
shop at Circus-Circus, under the name of Anthony Stuart. He
also held sway at the Dunes and at the Las Vegas Country Club.

It was the responsibility of the Chicago rep in Las Vegas to
provide the muscle. Not the brains, just the brawn. He was not
supposed to set any policy or be involved at all in the operation
of the skim. In Vegas, Chicago has what is called a "Mr. Outside" and what is called a "Mr. Inside." In the seventies, Spilotro was "Mr. Outside." If Chicago wanted something done
and it took a little persuasion, Spilotro was the man. And if one
of the "Mr. Insides" got out of line, maybe grabbed a little too
much skim, it was Spilotro's job to find him.

There were many "Mr. Insides" in Las Vegas in the seventies, all guys who were placed in the casinos by the Chicago
family. But the most important insider of all during those years
was Frank "Lefty" Rosenthal.

I had first met Lefty in 1961 when he was just a young kid

working for Donald Angelini, now a Chicago capo, and for Bill Kaplan at the Angel-Kaplan Sports Service on Clark Street. I had posed as a degenerate baseball gambler to uncover what was going on. Rosenthal left Chicago to run a sports gambling operation in Miami. While there he got in trouble fixing a basketball game in North Carolina. Then, on the recommendation of Angelini, Lefty was sent to Vegas. He was put in charge of the Stardust casino—although not officially. Things were a little rough for a while: Spilotro seduced Lefty's wife, and somebody bombed his car.

But Lefty got straightened out and did one hell of a job for the boys. He made sure the skim was huge and he kept his eye on Allen Glick, the guy who was fronting for the mob at the Stardust and the Hacienda. Glick was a legit young businessman from San Diego who went to college with one of the sons of Frank Balistrieri, the mob boss in Milwaukee. The son recommended Glick to his father, who recommended him to Chicago—and, presto, this young kid with no background in gaming gets a $62.75 million loan from the Central States Pension Fund of the Teamsters Union.

Glick became the owner of record at the Stardust, the flagship casino of the Chicago family. The Stardust caters to the low rollers in Vegas. Whereas Caesar's Palace, the Bally Grand (the old MGM), and (to some extent) the Vegas Hilton attract the high roller and the upscale gambler, the Stardust goes after the blue-collar bettor. It has many inexpensive rooms in its high-rise hotel. In back are other rooms that resemble Motel 6's, as well as many acres of hook-ups for RV's. The casino has two-dollar-minimum blackjack tables. In Las Vegas parlance, the Stardust is known as the ultimate "grind joint." They grind them in and grind them out.

(Incidentally, the garish blue lights of the Stardust shine down on the almost equally garish copper roof of the Guardian Angel Cathedral. On my many business trips to Las Vegas, I always visit the cathedral once a day. But I never get the feeling that I am in a particularly pious place. If you can depict a Las Vegas cathedral, Guardian Angel would be it. Maybe I'm being sacrilegious, but the figure of the Risen Christ on the sanctuary mural behind the altar reminds me of a disco dancer. I recently rode on a plane from Las Vegas to Reno with Mike O'Callaghan, the former governor, then a columnist for Hank Greenspun's *Las Vegas Sun*. He told me Guardian Angel was built in 1963 with contributions from the casino owners in Vegas; Moe Dalitz was a major contributor. It figures.)

Lefty Rosenthal was a natural for Vegas. He achieved the highest of profiles. He had a weekly television talk show, à la Johnny Carson and the ''Tonight Show,'' that was appropriately called ''The Frank Rosenthal Show.'' Lefty had Sinatra, Shecky Green, and many other entertainers from the Stardust itself.

But in 1978 he was forced out of the Stardust by the Gaming Control Commission. And with Rosenthal out of the Stardust, Glick himself was forced out. Into his spot stepped Al Sachs and Herb Tobman. I know very little about Tobman, who later ran for governor of Nevada. But Al Sachs I had known of for years. His dad was a stickman for Les Kruse, Gus Liebe and Rocco Fischetti at the Big Game, the casinolike gambling operation in Chicago that moved from place to place, one step ahead of the police. Little Al told us that whenever one of the mob had a friend or contact they wanted to wine and dine on the house (called ''comping'' in Las Vegas) they contacted Ralph Pierce, who called Al Sachs.

In 1980, the FBI sent a hard-hitting FBI agent to Las Vegas to be the special agent in charge. His name was Joe Yablonsky. At that time I only knew Joe by reputation. He had started in New York working for the famous Jack Danahy, the supervisor of the THP squad. Jack often tells the story about how he was driving John Malone, the SAC of the NYO at the time, in the eighties along Park Avenue. There was Joe Yablonsky, who should have been on the job, walking his dog up Park Avenue. Jack quickly diverted Malone's attention by pointing out an innocent passerby on the other side of the avenue as ''Potsy'' Pagoo, the notorious bookmaker! (Actually, Joe was on a surveillance and was using the dog as a decoy.)

After his stint in New York, Joe transferred to Miami where he worked for Ralph Hill and quickly made a great name for himself as ''the King of Sting.'' He was the role model upon which the Bureau based its current undercover agent program.

When Joe came out, he was assigned to Boston as assistant special agent in charge (ASAC) and then to that favorite city of mine, Cincinnati, as SAC. His next step was the gaming capital of America. In 1980, needing a very aggressive, knowledgeable hands-on SAC in Las Vegas, Judge Webster, the FBI director, assigned Yablonsky. Joe quickly assumed a high profile. He struck out at all the mobsters, both officially and unofficially. He got on television and in the press and lambasted the corruption in Las Vegas. And he achieved a great deal. The first sitting federal judge ever to be convicted of a federal crime was convicted by work of the agents under Joe's command.

But Las Vegas fought back. Senator Paul Laxalt, the closest friend of President Reagan, used his influence, unsuccessfully, to have Joe transferred. He announced that law enforcement in Las Vegas under Yablonsky was too aggressive.

In 1982, Yablonsky retired. But even then, his enemies didn't quit. They tried to lift his private investigator's license. He moved to San Francisco, and still they kept after him. They accused him of coming into Nevada to work illegally after his Nevada P.I. license had expired.

From the time the Chicago mob got its hooks in the Stardust, that became its flagship casino. And it would remain so into the eighties.

In 1976, the watershed event occurred that locked Chicago into Las Vegas and locked the other families out. The voters of New Jersey passed a referendum legalizing casino gambling in Atlantic City. For the first time, Las Vegas had a worthy rival.

In 1977 there was a meeting of the Commission, the ruling body of the national mob. Chicago advanced a proposition. "You guys in the East take Atlantic City. Chicago will take Nevada."

At first the eastern mobsters, the Gambinos in particular, protested. What they said in effect, was, "This is not fair. Las Vegas is a going thing. We know what we've got out there. We *don't* know what we've got in Atlantic City."

Joey Auippa was representing Chicago on the Commission that day. Joey had Tony Accardo behind him, and Accardo had prepared Auippa well for that meeting. When Auippa spoke, he said the lines that Accardo had prepared for him. "Number one," he said, "we will grandfather you guys in."

"Watch how you're talkin'!" the eastern families protested.

Auippa, who a couple days before did not himself know what a "grandfather clause" is, explained: "Hold on, by that we mean that what you got in Vegas today you got tomorrow. You keep it. Now, number two. We got Dorfman, we got the pension fund. You want to make a point of it, we can lock you out there.

Number three, we got our soldiers out there in place now. Spilotro and the guys he has brought out there with him. You don't want to fight them. Four, we got the politicians. It's our guys out there been contributing to them. They belong to us. And there are other reasons. Listen, you'll have a good deal. Go to school on what we done in Vegas, you got it all laid out for you. And remember, we already got most of Las Vegas, we could make a big play in Atlantic City, especially with our bank, and wind up with most of Atlantic City, too. Then where would you guys be?''

It was a strong argument. Although the Gambinos were the last to fall in line, they finally did. The pact was made. Henceforth, Chicago would have Vegas, except for those hotel-casinos "grandfathered in," and Atlantic City would be left for New York, Philadelphia, New England, and the rest of the East.

The way it has worked out, Chicago, with its close association with Detroit and Cleveland, and particularly through its working arrangement with the Civella family in Kansas City, made a great thing out of its prize. After 1976, Vegas was no longer an open city in mob parlance. It was Chicago's.

The eastern mobs did not prosper, but this wasn't the fault of Atlantic City. As a gambling capital, it soon developed into a mighty rival for Las Vegas. Due to its proximity to New York City, Newark, Philadelphia, Baltimore, Washington, and Pittsburgh, it is a great spot, for the low rollers. Anyone can bus into Atlantic City in the morning, spend the day in the casinos and the boardwalk, and be home late that night.

But for various reasons the eastern mobs were not able to make in Atlantic City what had been made for all the families in Las Vegas. One reason was probably ineptitude. No longer were Costello or Lansky calling the shots. They didn't have the bank, the Teamster pension funds. But perhaps more important, New Jersey regulation has been much tougher. New Jersey authorities went to school on what had happened in Nevada and even before the first brick was laid in Atlantic City, New Jersey had set up its Casino Control Commission and its investigative arm, the Division of Gaming Enforcement. Nevada, in contrast, waited until long after the hoods had become entrenched before it chartered its Gaming Control Commission and its enforcement arm, the Gaming Control Board.

Jersey made a decision to start tough and remain tough. Even though that state is hardly noted for incorruptible public officials, the eastern La Costa Nostra families have been unable to do in New Jersey what had been done in Nevada—make the town their own.

Several years ago* I saw the figures, comparing money and manpower the two states were then spending on gaming regulation. New Jersey was spending $3.4 million per casino in Atlantic City; Nevada was spending $32,000 per casino. The state of New Jersey had 92.3 employees policing each casino there; Nevada employed 1.1 person to look after each casino. All in all, Chicago outwitted their eastern brothers for quite a time.

In Las Vegas itself, Tony Spilotro cut a wide swath. Although Roselli and Caifano, his predecessors, were also flamboyant guys, Las Vegas woke up when Spilotro arrived in 1971. Spilotro did what none of his predecessors had done—he assembled in Las Vegas a bunch of thug burglars, known as the "Hole in the Wall Gang." Marshall Caifano has never been considered a bright guy but, in my opinion, compared to Spilotro he is brilliant. As far as I'm concerned, his nickname "The Ant" referred not to his diminutive stature but to the minuscule size of his brain. I told some of his colleagues in Chicago my opinion, sure that they would relay the message to Spilotro out in Vegas. I heard he didn't like it, but I never liked him either—especially after he and DeStefano tried to ambush me back in Chicago. There are mobsters like Hump and Pierce who had a sense of dignity. And then there were guys like Giancana, DeStefano, Alderisio, and Spilotro who would stop at nothing.

Soon after he hit Vegas, Spilotro corrupted a lieutenant of Metro, the Las Vegas police department. Not only did the lieutenant leak information on the Metro investigations to Spilotro, eventually he became the lookout for the Hole in the Wall Gang when it was committing burglaries.

Spilotro later became involved in narcotics. This was considered off-limits in Chicago. For decades, the Chicago family has decreed that none of its members is to become involved in any way with narcotics. Ricca set the policy in the 1940s. Anybody violating that order is dealt with as soon as his activities are

*From an article in the Reno *Gazette-Journal* (July 15, 1985, "The Other Nevada: Gaming, Politics and the Mob" by Ken Miller)

known. And violators receive the ultimate discipline. Yet Spilotro got away with it for several years.

Then Spilotro alienated a cohort, Frank Cullotta, a guy he had been associated with in Chicago and then brought out to Vegas to work with him. Cullotta knew where the bodies were buried—literally—in Chicago and in Las Vegas. He went to the FBI in Vegas.

Soon Spilotro was indicted in Vegas for his leadership of the Hole in the Wall Gang. He was indicted again in Kansas City for his role in the skimming of the Tropicana, which was perpetrated by Chicago's associates in the Civella family of Kansas City. And he was indicted yet again for the murders of two Chicago burglars named Miraglia and McCarthy (dubbed ''The M&M Murders'').

A number of others also became government witnesses. Among them was Allen Glick, the young San Diego businessman who became the top official of Argent, the holding company of the mob's Stardust and Fremont casinos. Joe Agosto, the mob's man in the Trop, became a government witness. Carl Thomas, the guy who knew more about skimming than anyone else in Vegas—and practiced his skim through members of his crew at the Trop, the Hacienda, and the Stardust—became a government witness. And another Spilotro underling, Sal Romano, became a government witness. All of these guys were supposed to be overseen by Spilotro.

What was he doing out there? Things had gone haywire.

In 1986, there was a new boss in Chicago, a new underboss and two new capos. Joe Ferriola, Rocky Infelice, Donald Angelini and Dominic Cortina, respectively. I have never met Infelice but I confronted the other three numerous times. They are three very, very sharp guys. Spilotro they recognized right away for what he was—a great liability for Chicago.

On June 14, 1986, Spilotro, (forty-eight at the time) left the home of his brother, Michael, in Oak Park, a western suburb of Chicago. His brother was with him. Spilotro's wife reported to the police that he had not returned home that night although he had been expected. His car was later found in a motel parking lot in the western suburbs.

On June 22, a farmer in northern Indiana noticed a soft mound of dirt in his field. Upon investigation he found two bodies in a shallow grave, both badly beaten and dressed only in under-shorts. Each had been brutally and fatally beaten. Dental charts and fingerprints were rushed by the FBI in Chicago out to Indiana. It was a positive identification—Tony and Michael Spilotro.

It was clear what must have happened. When Ferriola and his new crew came into power, they recognized that it was a mistake to be represented by Spilotro in Las Vegas. They soon made plans to dispose of him.

Today the situation in Las Vegas is entirely different than it was just several years ago. I feel quite strongly that the mess is pretty well cleaned up. But there are still questions about some of the casinos like the Palace Station, the Sahara, and the Hacienda. Those questions center around a figure named Paul Lowdon.

Lowdon owns what I call "the bookends," the Sahara at the top of the Strip and the Hacienda on the bottom. He has an interesting past. He was an executive at the Trop when it was skimmed by Joe Agosto, Carl Thomas, and other "Mr. Insides" of the Kansas City mob. He was not indicted, but he should have known what was going on there. He never blew any whistles; he never made any complaints anybody is aware of.

Then, all of a sudden, Allen Glick sold Lowden the Hacienda. He had been a lounge bandleader, then a mid-level exec at the Trop. Now he owns the Hacienda? The Glick syndrome all over again? While the Sahara and the Hacienda are not the best, they are certainly two nice multimillion-dollar properties.

It must be nice to be in the wrong place at the wrong time and come out smelling like a rose.

The Palace Station is located just west of the Strip on Interstate 15 and is somewhat isolated, but it is a large, attractive place and a big favorite with the locals. Its owner is Frank Fertita, another guy who was in the Trop during the days when it was being skimmed heavily by Carl Thomas.

Most of the big hotels like Caesar's Palace, Bally's, the Tropicana, the Vegas Hilton, and the Hilton Flamingo—Bugsy's old casino where it all started on the Strip—are now owned by legitimate public corporations. At this writing I have just finished working as the attorney in charge of investigation for Dow Jones and Company against Ramada, the owners of the Tropicana

Hotel in Las Vegas and Trop World in Atlantic City. Although I was a member of the defense team working against the libel suit brought by Ramada, I am convinced that the Trop is now cleansed of the mob influence that sullied its past history.

Hotel-casinos in Vegas that are not owned by large corporations—like Circus-Circus, the Dunes, the Alladin, the Golden Nugget, the Barbary Coast, the Frontier, the Sands, the Desert Inn and the Riviera—are currently owned by people who seem to be untainted with mob involvement. What used to be the flagship casino of the Chicago mob, the Stardust, and its sister casino downtown, the Fremont, are now owned by the Boyd family. The Boyds are an old-time Vegas family that also owns Sam's Town and the California Club. Nothing has ever shown up in their background to indicate mob association.

And the two new hotels, which will be the Strip's largest and perhaps most beautiful, the Mirage and the Excalibur, are Golden Nugget and Circus-Circus enterprises, untainted by the mob.

There is information that Donald Angelini is the successor to Spilotro as the Chicago family rep in Vegas. But Angelini has a very different style. I know from having arrested him twice and encountered him on numerous other occasions as late as November 1987.

Angelini knows well what problems Spilotro created for himself, and he is no mirror image of Spilotro. White-haired, a sharp dresser with a good command of the language, Angelini is level-headed and very well-read. He even possesses a real estate license. His respectability took a quantum leap when both of his sons became attorneys.

If Donald is the capo in charge of Las Vegas for the Chicago mob today, he will be hard to trip up. Yablonsky has told me that the FBI occasionally followed Angelini from Chicago to Las Vegas. Angelini would meet Spilotro at the airport, give him what appeared to be a few instructions, and then board a plane back to Chicago. Apparently he's doing the same today, running Chicago's interest in Nevada. But he's doing it with much more savoir faire than Spilotro ever demonstrated.

However, what Donald controls today in Las Vegas is smaller potatoes than what the Chicago mob entrusted to the three previous reps. But it's still a considerable part of Chicago's overall income. Chicago no longer controls the casinos through the use of licensees like Glick and Sachs. And when I last saw him, Dalitz was in physical decline. (I served a subpoena on him at the Las Vegas Country Club in 1987.) But many of the people beholden to Chicago are still working in the casinos as shift managers, pit bosses, floormen, dealers, and stickmen. Security can't be all places at all times. In some casinos, the security men don't even try to trace the action. The eye in the sky—the surveillance cameras in the ceilings that constantly film each table, and counting room—are not omnipotent. If anyone were to suggest that skim is a thing of the past he would be laughed at. The mob still gets its part, only now it's called stealing from the ownership, not skimming for it.

Law enforcement and regulatory authorities in Nevada are also concerned about the intentions of the Chicago family to locate new casinos in Nevada and to take over existing casinos. I have learned from a Chicago source that the Chicago mob has conducted a survey to find "pockets of potential." In fact, the most capable and experienced organized crime expert in Arizona, Lou Spalla of the Intelligence Division of the Arizona Department of Public Safety, has confirmed my information about pockets of potential. The Arizona DPS is concerned about such a development, because one of the prime pockets of potential, the town of Laughlin, Nevada, is located just across the Colorado River from Bullhead City, Arizona. Since legalized gambling and organized crime go hand in hand, what Nevada brings to one side of the river will certainly spread to the other unless Arizona law enforcement can prevent it from happening.

Another pocket of potential certainly targeted by the mob is the Lake Tahoe area. If I were a mobster and had the ability, I would definitely want a hotel-casino at Tahoe, which is one of my favorite spots in the world. It would be potentially lucrative all year round. There's skiing at Squaw Valley and Heavenly Valley in the winter. In the summer, there's golfing on the south shore next to the High Sierra, as well as boating, water skiing, and swimming in the lake. And there's hiking and jogging almost all year round. It's a beautiful environment, and Lake Tahoe is reputed to be the purest body of water in the world.

I hope the regulatory authorities in Nevada and California can continue to keep the mob out of that great region.

* * *

The concrete of the Strip in Vegas is vastly different from dusty old Highway 91—the Gay White Highway, as it was once called. Millions of neon lights light up the sky where once there were no more than several lanterns.

But modernization also brought the mob, and with the mob, corruption. I believe that enforcement should concentrate on depleting the mob's income; with less in the coffer corruption of public officials will be less possible. It is also my belief that corruption of public officials is the greatest danger organized crime poses to our society.

It's not only the citizens of Las Vegas who suffer because of the vast income the mobs have garnered there. Corruption also affects the people of Chicago, New York, Kansas City, Phila- delphia, Miami, Denver, Milwaukee, Tucson, and all the other cities where the mobs exist. Public officials, judges, law en- forcement officers, politicians, labor leaders, legitimate busi- nessmen—many are corrupted by "Vegmon," Vegas money.

17 A Different Mad Sam

"What wholesome girls!" said Jeannie. "The way they introduced their mom and dad seemed so well brought up. And the one with the most talent, that one in the middle, Phyllis? She really seemed so nice."

Jeannie and I were visiting the famous Chicago nightclub, the Chez Paree, for the first time. The sixties had just dawned, and we were waiting for the right act to appear—the McGuire Sisters came to the Chez! There were three sisters: Phyllis, Christine, and Dorothy—all sensations at the time. They were regulars on the Arthur Godfrey program and soon they would go on to make such gold records as "Sincerely," "Picnic," and "Sugar- time."

But our illusions about the group's wholesomeness were soon

to be dimmed. First we got a call from Frank Gerrity, the ace New York agent. Then we began to pick it up ourselves.

The McGuire Sisters had entertained in 1960 at the Desert Inn in Las Vegas, just about the time its owner, Moe Dalitz, was making the deal with Hump, Accardo, and Giancana that was to lead to more control by the Chicago family. According to the story we got, Phyllis ran up a sizable gambling debt at the D.I. Into her life came Mo Giancana. He told Dalitz to "eat the marker." Dalitz did, and she and Mo became close. Very close.

On July 11, 1961, Giancana and Phyllis went to Phoenix, where they stayed in a motel. It was bugged. On that occasion, Phyllis appeared to be the aggressor in the affair, which came as a big surprise to us. Henry Kissinger said one time, in explaining his abilities with the opposite sex, that power is the perfect aphrodisiac. In Mo's case, it is the only answer. He was a runty, bald, and big-nosed gentleman who talked in street-bully accents ("dem," "dese," and "dose"). But in the eyes of Phyllis and dozens of other women, he seemed to have a special charm. Through the bug, we learned that the pair would be leaving Phoenix the next day, July 12, and that they would be traveling on American Airlines, Flight 66. The flight would arrive at Chicago's O'Hare at 7:00 P.M. Mo would be traveling under the name Mooney Cecola.

We decided it was time for us to get down to business with Phyllis. We had done nothing to expose her relationship with Giancana, an exposé that we knew would be harmful both to her career and to the careers of her sisters. So we devised a scheme. Ralph Hill went to the Justice Department Strike Force in Chicago and cooked up a deal with them. They would give us a subpoena summoning Phyllis before the federal grand jury in Chicago on July 13. (We had a legitimate reason for this as the FGJ was then holding hearings that indirectly concerned Giancana—and her testimony about his spending habits, travels, associates, and other activities would be officially pertinent to that investigation.) Ralph Hill made an arrangement such that he could withdraw the subpoena if Phyllis otherwise cooperated with us—either if she cooperated right then, or if she indicated we could get her to help us out in the near future.

I headed out to the airport and made arrangements to secure a private room for the interview with Phyllis. Vince Inserra and Johnny Bassett would conduct the interview. Ralph Hill had

Giancana assigned to him at the time; Hill and I would conduct an interview with Mo and prevent him from interfering, using physical means if necessary. Our supervisor Harold Sell would be along to oversee.

Sure enough, right on schedule the king of Chicago and his princess appeared. Vince and John hustled up to Phyllis, handed her the paper, and explained the situation. She agreed to accompany them to the room I had arranged.

Sam had lagged behind in case of a tail. He did not want his relationship with the singing star—who was recognized anywhere—to become public knowledge.

I had never met Giancana before. I don't know whether he recognized Ralph or not. In any event, we presented our credentials to him and identified ourselves as Ralph Hill and Bill Roemer of the FBI. Giancana snarled at us, "I got nothin' to say to you guys."

Ralph said, "Mo, we are investigating the wiretap at the hotel room of Dan Rowan in Las Vegas. Do you know Rowan?"

Dan Rowan, of the comedy team of Rowan and Martin, was suspected of slipping out with Phyllis, cutting in on Sam's time. A bug had been planted in Rowan's room, and we suspected that Giancana had had the device planted to confirm his suspicions.

Giancana, in his usual surly manner, snapped, "I don't know nothing about nothin'. Leave me alone."

But it was not our function that evening to leave him alone. Ralph and I tagged along. Giancana began to get abusive and obscene. "Get out of here, I told you to leave me alone. Now get the fuck out of here!"

Very calmly I said to him, "Mo, this seems to be a public place. If you don't want us around, why don't *you* leave." I knew he would not leave until he found Phyllis.

He then turned to Ralph. "Who did you say you are?" Ralph gave him his name. "Oh yeah, Hill, I know all about you. You're the guy that's been fuckin' around with my girlfriends. I've got some affidavits, Hill, and I'm just waiting for the right time to use them!"

This was a bombshell. What was he talking about? That mention of "affidavits" caused Ralph to be fairly impassive the rest of the evening—a style that was very unusual for him.

Then Giancana turned to me. "What's your name again?" I

told him. He said, "Yeah, I know about you, too. You're the lawyer from Notre Dame."

He could have learned that from several people but I immediately suspected that tidbit came from John D'Arco ("I'm-too-big-to-be-embarrassed-in-this-town-by-the-FBI").

About this time, the last passengers to disembark from Flight 66 were leaving the American Airlines concourse. But Sam caught up with two young men who had just gotten off. "You dirty bastards," he yelled, "I spotted you guys right away for the G. You didn't fool me one bit, you assholes!" That caused a little stir among the dozens of passengers.

Giancana then began to search for Phyllis. Deciding that we must have escorted her away, he began to make remarks about the Gestapo. "A man can't even be left alone with his own girlfriend in this fuckin' country!"

He then turned to face Hill and me. "Have you guys figured out how many men I have killed? I understand you're always telling people what a killer I am." I quietly asked him, "Why don't you tell us, Mo?" He immediately shot back, "I might just add a couple more right now!"

Now, I began to get a little more animated. "Is that a threat, Mo? Are you threatening federal officers?"

He backed off. "No, no."

At this point, Giancana announced that he was going to "get the fuck out of here. I'm going to Cuba." With that he reboarded Flight 66, which was on a stopover enroute to New York. Phyllis had been scheduled to continue on to her home in New York; she had disembarked just to stretch her legs.

Five minutes later, Mo got off the plane again. He was carrying Phyllis's purse. Obviously he had changed his mind about continuing on the flight.

I then began to pursue a course that went somewhat beyond the policy of the FBI. I had gotten a little hot at this wise guy. As he approached the waiting room in the concourse, I said to him, "My, that purse certainly becomes you, Mo. I heard about you being a fairy but now we know, don't we?"

This provoked him, to say the least. He put his head right up under my chin and said, "You fuckin' cocksucker! Who do you think you are talkin' to! I could have Butch come out here with his machine gun and take good care of you right now!" (He was referring to his bodyguard, Dominic "Butch" Blasi, who had been convicted in Wisconsin of possession of machine guns. Butch was the closest guy to Giancana—his confidant, body-guard, appointment secretary, and driver.)

Again I asked if Giancana was threatening a federal officer and again he backed down, knowing that he was close to committing a crime.

Giancana then entered into a course of conversation that at the time was merely amusing to me but, which, more than twenty years later, would become controversial. I was to be filmed in 1984 on a "20/20" program on the life of Marilyn Monroe and again on a British Broadcasting Company program about the tragedy of Marilyn Monroe. On both programs, I was asked to explain what Sam and I discussed next.

"I suppose you intend to report this to your boss!" he said.

"Who's my boss?" I asked.

"J. Edgar Hoover," he replied.

"Yes, I imagine he'll see a copy."

"Fuck J. Edgar Hoover and your super boss!" he snarled.

"Who is that?" I said.

"Bobby Kennedy," he shot back.

"Might be he'll see a copy, yes," I said.

"Fuck Bobby Kennedy! and your super, super boss!" Giancana yelled.

"Who is my super, super boss?" I asked.

"John Kennedy!" he snapped back.

"I doubt if the President of the United States is interested in Sam Giancana," I responded.

"Fuck John Kennedy," Giancana shouted. "Listen, Roemer, I know all about the Kennedys, and Phyllis knows more about the Kennedys and one of these days we're going to tell all."

"What are you talking about?" I asked.

"Fuck you. One of these days it'll come out. You wait, you smart asshole, you'll see."

In retrospect, it is possible that Giancana, who obviously knew of John and Bobby Kennedy's relationship with Marilyn Monroe, was referring to that. Or he may have been referring to the fact that John Kennedy was bedding Judy Campbell (now Judy Campbell Exner) at the same time she was sleeping with Giancana.

Giancana then teased us by bringing up something else that

was to become at least as controversial as his knowledge of the Kennedys.

He made an oblique reference to Adlai Stevenson, the former Illinois governor who had become ambassador to the United Nations. I think Ralph came back in at that point and asked him what he meant by his mention of Stevenson.

"He's the guy who made that fuckin' mess in Cuba," Giancana replied. "He's a bookworm, got no common sense."

We looked blankly at Giancana, what was he getting at?

"The fucking United States government is not as smart as it thinks it is, is it? You made a deal with Castro to overthrow Batista if he would kick us out of Cuba, and now that deal has backfired on you, hasn't it?"

I continued to conduct myself poorly at this point by saying, "If he kicked your ass out of Cuba, that's one good effect, it seems to me."

Again Giancana blew his top. "You big fuckin' asshole! You think you're a tough guy. I know all about you, Roemer. You ain't gonna push me around. I know my rights!"

Since I was beginning to get some dirty looks from Harold Sell, I backed off.

Giancana then went into a diatribe about how the FBI was "persecuting Italians." I very calmly and quietly told him, "We're just as tough on Gussie and Hump, and they're not Italians."

That caused Mo to explode again. He objected to me thinking I was a tough guy, who could push his people around. "We'll get you," he said.

That threatened my patience. I had finally had enough. Since we were still in the public concourse of O'Hare, dozens of passersby had stopped to see what this ruckus was all about. They obviously wondered about the runty little guy yelling oaths and obscenities at the big guy. This was great theater but what was it all about? Who *were* we?

"All you folks," I yelled. "Come over here! I want you to see something!" The crowd numbered at least a hundred. "Take a look at this piece of slime! This is Sam Giancana! He is the boss of the underworld here in Chicago! Take a good look at this garbage! The big boss! Giancana!"

Then, lowering my voice a little as I calmed down, I said,

"You people are lucky, you're just passing through Chicago. We have to live with this jerk!"

I had pushed right up next to Giancana at this point, really hoping he would take a punch at me in front of all those witnesses. I hadn't decided whether I would respond by punching back or whether I would then grab him and arrest him for assaulting a federal officer. But the decision was taken from my hands. Harold Sell, my supervisor, made his presence felt. He pushed me back (he is bigger than I am) and kicked me in the shins. "Get back, Bill, you're going too far, get back and keep quiet."

Nobody had ever publicly insulted Giancana, the most powerful kingpin of the mob. He was quite upset, to say the least. Now he exploded, displaying the behavior that had caused him to be declared a constitutional psychopath when he was rejected for Army service in World War II.

"Roemer, you lit a fire tonight that will never go out!" he shouted. "I'll get you if it's the last thing I ever do! You'll rue this night! I promise you that!"

Sell continued to assert his authority by placing himself between Giancana and me. Thereafter I kept my distance and my cool, while Hill and Sell continued the "interview" with Giancana.

Phyllis McGuire then showed up. She had convinced Inserra and Bassett that she would keep an appointment with them in the near future, and she promised to help them with the investigation of Giancana. Based on that understanding with Vince and John, the subpoena was withdrawn. Phyllis never kept any appointments with the FBI. Vince and John never heard from her again. Years later, in 1986, when she called me from the "21" Club in New York to ask a favor, I did the favor and then asked for one in return. I wanted to discuss an investigation of her friend Senator Paul Laxalt that I was conducting as a private consultant after I retired. She agreed to meet me at her apartment in New York City. I went to New York as arranged, but she wasn't home. I think I "misunderstood" the arrangements just as Inserra and Bassett had "misunderstood" twenty-five years before.

When she arrived back on the concourse at O'Hare that night, she turned to all of us and said, "I have tried to act like a lady tonight. Sam hasn't acted like a gentleman. I apologize for him."

Holy smokes! This was not Sam's night! He lost his temper one last time. He grabbed Phyllis angrily by the arm, and said, "Let's get the fuck out of here!" And away they went.

But the night was not over. When we got back to the FBI office on Clark Street, Harold Sell called me into his office. He let me know in no uncertain terms how wrong he felt my actions had been. He was right, I had not acted like an FBI agent is taught to act, especially when I lost my cool by calling those people around to humiliate Sam.

As I was signing out to go home, I noticed a younger agent standing by the desk. I introduced myself and learned that he was a new agent reporting to the Chicago FBI office for the first time. It was about ten or eleven o'clock by then, and he hadn't yet made a hotel reservation. He had no idea where he would go that night. It just so happened that Jeannie, Bill, and Bob were in Cincinnati visiting Jeannie's parents, so I invited the new agent to spend the night in Bob's bedroom. He gladly accepted.

When we boarded the Illinois Central to go home, however, I had second thoughts. I might not be doing this guy a favor. If that crazy Giancana decided to do something tonight he knew where to find me. The mob had been to my home before. This new agent might get a Chicago baptism much sooner than he expected—in a baptism of fire! I decided I was being edgy. And as it turned out, nothing was to happen. At least not that night.

18 Another Penetration

Our spat with Giancana made us all the more eager to intensify our efforts to catch up with him. We did not plan to frame him or do anything else out of line. (In spite of my loss of cool for ten or fifteen minutes, we were still FBI agents: repeatedly we had been instructed that we must respect civil rights and civil liberties. Any disregard for those rights was subject to severe discipline in Mr. Hoover's FBI.)

The thing we could do, however, was to plant another Little Al. This time we aimed for the headquarters of Giancana. We already knew by this time where that was. We had tailed him and had also heard on Little Al that Hump, Gussie, and Strongy made meets with Sam at his place.

The headquarters was in the Armory Lounge on Roosevelt Road two blocks west of Harlem Avenue in a blue-collar suburb called Forest Park (not to be confused with Park Forest, which is a far southern suburb). The Armory had been a speakeasy in the days of Al Capone and was now owned by the capo in charge of Cicero, Joey Auippa.

We had code-named the place "Mo." Mo was on a corner, with a large parking lot to the west. As you came in from the parking lot there was a bar on the right with a restaurant straight ahead. In the rear to the north was a private room with a peep-hole—a reminder of the days when it had been a speakeasy. It was in this private room that Mo held court.

Ralph Hill, to whom Mo was assigned, got the "ticket." Maz was selected to help him. I had to look after Little Al, but I did become involved later.

Ralph and Maz went through the regular survey process that we had perfected when we installed Little Al at the tailor shop. Mr. Hoover had to be assured that the bug would be planted in a strategic spot and that there was no chance of embarrassing the Bureau by discovering the bug.

Of course there was no way we could guarantee not to embarrass the Bureau. But we certified that Little Al could be securely installed, knowing that it would be our downfall if, in fact, we did embarrass the Bureau.

Ralph and Maz were fully aware of the potential risk to their careers. It's no wonder that most agents in the Bureau wouldn't touch a Criminal Intelligence Program (CIP) installation. Their chances of being fired were much greater than the possibility of any substantial recognition.

In this case my partners had a real problem on their hands. First of all, we knew that many of the police in Forest Park were on Sam's pad. They ate at his place, they drank there after work, and they took turns patrolling the neighborhood.

So how to make the penetration? Ralph and Maz had a great

idea. After the lounge and restaurant closed at midnight a janitor remained there alone until he finished at about two. We would have from two to dawn to work. But how to get in? The outside was wide open to the police. If an honest cop caught them, they would be treated like intruders—but they could not identify themselves if they were caught. The rules were the same as at Little Al.

Ralph and Maz approached the janitor after he had left the area one night and asked if they could talk to him. Having identified themselves, they showed him an FBI "wanted" poster. They had found one with a subject who resembled the janitor. Ralph and Maz said they would like the janitor to accompany them downtown to the FBI office, where they would take his fingerprints and either identify him or eliminate him as a suspect. Knowing that he was not the subject of the wanted flyer, the janitor agreed.

When he got there, Ralph and Maz politely asked him if he would mind putting his wallet, money, and keys on the desk while he was fingerprinted in the mug room. He did. With a locksmith standing by, Maz had the keys duplicated while Ralph very clumsily took the guy's prints, prolonging the procedure as much as possible. After an impression of the keys had been carefully prepared, the fingerprints were found (surprise) not to be those of the subject on the wanted poster. The janitor was driven home.

Now we had the key. We were ready to plant Mo.

On this caper Ralph was the lead scout and went in first to secure the premises. Anybody inside was his responsibility, not mine. At least a dozen times we met in the area at midnight. Franklin McCormick, the late night disc jockey on WGN, the 50,000-watt Chicago radio station, came on with his show at midnight. His theme song was "Melody of Love." I heard "Melody of Love" at least a dozen nights as we waited for the all-clear from Ralph. Finally we got the signal and darted inside. Again, I don't want to identify the agents who were with us on this penetration because I know at least two who prefer not to be named. Again, there were numerous perils, and a lot of apprehension. During one visit, one of the guys snapped the wrong switch and the neon sign outside lighted up like it was Christmas. Another time, one of us inadvertently switched on the juke box. Fats Domino almost woke up the neighborhood!

In the Armory Lounge, we found the private room that was Giancana's private headquarters. We placed our old, pineapple-sized, World War II vintage mike behind the baseboard of one of the walls. We then began the tedious process of stringing the wire behind the baseboard, trailing it out of the room, down the stairwell to the basement, and then outside.

Finally, everything was in place. Mo was born!

We found that it was the practice of any prominent "made" guy who wanted to meet with Sam to get in touch with Butch Blasi. Blasi was the key. He lived in a very expensive home with a swimming pool in River Forest on Park Avenue. His home was probably two or three times as expensive as Giancana's at 1147 South Wenonah in Oak Park.

When Blasi contacted Giancana, they would set up a time for the meet in the back room at Mo. Mo would then tell us why the capo or other made guy was so anxious to talk to Sam.

On the other hand, if a politician wanted to see Sam other arrangements would be made. Butch would come in, tell Sam who wanted to see him and usually why. At the appointed time, Butch would drive Sam to a location (often a church yard along the Eisenhower Expressway) where the meeting would take place in the car. It wasn't that Giancana suspected Mo. He just didn't want the politicians to be seen coming to his headquarters. There was a rule—very well-spelled out—that every precaution should be taken to ensure protection of the identity of anybody legit who was a contact.

Things hummed along nicely for a year or so. However, every time there was a thunderstorm anywhere near the area, for some reason it knocked Mo out. Every month or so we'd have to go back in and breathe new life into Mo.

But the worst problem was when they decided to remodel the premises. The owners decided that the place was doing so much legitimate business—and the food was so good—that they needed to expand the kitchen. In doing so, they took away Sam's private room, which moved Sam out into the main dining area. Although his meets didn't slow down much, the quality of the reception from Mo did. Again, of course, we had to go in and rewire our old mike and realign it in the vicinity of Sam's table. It wasn't easy, and the reception wasn't as good as before. But the information we picked up still made it all worthwhile.

Now we could listen in on the general headquarters of the

mob on the Magnificent Mile and the special headquarters of the mob boss out in the suburbs. Many times, we would hear Frankie Ferraro (the underboss to Giancana) talking to Little Al. We'd hear him tell Hump or Gussie that he had to go, and an hour later we'd have Frankie talking to Mo.

One of the more frequent topics of conversation in that summer of 1961 (the early days of Mo) was Sam's confrontation with me at O'Hare. Sam loved to entertain his audience with a blow-by-blow account about how he had told me off. "That big bastard never lifted a finger. Why, if I was called all them names I called him I'd punched the shit out of him. Cocky asshole, thinks he's so tough. Guess I showed him." I'd grit my teeth as that kind of conversation came in. If I wasn't there when the voice was picked up, Ralph and Maz would always remember to needle me about it. "Mo says you ain't worth a shit, Roemer," they would tell me. "Yeah, I'd like to be there when he tells those stories," I said. "I'd tell a different side of it. And if Harold hadn't been there . . ."

Now, I knew that Harold had been a positive influence on the situation. But I often wondered how it would have all turned out if he had stayed back in the office that night.

Very soon we learned why Sam had been so knowledgeable about Cuba. We heard from other sources that Johnny Roselli had been approached by Bob Matheu, the former FBI guy who was Howard Hughes's right-hand man and was now acting for the CIA. The CIA wanted to do something about Fidel Castro. Roselli, the mob rep in the West (but not even as highly placed in the mob as a capo) could only bring such a plan to his boss. In this case, his boss was Sam. Giancana in turn put the CIA in touch with Santo Trafficante, the La Cosa Nostra boss in Tampa whom Sam had known well when the different families had their casinos in Havana. Roselli, Giancana, and Trafficante worked in concert on the CIA proposition.

Now a lot has been written about how the Chicago mob and the CIA formed an alliance to kill Castro. In Chicago we were never able to establish definitely that there was in fact such an alliance. But the Bureau in Washington gathered information from Chicago, New York, Miami, and Los Angeles to support this theory.

In my opinion, Giancana's part in the scheme was a ruse. From what I can see, Roselli was serious—but not Trafficante,

the mob boss in Tampa. We know that Giancana did not trust
or like Roselli. Little Al told us that. It appears to me that Giancana strung Roselli along. When Roselli approached him and
introduced him to his CIA "cut out," Giancana went along with
the idea of becoming a CIA "asset." Here was "the G" coming
to Sam to ask a favor. They would put themselves in his hands
and run up a "marker." What did Giancana have to lose by
going along?

But I don't think Giancana was about to risk his neck going
after Castro. In my opinion, he just let the United States government believe they had a viable strategy. Why not? It couldn't
hurt him—it could help—to have at least one part of the government on his side. (During our confrontation at O'Hare, Giancana had made a remark to that effect: "I thought we were all
on the same side." That had passed over our heads at the time.)

I think Roselli was probably never informed that Giancana
was not for real on the Castro plot. And Roselli had no power
of his own to do anything about killing Castro. His only power
came through the Chicago family and Giancana. He was part of
the deal because Bob Matheu, the CIA contact from Los Angeles, was acquainted with Roselli out there. Roselli was merely
a conduit allowing Matheu and the CIA to get to Giancana—
and then through Giancana to Trafficante. And Trafficante was
in touch with the Cubans who could have done the job if Giancana ever got serious.

If things fell easily into place, and there was good chance of
success with minimal risk, Giancana might have given Trafficante the green light. But it never progressed quite that far and
that easily. Giancana continued to give lip service to the CIA.
He did so with a little smile on his face. But the whole time, I
believe he was just playing along for his own reasons.

Eventually, Mo furnished us with a conversation during which
Giancana indicated that Frank Sinatra had made a commitment
to Giancana in 1960 when John Kennedy was running for president. The agreement was that if Giancana used his influence in
Chicago with the "West Side Bloc" and other public officials
on Kennedy's behalf, Sinatra felt he could get Kennedy to back
off from the FBI investigation of Giancana.

Whether or not Giancana got that commitment from Sinatra,
Giancana exercised influence through the group of politicians

known as the "West Side Bloc" or "Pat's guys" (as in Pat
Marcy, who held sway over the corrupt elements in the First
Ward and throughout the state). But much more important than
Giancana's influence was that of Mayor Richard J. Daley, whose
interests at the time just happened to jibe with Giancana's. To
say that Giancana's influence swung the election to Kennedy
would be farfetched; to say that Daley delivered Chicago and
thus Illinois may be true, but whether it swung the election is
highly debatable. An equally strong argument can be made for
Texas, which later in the evening added its large bloc of electoral
votes to JFK's tally.

To sum up our accomplishment in setting Mo in place, let me
say that it was a great source. Perhaps not quite up to Little Al,
but only because Al was giving us the whole mob family. Mo
was just broadcasting one guy's plans—but then, what a guy!
The boss! Through Mo we were able to keep abreast of what
the boss was planning, who he was planning it with, how he
was planning to do it, when, where, and why. If Giancana was
playing with Sinatra in Hawaii, we knew it. If he was in New
York for a Commission meeting, we knew it. If he was in Las
Vegas to meet with Dalitz or any of the inside guys there, we
knew it. If he went to Europe with Phyllis, we knew it.

   After Mo went in, Giancana had few secrets.

19 Margaret and Gus

   Soon after Little Al began talking to us, I began
to notice that somebody was missing: one of the major hoodlums who we believed we would be listening to frequently—my
friend Gussie. Occasionally there would be a mention of "Slim"
or "Handsome," as he was also called by his mob associates,
but we couldn't pick up his voice at all.
   Then we overheard a conversation in which Frankie Ferraro,

the mob underboss, made some oblique reference to "when Slim gets back." And then "when Slim gets well." It became obvious that Gussie Alex was ill and was confined somewhere in a hospital or clinic.

It was Sidney Korshak who let the cat out of the bag. He informed one of his associates that Slim was in a mental institution in Connecticut, a high-class place, and would be there for a while.

Gus Alex in a mental institution! I called New Haven, my old stomping grounds, and talked to my old handball partner, Bob Puckett. Where in Connecticut could this "high-class mental institution" be? He suggested I call Tom Murphy in Greenwich, a wealthy area of Connecticut. I did and Tom agreed to make a canvass of some of the high-class clinics and get back to me. A couple of days later he called back. He had found Gussie at the Silver Hill Sanitarium in New Canaan, the same place Joan Kennedy was to make famous years later.

Tom reported that the staff at the sanitarium would only confirm that Gussie was a patient, nothing more. But it seemed obvious from the conversations we'd overheard that he was there to recover from hypertension and related emotional stress. I then recalled that in a conversation with Tony Accardo, soon after we put Al to work, Tony had said to him, "Gussie, do what I do. When things here get to be too much I go up in the woods and chop wood. I chop and chop until I feel better and then I come back here."

We knew that Gussie's brother, Sam, the mysterious "Rip" we had so much trouble identifying, had a farm that Gussie called "Farmville" in Cassopolis, Michigan. We'd been watching the farm through the agents assigned to Detroit. In the past Gussie had spent many weekends flying to South Bend and then driving the twenty or thirty miles to Cassopolis. Now we knew why Gussie hadn't been at Farmville recently.

We learned from Korshak's associate that Margaret had remained in Chicago and that she and Bea Korshak continued to mind their modeling business. We also learned that Margaret had opened a high-class ladies' clothing boutique.

In the presence of Al, Frankie Ferraro mentioned that "Slim is very upset with Margaret. He thinks she's having a good time while he's away. She goes to see him on some weekends but not all the time."

Soon we learned that Gus and Margaret had gotten divorced!

I got an idea. Maybe this would be a good time to try to develop Margaret as an informant. Since she was no longer Gus's wife, she no longer came within the purview of our pact with the mob. We knew she could tell us a lot about Gus's role as the mob boss responsible for maintaining contact with Korshak. She could also elaborate on the close interplay between Alex and Ferraro; we knew they had grown up together and were inseparable.

Obviously, the fact that Gus's former wife was arguably the most beautiful girl in Chicago had a little to do with my interest in developing her as an informant. This would be a real change of pace, just as the burlesque queen had been. But with a distinct difference.

Eveything I knew about Margaret told me she was top hat, first class, premiere. I had heard not only that she was beautiful but also that she was a real lady. She was a catch for any man (unless he had Jeannie Roemer), not just for a top leader of organized crime.

I found her late one morning in 1960 at the boutique. I discovered that she sold women's wear that had been worn once or twice by high-society matrons, models, or entertainers. After wearing the garment to some gala event, they would then pass it on to Margaret, to sell on consignment. A five-hundred-dollar dress at the boutique could be purchased for one hundred dollars, for instance, with the cachet that this dress "was worn once by a movie star." In fact a big star, a friend of Margaret's through Bea Korshak, had given Margaret perhaps a dozen to twenty gowns and dresses for the boutique. Later, when the star had a daily television show, she hired Margaret to be her fashion consultant, and Margaret appeared regularly on the show, not only modeling clothes but also conversing with the star on the topic of the day.

I had also found that Margaret was a devout Catholic. She didn't eat meat on Fridays; she went to Mass regularly and she took Communion frequently. Also, she had been faithful to her husband.

The first approach was just touching base. I identified myself and she indicated that she knew who I was. I said I'd like to talk to her. She was busy. I understood. Maybe next week sometime? All right. Where would she like to meet, would she like lunch? No.

"I keep an apartment above the shop here, why don't you call me and we can meet there?" she said.

"Fine, how can I reach you?"

"This is my telephone number here."

"Thank you, I'll call you next week. It was very nice meeting you, and I'm looking forward to next week."

The next week we met in her apartment above the boutique. We had a nice conversation, and she fixed me a drink. Nothing momentous. Just two people meeting who had known of each other but had little in common. Except one thing. Gussie. She might be the only person in the world other than Frankie Ferraro who knew more about Gussie than I did.

We met five times in all in her apartment. On the third visit, I got a little more personal. She began to talk about Gussie and their life together. She loved him. But she could no longer endure the life he made for her. Before Apalachin and the Top Hoodlum Program, "Mr. and Mrs. Mike Reilly" had been able to separate Gussie's means of earning a livelihood distinct from their marriage. Nobody knew who Gussie was. When they went out for dinner with her friends, "Mike" was a quiet, reserved, very handsome husband. She had no reason to be ashamed of him. Sure, a few people like the Korshaks knew, but after all weren't they more or less in the same business?

However, after 1958, when the FBI got involved for the first time, things changed drastically. I found "Mike Reilly" at the Murray Hill Apartments and identified him as Gus Alex, the former mob hit man, the former "Greasy Thumb" Guzik bodyguard, now an upper echelon leader of the Chicago mob. That was the way the *Chicago Tribune*, the *Sun-Times*, the *Daily News*, and the *American* described Alex. Sandy Smith in the *Trib* even alluded to the fact that Gussie was married to a Chicago model. Soon the walls of privacy came tumbling down. It became a hot item of gossip in Margaret's circles that she was married to a hood! The respect she so rightfully earned through twenty years of climbing the ladder of professional and social success was now crumbling.

To make matters worse, Gussie was suffering. For almost thirty years he had been almost anonymous in Chicago. Once in a while the papers would print that he was being questioned by the police for a murder. But very rarely. Then when Mr. Hoover started the THP in November 1957 he drastically altered Gussie's life. The mobsters had to become accustomed to "heat from the G," but all of them adjusted. They suffered, they didn't like it, but they adjusted to it, more or less. Not Gussie. The constant pressure from the FBI, the fear of prosecution, and the fear of prison got to him.

The adverse publicity was a powerful weapon on our side. As I've mentioned, the intelligence we gathered from our mikes couldn't be used to prosecute the mob but served us nonetheless to put mobsters in the spotlight. We couldn't use it against Margaret (we were bound by the "family pact"), but we could sure use it to bother the emotionally fragile Gussie. If the public becomes aware of the identities of the mobsters and how they operate and with whom they associate, all the publicity turns over the rocks under which they hide. And the glare of public attention burns them. Public scrutiny becomes one of the most powerful weapons of law enforcement.

All that publicity combined with the fact that his home life was no longer ideal, and Gussie snapped. Margaret tried to be the dutiful wife. But Gussie could see that she suffered a great deal from a loss of prestige and dignity in her professional life, and that carried over into her social life. It affected their marriage. Hence the divorce.

After I left that third meeting, I began to shape a plan. It was obvious that Margaret loved Gussie but couldn't stand being married to a hoodlum. It was not Gussie she had drawn away from—it was his job, his life. What if we could make arrangements with Gus and Margaret so that he could *leave* that life? They probably had enough money to live very comfortably away from Chicago for the rest of their lives, probably even in the south of France or Zurich, where they had visited so often. They loved skiing in Switzerland. If we could get Gussie's cooperation and develop him as an informant on the condition that we change their identity and make them a new life, what a coup that would be! Gussie would be a gold mine of information. From the early days of Frank Nitti, through Guzik, right into the present—he knew everything. And even if he didn't care to cooperate, just to get him out of the mob, cut off his contacts and deprive the Chicago family of his many talents would be a great accomplishment.

I talked the idea over with Ralph, Maz, Vince, and Harold. They agreed. We called the Bureau. "Well, Roemer, see what she thinks," they said. "If she is agreeable, call us back with a progress report."

So, on my next visit to Margaret in her apartment I broached the plan. At first she was full of questions. How could it be done? Had it ever been done before? These were the days before there was such a thing as the witness protection program as handled today by the U.S. Marshal's Service. I said this would be strictly a function of the FBI. It would take many hours of work but no particular outlay of money since, presumably, Gussie had millions. It wasn't outside our capability.

We discussed it for hours and finally she agreed. She was ready if Gussie was. She was even willing to give up her current social life, which included a steady new male companion, a very wealthy, high-society gentleman (a Notre Dame graduate to boot). She agreed to talk to Gussie. I primed her for all his questions. I told her that I would come see him and make all the arrangements with him. But if he felt such animosity toward me that he preferred to have arrangements made by other agents, that was fine, too.

Margaret made contact with Slim. I awaited the results. "No way! A horrible idea!" was his reply. "My God, Margaret, how could you ever think of such a thing? You've been talking to Roemer? You could be killed for that! If Giancana ever found that out, what do you think would happen? You've got no sense at all! I can't believe this! No. No. No."

Margaret explained Gussie's reaction to me and told me that she must never see me again. She said her life was at stake.

Of course from the beginning I realized the relationship would be over if she went to Gussie and he had this reaction. But I chanced it anyway. It was worth the shot. Margaret had never disclosed anything of any value about Gus or his associates to me—as a source she was proving to be of little value. So I was willing to gamble all on this proposal.

Unfortunately, it did not succeed. I was never to see Margaret again.

But I was to see Gussie frequently. And soon. Although I knew there was little chance for a breakthrough, I felt there was nothing to lose by contacting Gus to make sure.

Shortly after my last meeting with Margaret, I knocked on

the door of Gussie's apartment. He had moved after he and Margaret were divorced and was now at 1150 Lake Shore Drive.

"Who's there?" Gussie asked.

"Bill Roemer, Gus."

"Go away. I've got nothing to say to you."

"Gus, just open up a minute. I'm alone and I've got something I want to talk to you about. I've got no paper."

"I know what you want to talk to me about, Mr. Roemer. But I'm not interested. I think you've been told that. Now, please, go away."

"Gus, it won't hurt to talk for a minute or two."

"Please, Mr. Roemer."

"Just for two minutes, Gus—just so I know you understand the whole situation. Then I'll go away and not bother you on this again. But let's talk face-to-face."

"Mr. Roemer, I'm trying to be a gentleman. Now please go away. Please."

And that was the end of it. If he wouldn't see me, there was nothing further I could do.

This experience may seem like a letdown. I had worked long and hard, not only trying to develop Margaret as a source but also to turn Gussie into a government witness. But I learned two lessons from this effort. For one thing, the government witness program, which was later developed, is much needed. (In this program, government witnesses who testify against the mob are protected, moved to a new location, and given new identities.) We had very little to offer Gussie at the time. He was obviously aware that the mob had much more chance of finding him than we did of giving him a secure life. Since those days, the new witness protection program has been critical in convincing mob figures that they can escape detection if they turn against their former associates. But at the time we were flying by the seat of our pants in trying to convince Gussie he could be safe from the mob.

The second thing I learned is that I had to improve the way I developed sources—one of the key attributes of a successful agent. Had I pushed Margaret hard enough to "turn," to inform on her former husband and his associates? Or had I let the fact that she was an attractive woman inhibit my aggressiveness in pressing her? There are very few law enforcement officers who excel at the development of sources, because it is pretty much an instinctive process.

And it's not something an agent can learn by rote in training school. Experience is the best teacher.

Although the experience with Margaret and Gussie proved fruitless, it did serve to prepare me well for similar endeavors in the future. Not all of them would be as frustrating as this one!

20 Hump

When Bobby Kennedy became attorney general, he ordered an intensification of the efforts to investigate all mob leaders across the country. It became apparent that I could not satisfy my responsibilities by focusing on both Gussie and Hump. The extent of the daily summary that was required on each was too demanding.

Soon all matters with the exception of the Top Hoodlum Program were stripped from C-1. The squad was beefed up from five agents to seventy. I was given five assistants to help me on Hump. Ross Spencer left us to take up his job as chief investigator to Dan Ward, the new state's attorney. Ray Connelley had received an office of preference transfer to his home area, and Harold Sell (a good man to work with) became the C-1 supervisor.

So Bob Cook and John Parish took over Gussie, and I devoted all my time to Hump. The reason I picked Hump is that he, as the leader of the connection guys, was more important to us.

The Chicago family of La Cosa Nostra probably reaches out further to rely on non-Italian or non-Sicilian mobsters than any other big family in the United States. New York, of course, has always had a Meyer Lansky or a Bugsy Siegel. But since the days of Al Capone there have always been three or four non-Italian top-level leaders in Chicago. There were ''Greasy Thumb,'' Fred Evans, Alex Louis Greenberg, and others in the thirties and forties followed by Hump, Alex, Ralph Pierce, Sam ''Golf Bag'' Hunt, and Les Kruse who I knew so well. Although these non-Italians could not aspire to membership in the La Cosa Nostra itself, there is no question that a Humphreys or an Alex were more important to the Chicago family than anyone in the 1960s other than Giancana, or his predecessors Accardo and Ricca.

In this regard, it should be noted that in most families of the LCN, all made members must be of Sicilian or Italian ancestry. In Chicago, this is the norm but not an absolute necessity. Today, for instance, Frankie Schweihs, Wayne Bock, and Lenny Patrick—to say nothing of Gus Alex—are prominent adjuncts to the Chicago LCN, whether or not they have been formalized as members. In fact, Schweihs (until he was indicted) and Bock were the hit guys for the mob. For decades Patrick fulfilled the role of a capo, taking charge of gambling activity, first in Lawndale and then in Rogers Park.

My friend Jimmy Frattiano has described how he was inducted, which is probably typical of the procedure in the eastern families. The inductee is led into a meeting between the top leaders of the mob. He is introduced and sponsored by one of the prominent people at the meeting. (Joe Bonanno was sponsor for Frattiano, as I recall.) The fingers of the new member and the sponsor are pricked, and their blood is commingled. The inductee then places a holy card common to the Catholic religion in his palm and it is lit. As it bursts into flame, he takes several oaths. One is the infamous oath of *omerta*, the oath never to betray the La Cosa Nostra by informing. Another includes a prohibition against coveting another member's wife or mistress. There's also an oath of loyalty to the organization.

In Chicago, there has never been this formalization of membership. Members get made when a prominent member or leader takes them into his faction. For instance, Dominic "Butch" Blasi told Mo about being made by Jimmy Belcastro, "the Bomber" (who torched and bombed many rival establishments for Capone and for Frank Nitti). According to Blasi, there was no ceremony. He was told by Belcastro that he was to work for him in a gambling joint in the Patch, the area around Taylor and Halsted on the near Southwest Side of Chicago in the First Ward, and that from that point on he was to consider himself "one of us."

We had come a long way in the investigation of "the Camel" since the inception of the THP. It took us a year and a half to locate his residence. And we were all so easily fooled when he had appeared before Dick Ogilvie's federal grand jury, leaning heavily on a cane, a patch over one eye and wearing a hat. He informed the swarming media that he had come in from Arizona to appear and that he was so ill and infirm in his old age that he could hardly walk. He asked for assistance from the press to enter the grand jury room.

It was his strategy, the wily grey fox, to further the idea that he was of no consequence to law enforcement, that he was retired in Arizona and on his last legs.

But on May 21, 1960, Little Al let us know that Hump had been in Washington, D.C., very recently and that he was planning a return trip for May 23. I heard him instruct his driver-bodyguard-appointment secretary and all around factotum, Hy Godfrey, to make reservations on American Airlines Flight 352 from Midway Airport in Chicago to National Airport in Washington. I called the Washington field office, and requested them to pick up a surveillance, which I would initiate at Midway.

I still have the photographs that I took of Hump that morning at Midway Airport as he sat reading the Chicago *Sun-Times*. He was dressed in a very conservative black suit with a black tie, wearing his glasses as always to conceal his blind eye. He had on a long-sleeved shirt, neatly showing an inch of linen. His shoes were bright polished, every inch of him looked like the CEO of Motorola or some other high-profile Chicago company.

It has often been said of Hump that he could have been almost anything he wanted in this world—an attorney, a congressman, a top legitimate businessman. I believe that.

As soon as Flight 352 took off, I called the Washington field office as prearranged and gave them a description of his clothing. Every field office of the FBI had a photo of Humphreys in what we called the ''LCN Index.'' It was therefore an easy matter for the six or so agents assigned to the tail to pick Hump up as he arrived in Washington. If we thought Hump would take a complex route I would have accompanied him on the plane and turned him over to the WFO upon arrival.

When Hump arrived at National Airport he immediately took a cab to the Woodner Hotel on Sixteenth Street NW and went directly to the elevator without checking in.

At five-fifteen that evening the WFO agents saw him leaving the Woodner carrying a package approximately the size of a dollar bill expanded to the thickness of two inches. Hump took a cab to 224 C Street NE. He rang the bell and was admitted. The Congressional Directory reflects that this address was then the local address of Congressman Roland Libonati of Chicago (7th District).

"Libby," as he was called by his associates, has been as associate of mobsters ever since he was photographed at Wrigley Field with Al Capone, talking to Gabby Hartnett, the Hall of Fame catcher who hit the famous "homer in the gloamin' " to win the pennant for the Cubs in 1938.

When Hump left 224 C Street he was not carrying the package.

The evidence that there may have been a payoff by Humphreys to Libonati was so circumstantial that we could not even consider presenting a case to the United States attorney's office (either in Chicago or Washington, D.C.) for potential prosecution. But our work did show us that Humphreys had a pleasant working relationship with the Illinois congressman and that we should keep an eye on Libby for future developments. (This was precisely the type of intelligence information that helped us in future investigations. In our investigation of Congressman Libonati just a few years later, we found that his key aide, Tony Tisci— the son-in-law of Sam Giancana while Giancana was the top boss in the Chicago mob—was the person we perceived to be the conduit of Giancana's orders to politicians who were counted on to provide favorable treatment to the mob.)

Hump had another congressional friend, as well.

At 7:50 P.M., Hump joined a person believed to be Murray Olf, Washington's most prominent bookmaker. Together they went by cab to the Hamilton Hotel, Fourteenth and K Streets NW. Hump went into the hotel by himself, made a phone call on the house phone, and was soon joined by Congressman Thomas J. O'Brien of Chicago (6th District). Hump and his partner then went to dinner at the well-known Fan and Bill's in Washington. When he returned to the Woodner later that night, he went to the room of a well-known Washington call girl where he apparently spent the rest of the night. The next day he took a Capital Airlines flight back to Chicago.

On June 6, 1960, I again tailed Hump when he left Midway on the same American Airlines flight to Washington. On this occasion he met with H. Clifford Allder, then a prominent

Washington attorney who represented many of the hoodlums subpoenaed before congressional committees.

On February 17, 1961, he was back in Washington again, meeting this time with Congressman O'Brien. O'Brien had been sheriff of Cook County early in his political career. He was called "Blind Tom" because he was never able to see any gambling in Cook County.

On August 24, 1960, Libby showed up at the U.S. federal penitentiary at Terre Haute as a member of the House Judiciary Committee. When he arrived, according to the warden, Libonati requested a visit with Paul "The Waiter" Ricca who was serving time at Terre Haute for income tax violation. When Libonati was taken to Ricca, the former top boss of the Chicago family, in the words of the warden, "there was a disgusting display of affection inasmuch as Congressman Libonati hugged and kissed Ricca." The warden was of the opinion that, in this case, congressional courtesy was being extended a little too far.

Libby is no longer a congressman but is now practicing law in Chicago.

Although at no time during the surveillances did we develop any information about the details of Hump's visits to the congressmen, we later learned that Libonati attempted to facilitate the early parole of Ricca from Terre Haute.

About that time, I decided that Hump's expenditures far exceeded what he had been claiming for income. I noted that in his most recent returns, he claimed an income of just $64,000. I knew I could show that he spent much more than that in the same year. Although a net worth and expenditure case—as this type of investigation was named—was strictly within the purview of the IRS, I would assist the agents of the Intelligence Unit of the IRS in amassing the information necessary to prosecute. I found that in one year alone he had spent at least $217,000 that I could document. In 1961, $217,000 was a lot of money to spend in one year.

By asking the Miami office to check public records, I found that he spent $128,321 refurbishing his Key Biscayne residence, where he kept his twenty-nine-year-old wife. He built a stone wall for privacy; a swimming pool and ramada; tore out the walls of one bedroom to make a master bedroom for Jean; and generally upgraded the home, which he had purchased previously for about $100,000.

When I got all my figures together, however, the United States attorney's office declined to prosecute. It would be Hump's defense that he had built up savings through the years. Using this argument, he could explain away the imbalance of expenditures to income. Since we were in no position to investigate the years prior to the initiation of the THP, we could not refute his defense. I have found through the years that the reason the percentage of successful prosecutions by the federal government is in the high nineties is that only those cases with almost an absolute chance of success are prosecuted.

Prosecutors are judged to a large extent on their percentage of wins. Few take the chance of losing by prosecuting cases where the chances of winning are iffy. For the investigative agencies, this is intensely frustrating. Many are the federal agents who work hard for months to built a solid case, only to have the prosecutor decline to prosecute. (This is what happened to my net worth and expenditure case on "the Camel." I got a "declination." I was upset at the time but later understood the weakness of my position.)

I was disappointed that the prosecutor would not go after Hump. It was the disappointment of a young, eager agent. I had to realize that even though I had a law degree and training at the FBI academy, I was not the *primus de pari* (the first among equals) when it came to deciding when and whom to prosecute. This function rested with the United States attorney's office; it was that office—not some FBI agent—that ultimately had the function of making such decisions. I was let down after spending all those weeks preparing my presentation. But I had lost battles before. I came to see that if I was to win a war I couldn't sit back and sulk—I had to live up to what have become the mottos for my life—"keep punchin' " and "keep the faith."

In 1962 I learned to my dismay that I did not know where Hump was residing. We heard on Little Al that he had moved, but we couldn't find out where. It had apparently become obvious to him that the FBI and the Bureau of Inspectional Service of the Chicago Police Department under Bill Duffy were both watching for him as he departed his apartment building at 4200 Marine Drive. Duffy's group in particular spent much time tailing Hump since surveillance was its big thing. (The Chicago PD was severely handicapped in developing mob informants, be-

cause any mobster with any experience knew that many cops
and their bosses were corrupt. No way would they jeopardize
their lives by cooperating with a Chicago policeman. And after
the Morrison Hotel bugging attempt, when the CPD unit was
immediately disbanded, Duffy shied away from attempts to plant
bugs or wiretap telephones. So the only technique for tailing
mobsters was surveillance, which is what they did most.)

Al told us that Hump moved because of the regular surveillance attempts. Al also told us that Hump was going to keep his
next residence so secret that "not even you guys are gong to
know!"—meaning his cohorts. We soon found that he would
stick to this vow.

I was always fearful that the Bureau of Inspectional Services
(BIS) would tail Hump or Gussie or Frankie or Ralph Pierce or
Les Kruse, the daily habitués of the tailor shop, to their meeting
place. I was also afraid they would tail the less frequent conferees like Giancana, Accardo, or Jackie Cerone. Should they do
so and then conduct an investigation, the attendees would probably pack up and move their headquarters elsewhere. But that
never happened.

I had "developed" a neighbor at 4200 North Marine. When
Hump moved, the neighbor was able to obtain the identity of
the moving company that carried his household goods away.
When I went to the company, however, my query was quickly
turned aside. I was told that I had to see the owner. All the
owner would tell me was that the goods were in storage for an
indefinite period. He said no orders had been received as to the
possible date they were to be moved to a new residence. I then
asked for his cooperation.

"Would you let me know when you hear from Mr. Humphreys?"

"No."

An emphatic no. That is unusual. Ordinarily, since people do
not openly court problems with the FBI, they lie if they do not
desire to cooperate by saying they will but then don't. This guy
was adamant: "No." And he looked me right in the eye.

As a matter of fact, it didn't make any difference. I later
learned he had been a cabareting buddy of Hump for decades.
He was also an associate of Frank Lee, the trucking company
magnate who had lied to me about having recently been with
Hump. The reason it didn't make any difference was that, as far

as I know, those goods are still in storage at that warehouse. When Hump finally did move, he left all of his household goods in the warehouse, obviously to make us believe that he had not yet pulled up stakes. Vintage Murray Humphreys!

I was angered by the stonewalling I had received at the storage company. "Okay, H, I'll find you. Make it tough on me, but I'll find you," I said to myself.

I went back to the artist's studio across the street from the tailor shop on the Gold Coast. When Hump came out I followed him. Frequently I lost him after he journeyed down Ontario Street to Mike Fish's Restaurant, then near the corner of St. Clair, next to the Eastgate Hotel, now the Richmont. But finally I got lucky. I tailed Hump to the Carriage House Hotel, on Chicago Avenue about one long block east of the Water Tower. Later, the manager confirmed that a man using the name Louis Scott, who fit very closely the description I gave him, was a resident there.

But I did not think for a minute that the Carriage House was Hump's ultimate destination. He wouldn't live in a hotel for the rest of his life.

Every good investigator has an instinct. He also gets to know the pattern of his prey. One day I read that a large residential building was being built along the Chicago River, just north of the Loop. In the article it mentioned that the builder was a guy who I recognized as an associate of Pat Marcy and John D'Arco. "I'll bet you a buck," I said to myself.

I visited the building, which was to be called Marina City. Presenting myself to the friend of Marcy and D'Arco—the guy who kept the records—I asked if anyone named Murray Llewelyn Humphreys had made application to lease an apartment there. No. Then I went down the list of Hump's known aliases— Brunswick, Burns, Hall, Harris, Lincoln, Hart, Hurley, Hyrley, Kelly, Logan, Murray, Ostrand, Plumer, Pope, Porter, Simmons, Singer, Scott, and several others.

"No."

"How about a man who looks like this?" I asked, showing a photograph.

"No."

I knew by now I would not be getting any cooperation from this guy. I asked him whether he would inform me if Hump did in fact make an application. He said he would do that. I was quite sure he would not.

In his office I looked hard at the three or four women secretaries and clerks. One in particular looked especially respectable, as if she might have enough civic responsibility to cooperate with the FBI.

That evening I waited for her to leave the building. I approached her and asked her if I could speak to her. She said she recognized me. I asked her if we could have a drink together. She agreed.

After an hour or so, when we had gotten to know each other, I told her about my problem. I didn't trust her boss. I showed her the photo of Hump, but she didn't recall observing anyone who looked like that. She also didn't recall anyone with the name and aliases of Hump. But she agreed to check. I also asked her to stay in touch with me. I asked her to please keep me up-to-date with the list of people who were applying for apartments at Marina City.

As 1962 turned into 1963, I could not believe that Hump would remain at the Carriage House. But he did. Nevertheless, I stayed in touch with my friend at Marina City.

On March 21, 1963, the secretary called me. It turned out that long before my initial conversation with the manager, a man named Ed Ryan had applied for a lease. If I had been a little smarter, a little more thorough I would have caught it. I *knew* Eddy Ryan. I had met him at the Palmer House a year or so before—by prearrangement—to talk to him about a close associate, Murray "The Camel" Humphreys. What Hump had done was to have Ryan make the application under Ryan's own name, using his own background. Eventually, then, Ryan would turn the apartment over to Hump. The manager probably knew that all the time.

In any event, according to my source, a man looking exactly like the man in the photograph—and even using the name Murray L. Humphreys—had come into the office a few minutes before she called. He was accompanied by Ed Ryan. Talking to our friend the manager, Ryan cancelled his application. It was thereupon assigned to Hump. He would be moving in tomorrow.

Tomorrow! That didn't give us much time. But we got up to his apartment, high on the fifty-first floor, and before the after-

noon was out we had installed another bug, a brother of Al and
Mo. I was ecstatic. "Hump, you thought you were so smart.
You almost beat me. But in the end I got you!"

The very next day Hump did in fact move in. The first thing
he did was install iron bars around his outside windows. He was
fifty-one floors up but taking no chances. He also installed a
burglar alarm. Had we come one day later, it would have been
much harder to penetrate "The Camel's" lair.

Ordinarily, a bug in a private residence is just marginally
productive. We had one in another residence—in the apartment
of a close Humphreys mob associate on Lake Shore Drive—and
it simply kept us abreast of his comings and goings. With that
one, we usually got just desultory conversation. It is not the
habit of the mobster to be open with his wife. He doesn't bring
the office home with him.

With Hump, however, it was entirely different. Hump hated
the Chicago winters. In fact, his serious case of shingles made
winter very painful for him. In Chicago, bad weather runs
through April. There is hardly ever a spring in Chicago, and
1963 and 1964 were fortunately no exceptions.

Since Hump kept himself housebound as much as possible,
he would have Hy Godfrey, the old prizefighter, come over.
Anything Hump desired, Hy got for him. Hy arrived early every
morning. He told Hump the identities of those who wished to
see him. He told Hump what they wanted to see him about.
Then Hump would tell Hy how he wanted each matter handled.

We named this bug "Plumb." Hump frequently referred to
"Joe the Plumber." When a matter of mob policy was to be
set, Hump would gaze back into his vast experience, recall how
Al Capone or Frank Nitti had handled a similar situation, and
say "Joe the Plumber says this," or "Joe the Plumber would
do this." Plumb was not the best bug we ever installed. Although I was to get another incentive award for my work in
birthing Plumb, he never matured to the point where he rivaled
Al or Mo.

But Plumb was real substantial help nonetheless. We had
Hump from about November through April. The only place he
would venture out was to see Al. From Plumb to Al and then
back home. By putting those two bugs in place, I greatly facil-
itated my investigation of the mob's master fixer, the elder statesman of Chicago. For the first fifty-eight years of Hump's life,

he had had a free reign. His last three to five years we had the
bit in his mouth. He didn't realize what a tight leash he was on.
But we knew his every move.

In the fall of 1965, I moved from a posture of strictly intelligence
gathering on Hump to a more aggressive position. I have always
considered myself an intelligence agent, not a policeman. Many
FBI agents develop the burning desire to lock people up, knock
them out. I really never did. My satisfaction transcended just
putting people away. If I could lock Hump into a relationship
with one of his crooked politicians and then work to neutralize
that politician and prevent him from extending favorable treatment to the mob, I got more of a sense of accomplishment than
if I put Hump himself away. I wanted to be the nemesis of the
crooked Chicago cop, politician, judge, labor leader, or public
official.

In my years of close listening, I developed a grudging respect
for Hump. I met with him on several occasions and always found
him to be a most interesting human being. I actually did like the
guy. Saying such things aloud, however, could get me in trouble.
I remember, years later, when I was a regular guest on a Sunday
night Jack Brickhouse radio program on WGN in Chicago, I
made some mention that I had a "grudging respect" for Tony
Accardo because he kept the Chicago family out of narcotics.
A couple of days later Mr. Hoover got a letter from a little old
lady in Peoria. "No wonder," she told Mr. Hoover, "we don't
have more success putting organized crime leaders in prison.
Here the top agent in Chicago respects them." I was immediately called into the SAC's office and required to answer Mr.
Hoover's angry query as to what that was all about. I covered
my tracks. But the truth was, I did have grudging respect for
Accardo. And I had even more respect for Hump.

My feelings for Hump did not impede my work. I think that
is obvious. As my target, he became almost second nature to
me. I thought about him a lot. The Marina City episode was a
prime example. I had gotten inside his skin—or inside his head,
at least—and was able to anticipate his move months in advance.

In the fall of 1965 came the chance to do more than gather
intelligence. I had the opportunity to put Hump away. I didn't
relish the prospect, but it was my job. If he put himself in a
stance where he was vulnerable, it was my duty to take him out.

Dave Schippers, the Justice Department Strike Force chief, gave me a subpoena calling for the appearance of Hump before the federal grand jury in Chicago.

In 1965, when I served the subpoena, we no longer had Plumb in place. Plumb, Al, Mo, and all of our other bugs had been taken out or turned off. President Lyndon Johnson issued an executive order declaring that bugging was a violation of civil rights. As I heard it, however, Johnson's motives were somewhat different. He found out that the FBI was investigating Bobby Baker, an aide of Johnson's during the President's Senate days, and that the Washington field office had placed a bug on an associate of Baker which revealed a lot of information about Baker. In my opinion, it's very possible that Johnson felt our bugs were getting too close to the flame and simply issued a blanket order shutting down all of them. I don't intend to use these pages as a forum to accuse Lyndon Johnson of graft or corruption. I admit up front I have no hard evidence of any such thing. He certainly did strike down our efforts to continue obtaining the valuable intelligence we were obtaining against the mob. He said he believed that such bugging was a violation of civil rights. And, after all, he was a great president for the advancement of civil rights. I'll leave it to the reader to determine if any possibility of our violation of the civil rights of some of the worst criminals in the history of our nation was a sufficient reason to tie our hands when it came to fulfilling our function to wage war against them.

To serve the subpoena on Hump, I visited his apartment on the fifty-first floor. The door was answered by his brother, Ernest, better known in the mob (where he ran all bookmaking on the Southwest side of Chicago) as Jack Wright. Wright would not let me in the apartment. But while I stood at the door talking to him, I noticed a royal blue blazer hanging on the back of a chair. I had seen Hump wearing that blazer, not in his travels around town, but when he traveled to Washington. Again, my knowledge of the minute-to-minute customs of my target was to come in useful.

Wright told me Hump was not at home. He said he had no idea where Hump was or when he would be home. I left. But I suspected Hump had been at home and would skip. I waited in the downstairs lobby of Marina City, near Johnny Lattner's Restaurant. I missed him.

I later learned that Hump had searched successfully for a way out of the building that was not readily observable. As a matter of fact, he had probably assured himself that such an exit was available when he first picked Marina City as his new residence.

Again I had a hunch. I went over to the Polk Street railroad station. Hump, when traveling to visit his first wife, Billie, always took the train to her farm in Norman, Oklahoma. I suspected he would run there to hide out. Of course, he could have flown to Oklahoma City and driven to Norman. But Hump's case of shingles had progressed to the point where he was blinded in one eye and could no longer drive. Guessing that he was going to travel by train to Norman, I put in a call to the Oklahoma City field office and was plugged through to the resident agent. The agents would meet the train. Again, my minute knowledge of my target enabled me to score.

Bingo! Hump *was* on the train. The next day we got the subpoena to Norman and it was served there.

Then we wondered whether we could add one more charge against Hump. If he had fled knowing that he was the subject of the subpoena, his action would constitute contempt of the grand jury. Suppose we could prove that he had been in his apartment when I appeared at the door and told his brother that I had a subpoena.

Enter the blue blazer. I hunted down the crew of the train on which Hump had traveled to Norman. "Luck is the residue of design," as Branch Rickey used to say. Yes, they remembered the passenger who fit the description of the man in the photo I showed them. Yes, he was on the train to Norman.

"What was he wearing?" I asked, holding my breath.

"A blue sports jacket," they said.

"Would you say it was dark blue or light blue or sky blue or baby blue or royal blue?"

"Royal blue," was the answer.

I had him. Then I had some additional luck. By chance one of the porters told me without my even asking that he recalled the passenger we were talking about: he had seen the passenger reading a Chicago newspaper in the dining car en route to Norman. When the porter picked up the newspaper after Hump had discarded it, he was surprised to see a photo of Hump on the front page. The article explained that a subpoena had been issued for his appearance before the federal grand jury in Chicago!

This was more than I had even hoped for.

I hustled back to Dave Schippers and his top assistant, Sam Betar. They agreed. We had enough to indict Hump for contempt of the grand jury.

An arrest warrant for Hump was issued. It was given to me. I did not want to execute it. I was fond of the guy and did not want to be the one who snapped the handcuffs on him. We were friendly foes and I had done my duty—I alone had put together the case that would probably put him in jail at this precarious time of his life. I wasn't at all ashamed of that, but I didn't revel in it either. So Maz Rutland, Denny Shanahan, and Tom Parrish—three big, strapping guys—were assigned to take him in.

It was Thanksgiving, 1965. The agents knocked on Hump's door. No answer. They began to make noises as if to knock it down. Finally Hump opened the door. He had a gun in his hand, and it was pointed at the agents!

Obviously, many agents would have shot him right there. Few agents would gamble that he was not going to pull the trigger. But this was the old gray fox, the elder statesman. What could he gain by shooting an FBI agent, or two or three? They grabbed the gun and quickly disarmed him. Hump was lucky his life did not end right there. But luck is fickle, and his was about to run out.

When a criminal is arrested inside his premises there exists the right of search "incidental to arrest." I had advised the agents that in Hump's apartment was a safe and that it contained some documentation of the identities of people who had provided favorable treatment to the mob. Corrupt pols and many others were likely to be mentioned in the documentation.

The agents advised Hump that they intended to open the safe. They asked him for the key.

Hump knew law. He had never finished Haven Grammar School in Chicago but it was "acknowledged" in Chicago in mob circles and law enforcement circles that he had a law degree. None that he acquired in any law school, of course, but if anybody knew the law from practical experience—having worked for decades with attorneys strategizing the defense of his associates—it was Hump. This leader of the connection guys knew his stuff.

However, he didn't understand the right to search "incidental to arrest." He was under the mistaken impression that the agents were required to produce a search warrant in order to show that a search of his premises was authorized by law. The agents, obviously well aware of their rights, insisted. When they suspected that the key to the safe was in Hump's pants pocket, they struggled with him and grabbed the key, tearing his pocket.

They searched the safe. Sure enough, it contained the documentation I expected. It contained the names of some judges, some politicians, and some labor leaders, along with private telephone numbers. The documents showed no indication that they were receiving money and were thereby on his pad. But the fact they were in the safe was a solid indication that the people on the list were available to him when he desired favors from them. There was certainly enough intelligence to make the search worthwhile.

The agents took Hump downtown for his arraignment. As he arrived at the Clerk of the Court's office to make bond, the press caught up with him.

I watched reporter Jorie Luloff attempt to interview Hump, shown later on the ten o'clock TV news that night.

"Mr. Humphreys, do you have any comment to make?" she asked.

"None, except, my, you are a pretty girl."

I laughed. "You can't keep that old guy down," I said to Jeannie. "Even under adverse circumstances, Hump has a quip. He really is a good ol' guy."

I went in to take my shower after the news was over. While there, Jeannie shouted in, "Honey, Sandy Smith is on the phone." The *Chicago Tribune* reporter was calling.

"Tell him I'm in the shower. I'll call him back."

"He says never mind, he just wanted to tell you Murray's brother found Humphreys dead in his apartment tonight. Heart attack."

I felt like I had taken a punch in the stomach. Honestly, it was as if a part of me died that night. "No more Hump?" What would my life be like? He was a major reason I enjoyed what I was doing. Besides that, if I hadn't pursued this two-bit case—contempt of a grand jury based on the guy wearing a blue blazer and reading a newspaper—Hump would still be alive.

Remorse set in. The oldest living member of the Capone mob was dead.

Morrie Norman, the restaurateur friend of Hump's, probably put it to me most succinctly. He said he felt if I had been there, as much as he respected me, the law could have passively been explained to him, he wouldn't have fought with the agents, as restrained as they were, and he probably would have lived many more years.

When Billie, his daughter Llewella, and his grandson Georgie came in for the funeral, they later went to Morrie Norman's for lunch. Morrie called and I came over. I told them all how much I had respected their husband, father, and grandfather and that I deeply regretted what had happened. Then I put my hand on Georgie's shoulder and told him that he could always remember his grandfather with respect. "He was a fine man."

In many ways I meant it. The man had killed in the Capone and Nitti days on the way up. He had committed my cardinal sin, corruption, many times over. But there was a *style* about the way he conducted himself. His word was his bond.

I surely was to miss him. My work would lose some of its glitter.

I had clearly developed an affinity for Hump—more so by far than I did for anyone else in the mob. Obviously, I had to lean over backward to ensure that my respect for the man did not outweigh my responsibility to do all in my power to neutralize his connections and minimize his role in the mob.

It is probably a common pitfall for lawmen to develop an affection for those of their adversaries who have more of the good human qualities than their other targets. Without question, I preferred working against a despised foe like a Giancana rather than a respected adversary such as a Humphreys. Each was a challenge—the difference being that I enjoyed the fruit of my success so much more against Giancana than I did against "The Camel."

I could be proud of my work. I fulfilled my duty as a hard-working FBI agent assigned to organized crime investigation. That was the work I had sworn to do to the utmost of my ability. That was the work for which I was being paid. But that didn't mean that I had to revel in it—or do a victory dance every time I scored a touchdown.

In Chicago there were always plenty more mobsters to choose as targets. But none like Hump.

21

Marilyn Monroe, Frank Sinatra, and the Rat Pack

It was August 29, 1985, and I was having breakfast at the Beverly Wilshire Hotel at the foot of famed Rodeo Drive in Beverly Hills.

My companions were Sylvia Chase, a commentator for the ABC News's "20/20" program; Bob Slatzer, a former husband of Marilyn Monroe, then an executive producer of Jaguar Pictures (a division of Columbia Pictures); and Jeanne Carmen, Marilyn's best friend.

I was in Beverly Hills to film a segment on "20/20" as part of a story on the life of Marilyn Monroe. We were shortly to go over to Century City where the filming was to be done in the plaza across Avenue of the Stars from the Century Plaza Hotel.

I had already filmed the same scene for the British Broadcasting Company, the BBC, on July 24.

My part in the story was to tell Sylvia Chase on film a part of what she referred to as "that famous encounter you had with Giancana at O'Hare." The part that interested her was where Giancana had asked whether I was going to make a report to my "boss, your super boss and your super, super boss." She was also interested in his reference to knowing things about the Kennedys that he and Phyllis McGuire might reveal some day. A simple five-minute narration on my part.

The producers of "20/20" contended that this dialogue—which we couldn't interpret clearly in 1961—must have referred to the story line of their show. They were out to prove that Marilyn Monroe had romantic affairs with both John and Bobby Kennedy. In fact, one theory held that the night she died of an overdose of drugs (in August 1962), she had been visited earlier by Bobby who told her he was breaking off the affair.

As our group discussed the program over breakfast in the Beverly Wilshire, it suddenly struck me—my Lord, this is all related to a conversation that Mo gave us back in 1962 shortly after Marilyn died!

Johnny Roselli, the representative of the Chicago family on the West Coast and in Las Vegas, had come into Chicago to confer with Giancana. After making the proper arrangements through the ubiquitous "Butch" Blasi, he met with Giancana in the presence of Mo.

The conversation was muted and I was unable to make a great deal out of it. But what I had gleaned was that Giancana had been at Cal-Neva, the Lake Tahoe resort, with Frank Sinatra and Marilyn the week before she died. There, from what I had been able to put together, she engaged in an orgy. From the conversation I overheard, it appeared she may have had sex with both Sinatra and Giancana on the same trip. During this conversation, Roselli said to Giancana, "You sure get your rocks off fucking the same broad as the brothers, don't you."

I know it is racist and I apologize for that, but at the time I assumed Roselli was using the phrase "the brothers" to mean black men. I never put it together that it might have referred to the brothers Kennedy. But the long preparations for that "20/20" segment brought that conversation to mind, and I realized that I had probably given it the wrong interpretation.

Although the BBC program aired in England and later on the cable network, SELECTV, in this country, the "20/20" program was ill-fated. After we filmed our part that day and the program was completed, Roone Arledge, the president of ABC News, declined to air it. Although he denied that complaints from his friend and tennis partner, Ethel Kennedy, had anything to do with his decision, he claimed that the program lacked merit. To this date it has never aired. Several people associated with the show, including Sylvia Chase and the producer, Stanhope Gould, resigned in protest.

Of course, what Roselli might also have been referring to when he mentioned that Giancana was bedding the same girl as the brothers, was not Marilyn, but Judy Campbell, now Judy Campbell Exner.

Judy has subsequently told all in her book—how she would bed down with Giancana in Chicago and wind up at the White

House with John Kennedy. Obviously this relationship between
the President and this young lady who was having sex with perhaps the most powerful mob leader in the country was potentially a powder keg.

We in Chicago stumbled onto it belatedly. I remember one
day I was tailing Butch Blasi because Giancana was "out of
pocket" (we hadn't been able to learn of his whereabouts for a
week or so). Blasi went to O'Hare where he met an attractive
young lady arriving on a fight from Los Angeles. Blasi took the
girl to the Oak Park Arms Hotel in Oak Park, a western suburb
of Chicago. She had been preregistered and she went right up
to her room. Blasi then left. I continued to follow Blasi that day.

That was probably a mistake. He undoubtedly had met the
girl and brought her to the Oak Park Arms for Giancana. Had I
stayed at the Oak Park Arms, I probably would have found Sam.

Later when I saw Judy Campbell's photo in the news, I realized that she was the girl I had seen Blasi procure for Giancana.

But the Bureau discovered the relationship. By checking the
long-distance phone bills of Johnny Roselli, the Los Angeles
office found he was making calls to Judy. Then in checking
Judy's calls they found many to Giancana and the Oval Office.

J. Edgar Hoover took that information on February 27, 1962,
to the President. In view of Mr. Hoover's personal dislike for
the Kennedys, I'm sure he loved that task. Although the logs of
phone calls from the White House showed many calls to Judy
before Mr. Hoover's visit there, only one, that same afternoon,
showed thereafter.

In a *People* magazine article in late February 1988, Judy
Campbell Exner claimed that she acted as a courier between
Giancana and Kennedy and that she knew of some ten meetings
between John Kennedy and Giancana. One of those meetings,
she said, took place in the Ambassador East Hotel in Chicago
in April 1961. The article was written by Kitty Kelley.

However, I doubt all of that and I said so when I was contacted
by reporters from *The Washington Post*, New York *Newsday*,
the Associated Press, and the Chicago *Sun-Times*. I also refuted
the article when I appeared on the "CBS Evening News" with
Dan Rather on February 23, 1988, and on three local Tucson
network affiliates during February, March, and November.

I hated to make a public refutation because I have very high
regard for Kitty Kelley but I don't believe the source—Judith

Campbell Exner. In fact, I find Judy's story very unlikely. John Kennedy was far above such stupid machinations as meeting with the Chicago godfather. On Dan Rather's program I said that "we in the FBI would have been watching Giancana closely during those days and monitoring his conversations through our microphones in his meeting places. Plus the Secret Service would have been escorting JFK on his trips to Chicago when he is alleged to have met with Giancana. I doubt that each agency would have screwed up at the same time."

I don't see that any purpose would have been served by personal meetings between the leader of the free world and the leader of the underworld. Even if Giancana, the West Side Bloc, and other politicians under his influence assisted Kennedy in the 1960 elections—which apparently they did—it wouldn't make sense for JFK to risk a meeting with Giancana. Nor would it make sense to have Judy as a courier between them when much more trustworthy messengers were readily available.

Furthermore, I recalled that Chuckie English, Sam's emissary, had brought me a message from Giancana in 1963. The message simply said that if Kennedy wanted to sit down with Sam he knew who to go through. It was obvious that the message referred to Sinatra.

I have yet another reason to disbelieve Judy's story (for which *People* magazine paid $100,000). As I heard on Mo, Johnny Formosa and Giancana met in October 1961 to discuss the efforts of Sinatra to intercede with the Kennedys through the father. If JFK and Giancana were meeting each other on a regular basis at the time, why would the services of Sinatra be needed?

Judy implies in the *People* article that, in addition to the help that Sam was allegedly giving to JFK politically, they were also discussing the involvement of the Mafia in the attempt to assassinate Castro. I can't swallow that. I feel certain Bobby Kennedy knew nothing about the CIA's plot against Castro until very late in the game. I also think that when Bobby learned of it he gave unequivocal orders to discontinue the scheme immediately. If Bobby didn't know of the plot, I find it most difficult to believe that his brother did.

As always, however, any action causes a reaction. Liz Smith, the gossip columnist for the New York *Daily News*, immediately tore into me. In her column shortly after the Dan Rather newscast, she took me to task for saying that both agencies would not have screwed up at the same time.

"Oh, really?" she wrote.

Then she misunderstood that I was in no way denying that Judy and JFK and Giancana were a triangle when I said I doubted that Kennedy and Giancana were meeting. She derided me for "being out of it," because I apparently did not know that it was J. Edgar Hoover who eventually reported the facts to the Kennedys. Of course I knew that. But "the facts" reported by Mr. Hoover certainly did not include meetings between Giancana and the President. Of this I am certain.

Once again I ran afoul of Ms. Smith in November 1988 when I appeared on the Fox TV Network show "The Reporters." I stated that from what I had heard over Mo I concluded that Sinatra and Giancana had been with Marilyn Monroe in the Cal-Neva in Lake Tahoe the week before she died. Liz announced on her local New York City TV show that she called Judy Campbell and Phyllis McGuire, and both denied that Sam was with Marilyn. Of course, that doesn't prove anything because I'm sure that as kinky as Sam was, he wouldn't have broadcast having slept with Marilyn to his other paramours.

Around the twenty-fifth anniversary of the assassination of JFK, in November of 1988, there was a flurry of broadcasts that espoused myriad theories about the Giancana-Campbell-Kennedy situation. I appeared on four such television and radio talk shows including Luke Michael's "West Coast At Dawn" on KDWN, the Las Vegas radio station. With me was a man who claimed to have a movie clip showing the Secret Service driver of Kennedy's car turning around and shooting the President twice with a .45. Luke said he saw the film ten times and confirmed that this was what it showed. Although I had not seem the films, I debunked it. My view gave balance to the five-hour talk show that otherwise consisted of similar claims.

Some people espoused theories that Castro commissioned Lee Harvey Oswald to kill Kennedy in reprisal for CIA attempts to kill him. Others insisted that Kennedy was killed by the Mafia. Some of these blamed Carlos Marcello, the New Orleans mob kingpin. But most blamed Giancana and the Chicago mob.

The sense of these latter theories is that the Kennedy administration (primarily Bobby Kennedy) put so much pressure on the mob that it was enough motivation for them to kill him. Since Giancana was the most heavily targeted of all, the theories insist that Giancana masterminded the plot. These theories are further fueled by exposing the acknowledged relationship between Jack Ruby and Lenny Patrick, a Chicago mobster who had met with me at Morrie Norman's about how the FBI had violated the family pact by informing his daughter's fiancé that his prospective father-in-law was a mobster (see Chapter 8).

When JFK was assassinated on November 22, 1963, I was working on organized crime matters in Chicago and keeping tabs on Giancana, Humphreys, Alex, and the rest of the Chicago mob. If the Chicago mob had anything to do with the killing of Kennedy, Giancana (as the Chicago LCN boss) and Humphreys (as the leader of the connection guys) would have been the persons in charge. In November 1963 we were listening to Giancana and Humphreys on Little Al, Mo, and Plumb practically twenty-four hours a day. Prior to November 22, 1963, we never heard any discussion of any attempt on the life of JFK—or RFK, for that matter.

The mobsters discussed the Kennedys constantly—almost as constantly as they talked about Roemer, Hill, and Rutland. But never in any way did they indicate they were interested in assassination.

After the assassination, they talked about it frequently. They weren't at all unhappy about it, but they gave absolutely no indication that they knew about it in advance or that they had anything at all to do with it. I recall Chuckie English, one of Giancana's very closest confidants, saying that it was the work of "a Marxist."

I don't subscribe to the post-assassination conspiracy theories. As I have said on television and radio shows, it is very titillating to espouse one of these theories. It gets a lot of attention from the many people who can't believe that it was the work of a simple little worm like Oswald acting alone and by himself.

But I do believe it. If there had been any connection to the Chicago family, I am quite sure we would have known about it. I firmly believe just what the Warren Commission found, after exhaustive investigation using the FBI, CIA, and all the other investigative bodies at its command. I believe it was the work of a lone, demented gunman, Oswald, and that Ruby's motivation in killing Oswald was just what he claimed—his anguish over the killing of the charasmatic leader of our country.

Giancana and Sinatra were close friends, apparently, in the late 1950s and early 1960s.

Sinatra had also been a friend of Joe Fischetti, a cousin of Al Capone, who was a made guy in Chicago and the brother of two Chicago capos, Rocco and Charley. Fischetti spent most of the time in the Miami area. However, after the election of Kennedy and the appointment of Bobby as the attorney general, it became obvious to Giancana that Sinatra could not control the Kennedys. Although Sinatra had apparently promised to have the Kennedys back off the tight investigation of the Chicago family boss, his promise backfired. As Giancana so aptly put it, "This is like Nazi Germany and I'm the biggest Jew in the country." His regard for Sinatra took a 180-degree turn for the worse when he found out that Ol' Blue Eyes wielded a lot less influence than he thought he did.

Giancana had played with Sinatra around the country—in Chicago, at Lake Tahoe, in Palm Springs, at least twice in Hawaii, and in Miami. I don't believe there was anything more sinister to it than play. They both loved the fast lane, beautiful women, song, and dance. Giancana had a big thing for entertainers. Their glamour rubbed off on him. With Sinatra it must have been the reverse side of the coin. From all I could ascertain, he enjoyed his relationships with powerful underworld figures like Giancana, Fischetti, Willie Moretti of New Jersey, Roselli, and others.

I remember the conversation of October 10, 1961, that Mo gave us. Johnny Formosa, one of the many Chicago reps in Las Vegas (he had additional responsibilities for the mob in Lake Country, Indiana) came in and talked to Giancana.

Formosa, talking about Sinatra, said, "Sam, I think you gotta start giving them orders—'This is it, Frank,' and that's how it's got to start. Aren't you going to be tied up with Cal-Neva?"

"I'm gonna wind up with half of the joint with no money."

Later in that conversation, again talking about Sinatra, Formosa said to Giancana, "I said, 'Frankie, can I ask one question?' He says, 'Johnny, I took Sam's name and wrote it down and told Bobby Kennedy, "This is my buddy and this is what I want you to know, Bob." ' Between you and me, Sam, Frank saw Joe Kennedy three different times—that's *Joe* Kennedy, the *father*."

Shortly thereafter Giancana said, "One minute he tells me this and then he tells me that. One minute he says he talked to Robert and the next minute he says he hasn't talked to him. So, he never did talk to him. It's a lot of shit. Why lie to me? I haven't got that coming."

"If he can't deliver, I want him to tell me, 'John, the load's too heavy,' " was Formosa's rejoinder.

There was a break in the conversation, a short silence. Then Giancana complained, "I got more cocksuckers on my ass than any other cocksucker in the country! Believe me when I tell you. I was on the road with that broad [Phyllis McGuire]. There must have been up there at least twenty guys. They were next door, upstairs, downstairs, surrounded all the way around. Get in a car somebody picks you up. I lost that tail, boom, I get picked up someplace else. Four or five cars with intercoms, back and forth, back and forth."

Formosa asked, "This was in Europe, right?"

"Right here! In Russia. Chicago, New York, Phoenix!" Giancana exclaimed.

Later Giancana told Formosa, "You see Dean [Martin], you tell him I want ten days out of him."

"What if he says he's booked?"

"Find out when he ain't booked," Sam replied.

"I'll tell him this is a must, right? Tell him you said it. Tell him, 'Hey Dean, this is a must. Sam wants you for ten days!' " Formosa said.

"Don't make a special trip. Call him," Giancana told Formosa.

"That fucking prima donna. You can't call him. I gotta go there and lay the law down to him. So he knows I mean business," Formosa said.

"It seems like they don't believe us. Well, we'll give them a little headache, you know? All I do is send two guys there and just tell them what they're working at. Bang, you crack them and that's it. Just lay them up. If we ever hit that guy you'll break his jaw. Then he can't sing," Giancana said.

I think that conversation pretty well summarized the way Giancana and his henchmen felt about entertainers such as Sinatra and Dean Martin. I also recall another conversation in

which Giancana and his conferee discussed "hitting" Sinatra
and "putting the other eye out of that nigger," referring to
Sammy Davis, Jr. On that occasion they decided that rather than
use force, Giancana would influence them to entertain at one of
his nightclubs, the Villa Venice in the northwest suburbs of Chicago.

Sinatra and Davis came in and drew large crowds to the Villa
Venice while segments of the crowd were bussed to Giancana's
casino-type gambling establishment that he set up several blocks
away. Using the entertainers as a lure, he made a mint at the
gambling den from the high rollers who attended the performances.

It appeared to us that Giancana humiliated Sinatra and Davis
by forcing them to put on their act, then paying them scale rather
than their usual high fees. It was my general impression that
Giancana treated Sinatra and his "Rat Pack" with contempt, at
least in the latter stages of their relationship in the mid-sixties.

22 The First Ward

In the spring of 1962 it became very apparent to
us that we had a great combination of bugs. In order to completely blanket the Chicago mob, however, it would be necessary to put one more microphone in place. In view of my
obsession with combating the alliance between the mob and
politics, I recognized that there was one glaring shortcoming in
our network.

That, of course, was at the Regular Democratic Organization
of the First Ward's headquarters. First Ward, for short, *had* to
mean Democrats, because the Regular Republican Organization
of the First Ward's was merely a weak sister of its "rival." The
Republican organization in that ward was virtually nonexistent.

The alderman and First Ward committeeman in 1962 was
John D'Arco, the guy I had first visited in 1959. His name was

on the list of hoodlums that was found on Sam Giancana when he returned from Mexico. D'Arco was the public official who "couldn't be embarrassed in this town by the FBI." Nonetheless, he was really just the figurehead in the First Ward. The mob's real power lay in the hands of their main associate, Pat Marcy. Many years later, in 1983, I testified that Marcy was a made member of the Chicago mob that ordered him to infiltrate politics. (Marcy actually is not his true name. It is Pasqualino Marchone.)

There was one other key man in the First Ward in 1962. He was Buddy Jacobson, who has since died. Buddy had been there from time immemorial, since the days of "Hinky Dink" and "Bathhouse John," the two Capone officials whose reigns lasted through Frank Nitti. Those two, in turn, were controlled for Capone and Nitti by the boss of the connection guys at the time, Jake "Greasy Thumb" Guzik. And it was Guzik who put Buddy Jacobson in place in the First Ward.

It is easy to see why we felt it was important for us to bug the First Ward headquarters. It was the only real gap in our development of Chicago intelligence, and we felt strongly that if we accomplished this task we would achieve the perfect score. If we could put a Little Al, a Mo, or a Plumb in the First Ward we would have such complete coverage of every aspect of the mob that no other field office of the Bureau would be able to match our records.

So we went about our task. Just as I had the ticket for Al, Ralph Hill had had the ticket for Mo and I again for Plumb, Marshall Rutland was given the assignment for the First Ward. I agreed to work with him. We would be jointly responsible for the installation work, but he would be solely responsible for the paperwork. As always, the Bureau in Washington required that we furnish them with the "survey." The survey included a letter stating how we would prepare the site; the reasons why it was important for us to make the installation; and the all-important caveat, the sine qua non, the reasons why our bug "won't embarrass the Bureau." Then, and only then, would the Bureau approve the penetration of the premises and the installation of the mike.

Mr. Hoover's power to authorize us in this regard was absolute as far as we were concerned. In later years it became somewhat of a gray area, but in those years we knew we were working under the direct authority and orders of Mr. Hoover. Always, the SOG directed what we were doing.

We had encountered severe problems in placing Al, Mo, and Plumb—problems that had made these installations appear to be virtually impossible when we started. The same situation prevailed here. The First Ward headquarters is located in an area subject to a blanket of police protection. Not only is it located across the street from City Hall, but La Salle Street in Chicago is the heart of the financial district. Several of Chicago's major banks are on La Salle Street. Many of the most prominent law offices are on La Salle Street. It is the site of jewelry and fur stores, and therefore the natural target of thieves.

In addition to all the police, there were guards stationed in the lobby of the building. Any off-hours visitor was required to give a good cause for his presence. We couldn't just walk into the building, at least not during nonbusiness hours (which is when we would have to make our move), and get onto an elevator.

There was restaurant on one side of the building, now called Counselour's Row. A bar called the Normandy Inn was around the corner on Washington Street, with an entrance into 100 North La Salle. The Normandy Inn was a special hangout for Pat Marcy, Gus Alex and Frank Ferraro. This site was a natural since it could be entered without going out on the street, and it stayed open into the wee hours.

I took over the problem, as I had with Al, of making the arrangements to gain entry to the building. The arrangements were made with a private citizen whose life, even today, would be in extreme jeopardy if I were to reveal his identity. As always, we were extremely grateful for such civilian help. Private citizens who help out a law enforcement officer are indispensable in my line of work, and I regard them with the same high respect that I accord to my best associates in the FBI.

The Chicago mob has murdered at least one private citizen and bombed the home of another who they suspected of lending us aid. At this late date I am not going to risk another.

With the help of our civilian contact, we were able to get into 100 North La Salle. Once I had solved the problem of entry, we were more or less home free—because of our experience with installations, the work went smoothly.

We named this new source "Shade." For two reasons, really.

First, our bug was to live his life in the "shade" of City Hall, right across the street, and he would tell us about the mob involvement with City Hall. Secondly, the atmosphere he would live in was as "shady" as you can get. Shade bounced a big surprise to us immediately. As I've mentioned before, we obtained information that led Maz, Ralph, and me to conclude that Tony Tisci, the administrative aide to Congressman Roland Libonati—Hump's host at his home in Washington—was the conduit of orders from Giancana to D'Arco, Marcy, and Jacobson in the First Ward. Whereas D'Arco and Marcy would go directly to meet with Ferraro, Pierce, Kruse, and Humphreys (then still alive) it was Tisci who served as the courier between Giancana and the First Ward bosses.

Tisci was a regular in the First Ward offices. The conversations we heard explained how Giancana dominated the First Ward. Through the ward he influenced dozens of politicians, members of the judiciary, labor leaders, and public officials who provided favorable treatment for the Chicago mob. We were able to learn the identities of many of the individuals who were influenced in this way. We not only were privy to the orders that Tisci brought, particularly to Marcy, but we were there when Marcy carried out the orders by giving them firsthand to the intended recipient.

For example, orders from the First Ward determined who should be selected as candidates for judgeships. Such selection was tantamount to election. The First Ward leaders also handed down instructions to contact the commander of the central police district of the Chicago PD in regard to a problem the mob was having with their strip joints on South State Street in the Loop. A particular legislator in the Illinois General Assembly in Springfield, the state capital, was told to vote a certain way on a bill of interest to the mob. D'Arco was instructed how he was to vote in the Chicago City Council. A relative of a mob boss was given a city job as part of other First Ward patronage privilege. Paul Moss, the president of Anco Insurance Company, was told that he must solicit a particular businessman for insurance before the First Ward would sponsor his application for a canopy over the sidewalk from his building. Pat Marcy was told to approach a particular judge directly to intervene in a case involving a mob member. Marcy was instructed to meet with the commander of the central police district in order to

secure the promotion of a police officer who could be counted
on to provide favorable treatment to the mob. And Marcy was
also instructed to meet with the alderman and/or ward committeeman in any of the other wards in Chicago under the influence
of the mob to ensure that the mob's requests were carried out.
(I have testified before the Senate that the other Chicago wards
under the control of the mob were the 25th, 36th, 39th, and
28th.)

Buddy Jacobson was used extensively to run the orders to
those who, for reason of logistics, were less conveniently located. For instance, the Criminal Courts Building, where judges
hear criminal trials in Cook County and where the assistant
state's attorneys prosecute them, is located at Twenty-sixth and
California. That is about fifty-six blocks from La Salle and
Washington. We would hear Marcy or occasionally D'Arco receive Giancana's orders and pass them on to Buddy Jacobson.
He then transmitted those orders to the corrupted public official
or judge; shortly thereafter, we would hear Buddy return to tell
of his success.

What we learned—which came as a surprise to us—was that
Marcy was the boss of the First Ward. So the boss wasn't
D'Arco! D'Arco took his orders from Marcy.

However, the biggest surprise of all was that the First Ward got
its orders from "the west side." In the parlance of the Chicago
mob, the west side refers to their leadership. For one reason or
another, the big boss of the Chicago family, ever since Capone,
has always lived in a western suburb. Ricca and Accardo lived in
River Forest until Accardo moved his part-time residence in Chicago to Barrington Hills. Alderisio lived in Riverside; Aiuppa and
Ferriola in Oak Brook. Cerone lived in Elmwood Park, Giancana
and Battaglia in Oak Park. In the mid-sixties, Giancana *was* the
boss and he was "the west side."

The reason it was such a big surprise was that we had assumed
from the traffic at the tailor shop that the connection guys (Hump,
Alex, Ferraro, Pierce, and Kruse) were handling the bulk of the
corruption. Now we were to find that their manipulations
weren't the half of it. Little Al was feeding us a combination of
mob activity and corruption. What Shade fed us was pure corruption. Never would a public official, politician, labor leader,
or law enforcement official appear at the tailor shop. But these
people would appear regularly at the First Ward.

The business of Pat Marcy is corruption, pure and simple. Only occasionally does he get involved in the alleged business of the First Ward, the business of its citizens. Rarely did some denizen of the First Ward who came with a problem get to see Pat Marcy. He might see Buddy or Joe Laino or, if he was lucky or had some clout, he'd see D'Arco. But he would rarely see Marcy. The clout it generally took to be ushered into Marcy's presence was that the visitor had to be corrupt. He had to be crooked. Or at the very least bendable.

We also learned that many of the corrupted appeared on a monthly basis for their "envelope," their payoff. For that they came to Marcy, who was the payoff man. For the most part these guys receiving payoffs were cops from the central district, located in the same building as police headquarters, at Eleventh and State.

We found that Pat would meet officers of the vice squad of the central district at 100 North La Salle. But when it came time to meet with the commander of that district he found a different meeting spot, Maxim's, a nearby restaurant. It had both a ground level and a basement level. Pat would meet the commander in the basement.

We also confirmed what we had gleaned from Al. Although D'Arco (I assume with the concurrence of Marcy) had recommended to the connection guys that the mob support Richard J. Daley when he ran against Martin Kennelly for mayor in 1955, Daley's election had not worked out well for the mob.

I remember when Ross Spencer was appointed chief investigator for Dan Ward, when Ward was elected state's attorney. I joked with him (knowing he knew better), "Watch out for John D'Arco." He replied, "That's exactly what Dan Ward told me. And what he had been told by Mayor Daley!"

I always thought Dick Daley had a blind spot where the First Ward was concerned. He knew what D'Arco represented, and he kept him at arm's length. But whereas Daley had vast political power in Chicago, he never did anything to lessen D'Arco's influence or the influence of the First Ward. With his great power, Daley could have chopped the head off D'Arco, made sure his subordinates realized who D'Arco represented, and prevented those subordinates from doing his bidding. At the very least, Daley could have developed someone in the First

Ward who would outpoll D'Arco—someone honest. But Daley never lifted a hand to do anything about D'Arco. I blame him for that. And it's a mortal sin. In my view that was a great blot on Daley's accomplishments for Chicago.

Other than that, I felt that Daley was also the personification of the axiom that the ends justify the means. He was political through and through. Expediency was the answer to everything. If it made good sense politically, it made sense, period, in Daley's view. If John Jones was electable it didn't matter that he used narcotics or kept a mistress or abused his children (unless that character defect might be exposed). Daley would appoint judges to the bench who were alcoholics and worse.

Under Daley's reign of political expediency, Chicago was the "city that worked." The streets got cleaned; the snow was removed promptly; the city police knew they had City Hall's support in their war on rapists, burglars, robbers, and muggers; and the parks were kept clean, landscaped and as well-guarded as they could be in such a city; the elevated trains and buses were relatively safe to ride and they arrived on time. Jobs were plentiful. The city and the business community coexisted on a level playing field, the Chicago Board of Trade had no complaints, and the Loop thrived. At least until the Days of Rage in the sixties when the blacks and the hippies rioted (for which I did not blame Mayor Daley), Chicago was a safe city in which to live and work compared to other major cities.

Despite Daley's blind spot—John D'Arco and the First Ward—he did keep the ward guys at arm's length.

The mob thought they were going to get a lot more from Dick Daley than they did. D'Arco clearly indicated to the connection guys that if they worked for him when he was first running for mayor in 1955, he could control Daley. But D'Arco couldn't influence Daley any more than Sinatra could influence John F. Kennedy.

As Hump was to say to D'Arco, "We can't get our toe on the fifth floor," the site of the mayor's office in City Hall. "We" meant D'Arco—even under the worst Chicago mayors like Ed Kelly, the mob chiefs didn't embarrass him by appearing in his office. Not that D'Arco didn't "get his toe" in the mayor's office, but when he did, he did not receive a big smile, a hearty hello and a firm handshake. It was sometimes even a cold shoulder.

So my recollections of Mayor Daley are mixed. Decades later, in 1983, I was to testify before the U.S. Senate Permanent Subcommittee on Investigations. I compared Daley favorably with the then current mayor, Jane Byrne. Her office was open to D'Arco anytime he wanted to enter, even without appointment. The big difference was, from her D'Arco was to get a warm, comforting shoulder.

On December 31, 1979, with Byrne installed as mayor, Joe DiLeonardi was the acting superintendent of the Chicago Police Department. Bill Duffy was a deputy superintendent. On that date, DiLeonardi said he was summoned to City Hall by two aides of Mayor Byrne—Michael Brady and William Griffin. He was advised that Mayor Byrne desired that he dump Duffy. When asked why, the Byrne aides replied, "Because John D'Arco wants it." To my ears, that is like saying to Jesus Christ that he should dump St. Peter because the devil wants him dumped! But that is what Superintendent DiLeonardi said he was told by the two aides of Mayor Byrne.

When DiLeonardi refused to dump Duffy, knowing that Duffy was exactly the man for the job and knowing who D'Arco represented when making such a request, DiLeonardi was himself dumped. He was demoted from superintendent and resumed his civil service rank of captain. Then he was assigned to an innocuous post at O'Hare, many miles from the seat of power. Mayor Byrne replaced him with Richard Brzeczek. On April 15, 1980, Brzeczek dumped Duffy.

Duffy was then reassigned, demoted from the post of deputy superintendent to the post of watch commander on the swing shift at the 13th District, in a Hispanic neighborhood on the West Side. And that's where he remained until he retired in 1988. In other words, he was completely removed from the area of his greatest expertise, the investigation of the Chicago mob. The Chicago Police Department's number-one resource in the fight against organized crime was completely wasted. The mob's wishes in the days of the Summerdale Scandal ("Anybody but Morris or Duffy!") were fulfilled.

In the sixties, Dick Ogilvie, the former federal prosecutor who directed our investigation of Tony Accardo in 1959, was first the sheriff of Cook County and then the chairman of the Cook County Board of Commissioners. In this post he was called "mayor of Cook County," since the Board of Commissioners ran everything in the county outside Chicago. Dick went on from there to become governor of Illinois and then to other important posts. He was the whip for President Ford at the 1976 Republican Convention in Kansas City.

Ogilvie could have been president of the United States, and one of the very best in our history, if he had not instituted the state income tax while governor. He did the honest thing, the thing that had to be done to restore fiscal responsibility to the state treasury, and the voters held it against him when he ran for reelection.

In the sixties, however, I met regularly with Dick Ogilvie, using him as a sounding board for the reams of information we were gathering, especially from Shade. Our meetings were clandestine. Dick was known by everybody and especially the FBI to be "Mr. Clean" in Chicago politics, but he had criticized, at some point in his career, the training program of the FBI for the national academy, our training school for police officers. To criticize one of J. Edgar Hoover's programs was a no-no to the nth degree. Mr. Hoover cautioned us to steer clear of Mr. Ogilvie, so no Chicago FBI official at that time could be seen near Dick Ogilvie. An agent's career would be in jeopardy if word got back to Mr. Hoover.

Dick and I devised a scheme for setting up meetings. He would call me, and then I would call him back using the name "Mr. Richards." To meet him I would go in the side door of his office, out of sight of those in the anteroom, and he would open the door at my knock. I wasn't trying to hide from his associates, but *mine*. (Following the death of Mr. Hoover, things changed and Dick Ogilvie was then recognized by all in the FBI as an outstanding authority.)

Dick Ogilvie in the sixties was my mentor. When he died of a heart attack on May 10, 1988, I felt as if a wise and generous man had left my life forever.

My conversations with Ogilvie were always two-way. For instance, if we learned that Judge Kowalski was "Pat's guy" (using the political parlance meaning he is corrupt), I would ask Dick Ogilvie, "How can we neutralize him? What can we do to see that he does no harm?" Or I might say to him, "Dick, there's a guy named Paul Ross in your party. Stay away from him, watch what you tell him, he's not your kind of guy." He would know what I meant, not that I got it from Shade, but that it came from a reliable source.

The problem with the hot and heavy information that was coming from all our bugs was that it was inadmissible in court. It could not be used except for intelligence, and even in that use we were extremely limited because we could not do anything to compromise the sources.

Once we put a bug in, for instance, we would never again place surveillance on the site. If we were on Giancana and he eventually headed for Mo, we pretended to lose him. That was easy to do since he "dry cleaned" himself thoroughly as he neared that sensitive spot. He would not believe we had uncovered his headquarters; he felt that he was sanitized there.

Same with Hump at Little Al's. Very rarely did we follow through with a surveillance of any of the hoodlums when they headed for the location of an installation.

Due to the inadmissibility of the information for prosecution, we would not even discuss it with members of the Justice Department. They could make no use of it, they were not on a "need to know" basis. We trusted them, but loose talk was dangerous.

Many department officials use their careers as assistant U.S. attorneys and Strike Force attorneys as a springboard to private practice. Several former assistant U.S. attorneys in Chicago have gone on to represent the mob leaders. I was not about to share my secrets about my sources of information with a U.S. attorney today, knowing he may be sharing his secrets with his new client, Mr. Mob Boss, tomorrow.

A prime example: I investigated Anco Insurance, the First Ward insurance company whose policy was set by Giancana when he was the mob boss. I wrote a report that was thereafter sent to the Justice Department Strike Force in Chicago for possible prosecution. In it I reported that a restaurant owner in the First Ward wanted to put a canopy over the sidewalk in front of his restaurant. I mentioned that he applied for a permit to do so.

Months passed, and nothing happened. Then, one day, he was visited by a First Ward precinct captain, who was soliciting the restaurateur's insurance business.

"I've got all the insurance I need. Why should I get more?" the owner asked naively.

"I hear you've got a permit pending for a canopy," was the reply.

"What's that got to do with insurance on my restaurant?"

"Think about it. Ask around."

The man asked around. He took out dram shop insurance (which is protection against liability for owners of establishments which sell liquor) with Anco, the company represented by the precinct captain. Two days later he got the permit for his canopy. He became an enthusiastic link in the chain of "word of mouth" that makes Anco the prime insurance business in the First Ward.

I also reported an item that John Bassett had developed. John's source gave it to him on the condition he not be identified.

The source was the owner of a building in the First Ward. While the building was going up, a work stoppage by the building trades unions prevented further progress.

After some time elapsed and no further progress was made toward negotiating a settlement, the man got a visit from another precinct captain of the First Ward. Their conversation was similar in tone to the first. "If you already think you've got enough insurance, fine. I hear you're having a labor problem? Bad one, huh? I'm sorry. Ask around, you might get some ideas about how to solve the problem."

The man "asked around." He got the idea. He bought some liability insurance through Anco. The workers went right back to work. Today he continues to buy his insurance from Anco. All kinds. He owns a lot of property in the First Ward.

Soon after that section of my report went up to the Strike Force offices in the Dirksen Federal Building, I got a call from Sam Betar, the chief deputy Strike Force attorney.

"Roemer, who is your source in this section of your report?" he asked, referring to the information John had developed. "Who is the precinct captain and what is the name of the building?"

"Sam, I'd like to tell you, but Johnny Bassett got that information on the condition that all of those questions be covered. I can't help you. Sorry," I told him.

"Roemer, we work on the same side. I'm in a position to demand you tell me. I'm the chief deputy Strike Force attorney, for Christ sake. If you know what's good for you, you'll tell me," Betar shot back.

"No way, Sammy. If Johnny wants to tell you, fine, but I know he won't. We developed that info with a promise. We keep our promises."

"Fuck you, Roemer!" Betar slammed the phone in my ear.

Sam and I didn't communicate for the rest of my time in Chicago. I disliked the way he put it, but I understood his frustration. He was trying to build a case against Anco, and by upholding a commitment John Bassett had properly given to his source, I had impaired Betar's progress in this regard. I thought at the time he was a jerk for displaying his temper as he did. I also thought he was stupid to talk to me like that. But, I did little about it except to tell my peers that I wouldn't be working with Betar any further. Actually I don't recall that anything happened as far as prosecution of Anco or any of its principals is concerned.

Many years later, after I had left the FBI and became an attorney representing clients having problems with mobsters, I had to serve a subpoena on Jackie Cerone, the boss of the Chicago family. He referred me to his son, Attorney Jack P. Cerone. When I called him, he told me. "There's another attorney who will handle this for us. Give your subpoena to him. He has my father's authority to receive it on his behalf." The other attorney turned out to be Sam Betar. He wound up representing the mob boss, the guy who in previous years he was responsible for prosecuting.

Sam Betar did what he felt was best—both when he was with the government and now that he is in private practice. But just as I wouldn't divulge my secrets to him when he was a governmental attorney, I certainly won't today when he has been an attorney for Jackie Cerone.

As we reaped the benefits of Shade, it became increasingly obvious that John D'Arco, the guy "who couldn't be embarrassed in this town by the FBI," was up to his gonads in corruption. I was determined to bring him down.

In late 1962, a situation began to develop that was to give us our chance. Giancana, on the advice of Pat Marcy, his man in the First Ward, decided that D'Arco was incapable of having sufficient impact in the City Council. Marcy felt, and Giancana came to agree, that D'Arco did not have the influence required of a First Ward alderman.

"With you behind him, Mo," he told Giancana, "anybody can be as good as he is and can get done what he gets done."

During the day, Marcy would commiserate with D'Arco, who was demolished by the thought that he might have to go to work for a living (something he had never done in his fifty-some years), while at night Marcy would counsel Giancana to "dump D'Arco."

We were amused with this situation until Mo and Al began to report on the same thing. This was in 1962, when Hump was still alive. He, Gussie, and the other connection guys became quite concerned. In their opinion D'Arco was a definite asset to the mob. He had worked for them in the Illinois General Assembly. He had worked for them not only in the City Council but as the ward committeeman, handling the important job of dispensing the patronage in the First Ward. If a son or a nephew or a cousin of Joe Mobster needed a job—a "ghost" job, a "payroll" job—where he could report to work for the city of Chicago at seven o'clock and go home at eight o'clock for eight hours' pay (or even better, never report), then good old John D'Arco could be counted on to find such a job. Although a new man might be better than D'Arco, he would need time to learn how all these things were done. He would also have to develop the contacts.

"If it's not a problem, don't fix it," was the attitude of Hump and Gussie. They sent that message to Giancana after D'Arco had met with them to plead his case.

Now we began to become more interested. We considered the connection guys, Hump especially, to be the real oracles of corruption in Chicago. We considered Giancana much less able in exercising good judgment. Therefore, we felt that the cause of good government would be enhanced if the will of Hump and his group, the experts in the field, was thwarted—even if that meant Giancana would prevail. When we weighed the good against the bad, we decided that "Dump D'Arco" should be our motto.

How to accomplish that was another matter, however. After all, we didn't exactly have influence over Giancana. I couldn't walk up to him and say, "Hi, Sam, my name is Bill Roemer. You might remember we met at O'Hare a year or so ago. Look,

I want a favor. Dump D'Arco.'' Although Giancana was already inclined to do so, that would have caused him to change his position 180 degrees.

Then we recognized our opportunity. One day I was listening as Marcy told D'Arco:

''Sam has agreed to your request to meet with him. I haven't been able to do much to change his mind and I don't think you can either. But he will meet you at the place in North Riverside. The Czech Lodge. Meet him there at one o'clock tomorrow afternoon.''

I yelled to Maz and Ralph. We had a big decision to make. Here was a golden opportunity to compromise D'Arco forever in the eyes of Giancana. But if we acted on our information, we risked exposing Shade. However, we made a conscious decision, after a lengthy conference with Inserra, to take the action we did. We were confident of our reasoning that this was a real opportunity to knock D'Arco out of the box, and we believed our best course of action would help to further good government and good law enforcement.

In our discussion with Inserra, I was the leading proponent of that course of action. It needled me that a guy could say to my face that the FBI could not embarrass him in Chicago. This is precisely the role I relished: I wanted to be the mob's nemesis, thwarting them at every turn when they endeavored to manipulate politics and governmental affairs.

Maz and Ralph agreed we could probably take action without revealing our information source. We were getting so much intelligence from so many sources indicating that D'Arco was ''in trouble'' that we decided the mob would never figure out where our precise information came from.

Also, other agents on C-1 who had tailed Giancana told me that Giancana had just recently begun to use the Czech Lodge as a meeting place. So it was not as if Giancana was using the Czech Lodge for the first time, just for his meeting with D'Arco. It had become a ''known'' meeting place for Mo.

The next day we three amigos went out to the Czech Lodge. It is a large restaurant, featuring Old World food. As you enter from the front, there is a long bar surrounded by a large public dining room and two public rooms on the ground floor. There are several private dining rooms—one on the ground level and more upstairs.

Ralph, Maz, and I walked around the public areas. Nothing. Then we went up to the bartender, told him who we were, and showed our credentials.

"We're looking for Sam Giancana," we announced.

"Don't know him," the bartender replied, somewhat surprised.

We decided to tackle the private rooms. Ralph and Maz sprinted up the stairs. I took the downstairs room. Bingo! Standing right outside the door, who did I spot but Buddy Jacobson! This must be the place! The room behind Buddy was within earshot of the bar, and I was afraid our prey had been alerted when we identified ourselves. But apparently Buddy—no spring chicken in 1962—was hard of hearing. He proved to be not much of a lookout and no guard at all. I brushed him aside and stomped into the room. I had thought I would wait there for Ralph and Maz to let them in on the fun, but I was afraid the birds had already flown the coop.

There were Giancana and D'Arco, all alone in the room. They were hunched over, faces close together in earnest conversation. This I thought might well be the Last Supper for John D'Arco.

"Ho, ho, ho, it's Mo!" I shouted at the top of my voice from the doorway.

As I strode to their table, Giancana recognized me at once. He glared at me, obviously enraged. He had not seen me since O'Hare, and this was the last place he wanted to encounter me. Maybe he wanted to see me in hell, but not here.

I stuck out my hand to D'Arco. "Nice to see you, John," I said sarcastically.

With the reflexes of a politician, D'Arco jumped up, took my outstretched hand, and shook it. I smiled brightly.

"You fuckin' idiot!" Giancana snarled at D'Arco. "This is Roemer!" Then he kicked D'Arco in the shins! Hard!

D'Arco sat down. The smile, weak as it had been, evaporated. He was beginning to realize the impact of this development. Here he had been, trying to plead that he could handle the job if Giancana would let him, and the FBI busts in. Talk about the smoking gun! Meeting with the mob boss in secret! Caught with his pants down. How could he maintain the corrupt politician's stance of innocence when he was caught meeting privately with the biggest hoodlum in Chicago? How could he deny his association now?

My mission accomplished, I strode happily from the room. On the way out, I shook hands with Buddy. "Can I buy you a drink, Buddy?" I asked.

Buddy hadn't quite realized what was going on. He joined me at the bar. Maz and Ralph came back downstairs in a few minutes. I introduced them to Buddy and filled them in.

Soon, Giancana came out of the room. He stood five yards away and glared at us. I hoped he would start O'Hare all over again. Harold Sell was not there to kick *me* in the shins this time. We glared back. Then I laughed. And laughed again. Louder and louder.

I felt sure Mo was going to lose it again. I sure hoped so. He didn't. He turned on his heel and bounded out of the restaurant.

I turned to Buddy Jacobson. "Never met you before, Buddy, but you have a great reputation. Used to be with Greasy Thumb, didn't you?"

Buddy took that as a fine compliment.

I continued in the same vein. "Fine reputation. I guess you can fix just about anything in Chicago."

"Yes, I can. You want something done in Chicago, mister, you come to Buddy Jacobson."

I felt a little sorry for him. No sense beating a dead horse. We had done everything we had set out to do and more. I began to hope that John D'Arco could soon screw up his courage and come out of the room so Buddy could take him home. He did, eventually, and he had to pass us. He looked pasty-faced. I felt sorry for him also.

"Are you all right, Alderman?"

He nodded his head, jerked his thumb at Buddy, and together they left the premises.

Maz, Ralph, and I hoisted beers and shook hands. The bartender left us and went down to the other side of the bar. He knew we were the FBI, and he also knew that Giancana, who was undoubtedly a great tipper, was mad at us. We were not the bartender's friends. He let us know he'd just as soon we dropped dead.

We didn't care. The ride back was a happy one.

The next day, it was announced in all the papers that John D'Arco had suffered a heart attack and was in a West Side hospital. He would not be running for alderman in the upcoming elections. If I believed that I had caused the heart attack, it would have disturbed me. Nobody deserves a heart attack.

He did hospitalize himself, but I believe he had what law enforcement people call a "mob illness." When it comes time to appear before Congress or a grand jury, the suffering mobster finds a doctor who will testify that the mobster has a crippling illness—even though he may have been playing golf the day before.

What made Maz, Ralph, and me so happy was that just perhaps John D'Arco was hoisted on his own petard. No longer could he be certain that "there is no way that I can be embarrassed in this town by the FBI." We wondered if perhaps—just perhaps—he might have changed his mind.

But our day was not over yet. After one beer at the Czech Lodge, we hustled back to the office to monitor the reaction from Shade. We had beaten Buddy back downtown. Apparently, he had dropped D'Arco off at home before coming into the First Ward office. What we heard was Buddy telling Pat Marcy—the guy responsible for the smooth operation of the mob's interests in the First Ward—his version of the confrontation at the Czech Lodge. These were his words, verbatim from the official FBI tape:

". . . and all of a sudden, there they were! These guys walked in and Mo, why he kicked John in the shins! And John says I don't know them. And *I* don't! How he knew me I don't know. The same guy as always. Roemer. With those two guys they say are always with him, Hill and Rutland. I didn't know what to do or how to do it! The thing is they are so fucking smug! . . . world by the ass. And how do you fight them, you can't stop them . . . like fucking gangbusters!

"Smart cocksuckers. Why, John is sick, dead. Said we know you, Buddy. Used to be with Guzik. They been giving Mo fits. He hates them. Hill. And they say Rutland is the one caused Frank Ferraro all that trouble.

"They can't do nothin' with those guys. They never seen such guys. Nobody can sit with them.

"You know it wouldn't be so bad, but how do you fight that kind of thing? In the forty-one years I been here I ain't seen nobody like them three. They walked into that place like the goddamn Marines!

"I never saw them before but right away I said to myself, we're in trouble. See, I can spot a wrong guy after all this time.

"Three big, cocky, arrogant, like get the fuck out of the way, you fucking bastards! I knew they had to be heat, and I heard Roemer say to the bartender, FBI! I knew we was dead right then. Fucking cocksuckers!

"If only there was some way somebody could sit down with them. And what do they get out of all this? Like a bunch of Boy Scouts. Hump says he can't do nothing with them.

"And sweet talkers? You'd think they was the three nicest guys in Chicago. But dirty? They would burn their mothers if she crossed the street on a red light, what with their honor! I think they would. Dirty pricks! I *never* seen Mo so mad!"

Now that D'Arco appeared to be out of the picture (an assumption that would prove to be half-right), who would be tabbed by Giancana to replace him? The alderman must be elected by the populace, the voters of his ward. In the First Ward that is a farce. The mob picks the candidate and then does whatever it takes—bloody beatings or phony ballot counts—to get the job done its own way.

Giancana chose his nephew, Anthony DeTolve. *Now* we believed we knew why he wanted to replace D'Arco against the advice of all but Marcy—to put his own kin in there. If Henry Ford can put his son in to run the Ford Motor Company, Giancana could draft his nephew to run the First Ward. After all, the nephew didn't have to know anything.

DeTolve was ordered to keep a low profile. "Stay low," they told him. "Don't stir anything up. Keep your head down. You're a sure winner, it ain't like there's going to be a real election here."

So DeTolve kept his head down. He granted no interviews to the press. He even put his campaign office in an old speakeasy that had iron bars on the doors and peepholes. The telephone could ring and ring.

Frustrated, the press began to ridicule the candidate. Buddy and Pat realized that was the one thing no candidate could face and remain credible. What Giancana was trying to do—so he said—was to get a more articulate man in the City Council, one who could influence his associates.

So DeTolve finally granted one press interview. He told the press, "I haven't been hiding. I've just been busy, busy, all the time busy."

To the press Anthony DeTolve became "Busy-Busy" DeTolve. Like Tony "Big Tuna" Accardo or Joey "Doves" Aiuppa, it made him sound like a hood. "Busy-Busy" DeTolve—what a name, even for a Chicago politician.

Giancana realized his folly. "Busy-Busy" wasn't going to be a serious player in the council. The press had ruined him.

So Giancana dumped Busy-Busy and entered a write-in candidate who looked like a highly qualified attorney and a first-class person. His name was Michael Fio Rito. We were told by knowledgeable people in the legal fraternity that Fio Rito was highly regarded. Since none of our intelligence indicated otherwise, we couldn't understand how Giancana and the First Ward could have induced a man with the fine background of Fio Rito to accept the job. We finally concluded that the First Ward had become such a comic opera that the only way the bosses felt they could restore some respect was to go for a high-class, gilt-edged candidate.

Obviously, they also had some reason to believe they could control him, though we couldn't fathom how.

Fio Rito was elected by a landslide even though he was unknown in the First Ward.

In fact, he didn't even live there! And technically that made him ineligible as a candidate. Fio Rito was running illegally.

I was ambivalent about what to do. On the one hand, a man with integrity in the First Ward was a plus for good government. An articulate orator in the City Council could be good.

But it could be very bad if he supported bills that would benefit the mob. Finally, I was guided by the fact that he had violated the law. (I learned from the press that Fio Rito claimed his permanent residence to be the Conrad Hilton Hotel, the old Stevens, now the Chicago Hilton and Towers.) So I called Dick Ogilvie who was then the sheriff of Cook County and I asked "Mr. Richards" if he thought the sheriff might be interested if I could prove that illegalities existed in the election of the new First Ward alderman. I knew Dick knew as well as I knew what the First Ward represented. Dick indicated that, yes, the sheriff might just be interested. I told him that I knew Fio Rito's use of the Conrad Hilton as his permanent residence was a fabrication—that he was actually a resident of Wilmette, a silk-stocking northern suburb of Chicago. Investigation there of neighbors, of employees at the Conrad Hilton, and especially of the registration cards at the Conrad Hilton would prove that. Dick Ogilvie was never at a loss for action. He plunged his men into the task posthaste.

In the meantime, Maz and I sat down with Fio Rito and had a friendly lunch.

"Mr. Alderman," I said, "here is what is going to happen. You've got a capable man probing you in Dick Ogilvie. He won't let an easy one like this get away. But let's say it doesn't happen, that you squeeze by. You are an honorable man. An attorney with a fine background, a good reputation and a bright future. Now you're going to sit in the First Ward offices and take orders from Pat Marcy for the rest of your term? How can a man like you do that?

"We'll let you digest that.

"But there is one more thing. The FBI is well aware of what the First Ward of Chicago represents. The city of Chicago might not do anything about this. But the FBI will. We'll be on your case, watching. If you continue to front for the mob, we'll continue to watch you. If you feel you can take that kind of stress, that pressure, fine, go right ahead. But we felt like a nice friendly warning today might be heeded by a level-headed, clear-minded guy like you."

That nice, friendly warning was indeed heeded. After a total of nineteen days in office, Mike Fio Rito realized the mistake he had made.

He gave up the ship. He made the right decision. From a dunderhead like D'Arco to a nitwit like "Busy-Busy" to an intelligent Mike Fio Rito, the First Ward had been run from pillar to post.

The First Ward became a farce. Mention the First Ward at that time and it was like saying the "Funny Farm." The press had a ball. Four daily newspapers in Chicago all competed to ridicule the First Ward.

It was that kind of action, to neutralize the alliance between organized crime and politics, that gave me my pleasure.

But much of the old gang is still there as of this writing. D'Arco got out of the hospital. Giancana, perhaps to spite us, gave him half a loaf. Though Giancana had replaced D'Arco as the alderman in City Council, he let him remain as ward committeeman, which was really the most powerful post. Even more important to D'Arco, Giancana let him keep his share of Anco, the lucrative insurance company.

Marcy likewise is still going strong in 1991.[1] I ran into him at The Spa in Palm Springs a few years ago, but he didn't seem to recognize me and I didn't push it.

Donald Parillo became the alderman for a while, until he was replaced by Fred Roti. Parillo's father was an old Humphreys associate and Roti's father was the notorious Bruno "the Don" Roti, a somewhat mysterious figure, at least to me, who coexisted with Frank Nitti in the Patch on the near South Side. I suspect why he got the name "the Don," but I don't really know—his day preceded even CAPGA. I don't visit the sins of the father on the son; Parillo and Roti might be clean as the driven snow. Marcy and D'Arco are still in place in the First Ward, so there's a good chance things are still status quo there.

Shade died in July 1965 with the rest of his brothers, courtesy of Lyndon Johnson.

[1]Talk about deja vu all over again, as they say. On July 13, 1989, the big news in Chicago was that a busboy had stumbled on a hidden video camera pointing at Booth No. 1 in the Counselour's Row Restaurant. This is the restaurant frequented by many of the pols who do their business across the street at City Hall—and some who do their business in the adjacent building at 100 North LaSalle, the location of the headquarters of the First Ward. Also uncovered in the search which followed was a bug in the telephone located next to the booth.

Obviously, the law enforcement agency which planted the devices had an official investigative interest in monitoring conversations of the pols who regularly reserved Booth No. 1. Most often that was Fred Roti, the First Ward alderman who coexists just upstairs with John D'Arco and Pat Marcy. Of course, the FBI got the blame—or, in my viewpoint, the credit—for these installations. Obviously, there continues to exist in Chicago an official investigative interest in crooked politics—and especially in the First Ward. The more things change, the more they stay the same in Chicago.

23 Bobby Kennedy

It didn't take Bobby Kennedy long to realize that he wouldn't have to drag J. Edgar Hoover kicking and screaming into the fight against organized crime. By the time Bobby put his feet up on his desk in the Justice Department and started reading the reports of Ralph Hill on Sam Giancana, John Roberts on Tony Accardo, Vince Inserra on Ross Prio, Marshall Rutland on Frank Ferraro, and Bill Roemer on Gus Alex and Murray Humphreys, investigations that were duplicated across the country, I'm sure Bobby got the idea that Mr. Hoover certainly did recognize there was organized crime.

I read in 1987 that William Webster, then the director of the FBI, gave a talk in which he said that when he was the United States attorney in St. Louis in 1960 under President Eisenhower, he "called on the SAC of the St. Louis field office of the FBI and asked him to tell me about organized crime. His response—the official FBI response—was that there was no such thing as organized crime, only some loose, familial relationships. And that really was about all that was known in those days."

Wow! Did I jump at that! No *way* could that have been the "official FBI response" in 1960. I have no doubt the SAC in St. Louis told Judge Webster what the judge recalls. But the SAC in St. Louis could not possibly have been up-to-date on what was happening.

Immediately, I wrote a letter to Judge Webster. I had spent some time with him at a cocktail party in Chicago, but I didn't really know him. In my letter I pointed out how far we had come in 1960. We had already installed Little Al and had overheard Giancana and Accardo discussing Giancana's observations of the national Commission of the mob—a discussion that was disseminated all over the country (as I have reported). It was likely that we had not sent a copy of our daily summary airtel to St. Louis, since the LCN did not have a Commission member there. But in 1960 a Top Hoodlum Program had been under way for over two years in St. Louis. Any self-respecting SAC should have been well aware of the developments under that program.

I received a very nice letter back from the judge, just as he was moving from the FBI to take over the CIA. He told me that I should "take great pride in the vital role you played in the Bureau's involvement in organized crime investigations" and thanked me for bringing my thoughts to his attention.

I wrote because it really gets under my skin when I read of the popular belief that Mr. Hoover dragged his feet on organized crime investigations until Attorney General Robert F. Kennedy forced him to take action. The FBI is the greatest law enforcement organization in the world. And Mr. Hoover was the greatest law enforcement administrator of all time. He had his idiosyncrasies, and he was a tough man to work for. But as I often said then, "If you don't want to work for the man, don't, just get out."

Many did, after just a few years. Those of us who stayed the course realized that he was the way he was because he wanted only the best. He wouldn't tolerate mistakes because they detracted from the reputation of the Bureau. And that was a reputation he worked hard to build and maintain.

I also know that although Bobby Kennedy came into office at the time when there was a well-organized fight by the FBI against organized crime, it had wound down a bit from its early fast start. I give Bobby credit for renewing the fight. As I have reported, we had dwindled down from ten to five agents on the THP, and the five of us were being assigned other criminal investigations in addition to our THP duties. But within a year after Bobby came in, we were up to seventy agents in Chicago. I'm sure similar increases were replicated all over the country.

In any event, we soon got word that RFK was going to make a swing of inspection visits to FBI field offices. He wanted first-hand information from agents working on organized crime.

Marlin Johnson was the special agent in charge of the Chicago FBI office at the time of Bobby Kennedy's visit. He called us in.

We were all instructed to make presentations to the new attorney general about our targets. I was to speak not only on

Hump and Gussie but also on the alliance between organized crime and politics. Since these links were my special interest, it was expected that I would share my opinions with Mr. Kennedy, for obvious reasons.

Bobby arrived with Ed Guthman, his press relations man, and Courtney Evans, the assistant director of the FBI, who was Hoover's man in charge of what was now to be called the Criminal Intelligence Program (CIP).

Marlin Johnson was at his desk when Kennedy and his aides entered. He arranged the seating so that Kennedy and his two aides had chairs facing him and the rest of us were horseshoed around the Kennedy group, most of us facing their backs.

Marlin greeted Kennedy and then began reading from a prepared statement, beginning to tell the attorney general of all the great things that we had done in Chicago to date.

After Marlin got about thirty seconds into his speech, Bobby Kennedy stood up and said, "Mr. Johnson, I didn't come here today to hear a canned speech about how magnificent you are. I didn't come here to hear from *you* at all. Now why don't I just step around there and take your desk. You can sit over there in the corner and we'll listen to the agents who are out on the street, the men who are doing the work you think is so great."

After we were rearranged to Bobby's specifications, so that he was now facing us, we began talking one by one, extemporaneously as we had expected to anyhow. Bobby listened attentively, asking many pertinent questions. He was obviously well-prepared. He impressed all of us: his questions showed that he had been reading our daily summary airtels. He was most knowledgeable about the Chicago mob.

At the time I was surprised that he knew so much about one guy in particular: Giancana. Ralph Hill started the day off by giving his discourse on Giancana; Bobby was on the edge of his chair the entire time. He pounded Ralph with questions, sometimes not even letting Ralph finish his sentences.

After four or five of our presentations, it came time for lunch. Mr. Johnson stood up. "Mr. Attorney General, if you will come with me, I have prepared a lunch in our conference room here with my supervisors who are waiting to meet you."

Bob got up and moved off with the SAC. The rest of us, who had not been invited, remained in the room getting ready to go out for lunch. Before we could leave, Bobby bounded back in

the room. He had just realized that we were not expected to
attend the luncheon, that it was for the administrative staff only,
not for the agents. And he would have none of that. He shooed
us in and shooed them out. Between mouthfuls of turkey salad
sandwiches and potato salad, he wanted to be with us to talk
more about organized crime.

I knew I could grow to like him; he was my kind of guy!

It didn't take long to shovel down those sandwiches. Back we
went to Mr. Johnson's office. When we were finished with everything else, about four or four-thirty, we were ready for the
coup de grace—my third presentation, the one on the alliance
between the Chicago mobster and the Chicago pol.

I gave Bobby the general stuff we had gotten from Al and Mo
and especially, of course, from Shade. I didn't need to prepare
him by telling him generally about politics in Chicago. He knew
about a hundred times more about that than I did.

Then I gave him the goods we had saved for the final scene.
I played a tape that we had obtained from Shade at the First
Ward headquarters. To lay the groundwork for him, I explained
that this was a tape of a conversation we had procured by placing
a microphone in the headquarters of the Regular Democratic
Organization of the First Ward.

The tape was the last in the series of conversations Pat Marcy
had had with two members of the central district vice squad of
the Chicago Police Department. I explained who Pat Marcy
was—a made guy, stationed in the offices of the First Ward
Regular Democratic Organization to run the ward for the mob.
Kennedy didn't blink an eye. If that shocked him, he wasn't
letting on.

Then I let the tape run. The recording revealed a number of
interesting facts about leading characters. Gussie Alex oversaw
numerous arcades and strip joints on South State Street in the
First Ward (prostitution, gambling, porn, all kinds of vice existed in 1960 in that area). Pat Marcy had all the members of
the vice squad of the central district, which patrolled South State
Street, locked in. They wouldn't be on "vice" if he didn't want
them there, and he gave them their monthly envelopes besides.
In addition they picked up other gravy from the pimps, whores,
and operators themselves. Vice is a highly valued assignment
among corrupt officers in many police departments, and Chicago is by no means an exception.

There was one vice officer who could not be controlled, however. Pat couldn't bribe him, couldn't intimidate him—his peers couldn't either. During the conversations leading up to this one, Marcy and the two Chicago vice cops discussed their efforts to control this guy. Now they had run out of all patience. They decided to kill him. A Chicago Democratic politician and two Chicago police officers were plotting to kill another Chicago police officer! It was loud and clear!

Now Bobby *was* shocked. If we had told him about this plot, rather than let him listen to it, I believe he might have been highly skeptical about the credibility of the source.

But here it was, verbatim, loud and clear. When the tape ran down, Bobby looked at Guthman, his aide, and then looked at the floor for ten seconds or so. He then asked that the latter part of the tape be replayed—the crucial part where the decision to kill was made. As it was played he looked at me, then at Ralph, then at Vince, then at Denny Shanahan, then at John Roberts, then at Maz, then at Christy Malone as if to say, You guys hear this? What are we going to do in Chicago about this kind of thing?

We got the message.

Later on, we saved that police officer when, being very careful not to compromise Shade, I went over to Eleventh and State, CPD headquarters where the central district is quartered, and made sure that it was clear Roemer and the G were close to the man, "they stay with him," so that anyone plotting his harm would know that the G would be extremely interested in finding out what and how and why and who. He was never touched, only transferred.

Whenever Bobby would come into Chicago after that he would have Ed Guthman call ahead and arrange for Ralph, Maz, me, and other members of C-1 to pick him up at O'Hare and be his escorts during his stay in Chicago. After greeting him at O'Hare, we would usually take him to the Conrad Hilton, although he also liked the Drake. In the presidential suite at the Conrad Hilton he would take off his shirt and dig into the refrigerator for bottles of Heineken. Then we would sit and talk about what the mob was doing in Chicago, what corruption was taking place, and what we were doing about it.

One time when he came in, Bobby, Ralph Hill, Maz Rutland, and I had dinner with Mayor Daley at his club. Another time, Bobby took us with him while he judged a Puerto Rican beauty contest. On a third occasion we accompanied him to the University of Chicago where he spoke to the student law association.

But Bobby and the Chicago agents did not become lifelong friends. Actually, the seeds of the destruction of our relationship with Bob were sown in that very first meeting—the meeting we concluded with the tape of Pat Marcy and his crooked cops plotting to kill another cop. As time went on, Bobby Kennedy and J. Edgar Hoover liked each other less and less. I don't know it for a fact, but I have been led to believe that Bobby conducted himself in the presence of Mr. Hoover like he did with Marlin Johnson. Brass in the FBI meant little to Bobby Kennedy.

I don't recall exactly when it occurred, but Bobby—apparently catering to the more liberal faction of his already liberal party—made the statement that he was totally unaware that the FBI conducted any bugging operation of any kind. Had he been aware of the practice, he said, he would have ordered it stopped. That was hard to believe, after what he had listened to in Chicago, but that is what he said. And repeated.

Now Mr. Hoover had him. Hoover had been informed of what we had presented to Bobby that day. He immediately called the Chicago field office. He told the SAC that all the agents who had participated in that presentation, heard that tape, and knew that Kennedy had heard it were to prepare sworn affidavits attesting to these facts.

I was dismayed. Bobby was something less than a close friend, I guess, but he was certainly a friend. On the other hand, the truth was the truth. Bobby knew what we'd done; he had seen the tape spinning on the reel. He had asked for the tape to be played back. Could he have believed some other agency had installed and recorded the bug?

After all—at that first meeting especially—we had wanted him to know we were working hard in Chicago and that we were producing. No way did I want him to believe somebody else was doing our work for us. Besides, what other agency in Chicago could have produced Shade and his brothers? I wasn't about to hide our accomplishments.

Since it was the truth and since it was Mr. Hoover that we worked for, we all did what we were instructed to do. We prepared the affidavits and we sent them along to Mr. Hoover. He

Tony "Joe Batters" Accardo, bodyguard to Capone, absolute boss of Chicago Mob in the 1940s and 1950s and current consiglieri.

Here I am winging a left at Gus Cifelli while winning my fourth Notre Dame Boxing Championship in 1949 on the same day our son Bill was born.

Jeannie, the lovely bride, around the time of our marriage.

As a new agent at the FBI Academy, Quantico, Virginia, October 15, 1950.

Al Capone in the 1930s.

Frank "The Enforcer" Nitti in 1932. He was the successor to Capone as boss of the Chicago Mob. Committed suicide in 1943.

Murray "The Camel" Humphreys circa 1940; he was "Public Enemy Number One" in Chicago in 1932.

Paul "The Waiter" Ricca, aka Paul DeLucia, about 1952; he was boss of the Chicago Mob in the mid 1940s.

Jake "Greasy Thumb" Guzik, financial wizard of the Chicago Mob from the Capone era until he died in 1956.

J. Edgar Hoover, who sent this autographed photograph to me in 1950.

A family portrait at 47 Green Garden Court, East Haven, Connecticut, September 21, 1952. Bill was three years old and Bob was nineteen months.

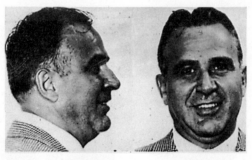

Gus Alex in 1958; he is the current leader of the Chicago Mob's "connection guys" and former Mob boss of Chicago's Loop.

Members of the top Hoodlum Squad in Chicago, 1959, receiving incentive awards. *Second left:* Ralph Hill; *middle rear:* Bill Roemer; *middle right front:* John Roberts; *right:* Vince Inserra; *middle left front:* Special Agent in Charge Julius Lopez handing out the awards.

Sam "Mo" Giancana as he appeared in 1955, ready to assume his role as absolute boss of the Chicago Mob.

Murray "Hump" Humphreys, circa 1959; he negotiated the family pact between the Chicago Mob and the FBI.

Lenny Patrick in June 1955; he was Chicago Mob gambling boss in the Rogers Park area and an associate of Jack Ruby.

"Mad Sam" DeStefano, the worst torture murderer in the history of Chicago, circa 1960.

John D'Arco, former alderman of Chicago's First Ward and current Democratic First Ward Committeeman, in 1960.

I received an incentive award in 1959 from SAC Julius Lopez for my work installing "Little Al."

Frank "Franky Strongy" Ferraro, underboss to Giancana and a "connection guy," circa 1960.

Ralph Pierce, member of the "Connection Guys" and boss of the South Side of Chicago in the 1950s, 1960s, and 1970s.

Les Kruse, "Killer Kane," Mob boss of Lake County, Ill. from the 1950s through the 1970s and a "connection guy."

Johnny Roselli, a Capone mobster who became Chicago's overseer on the West Coast and in Las Vegas 1930s to 1950s, circa 1925.

Tony "The Ant" Spilotro, the Chicago Mob's overseer in Las Vegas, 1971–1986.

Chuckie English, true name Englisi, right hand to Sam Giancana when Giancana was Chicago boss 1957 to 1966.

Tony Tisci, former congressional administrative aide and son-in-law of Sam Giancana, cira 1960.

Dominic "Butch" Blasi, bodyguard, driver and appointment secretary to Accardo, Giancana and Aiuppa, Chicago Mob bosses from the 1940s to the 1980s, circa 1970.

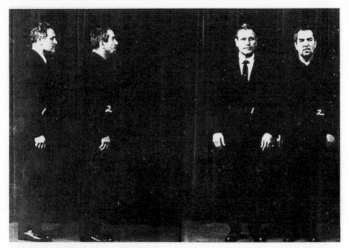

Charles Nicoletti (#1) and Felix Alderisio (#2), hit men of the Chicago Mob, circa 1965.

Left to Right: John Bassett, Felix "Milwaukee Phil" Alderisio, Dennis Shanahan and me leading Alderisio, top boss of Chicago Mob into police lock-up after his arrest in 1969.

Gus Alex, the Chicago Mob's chief of corruption, on his honeymoon in Switzerland with second wife "Shatzie."

FBI surveillance photo of Murray Humphreys, boss of the "connection guys," near his home in Key Biscayne, Florida, circa 1962.

Chicago FBI Criminal Intelligence Squad agents enjoying some free time at a local pool, circa 1963; left to right: Vince Inserra; Marshall Rutland; Ralph Hill; Gus Kemkpff, myself; John Bassett.

Dick Cain, "made" mob member whose function it was to infiltrate law enforcement.

Pat Marcy, true name Pasqualino Marchone, "made" member of the Chicago mob and their man in the First Ward, circa 1959.

Sam Giancana as he arrived in Honolulu to meet with Frank Sinatra in 1964.

William "Action" Jackson, whose brutal torture-murder was discussed by the Chicago mob's hit team in Miami and overheard by the FBI.

Jackie Cerone, Chicago Mob hitman and absolute boss on two occasions in the 1970s and 1980s.

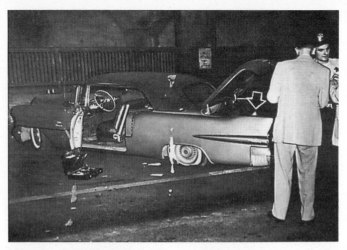

The body of William "Action" Jackson was discovered in the trunk of his Cadillac on lower Wacker Drive in Chicago.

"The Big Tuna," Tony Accardo, circa 1950; Accardo is the Chicago Mob's dinosaur, their most influential leader from 1945 to the present.

Bernie Glickman after he took a beating from "Milwaukee Phil" Alderisio in the mid-1960s.

Joey "O'Brien" Aiuppa, boss of the Chicago Mob from the 1970s until 1983.

Sam Giancana as he appeared in 1975 just before he was murdered by his own.

Dominic "Butch" Blasi, a prime suspect in the murder of his boss, Sam Giancana, circa 1954.

Bill McGuire, former Chicago cop and later a gambler and close Mob associate.

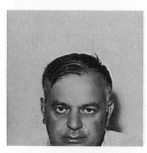

Joe "Negall" Ferriola, Mob boss in Chicago from January, 1983 to March 11, 1989 when he died of natural causes.

Donald Angelini, "The Wizard of Odds," a current Chicago Mob capo and their overseer in Las Vegas today, circa 1968.

"The Last Supper," photo of top Chicago Mob leadership in the mid-1970s:

Front row: Tony Accardo (Consiglieri), Joe Amato (Far West Suburbs), Joseph Caesar Di Varco (near North Side; Rush Street nightclub area), Jimmy "Turk" Torello (West Side and South Side)

Middle row: Joey "O'Brien" Aiuppa, Boss; Dominic Di Bella, terminally ill boss of North Side; Vince Solano, just named Di Bella's successor, his induction being formalized on this occasion; Al Pilotto, Far Southern Suburbs

Rear: Jackie Cerone, Underboss; Joey Lombardo, in charge of Mob's interests in Las Vegas and over Teamsters Union

Edward Vogel, circa 1963.

made the most of them, blasting Bobby. I never saw Bobby Kennedy again.

I was heartbroken when I heard the news in 1968. "My kind of guy" could have been in the White House. I don't know what else could be done about his favorite subject, organized crime. But under the innovative RFK, there undoubtedly would have been something. It was a shame we never had the chance to find out what he would do.

24 Dick Cain

Was he the most interesting guy I ever knew? Very well might have been. Dick Cain, whose true name was Ricardo Scalzitti, was an enigma. One of those guys you dislike immediately. He was almost too handsome, too charming, too sure of himself—a little too much of just about everything. But once you got beyond that facade you could get to like him. So they told me before I first met him. I first encountered Cain when I was working for Dick Ogilvie and Ogilvie was investigating Tony Accardo in 1959 for income tax fraud. At the same time, Ogilvie was running a special federal grand jury investigation of interstate illegalities in the bar and restaurant business. Cain was also working for Ogilvie at the time.

Cain's grandfather was an Italian who changed his name. Ole Scully, as the grandfather was known, became a leader in the Italian ghetto known as the Patch.

Ole Scully formed an organization of fellow citizens in the Patch, called the White Hand Society, designed to counter the evil of the Black Hand that terrorized the Italians in the neighborhood. Some time after the group was formed, the son of a prosperous Italian contractor, a lad named Billy Ranieri, was kidnapped. The police were ineffectual in finding him. So the elder Ranieri turned to Old Scully and his White Hand Society.

The society soon fingered a Capone mobster named Angelo
Pettiti, a bulky thug who preyed on the neighborhood.

Rather than use the intimidation tactics of the Black Hand,
Scully took his information to the authorities. Pettiti was ar-
rested. The night before Pettiti's trial was to begin in September
1928, Ole Scully joined other fellow members of the White
Hand Society for a few beers at a restaurant-bar in the Patch.
Five men burst through the door with shotguns. They caught
Scully in the back with five separate blasts as the gallant vigi-
lante tried to flee for his life.

That was the heritage of Dick Cain. He was born to Lydia,
Ole Scully's youngest, who was seventeen at the time of her
father's death. Some records show Dick's birth as early as 1924,
some (his passport) as late as 1931. He grew up to be a blond,
fair-complexioned Italian—medium height, medium build but
wound tight. If you knew him only as Dick Cain you would
never take him for an Italian.

Cain never finished high school but he had an IQ of 145. He
read everything he could get his hands on—and remembered
everything he heard, read, and saw.

For reasons that are hard to fathom, Cain was made into the
outfit at a very early age. The outstanding authority on organized
crime, Ralph Salerno—the former supervisor of detectives of
the Intelligence Unit of the New York Police Department and
congressional investigator—has believed that Cain was made
early because he may have been the illegitimate son of Sam
Giancana. (Ralph is quick to say this is just a hunch, he has no
documentation for his suspicion.)

Cain was respected for his very unusual intellect and the manner in which he carried himself. He had a confident air, a jaunty
step, a big smile—the ability to look you in the eye and ingratiate
himself.

Before Cain could become recognized as a hood, he was given
a most unusual assignment. The job: infiltrate law enforcement,
join the enemy camp, and be a spy. He was supposed to join the
guys they hated the most and get up as high as he could in their
ranks. Cain's was a reverse undercover assignment—"sting"
the cops.

In 1953 Cain joined the Chicago Police Department. This was
easy. He had all the qualifications. He didn't even have to come
to the First Ward for a sponsor. He obtained a political "rabbi,"

who was respected by the Irish cops, one who didn't raise eyebrows. He came into the job clean.

In the academy his grades were so good and his moves so quick that he was assigned to the 35th District, Chicago Avenue, on the Near North Side, now the 18th District. The 35th was a most desirable district, especially in 1954, because it encompassed Rush Street, the nightclub area; Michigan Avenue, the Magnificent Mile (now more and more referred to as the Gold Coast); and Division Street, where the homosexuals hung out in the pubs. It was very unusual for a young cop, just out of the academy, to be sent to the 35th.

Dick quickly became the guy who carried the "satchel," the "booty," or the "bag"—synonymous terms meaning he was the mob's payoff man. He had to remember the names and amounts without having to write them down. For instance—the commander at central, $1,000 a month; the "bull dick" at Austin, $500 a month; the lieutenant on the vice squad at 22, Maxwell, $700. On it went. Each month, the mob boss in each district gave Cain a bundle wrapped with a rubber band and dropped it in his satchel. When Cain collected all the bundles he closed his bag and then reversed his journey. The next step was disbursing the booty, emptying the syndicate satchel. That job took most of his time.

Anyone unfamiliar with the Chicago Police Department would wonder how a man with that kind of an all-consuming underground assignment had time to build a career within the department. But on the job, he was the kind of guy who advanced.

There are some Chicago police officers who will despise me for saying that. But there are more who will agree wholeheartedly. All will know what I say is factual. And it won't be the good cops who will despise me, it will be the bad ones for disclosing it. There are hundreds of good cops in Chicago. Scores of them are better men than FBI agents. Not only are they good cops, they are also family men who live clean lives, have a lot of brains, and contribute a lot as volunteers. But even the best cops know what the situation actually is on the job. They know what it takes to go to the top in the Chicago Police Department.

However, Dick Cain was soon to go a little too far. He began to outstride the role the mob had cut out for him. He shook down a jack-roller, a guy who was preying on homosexuals.

After Cain finished with the man, he never woke up. Cain beat him to death.

Cain then got involved in a raid on a whorehouse on the South Side. The madam claimed he ran off with her cache, and not for prosecution purposes. The money never wound up in any evidence room.

In 1960, Cain took a furlough from the Chicago PD, which was dominated from top to bottom by Mayor Richard J. Daley, a staunch Democrat. Cain went undercover for Republican State's Attorney Ben Adamowski, a fierce opponent of Daley's. It was Cain's role to investigate his own department and also to investigate Daley's commissioner of investigations, Irwin Cohen. Cain bugged Cohen in City Hall—not an easy job.

Cain got caught. When he was fired from the CPD, the mob got angry with him. Had he just done what he was told, he would have been pushed up the ladder, and there is no telling where Dick Cain would be today. But his brains and arrogance got beyond him, and he ended up with no friends in the mob, in City Hall, or in the PD.

It was now 1961. The year the exiled Cubans, the so-called "Cuban Brigade," were being trained in Florida for the Bay of Pigs. A private detective agency in the Miami area covertly recruited for aggressively well-trained former military officers and law enforcement people. The salaries were attractive, and Cain joined. Whether he actually invaded with the Cubans, I don't know. But after Bay of Pigs, Cain came back to Chicago. That was about the time Dick Ogilvie won the election (having left the federal government) and became Cook County sheriff.

Ogilvie offered me the job of undersheriff, the number-two position in the S.O. I really thought it over. I had been in the Bureau twelve years at the time. I remember lying in bed in Cincinnati on annual leave, pondering my decision. But I loved the Bureau and I have never had reason to regret that sentiment. I finally decided to turn down Dick's offer.

It was a tough decision, however. What Dick Ogilvie offered me was not only the job but also the guarantee that I would be the Republican candidate for sheriff the next election. (Sheriffs were then unable to succeed themselves.) As part of the deal, I would be publicly built up as the official spokesman for the sheriff, announcing all arrests, raids, and other achievements.

All things considered, it really was a very nice offer, but my paramount loyalty was to the Bureau.

My decision, however, was to have far-reaching consequences. Dick Ogilvie subsequently gave the job he offered me—though not the same title—to Dick Cain.

Unknowingly, Dick Ogilvie, the most respected public official I have known, had given the job of chief investigator of the Cook County sheriff's office to Dick Cain, the made mob member. Of course, no one outside a few family members knew then that Cain was made. I certainly did not, nor did Ogilvie.

Although I did caution Dick Ogilvie against such a move on the basis of Cain's questionable record on the police force, Dick Ogilvie felt he could control Cain. After all, he said, "Cain sure knows where the bodies are buried."

I recall Bill Duffy calling me when it was rumored that Cain was to be the appointee. "Don't let Ogilvie do it," he said. "He's a big hope for law enforcement in this town. Don't let him appoint a guy like Cain."

I then called Dick Ogilvie, passed along Bill's concerns and added mine as well. He listened. But for once in his life—maybe the only time in his life—he made a significant mistake.

The mob loved it. Cain had performed his task to perfection and without any mob help at all. No mob-tainted politician ever had any clout with Ogilvie. Yet he'd been taken in by Cain because he knew Cain to be a very capable law enforcement man. Ogilvie had been impressed with Cain when he had worked with him on the Accardo investigation three years before.

At first all seemed to go extremely well. It looked like a magic choice. Cain raided gambling houses all over the county, wherever the sheriff was the prime law enforcement officer. Bang, down went the doors, crash, went the crap tables; crack, went a few heads. The press, the paparazzi, were always right there on the scene, tipped off ahead of time by Cain. He always told them where there would be "good news tonight." Only a few suspected that the mob was setting up those situations for Cain.

In no time, he became the darling of the press. Cain was dubbed the "Super Sleuth of Cook County." He could do no wrong. The statistics far surpassed the record of any previous sheriff, although that was not a particular distinction in view of the history of Cook County sheriffs like "Blind Tom" O'Brien and Tommy Harrison. (The reason the law limited Cook County sheriffs to one four-year term was that in four years a sheriff in Cook County could make so much graft money!)

Unfortunately for both Ogilvie and Cain, however, the bubble was about to burst. In the fall of 1963, there was a major theft at the Zahn Drug Company in Melrose Park, a Cook County suburb to the west of Chicago—$250,000 worth of drugs were stolen. It was headline news for a while and then it slipped into the back pages. Four months went by. The police were baffled. Then one day each of the four Chicago daily newspapers was called. All of the TV stations. They were told to meet Dick Cain at the Caravelle, a motel in Rosemont that had been owned by Giancana some years previously and the site of many of his shack-ups.

When the press arrived, Cain was waiting for them. "Come with me!" he shouted. Equipped with machine guns, axes, and all kinds of heavy equipment the group headed into the motel. "Stay behind, who knows what we are liable to run into here, keep your cover," Cain warned the press. Then, as if realizing he didn't want them too far behind—his purpose was not to do this thing without great publicity for himself—he added, "We'll protect you, don't be afraid, we're in front of you."

When the strange caravan at the Caravelle approached a particular door, Cain blasted it with his ax as his men stood by with machine guns at the ready. Tension! Stress! What will happen now?

Down came the door. In rushed Cain and his men. There was a big portion, $43,000 worth, of the stolen loot! No culprits, but by God at least somebody had done something about this major theft. Finally!

The reputation of Cain was now just about cast in stone. The guy produced. Where had he been all these years? The papers lauded him to the skies. Columnists fawned over him. The favorable press was overwhelming. His photo was on the front page of all the papers; the TV stations fought for interviews. He was too good to be true.

Months went by. Finally, a certain FBI agent put a bee in Ogilvie's bonnet again. I'd been doing my job and had begun to put two and two together. I suggested to Ogilvie that someone should go out and check the registration card for the room at the Caravelle where that Zahn loot was found.

Cain's house of cards came falling down. I couldn't believe

this sharpie had been so careless as to make such a mistake. Sure enough, the room was registered to one of his own deputies!

Soon Cain and two of his helpers were indicted for perjury, conspiracy, and obstruction of justice. They were all convicted in 1964. Ogilvie swallowed hard, admitted his one big mistake, and fired Cain. It made a big difference to Cain—but not to Ogilvie—when the state Supreme Court reversed the verdict years later.

In 1963, while Cain was still the chief investigator for Ogilvie, the Franklin Park Savings and Loan Association in a northwest suburb of Chicago, was robbed of $43,000 by a half-dozen gunmen. Shortly thereafter, Tom Green and Ramon Stratton, two ace FBI agents assigned to C-3, solved the case. All the robbers were apprehended.

Due to the speed with which Green and Stratton did their jobs, it appeared to Willie "Potatoes" Daddano—the made guy who (as we knew) was responsible for matters involving burglars in Chicago—that one of the robbers may have been an FBI informant. Daddano therefore reached out for Dick Cain. Cain was vacationing in Paris at the time. What Daddano wanted was to have the robbers put on the lie detector to determine whether his suspicions were of any merit. An expert polygraph operator himself, Cain would have responded to Daddano's request personally except for the logistics involved. Cain called Bill Witsman, one of his subordinates in the sheriff's office, and instructed Witsman to meet with Daddano and to carry out his wishes.

Witsman did as he was ordered. In a west suburban motel, he put all the robbers on the box (the lie detector) and announced to Daddano that he had identified the culprit as Guy Mendola. Mendola was *immediately* shot dead outside his home in August 1964.

This infuriated Stratton and Green and the rest of the agents on C-3 working under Kenny Grant, the supervisor. They learned of the involvement of Witsman and began to work on him. Eventually they turned him and developed the story from him.

Green and Stratton then went to the U.S. attorney's office where they devised a careful, ingenious strategy. A charge of conspiracy in the robbery of the Franklin Park bank was lodged against Cain and Daddano. They were charged for ordering the lie detector examination of the robbers, and Witsman was to be the key witness against them.

Cain was indicted in December 1967. I was assigned to arrest him even though I was not on C-3 and had nothing to do with the investigation of bank robberies. Accompanied by another agent, I went out to Cain's home on the Northwest Side of Chicago very early one morning. I woke him up, placed him under arrest (without any incident) and brought him downtown.

Cain remembered me from the days when we had worked together for Dick Ogilvie. But he also knew that I had cautioned Ogilvie against hiring him. Since he knew me, he must have decided I would do him a favor.

A couple weeks later I got a call from Cain. He wanted to see me downtown. I suggested I walk over to the corner of Adams and Clark and meet him inside the lobby of the Banker's Building. When I arrived, Dick was already there. Then he told me that he and Daddano were ready to make a deal. I immediately told him that, number one, the FBI was not the agency to deal with, he would have to go to the United States attorney. Number two, this was not even my case. I told him I had no authority, I was just a supernumerary, that Tommy Green and Ray Stratton were the agents who had the "ticket."

"But you carry a lot of weight, Roemer, that's why we want you to handle this," he replied.

"Not nearly as much weight as you might think, Dick—Green and Stratton are heavier guys than I am. But as I say, Tom Foran, the United States attorney, is the guy," I said. "What's the deal anyway?"

"Potatoes and I were both born in Italy."

"Whoa," I said, surprised, knowing that he was Ole Scully's grandson.

"Yeah, really. We'll produce birth certificates showing our births there. And then we will agree to be deported, without fighting it. We'll stay away for the rest of our lives if you people will drop those bullshit charges. They can't hold up anyway. It's a good deal for you."

A typical Cain maneuver. It didn't make much difference to me. At the time, I had little or no investigative interest in Dick Cain. But I promised to talk to the appropriate people and then to get back to him.

I went to Green and told him what had transpired. I suggested he take the proposition to Tom Foran. He suggested that since I had gotten the call and knew the deal that I take it to Foran. I did.

Tom Foran was the finest United States Attorney I was to know in Chicago—a feisty, tough-talking, tough-acting attorney who knew his business. Unlike most attorneys who are in it for future political gain and don't particularly want to get their hands dirty, Tom rolled up his sleeves and he and his assistants worked around the clock if that's what it took. He was the favorite of all federal agents who brought cases into his office.

Tom looked at me. "Sounds like a lot of bullshit to me, Bill. We've got Cain and Daddano right where we want them. I think I'd rather have them in the slammer for a few years than enjoying the sun in Rome. But, what the hell, let's you and me talk to him and we'll see."

I called Cain. He met Tom and me at the Bull and Bear, a restaurant that was then located near the Federal Building. Nothing Cain said changed Tom's mind. As for my role, I don't know if I even ventured an opinion. It wasn't my business. I merely served as an intermediary, putting Cain together for his day in court before his day in court. Tom Foran looked him straight in the eye with that bulldog look and said, "No."

That was the end of it. Cain and Daddano were both found guilty and put in prison. Daddano, whose involvement was much greater, got fifteen years. Cain got four and was shipped off to the federal prison in Texarkana, Texas.

While there he wrote poems that he sent to Jack Mabley, the noted columnist with the daily newspaper *Chicago Today*. Cain also taught languages—he spoke five fluently—to his fellow inmates. I forgot about him. But only for a while.

By 1966, we no longer had our listening devices. President Lyndon Johnson had killed Little Al, Mo, Shade, Plumb, and all their brothers all around the country. It was a heinous slaughter, devastating to our coverage of the mob. Never before in history has any mob been so thoroughly blanketed—and it was never to be again. (Even though our devices never produced conversations that were admissable as evidence in court, the bugs did point us in the right direction. Many times.)

Now, all the intelligence that had been available as a result of our long, hard hours of installing and monitoring these devices was no longer on tap to us. No longer were we able to track our targets from hour-to-hour, day-to-day. July 11, 1965, had been the fatal day!

When I received word of Johnson's executive order, I was flabbergasted. How could anyone put such a roadblock in the way of our efforts to track the mob? I could hardly believe it. When it was explained to me that the Washington field office had placed a bug on a Fred Black who was a friend of Bobby Baker, Johnson's chief aide when he was majority leader in the Senate—and that the device was picking up conversations involving Baker—I was given to understand that Johnson became alarmed. I can only surmise he was afraid that sooner or later the bug would reveal something of his activities, not necessarily pertaining to the presidency but to the days when he was amassing his wealth as a senator from Texas. Here was a man who entered public life poor, spent his whole career there and emerged with a net worth of $43 million. It was enough to raise suspicions that he had some things to hide somewhere along the line. There were those who even thought he might have been on the take, that the mob had gotten to him. I doubt that. However, if you judge a man by his acts, here was a man who did more to hinder the government agency fighting organized crime than any other president or leader in our history. Of course, he trumpeted the cry of civil rights, claiming that we were breaching the civil liberties of our targets. The fact that our targets were members of the La Cosa Nostra, the Mafia, organized crime, made no difference in his eyes.

As I have said before, we had three primary avenues of investigation—electronic bugs, informants, and physical surveillance. Mr. Hoover did not allow undercover work by his agents due to his belief that u.c. tended to corrupt agents. In 1965 we in Chicago had no informant of any value to replace the information we got from our bugs. Some gamblers and a couple of bookmakers were informants, along with several burglars and thieves, but we had no informant who was a made man in 1965.

That is the situation that hobbled us in 1966 with Sam Giancana. First, we saw him and then for a long time, we didn't. We had no way to catch up with him: President Johnson had seen to that.

We had another problem in 1966. Marshall Rutland left us.

First Ralph Hill had gone on in 1963, and now the other great organized crime agent left and took his talents with him.

Maz and Peggy were from Connecticut. There was no reason why they would want to live in the Chicago area. Besides that, Maz felt that now would be a good time to advance in the Bureau. He and I differed diametrically on what we wanted from the Bureau. I wanted the challenge and adventure of the street, he wanted to progress in status and salary. So when he made it known that he would accept a promotion to Washington as a supervisor, his offer was snapped up immediately. That was understandable; he was at the peak of his game, though, and I really hated to see him go.

Advancement in the Bureau means many sacrifices. First of all, an agent must ordinarily become a relief supervisor; that means he sits on the desk of the squad supervisor in the latter's absence. The next step is a return to the SOG in Washington, where he becomes a supervisor handling certain specific operations of a particular field office. For instance, he might oversee the investigation of bank robberies in Pittsburgh from his desk in Washington.

After about a year of that, he would become an inspector's aide, traveling throughout the field inspecting offices while leaving his family in Washington. This would continue for a year, the usual tour of duty, although he would return to Washington for a week or so every six or seven weeks. At the end of a year, he would find himself again as a supervisor in charge of a particular squad in a field office.

After another year of that, back out with the inspection team in the field, but this time as the chief inspector. Another year: back to Washington, this time as a unit chief or section chief. The stint in this position was indefinite. And that's where Maz was finally to end his advancement.

But most of those determined to advance their careers stayed on the ladder. If they continued to climb, the next step was to go out into the field as the assistant special agent in charge of a small office. After a couple years of that, they got promoted to ASAC of a larger office. Two more years or so and then on to SAC of a small office. Then after another few years, SAC of a larger office and then again after two or three years, SAC of a major office.

The ultimate promotion would be to assistant director, usually once again back in Washington (although a couple of AD's are assigned to our largest office in New York).

Obviously, advancement in the Bureau is not for those whose families come first. The almost constant transfers mean uprooting children and wives from one community to another. This is toughest (in my opinion) on the kids, especially if they are active in extracurricular activities such as athletics. I know I couldn't have contemplated that kind of moving around when Bill and Bob were in high school. To take them away from their close pals and girlfriends would have been difficult for me. Besides, I was selfish. I didn't want to give up my own work: I wanted to be the nemesis of the mobster and the crooked politician. I wanted to be able to continue to walk into City Hall and the County Building with a big smile on my face and say to myself: "Watch out all you crooks, here comes Roemer!"

The fact that we couldn't find Giancana for weeks in 1966 was especially embarrassing to me. I had taken over the ticket on Mo after Maz departed. So I sent out leads around the country to be on the alert for him. But he wasn't seen in Las Vegas with Phyllis McGuire or at the Cal-Neva in Lake Tahoe with Frank Sinatra or in New York or Miami, his favorite spots.

I was to learn later, when I finally got a breakthrough and developed a top-drawer source, that he had left Chicago. He said good-bye to his daughters and to everybody and everything. He utterly abdicated his spot as the supreme boss of the Chicago family, just as Tony Accardo his predecessor had done nine years earlier. The difference was that Accardo had left the Chicago family in great shape. At that time the family was not under the spotlight; there was no investigation of any significance. It was the bad luck of Giancana to take over at the time he did, in 1957, when Apalachin caused J. Edgar Hoover to bring the FBI into the fight against organized crime for the first time in history. A bad break for Giancana. However, he compounded the problem with his high-profile manner. By 1966 when he abdicated, the mob was tired of him and happy to see him go.

As I was to learn much later, he was driven to a hotel in St. Louis by his two closest pals, Butch Blasi and Chuckie English. He was subsequently joined at the hotel by Dick Cain. We later learned that Cain was selected by Giancana to be his lifelong confederate from then on. It was a "natural," especially if Ralph

Salerno's hunch that Giancana may have been Cain's father was true. But whether or not there were blood ties, they were a good match. Though not as volatile as Giancana, Cain was an aggressive guy who deserved to be more than a lackey. It was Giancana's plan to make an empire for himself by organizing the mob gambling operations all over the world. Cain would be the perfect man to assist him. He could talk to his fellow law enforcement agents in their own languages. He knew the mob and he knew the mob fighters.

After a couple of days in St. Louis the pair flew to Mexico City, where they planned to set up their base. Giancana adopted the alias Sam Ginco.

Giancana and Cain rented an apartment on fashionable Amsterdam Avenue in the Mexican capital. Then they set about to find a way to handle their finances. They retained Jorge Castillo, an attorney in Mexico City who Cain had scouted out beforehand. Castillo was a well-established lawyer with strong connections to the political structure in Mexico. He was especially close to Luis Echeverria, who was later to become the president of Mexico. Castillo became Giancana's counselor in Mexico.

The first problem they encountered was how to obtain temporary resident alien status. A noncitizen cannot live in Mexico permanently without obtaining resident alien status. He doesn't have to renounce his prior citizenship, but he does have to make proper arrangements in order to remain in Mexico indefinitely. Castillo's function, among others, was to handle that little item. We suspected he handled it by making a "drop" (giving cash) to the appropriate Mexican official.

From their apartment on Amsterdam Avenue, the pair then began to travel in order to explore the possibilities of building a gambling empire outside the United States.

Their first excursion was to the Mexican Caribbean. They loved Cozumel, which was virgin territory at the time. Also Cancun, another garden spot in the Mexican Caribbean. Then they visited St. Martin, St. Thomas, St. Croix, and the other Caribbean islands. They decided to invest Giancana's millions in cruise boats plying the Caribbean.

Cain went back to Chicago and got hold of Hy "Red" Larner, an old Eddy Vogel associate who was an expert on slot machines and other coin-operated machines. When Larner indicated his eagerness to contribute his expertise for a cut of the proceeds, he was brought to Giancana. Eventually, the cruise ships were purchased and outfitted with the latest in casino gambling. They began cruising the Caribbean.

Now off to a great start, Giancana then returned to Mexico. He retained the Mexico City apartment, but Castillo had meanwhile found something a lot more to their liking in Cuernavaca, not far from Mexico City—a town where many Americans have bought homes. Cuernavaca has the charm of Mexico, but with all the amenities. Maids, butlers, and gardeners can be hired for a fraction of what they cost in the United States, and the land is inexpensive. Not that that made a lot of difference to Giancana and Cain.

Castillo had found just the spot for the two wanderers in a luxury development called Las Nubes #2. The home was large, although not overly pretentious. It was surrounded by a high masonry block wall, with high iron grille gates providing security and privacy. It had large gardens and the obligatory swimming pool. Giancana bought it through a private corporation that had been set up for him by Castillo. Pretending to be a retired banker, he assumed the name Sam DePalma. For a while he returned to his favorite hobby, golf. (He shot in the high eighties, but he was not averse—as we had observed at Fresh Meadow—to kicking his ball out of the rough onto the fairway.) Even though Giancana joined the country club in Cuernavaca with its plush fairways, he played winter rules all year round, picking up his ball before each shot to improve its lie. To be fair, however, he hit a straight ball, not much over two hundred yards, but usually down the middle. His approach game was good and he was a fine putter. I recall when he brought us into court in Chicago, his attorney George Leighton had pleaded with the judge to demand an injunction against our "lockstep" surveillance. "How would you like it, your honor, to be lining up your eighteenth putt and to look up to see FBI agents watching you?" the attorney asked. Judge Austin, with his wit, replied, "I don't know, I never took more than four putts myself."

Now that Sam was settled, it was time for his romance with Phyllis McGuire to heat up again. Actually, this is the way we found Giancana. We tailed Phyllis to the airport in Mexico City where she was met by Dick Cain. The pair were not strangers, or at least they didn't act like it. In fact they seemed to be much more than just friends. If we hadn't known better, we would have thought Phyllis had come to Mexico to see Dick. But he eventually took her to Cuernavaca and deposited her with Sam.

Dick Cain didn't do so badly for himself, either. By this time, he had divorced Harriet Blake—or rather, the other way around—and had met a very lovely Chicago entertainer who we shall call Joanie O'Brien. Joanie is a lovely woman, very talented, and a graduate of one of our finest colleges. Cain was very lucky, but given that he was handsome and articulate it was not hard to imagine why he could attract the best. Joanie came down to Mexico to visit also. She was as fine a complement to Dick Cain as Phyllis McGuire was to Sam Giancana and a lot less volatile.

Other visitors to Cuernavaca included the Giancana daughters, Antoinette, Bonnie, and Francine. Butch Blasi also came, of course. Giancana had visits from Chuckie English and Johnny Mattassa (another former Chicago cop who had made his way into the mob).

Giancana and Cain often visited Acapulco where they stayed at the apartment building of a Los Angeles friend of Sidney Korshak's, Moe Morton. The building was called Acapulco Towers. On one occasion we learned that Meyer Lansky, the New York and Miami mob genius, met there with Giancana and Cain to discuss Giancana's burgeoning gambling empire.

Giancana and Cain settled into an idyllic life. Swimming, golfing, romancing—it was the cat's meow.

But that little birdie who had flown over Chicago since early 1958 now flew over New York. Sandy Smith, my newspaper friend, was now a reporter working out of New York for *Life* magazine. I gave him a tip that Giancana and Cain were in Cuernavaca. He quickly hustled up a photographer and together they flew from New York to Cuernavaca in September of 1967. They photographed the home and the golf course and the favorite restaurants of Giancana and Cain. Sandy came back and wrote a series for *Life* describing how the big mobster from Chicago was now enjoying life in Mexico.

Giancana's anonymity was shattered. Suddenly, Sam was exposed for what he was, a gangster in exile. Castillo came by to announce that this exposure was going to make things a lot tougher: the "drop" was going to have to go deeper. As in the United States, the reaction of the American colony was mixed. Reputable people shunned the pair, but some others gravitated to him. A real live Capone gangster from Chicago! they

thought—how exciting! Some of the women giggled when he
approached; others turned their backs. Some of the men left the
gin-and-bridge games when he showed up; others yelled to him
to join them. Some of the colony would have loved to have heard
his stories. They wanted to know how he had beaten the FBI in
court or how he hobnobbed with Sinatra, Leo Durocher, and
Dean Martin. And of course they wanted to know all about
Phyllis McGuire, who had been down here with him.

Many Americans love to touch the garment of the hood and
to live vicariously with him. They are a sad commentary on our
society—part of the reason, I guess, why organized crime can
flourish. Many of the mob's admirers are public officials, judges,
even law enforcement officers. They enjoy the camaraderie of
the hood, and worse, don't mind taking his "drop."

In any event, Sandy Smith's articles caused Giancana and
Cain to leave Cuernavaca for a while. Not only to let things cool
down a little but also to find more empires to conquer. They
traveled to the Bahamas, to Rio de Janeiro, and finally to Haiti
where Papa Doc entertained them royally. The dictator remembered the large amount of money Giancana's ambassadors Les
Kruse and Lou Lederer had spread around the country when
they had visited him on a side trip from their venture to the
Dominican Republic. (Giancana had sent them in 1963 when
they were studying the feasibility of setting up a gambling
stronghold in the Dominican Republic to replace the one lost in
Cuba.)

The duo then took off for Europe, visiting Paris, Geneva,
Zurich, Vienna, London, Munich, and Rome. I remembered
the conversation in the early sixties Giancana had had with Milwaukee Phil Alderisio when he returned to Chicago after a visit
to Greece. Alderisio asked him, "Did you get to spend any time
seeing the ruins?" Giancana, the sophisticated world traveler,
had replied, "The ruins ain't shit!" (I recall that when Ralph
Hill had transcribed that conversation from Little Al, he had
penciled in the margin: "Intelligencia!")

We didn't try to keep up with Giancana and Cain during those
travels. Surveillance outside the United States by the FBI, at
least in those days, was virtually impossible. There would have
been only one way to do it—develop one of the world travelers
as a source.

I had the ticket on Giancana in those days, not that it amounted to a lot of work. We had a "legat" in Mexico City, an FBI group there assigned to the embassy, but they had a lot more to do than keep tabs on two self-exiled Chicago mobsters. But we would get a report now and then, and Sandy Smith would bring us up to date with his photos. His trip to Cuernavaca had not been set up with my help just for harassment purposes. We found that Giancana came back into the country on occasion. Once he came through Nogales, when the home of his daughter and son-in-law, Tony and Bonnie Tisci was bombed in Tucson. It turned out that an FBI agent named David Hale, assigned to the Tucson resident agency of the FBI, had formed a vigilante group that tried to foster a mob war. They first bombed the homes of Joe Bonanno, the New York boss, then living in Tucson; and then the Grace Ranch home of Pete Licavoli, the Detroit capo. This was all an attempt to get something going between the two families of the La Cosa Nostra—an attempt that in my estimation was foolish and stupid.

Giancana, who had no love for his fellow Commission member, Bonanno, flew into Tucson to see what was up. He believed, as most did at the time, that it was a mob war. He did not want his family involved.

We don't know what he accomplished. At the time we had no idea that it was an FBI agent who was responsible for the outbreak of bombings, and I'm sure Giancana didn't find that out either. When it was exposed and the agent was fired, it probably solidified Giancana's opinion that the FBI would go to any lengths to get the mob.

And that just wasn't true. We would go to any legal and ethical lengths, but we would never endorse what Hale had done.

Giancana and Cain continued to live in Cuernavaca under the resident alien status that had been arranged for them by Jorge Castillo. Now they found that they had become targets of the curious who were aware of their Chicago gangster role and would stand on a hill nearby Las Nubes #2 and peer into their compound. Searching for a more secure place, they finally found a large estate in the La Quintas section of Cuernavaca called San Cristobal. It was just what they were looking for—very high wall, more expansive cactus garden, swimming pool, iron gates—a virtual castle. The only thing missing was a bridge over a moat. That house rivaled the home Tony Accardo had built in

River Forest decades before when it was not considered ostentatious for a hood to live in grand style. Tony's house had twenty-four rooms, a greenhouse, bowling alley, and guest house. Giancana's house, in his second career after retiring from the mob, was just about as nice. And it only cost $150,000, which was a lot of money in Mexico but just a pittance to Giancana.

Giancana and Cain loved their new digs. This was the life! Golf and swim during the day; a nap in the late afternoon; out for dinner; and then "bumming," as they called it, in the nightclubs of Cuernavaca and Mexico City. Interspersed with trips around the world, they had it made. They even joined a country club in Teheran, Sam registering under the alias of Sam Ginco. (That was in order to be close to a gambling casino they set up there, after making the proper arrangements with their new friend, the Shah of Iran. Lou Lederer became their man in Teheran.)

Whenever he needed money, Giancana sent for it through his aunt, Rose Flood, who served as his courier from Chicago to Mexico. This was the same Rose Flood who (much to Sam's dismay at the time) was informed by Ralph Hill that Giancana had murdered thirteen people. When that came up at the O'Hare encounter in 1961, Giancana had hammered Hill with it. "What business have you got going around telling my relatives I killed thirteen people?"

About this time Giancana dumped Phyllis McGuire after he fell deeply in love with a member of the American colony in Cuernavaca. We later talked to his new girlfriend at her home in Santa Monica. She was a refined, very attractive former wife of a Broadway music publisher associated with Alan Jay Lerner, the composer. She had been an actress in her younger days and for some time, so the story goes, she was the roommate of Lauren Bacall. She was about fourteen years younger than Giancana, who at this time (1970) was sixty-two.

Cain left his buddy Giancana in 1968 when he stood trial for his conspiracy in the Franklin Park Savings and Loan Association robbery. He was convicted that year and sent to prison where he was to remain until 1971. Almost as soon as he got out, he rejoined Giancana. But when he returned, unbeknown to Sam, he would be working for someone else.

25

Cain Comes Over, and Then Goes Over

When Dick Cain came back from Mexico in 1967 to represent himself in the Franklin Park bank robbery conspiracy case against him, he got in touch with me. We had met in the late fifties; he had heard about me from Dick Ogilvie when Ogilvie offered me the job of undersheriff, and had even been arrested by me. We were not exactly strangers. But I was puzzled when he contacted me again, and that puzzlement was not satisfied by our conversation during a casual lunch at Staley's.

Then he went away to prison. Since he wrote people like Jack Mabley, the columnist, and Jack wrote about him, I was aware he was in Texas. But not much more.

In 1971 he came out. When he got to Chicago he called me again. He wanted to meet and he suggested The Little Chalet, way up north. I met him, we chatted for a while, and then he got down to business. He started talking about his being a soldier of fortune in his own mind. He said he considered himself an intelligence officer, no matter who he was working for. When working for Giancana, he said, he did not consider himself a hoodlum but an intelligence agent. He simply worked on whatever project Giancana would assign him. It seemed to me that he was deliberately opening the door.

"What if you were to work with me?" I asked. "Would you consider a role as intelligence officer for the FBI?" We had known each other for twelve years and had sparred long enough in my opinion. I came right out and hit him with it.

"Under certain conditions, yes, I would consider it," he replied.

"Under what conditions?" I asked.

"I'd give it some thought, you understand, if you could guarantee me the salary of an FBI agent like yourself and the status of an FBI agent."

"Dick, I don't know about the salary . . . that part might be arranged. But I'm sure the Bureau is not going to confer on you the title of special agent if that's what you mean."

"Then there's no sense talking about it," he said. Then he asked, "Why not?"

"Your background. You're a made guy of the Chicago LCN. You're an ex-convict. You don't have a college degree. That's for starters," I told him.

We sat in silence. He called for the check. But I couldn't let this get away. There is no way the Bureau would ever confer on Dick Cain any official status. But the door had been opened.

"Richard," I said. "Let me think about this. My old partner is now the Bureau official back in Washington who makes the first recommendation on something like this. I'll call him and talk to him. Why don't we meet here again before you leave? Say in three days at noon?"

He agreed. Maz Rutland was now back at the Bureau and had been recently promoted to supervisor of all organized crime investigations of the Chicago office.

I hustled back to the Federal Building in the Loop and got on the phone to Maz. He knew all about Dick Cain and how he was the confidant of Giancana. I told him Dick had indicated that he was leaving to rejoin Giancana in Mexico. I told him of Cain's offer. He rejected the special agent status, as I expected, out of hand. But the money wouldn't be much of a problem on a COD basis. When Cain gave me some information that I felt was worth it I could pay him, not to exceed $23,114 a year prorated, the salary I was making in 1971. I would have to report each piece of information he gave us, explain its significance and value and thereby justify my outlay to him.

I went back to Cain with half a loaf. I told him that I would consider him a special agent of the FBI. I said so would Rutland back in Washington. But I added that it had to be kept so confidential that the two of us would be the only ones to know of his cooperation. Therefore we could not accede to his request officially but only informally. Three of us would know: Rutland, Roemer, and Cain.

I don't think I conned him any. And I really wasn't trying to. I had already learned my lessons, and I always tried to be sincere with potential sources. So what I said had the ring of truth to it.

As far as I was concerned, I would consider him an SA if that's what he wanted.

He went for it. "Starting when?" he asked. I told him right now, although I'd have to call Maz and get a "blue slip" approved. He told me where he was to meet Giancana—in Cozumel, the Mexican Caribbean island. I told him that was worth $250. He told me that Giancana was there to meet "Red" Larner to learn what Larner was doing with the gambling casinos on Giancana's cruise ships. "What cruise ships?" I asked since this was the first indication we had of Giancana's branching out into that. That was worth $750. I already owed him $1,000.

"How much money would you have spent, assuming you knew enough to even think about it, to send an FBI agent or two to Cozumel and uncover what I just told you?" Cain asked me. I said he had a very good point. I could have gone to Cozumel, which I have never heard of, and stumbled around for weeks without learning what he had just told me. The thousand dollars had been well spent.

Before Dick took off, I met with him twice more. On Maz's instructions, I took Johnny Bassett with me. Maz wanted Dick Cain recorded so that he could satisfy himself that he was as good as he sounded.

John and I met with Dick in November of 1971, first at the Essex House, a motel on south Michigan Avenue near the Conrad Hilton, and then at the Palmer House, two blocks from the Federal Building at State and Monroe. On the tapes, Dick described the entire situation in Chicago from his unique perspective as a made member of the La Cosa Nostra. He told us what had occurred from the time when he was made to the date of the interviews in 1971—how he "carried the satchel" when he was a member of the Chicago Police Department. He told us who the police officials were on the mob payroll. He named those he paid off on a monthly basis and told us how much they received. At great length he described his relationship with Pat Marcy and the relationship between Marcy and Giancana. He identified the judges in Chicago who were Pat's guys. He also named politicians, labor leaders, crooked attorneys, and law enforcement officials. He identified the made members of the Chicago mob, telling us something about their background and indentifying their responsibilities. He talked at some length about Las Vegas and the Chicago influence there.

We taped for two whole days before Cain left Chicago to hook up once again with Giancana in Mexico.

Cain wanted me to surface his role—to tell the world and especially the mob of his status with the FBI. He told me as much. One day he said, "Bill, if anything ever happens to me, I hope you will let those cocksuckers know that I was one of you, an intelligence officer working undercover in the mob. I want them to know that I doubled."

Dick, for you I am telling the world now. You were a made guy who became a double agent and worked for us. It's that simple. If there is nothing else this book does, it fulfills my promise to you.

Before he left for Cozumel again, Dick asked me for another favor. He had developed a romantic attachment to the well-known Chicago entertainer we are calling Joanie O'Brien herein. Dick wanted me to look after her and help her out if she needed it. I'm sure he also preferred that she not look for a new boyfriend while he was gone. She was to visit him in Mexico but because of her performances, she would have to spend almost all her time in Chicago while he was flitting around the world with Giancana.

The problem that immediately presented itself was that obviously I could not let Joanie know I was an FBI agent. That, of course, would blow Dick's cover. He suggested that he tell Joanie that I was a close friend of his named "Cappy," and without making it clear to her indicate that I was an associate in the same line of work, i.e., a mobster. Off he went then, knowing that I would make myself known to Joanie as his mysterious friend Cappy.

In the meantime, we made arrangements for him to telephone me periodically using the pseudonym "Marquis."

One evening shortly after Dick left to rejoin Giancana, I took in Joanie's performance. At the intermission I went up to her and said, "Joanie, my name is Cappy. I believe Dick told you I would be in touch with you."

She was very pleasant and seemed pleased that I had introduced myself. She joined me at my table during intermission and we had a nice chat. She is a well-educated young lady, very articulate and personable. As she had to go back to work, I suggested we get together for lunch at Grassfield's.

We did. The next week and for many years thereafter. On the third or fourth occasion, she mentioned that her best friend was a lady we shall call Roberta Holland. It just so happened that I knew Roberta Holland from an investigation of Eddy Vogel I had conducted. Roberta was a sometimes companion of Vogel. I had interviewed her and had taken her to lunch once or twice. Apparently, I let it slip to Joanie that I knew her friend Roberta.

Now Joanie had never fully accepted that my name was Cappy and that I was a friend of Dick's from his hoodlum world. I guess I just didn't carry that off too well. When I indicated that I knew Roberta, Joanie talked at length to Roberta trying to figure out exactly who I was. She described me in great detail.

Roberta was in the dark. She had been led to believe that I must also be a friend of Eddy Vogel's if I knew both Dick Cain and her. But she recalled immediately when Joanie finally mentioned that I wore a Notre Dame class ring. Bingo!

One day before I'd come to pick up Roberta at her place on Lake Shore Drive, I had stopped to wash my hands in the men's room at the Drake. While washing my hands, I left my ring in the washroom and almost as soon as I picked up Roberta I noticed it was missing. I therefore had rushed back to the Drake and retrieved the ring. Roberta remembered that. Since I had openly identified myself to Roberta, she knew who I was. She told Joanie.

The next time I picked Joanie up, as we were coming down the elevator in her high rise on our way to lunch, she turned to me and asked, "Is your real name Bill Roemer?"

"Joanie," I said, "let's not worry what my real name might be. We're enjoying the situation wherein I am just Dick's friend Cappy. If he wants you to know more about me, he'll tell you. But keep in mind one thing. Whoever I am, it's in all our best interests, and especially Dick's, that you keep to yourself any suspicions you have. Look, Dick pays off a lot of law enforcement people to operate as he does. How would it look for me if you went around telling people that I might be somebody named Bill Roemer? That would throw suspicion on me that I'm corrupt. So for everybody's sake, I'm just plain ol' Cappy."

Joanie and I remain friends to this day. She is still a top-flight entertainer, one of the most popular in Chicago. Whenever we're in Chicago, Jeannie and I stop in and catch her act and spend intermissions with her. I don't know whether she ever has figured out whether I was the bad cop, fraternizing with Dick Cain, or whether he was the double agent he was. If she reads this she will really know the truth for the first time.

After Dick Cain left to gallivant with Sam Giancana, I heard from him regularly. He somehow found chances to slip away from Sam and mail me reports of what he and Sam were doing. These reports would come to me at the FBI office signed "Marquis."

On one occasion we were able to get together. Giancana sent him back to the United States to meet in New York with "Jimmy Blue Eyes," a New York capo whose true name is Vincent Alo. The message Sam was sending to Alo concerned a well-known Chicago company with hoodlum ties to Geraldo Catena, the New Jersey boss, whose interests in 1971 were being handled by Alo. Cain was able to divert himself from his Giancana business to see me in Chicago.

Later that year, he came back for good. He moved into apartment 1401 at 233 East Erie, about three blocks east of Michigan Avenue. He picked the location for good reasons. First, it was a fine apartment, with a partial view of the lake. It could be entered and exited secretly. He found that you could reach his building by entering a building to the west. It was possible to go into the basement of the adjacent office building, cross into the basement of Dick's building and then take an elevator up to the fourteenth floor without ever stopping at the lobby of 233. You could lose any tail on Ontario Street, a block away, just by entering the other building, and never be seen in Dick's building at all. It was ideal.

Every Wednesday at noon, I would use this method of going to Dick's apartment. When I arrived, he would have a couple of cold beers, cold cuts, and potato salad set up. We would put our feet up, drink our beer, eat our sandwiches, and talk about the mob. One time, just to show me how tight he was with Phyllis McGuire, he called her in Las Vegas and let me listen to their lovey-dovey conversation. Other times, he would go to the phone and call the hood, attorney, or well-known congressman he was telling me about to confirm that they really were that tight.

Dick met with them all. From Louie Lederer to Gussie Alex to Angelo Volpe to Caesar DiVarco to Turk Torello to Fifi Buccieri to Al Pilotto, who had taken Frankie LaPorte's spot in the southern suburbs. He did business with them all.

He told me that Sam Giancana had given him rights to any gambling operation he wanted in any territory in Chicago. I found that difficult to believe, since I didn't grasp that Giancana had the power to allocate such responsibilities. I thought he had abdicated his role as boss. But I assumed Giancana had made some agreement with the current leadership on behalf of Cain.

Cain put a proposition to me. He told me that he was going to take over *all* the gambling in the Chicago area. That would be a massive undertaking, and it meant he would come in conflict with the rest of the Chicago mob. He asked me if we could grant him immunity from investigation, allow him to work unimpeded by the FBI while he put his organization together. In return, he would "spin off" his competitors to us. In other words, he would advise us of the operations of all the other mobsters in Chicago in return for leaving him alone. I told him I personally did not have such authority. However, I told him I would discuss it with my superior.

I went back to the office and did just that. My supervisor thought the idea had some possibilities. I then put him in touch with Cain and they worked it out. Cain would not have immunity; we couldn't grant him the right to break the law. But it was agreed that if we weren't aware of what he was doing, we obviously couldn't investigate his activities. In other words, Cain was not granted any immunity from investigation by the FBI or any other agency. He was given no promises whatsoever. But, if he would furnish us information about all aspects of the mob's control of gambling, we would obviously be in a position to come down hard on *those* hoods rather than those in *his* organization.

Everything went well for two or three weeks. He began to give me information about his competitors, but per our arrangement we knew nothing about what he was doing himself. What we didn't know didn't hurt him is the way it worked, although if the other FBI organized crime squad, C-10, developed information as to his operations, he was fair game.

Then Chuck Carroll was murdered. Carroll was an operative of Ralph Pierce, the mob boss on the South Side. We never knew for sure, but we suspected that Carroll might have been killed when he resisted Cain's attempts to muscle into his operation.

We decided that I should question Cain about the Carroll murder. He, of course, denied any involvement whatsoever. I was not sure. We decided to tell Cain that, friend or no friend, we were going to initiate an investigation into his gambling activities. When it came to homicide, he was no different than any other hoodlum. If he was in any way involved in the Carroll murder, we would come down on him with both feet.

When I told him that, Cain was furious. I was seated in his apartment at the time. He jumped up and actually pounded his fists into my chest, not really trying to hurt me, just venting his rage. He could see all the effort and money he had expended going down the drain. I jumped up, grabbed him, threw him onto the sofa, and sat on him. Finally, he calmed down. I made it clear to him that if we learned that he was involved in any illegal activity, then he was fair game. "You do the crime, you do the time," I told him. When I left him that afternoon, we were not on friendly terms to say the least.

However, the next Wednesday afternoon I went to his apartment as usual. He opened the door, obviously expecting me to keep our regular appointment. He had the cold cuts and the cold beers, and we soon settled back into a reasonably friendly relationship once again. I never knew whether he suspended his gambling venture or whether we just never could find it. I suspect the former.

Then he began telling me about a venture he had taken up with Marshall Caifano, the former Chicago mob representative in Las Vegas. Caifano had gone to prison and was now out. However, he had reduced status with the mob—that is, almost none whatsoever—although he was still a made guy. It was now late fall of 1973, about two years since Cain had been released from prison and begun cooperating with me. When he described his venture with Caifano, he was very vague. I knew they had invested in some sort of a soft drink bottling company and that there might be something more to it than that, but I was never sure exactly what it was.

On November 17, 1973, I got a call from Cain at the FBI office in the Federal Building. He was agitated. He wanted to meet immediately, rather than wait for two days, our regular Wednesday appointment. We had set up an emergency meeting place, which we had used three or four times over the two years of our relationship. It was The Den, a dimly lit lounge located in the upper lobby of the Palmer House Hotel now called Windsor's. In the midafternoon, we were generally the only patrons in the place. It was a cozy, almost private place to meet. When I got there, Dick was waiting.

"Something's wrong, Bill," he told me. "I had a meeting at noon today at Rose's Sandwich Shop, near our office on Grand Avenue. When I left, all hell broke loose. Tires screeched, cars raced, somebody was after me. Was it you guys?"

I told him I didn't think so. It could have been our agents on C-10, but if it was I couldn't tell him even if I knew, since I couldn't blow their investigation. He was really upset. It bothered him to think that a law enforcement agency was apparently so close to him. But he eventually settled down. We decided to skip our regular meeting for the next day, and he then gave me the information he had accumulated that week. In my haste to leave the office, I had neglected to bring writing paper. I therefore used several cocktail napkins from The Den imprinted "I'm Arlene, Welcome to The Den."

I still have those cocktail napkins, brightly colored orange with the notes of that meeting. They show that on that day he told me more details about Giancana's Caribbean cruise ship venture; of a new hangout at North Avenue and Twenty-fifth in Melrose Park that the mob was now using; about another restaurant at Kinzie and Franklin that was a mob hangout; about some new operations of Guido DiChiaro, a west suburban made guy; he also revealed that DiChiaro's territory was Northlake, Stone Park, Schiller Park, and Melrose Park and that Louie "The Mooch" Eboli was DiChiaro's man in Melrose Park (Eboli being the son of Tommy Eboli, the New York capo); that Turk Torello had taken over Fifi Buccieri's faction of the mob on the West Side and that Frank Buccieri was the coequal of Torello in some respects in this regard; and that Joey Aiuppa was making noises like he might want to step down as part of the triumvirate running the mob at that time; that Larry "The Hood" Buonaguidi, a Near North Side mobster, was making $50,000 a day taking bets on football games. About Giancana, Cain revealed that the mobster had been in the United States on December 12, a few days before, and that he would be spending New Year's Eve in Honolulu. I found out that Giancana would be in Santa Monica for Christmas with his new love. He had grown a beard, which was almost white. Cain told me the name of another of

Giancana's cruise ships that was cruising off St. Thomas in the Caribbean.

Many other things came to light during that long meeting with Cain. He said that Cliff Jones, the former lieutenant governor of Nevada, was now associated with Lou Lederer in the casino in Iran. Johnny Roselli would now be living with his sister in Florida and would move soon from his residence in California. Caifano and "Cowboy" Mirro had a deal with the head of security at one of the Chicago racetracks and would be booking there with the okay of a former Chicago police officer.

Turk Torello had told Cain, just that week, of a new arrangement the Chicago mob had at the Stardust in Las Vegas. Cain knew that two Chicago hoods were meeting Hy Larner in Miami once a month and giving him a cut of a coin-operated machine business they were operating for Larner in Chicago—the same business Larner had had to leave when he became Giancana's man in the Caribbean. Cain revealed the identify of "another Jew named Red," who was Larner's man in Miami. It turned out that Larner was Giancana's man for cigarette machines, coffee machines, pool tables, and pinball machines in Cook County, Jamaica, Panama, Guatemala, Ecuador, and Brazil. But Butch Blasi was getting $25,000 per month from these operations.

The Hotel, Restaurant and Bartenders Union was making a big play to organize in Atlanta, according to Cain. They would use "Chicago methods," meaning muscle and bribes. Cain gave me the names of several organizers of that union who were controlled by the mob and whose jobs had been obtained for them by mob people. He said Ed Hanley, the president of that union, had just purchased a million-dollar jet airplane, which he would personally use. (Johnny Lardino was the made guy who put Hanley into that union.) I also found out that an official of the Illinois Department of Labor was associated with the Chicago mob; that Angelo Volpe was in trouble with the mob because his policy operations had lost $300,000 recently; and that the next move of Larner and Giancana would be in Bogotá, Colombia. Cain told me he had a new bodyguard named Mike Jalardi. He knew that Giancana was now up to one million dollars a month in profits from his Caribbean venture, and Cain said Giancana was sending Gussie Alex a piece of this. Another mobster, Joe Ferriola, was moving up under Turk Torello. Cain thought Joe was a man to keep an eye on.

Cain said Giancana's casino in Iran was making a profit of $125,000 a day, but that the Corsican mob was attempting to muscle in on it. This was a situation that would have to be countered by Giancana.

And finally, Cain told me that a tavern called RagTime, east of Harlem Avenue on Roosevelt Road, was a hangout for Tony Spilotro when he was in town reporting to the mob on his Las Vegas activity.

This was a good sample of the type of information Cain was furnishing me at that time. In fact, that was a shorter list than usual, since we'd met forty-eight hours short of our regular Wednesday get-togethers.

That was on December 17. On Thursday, December 20, I started my annual Christmas vacation. I was at home in the early afternoon, shadowboxing down in the basement. I had the radio on listening to country music. Ray Price was singing his great version of "For the Good Times." It was interrupted by a news bulletin.

"Dick Cain, the gangster, was shot and killed at noon today. He was having lunch at Rose's Sandwich Shop when two men entered the restaurant, announced a holdup, lined the patrons up against the wall, went over to Cain, and shot him in the head with two shotgun blasts. He was killed instantly."

It hadn't been a law enforcement agency that "squealed its tires" three days before. It had been his own people!

It was as if I had been punched in the stomach. I sat down on the cellar floor. If I had felt disappointment when Hump died, I now felt devastated! Hump had been the friendly enemy. Dick Cain was a friend. There were few people I felt closer to.

I immediately searched my conscious mind to see if there was anything I had done that might have precipitated his killing. The first thing I thought of was that after I went back to the office the previous Tuesday, I shot off a teletype to our agent in Honolulu, Barry Goodenow, asking him to be alert for the arrival of Giancana for New Year's. I suggested that if Frank Sinatra were in town, he would probably be found with Giancana.

Now I wondered whether Barry had done some work, tipping off Giancana that we knew he was to arrive. However, I had cautioned Barry that this was closely held information and that he should be most discreet in handling it in order not to compromise the source, who, of course, I did not name.

I was later relieved to get Barry's report showing that he had done nothing in response to my request until after December 20, the date of Dick's murder.

I conducted my own personal investigation of the death, to no avail. It wasn't until a couple of years after I left Chicago, when the Chicago office developed a source close to Caifano, that we were to learn what had happened. According to the source, Caifano had set up Cain.

Dick had gone to Rose's Sandwich Shop, as was his custom at that time, to meet with Caifano. When Caifano left Cain, he sent in two Chicago made guys, one of them Joey "The Clown" Lombardo (the same guy whose wife had fixed Johnny Bassett and I a wonderful Italian lunch when we went to arrest him). Lombardo and the other killer had then gone into Rose's. Using the robbery as a ruse, they lined up all the patrons against the wall. Then they put a shotgun under Dick's chin and blew his brains out the top of his head.

The reason for the killing, it seems, was that Cain knew that Caifano was the leader of a crew of burglars. Caifano himself did not actively participate, but he directed the crew. On a house invasion just days before the shooting, the Chicago Police Department had ambushed the burglary crew. The police had been awaiting the burglar's arrival in what was obviously a set-up.

When I learned the name of the sergeant who led the ambush, I realized he was a cop Dick had mentioned to me previously as a friend. I suspect that when we told Dick that we were going to investigate him, he may have made some arrangement with the Chicago Police Department. Perhaps he made a deal to spin off some law violators in return for a "pass," similar to the deal he had tried to make with us. So Cain must have decided to sacrifice Caifano's crew for his own security. Caifano apparently smelled this out, and Dick was killed as a result.

Although all of this made it clear that I had nothing to do with Dick's death, it did nothing to relieve the sorrow I felt in losing a good friend.

Losing a bitter foe would create another type of feeling. That was to come next.

(Author's Note: In order to give continuity to the saga of Dick Cain, a story within a story, I have taken a flight through time, skipping the chronology of other events, particularly the events which lead Giancana to abdicate and flee the country. We now step back more than a decade to continue our story.)

26 "Wining and Dining on Mo"; Changes in the Office

Shortly after we put "Mo" in place, I was listening one afternoon to Sam Giancana when I heard another voice that surprised me. I had a very good friend who was no part of the Chicago mob. He was a wealthy Chicago industrialist I will call Angelo Girabaldi. He and his wife had become very good friends of ours, and although I sensed that Ang might know "some of the boys," I had no idea he would be meeting with the absolute boss of the Chicago family of the La Cosa Nostra.

But there he was. I couldn't mistake his voice, nor what was said.

"Girabaldi, we have known each other for some time, is that right?" Sam asked.

"That's right," my friend answered.

"I'm getting some information that you also know somebody else I know. A guy with the 'G', named Roemer."

"Zip? Sure I know him." Girabaldi said. "Zip" is a nickname I picked up in the eighth grade. It was supposed to connote my swiftness when I was a kid.

Giancana continued his line of thought. "Know him good, I hear."

I think Angelo at this point felt he was on the carpet, that perhaps he was about to be accused of being a stool pigeon. To his credit he faced Giancana down—at least that is the impression I got from the sound of his voice. "Yeah, I know him good. He's a nice guy. I doubt he even knows I know you. Your name has never come up."

Giancana went on. "I understand you go bummin' with Roemer and his wife."

"Yes," was the short and simple answer from Angelo. He

239

was obviously waiting for the other shoe to drop, and probably with some anxiety.

"Ang, relax," Giancana said. "Here's what I want. I want you to wine and dine Roemer."

"Wine and dine him?" Girabaldi questioned. "I don't get it."

"Take him out for drinks, dinner, nice places. Loosen him up a little. And then listen. That's all. He's bound to say a thing or two about what he's doin'. Get him to invite his partners along. They got a guy named Hill. Rutland. Those guys are the ones workin' on us guys."

"Sam," Girabaldi said, "it ain't gonna work. He don't talk about such things in front of me. We're friends, he would be surprised I know you or Butch or Chuckie English."

"Open him up a little by telling him you used to know us. See what he says," said Giancana.

"Sam, I got to think about it. I don't like it."

Giancana exploded. "You don't like it! I'm asking you for a favor here and you don't like it! Butch, come in here!"

A moment later I heard Butch Blasi mumble something to his boss.

"Angelo here, he don't know if he wants to do me a favor! What do you think of that!" It wasn't a question. Sam went on: "Have we ever asked you for anything before, Mr. Girabaldi? The Italian people in Chicago support you, Mr. Girabaldi. Where would you be without the Italian people, Mr. Girabaldi? I think you better make up your mind who your friends are. I'm not asking you to take a gun and go out and hit somebody. I'm not asking you to commit no crime here. I'm asking you to take my money, go to the best restaurants in Chicago, go with some people whose company you seem to enjoy. I don't ask you to do nothin'. Just listen. *Just listen!*"

At this point, I chuckled to myself and picked up the phone. Ralph Hill was in the office, but Maz was not: "Ralph," I said, "get in here, quick." I knew he would be as interested in this as I was. As I turned back to the conversation, I was thinking to myself, "Ang, do what he wants, for Pete sake."

Ang must have read my thoughts. "OK, I'll do it."

Giancana heaved a sigh of relief. "You had me worried a little there, Ang. A man has to choose his friends in this world of ours. The favor I ask here is so small, it's hardly a favor at all. If a man can't do such things for another, he ain't worth much. All right, here's what you do. You spring for the tabs, tell Butch what they are from time to time, and he'll make it up to you. Get Roemer to be loose with you. Who are they workin' on, where, what kind of situation? That's all. I don't expect he's gonna give you the shirt off his back, he ain't gonna give up nothin' big, like a stool pigeon. But for a few hundred bucks from time to time, it's worth it to us just to know where he's been, who he's workin' on. And get him to bring Hill and Rutland and anybody else he wants. Go to the best places. Don't worry about the bills, just get 'em loose."

It was settled. Ang left. Giancana turned to Butch Blasi, his closest aide.

"Can you imagine that cocksucker? He don't know if he wants to do me a favor? Keep your eye on him, Butch. If he comes through, fine. If not, we cut the balls off his business."

Ralph and I looked at each other and laughed. "Wine and dine 'em," huh? We could make a real good deal out of this. "Wine and dine on Mo!" And we could turn it to our advantage—plant a little disinformation that would get back to Giancana, throwing him off the track. Not so as to get Ang in trouble—we would have to be very careful—but we definitely could turn it to our advantage.

Sure enough, Ang called shortly thereafter. "How about you and Jeannie joining us at the Imperial House Saturday night? Let's have dinner, and then maybe we can catch a show at the Chez?" Sounded good to me. And to Jeannie. We went and had a great time. And Ang never asked me a question, never mentioned the name of anybody remotely connected with the outfit.

Two weeks later. Ang again: "How about lunch? Would you like to bring a couple of your friends along? Make it the 'Well of the Sea' in the Sherman? See you at noon." Again, nothing about anybody in the syndicate.

Two weeks go by. Ang calls again. "I'm looking to have a party at my house. Thought I'd do this one for the FBI. Why don't you get up a guest list of about a dozen or so of your people and invite them?''

We did. We had Ralph and Billie. Maz and Peg. Vince and Marilyn. John and Annette. Denny and Bettye. Christy and Fitzie. Zip and Jeannie. We had a very, very nice time.

The next time Ang called, I decided to take the bull by the horns. We were at the Chicago Athletic Club. I eased into the fact that we had been working the previous day watching Giancana at the Fresh Meadow Golf Course, a fact I knew Sam knew because he had made us. It was a harmless piece of information but one which I knew Sam would know was true. From then on, as we "wined and dined on Mo," I began to slip stuff in along with a piece here and there to throw Giancana off.

Except it never got back. None of it. For a year or more I had assumed that Ang was reluctantly doing what he had been asked. But one day we heard Giancana and Blasi in front of "Mo": "If you and I go out with a guy and especially with a guy drinkin' at least a couple beers, we'd come back with somethin'! The guy must crack for somethin', sometime? This guy goes out, comes back, 'they don't say nothin',' he says. They gotta say somethin'!''

But Ang didn't say nothin'. He was so loyal to me that for two years or more he never brought a word back. He would meet with Butch, apparently, and tell him that he was "wining and dining" us regularly but that we were not saying anything about anybody. Giancana could hurt him or help him, whereas I sure couldn't. But he was more loyal to me than he was to Giancana. How many friends like that does a guy make in a lifetime? My job shows me the seamy side of life. It also shows me the wonderful side. There are animals in this world like Sam Giancana. Thank God for the "Angelo Girabaldi's"!

Several years afterwards, I let Ang know that I had been aware of the entire situation from the beginning. I told him how much I appreciated how he had handled the whole matter although I also indicated that I was sorry he had not taken what I had told him back to Giancana. He was embarrassed that I felt so strongly as to what a good man he really is. Without saying it, but by giving me a bear hug, he let me know that I was his true friend, not the likes of Momo Giancana. Although we are far apart geographically today, we are still pals and in frequent communication.

About this same time I was to lose the constant companionship of a great agent and a great friend, Ralph Hill.

Ralph had been a part of C-1 from the first days of the Top Hoodlum Program into the early days of the Criminal Intelligence Program. (The name of the organized crime program was changed after Bobby Kennedy became involved.) Ralph was part of the backbone of the program. He had first taken on Sam Giancana. Nobody knew as much about "Mo" as Ralph did when he decided to move on in 1963. His loss, just from a professional standpoint, would be very hard to overcome. The program would surely suffer, and I would suffer also. We depended on him to help monitor, transcribe and analyze all of our bugs.

There were only three of us who did the monitoring—Ralph, Maz and I. John Roberts and Vince Inserra did a little but I can't recall that any of the other agents participated. For some reason, they either didn't want to become involved in this work, or they didn't have the depth of knowledge to be qualified. From my viewpoint, the bugging has always been the most important thing we did. How much more could you expect than to be in the same room with four or five top leaders of the Chicago family and listen to their every word?

Actually, the reason it went that way was that Ralph, Maz and I so reveled in the assignment that we didn't look for any other help. It was a large assignment, but we could do it. We had pride of ownership.

After we put the bugs in, we were the ones to exclusively handle the "daily summary airtel" that went to the Bureau, the Department, and to Bobby Kennedy.

But then Ralph left us to go back home. He loved Miami: he had grown up there and had attended Miami University. When he had the chance to become the supervisor of the organized crime squad there, the opportunity was too good to pass up. His great work on C-1 had made a lot of points for him in the eyes of the Bureau; as soon as he applied he was transferred. They needed him in Miami also.

* * *

The passing of the great Hill was not the only change on C-1. Harold Sell decided that a Bureau career was not what he was looking for and he resigned to take a very nice opportunity in private industry. The background and experience a young Bureau agent acquires in a short number of years is very helpful in obtaining jobs outside law enforcement. And the income, most times, is much better. Harold went that route and we were to miss him.

Vince Inserra was chosen to take his place. Vince had become Harold's relief supervisor and was the logical choice. He wanted the job and he was well qualified, having been on the THP even longer than I had. (He was on C-1 when Mr. Hoover formed the program on November 27, 1957.) Whereas it took me four weeks or so to move from S-1 to C-1 after cleaning up my work and taking my Christmas leave, Vinny was on the THP the next day. He was the senior agent within four weeks or so. He had been a fine agent, with an outstanding memory, the original photographic mind. He wanted the desk and all of us were glad he got it.

The SAC at the time was Jimmy "Blue Eyes" Gale. A redheaded whirlwind, he was a "hands on" SAC. He knew the highest priority in the Bureau was during those Kennedy years—organized crime. He threw his door wide open to those of us who were handling the bugs because he wanted the hot skinny right now so he could call the seat of government and give it to them almost as the mob was saying it.

What I never wanted at any time in the Bureau—and this was a continuation of my mindset during my early days in New York—was advancement. I always felt that some day I would burn out as a "brick agent" on the street. I thought I would get tired of the action out there, want to put my feet up on the desk as a supervisor, and read the reports of other street agents. But that day never came. After thirty years in the Bureau, I had yet to burn out. I still relished the challenge of the street and didn't want the detail of the desk.

Most agents, and most supervisors, will tell you that the Bureau is unique in that respect. Almost all agents come into the Bureau to make arrests, conduct surveillances, and solve crimes. That is the challenge they accept when they go to the FBI Academy. What most of the agents and supervisors will tell you is that a supervisor is a mere glorified clerk.

I don't go that far. Thank God there are FBI agents who will give up the action and become supervisors. We need them. Somebody has to shuffle the papers, make the assignments, attend the SAC conferences and bring the word back to the agents. Somebody has to tell the lazy agent (and there are some of those in the FBI, including yours truly, at times) to get on the ball. Somebody has to tell the experienced, tough agent to hit the front door on an arrest and assign the lesser agent to the back door. Somebody has to recommend the action agent for incentive awards or a highly prized quality raise. Somebody has to sit in the smoke-filled conference to iron out the mundane office problem. Thank God there are the Vinny Inserras who are willing to leave the action on the street and assume the duties of that somebody.

Actually I had every opportunity to climb the career advancement ladder, as it is called in the Bureau. When Harold Sell became C-1 supervisor, early in the 1960s, he asked me to be one of his relief supervisors. That was the first step up the ladder.

I declined.

Again all during Vinnie's long reign as C-1 supervisor, I could have been a "relief." But I didn't look for the job.

And, when Jim Gale left Chicago to become the Assistant Director in charge of the Bureau's organized crime investigations, he asked me whether I was interested in following him to Washington. Again, I declined. I told him I was interested in staying on the streets and that I didn't want to move my family. He must have had me a tickler in his file, because almost immediately when Jeannie and I became empty nesters (when Bob entered Notre Dame), I got a call from a supervisor in Washington. He told me that Gale felt I no longer had an excuse not to accept promotion and that he had been instructed to tell me that. However, I was able to again decline.

Finally, in 1975 when Dick Held was the SAC in Chicago he called me into his office and told me he wanted me to accept a new supervisory position he intended to create—supervisor of all training. I would get a few thousand dollars per year raise, an office, secretary and car. Once more I declined, something which caused friction between Held and me for several months. I was never able to separate myself from the action on the streets. I guess I never grew up.

In any event, in the early days of Vince Inserra's long reign as supervisor we got along fine. When I was in the office at noon—as I was so often, working on our bugs and getting out that burdensome "daily summary airtel"—we'd have lunch together, usually at a spot in the Palmer House. We'd have one draft beer—although that was prohibited by Bureau rules—and a big sandwich. Vince knew his job, he knew the program and he liked his desk.

In the early 1960s, Mr. Hoover had not yet decided that FBI agents needed exercise to keep in shape for their demanding jobs. But he had decided that there were too many overweight agents in the Bureau, and he instituted a very strict weight program. I had won the heavyweight boxing championship at Notre Dame weighing 215 pounds, but my assigned weight in the Bureau was 190 pounds. "Making weight" was a bear of a job. The time for my required annual physical was in July each year, usually at Great Lakes. The naval corpsmen weighed me in each year. Unless I could talk them into "what's-a-couple-o'-pounds," I had to make 190 or jeopardize my salary increases. Being overweight could even lead to a disciplinary transfer—and there were some of them. We had one fine agent on C-1 who was transferred to Cleveland solely because he didn't meet the weight requirement.

In order to keep within sight of 190 when I was most comfortable at 215, it took a lot of working out. And I was soon about to get the exercise of my life. Giancana was about to give us a real run for our money.

27 Lockstep

It was early June, 1963, during a lull in one of our monitorings. Maz Rutland and I were overhearing Giancana as he talked about building a gambling stronghold in the Dominican Republic. He had sent Lou Lederer and Les Kruse, two of his top gambling experts, down there to make a feasibility study. Lederer and Kruse were the true gambling casino experts in the Chicago mob.

Should Giancana establish large-scale gambling operations in the Dominican Republic, we were sure the millions he made there would be used to corrupt more public officials in Chicago. The more money the mob made, the more officials they corrupted. It was a Catch-22 for them. The more they created operations which needed protection, the more protection they needed to buy.

We had brought Giancana's moves in this regard to the attention of the Bureau, which had passed the information on to the Justice Department which in turn passed it on to the State Department: "Sam Giancana and his associates in the Chicago family of the La Cosa Nostra have made contact with an official of the Dominican Republic and certain agreements are being made for the Chicago family to have access to certain property there for purposes of building and maintaining gambling casinos." State was looking into it. In the meantime, Giancana was making arrangements to meet with Porfirio Rubirosa, the Dominican Republic diplomat.

We felt that if we waited for the State Department to get moving, the game might be over before we got started. During a brainstorming session, Maz and I decided that a real tight, round-the-clock, put-him-to-bed-and-be-there-when-he-gets-up surveillance was what was needed to prevent Giancana from meeting anyone. We wanted to keep him away from Rubirosa as well as his associates, like Kruse and Lederer, who were assigned to carry out the Dominican Republic gambling venture.

Maz had taken over the "ticket" on Giancana with the transfer of Ralph Hill. I had more than enough to do, given the requirement of the "daily summary airtel." (Humphreys was still very much with us in June of 1963—and would be for another two and a half years.)

Maz went to Vinnie with our thoughts, and Vin took up the subject with Marlin Johnson in the front office. Johnson had replaced Jimmy Gale, who had been recalled to the SOG to become the assistant director of the entire CIP.

I don't think Marlin was for or against the surveillance plan. But, he said, if that was the way we wanted to handle this, well "it's your baby." He called SOG and told them what we wanted to do. They put a handle on it, called it "lockstep" and wondered whether we could actually stay with the madcap of the underworld long enough to make it work. Chances were, he'd be out of the country in a couple days, away from our lockstep. But if that's what we wanted to do, OK.

It was decided that Maz would run lockstep. I would be in charge on the street and would call the shots out there. Not an unusual job for me, of course, as I was very familiar with the streets of Chicago.

Lockstep is a good example of the role I saw for myself throughout my intelligence work. I was a counterintelligence agent more than anything else. I was an agent who always tried to discover as much as I could about the mob's strategy, to find out how they would attempt to implement it; and then I would set about neutralizing that design.

I won't deny that part of my scheme was to make life miserable for the guy I now considered my arch enemy. I would never forget the way Momo Giancana had shouted at me that I had "lit a fire" and that he would "get me" if it was "the last thing" he did. Anybody with any balls at all doesn't forget a challenge like that, and I sure didn't. If he wanted to threaten, I was there to spar with him, not run from the challenge.

After overhearing Giancana's concocted story of how he had shouted obscenities at me, after hearing him say I wasn't "a man" for not doing more than I did, I believe that I wanted to force another confrontation like the one at O'Hare and see what happened this time.

I'm sure Maz Rutland had an inkling of my thoughts since we were as close as brothers. But no one else knew. Again, as hard as this may be to believe in a world which has come to believe that Mr. Hoover was no civil rights libertarian, he stressed to us all at the Seat of Government (SOG), that he would not stand for harrassment even of mobsters. That was a given. So even though I wanted to give Giancana another shot at me, only Maz knew about it. As far as my overt course of action, my only design was to seal off Giancana from his peers and subordinates to prevent him from governing and expanding his domain.

We learned that Mo would be coming back into town after a short absence, and that Butch Blasi, his shadow, would be picking him up at O'Hare on the evening of June 10, 1963.

I went out to O'Hare with five other guys and set up. When Giancana got off the plane, thinking "Here we go again," I moved right up to him. I reached him before Butch did. I didn't say a word. I walked right alongside him as he exited the airport concourse.

"What the fuck is this now?" Giancana snarled at me. His first thought was that I had a warrant for him. He had been followed many times by 1963 but this was new. This time, Roemer and his pals were not only following Mo—they had him surrounded, too.

Mo entered Butch's car. We followed quickly in three cars and soon caught up with them. As they proceeded to Giancana's home at 1147 South Wenonah in Oak Park, we were right with them. There was a car on their rear bumper, with one car behind that and another behind that one. When they arrived at Mo's home and entered, we parked one car east of the house, on the corner, and another to the west, a half block down. The third car was parked to the south, right on the corner.

Pretty soon, Giancana came out. He couldn't help but see us, as we were practically in his yard. He went for a walk. I suggested to the others that one man stay in each car and one man join me on foot. I bounced right up to Giancana, a half step behind and a half step to his left.

He whirled on me: "Get the fuck away from me, you cocksucker!"

I think that was his favorite word, as he sure got a lot of use out of it.

"You use that word a lot when I'm around, Mo. You must have something on your mind, is that what you do?"

My, the man took offense easily! He actually began to drip spittle from his mouth. I won't repeat what he said to me that night. The man had a vocabulary of obscenities, and he wasn't adverse to using them all.

As we walked, he led us into a park a block or two from his home. There I made my first mistake of "lockstep." As he harangued me, I began to lose my cool again as I had at O'Hare. In reply to some obscene suggestion to me, I said that he should just get out of the country. I said that nobody wanted him around, not even his own people. He had become so much a burden on society that society would be much better off if he found some other country in which to live. This slip was to haunt me later.

For the next six weeks we stayed on that man. We *literally* lockstepped him. We used nine men on each twelve-hour shift, twenty-four hours a day.

If he went to dinner, we went with him. If I was on the shift and he got up from the table to go to the men's room, I'd get up and be at the next urinal. I found that really bugged him. He had shy kidneys. He couldn't do it when I was right there.

At first, he tried his best to elude us. He tried car-switching with Butch Blasi. Tires screaming, they would race the wrong way down one-way streets, into alleys, frequently backing up as they attempted to intimidate us, long stretches at over 100 miles an hour out on country roads.

It got to be ludicrous. One day he took his car right through his favorite car wash. He drove through the spray from one end, shot out the other side and just kept right on going. The attendants knew him as a regular patron, and they recognized us as the law.

"Go, Mo, Go. Go, Mo, Go!" they yelled as he sped away.

The madder he got, the more I loved it!

After a couple of days, he got in the habit of heading, each morning, for the golf course at Fresh Meadow way out in Hillside. There he would meet his cohorts, Chuckie English, the guy he grew up with, along with Butch Blasi. Sometimes he saw John "Haircuts" Campanelli and Sam Pardee. Once or twice he was joined by his daughter, Bonnie Lou. (She would go on to become the city ladies golf champ in Tucson in the late 1970s and early 1980s.) Mo and his companions of the morning played in a foursome. They waited until they got to the seventh hole or the fourteenth hole, both of which run along roads—then Blasi would show up.

The first day, Sam jumped into Butch's car and sped away.

Luckily, we had foreseen such a possibility. We had a car waiting and were able to keep Sam "in the pocket."

On subsequent days, Blasi would drive up, but only to deliver messages.

Several of us were golfers. We began bringing our clubs and using our credentials to get the tee time right after Mo's foursome.

How I loved to bang my tee shot into Giancana as he was waiting to hit his second shot. I never hit him on the fly; after all, I didn't want to hurt him. I just bounced my drive past him. Then, as he was lining up his putt, I'd bounce my approach onto the green. Or yell "fore!" just as he started his backswing. That was a nice summer!

I usually overlapped the shifts. I'd come on about nine in the morning, before Giancana generally got up, and hang on until midnight or so. I didn't get home as long as Mo was still out. When he had settled in, apparently, for the night, I let someone else take over.

One Saturday evening he headed for the Czech Lodge, the place where he had met D'Arco. This time he was with Butch, Chuckie English and one or two others. It was about five weeks or so after we had started lockstep. I was happy he had picked all the nice restaurants he had picked, because that gave me the chance to eat there too and charge it to the government.

This time, when he left the Czech Lodge, he got in Chuckie English's car. To our surprise, he went to the Armory Lounge. The lounge was in the 7400 block of West Roosevelt Road, across from the Armory where guns and ammunition were produced for the military. Generally, Mo never took us there because he didn't want us to know that was his headquarters. That was where he spent every evening when he was in town.

English let Giancana out of the car in the parking lot adjoining the west side of the Lounge. Mo proceeded inside. We pulled in right behind, me in one car alone and Maz in another, each of us alone. As we parked, Chuckie was waiting for us.

"Look, you guys, this has gone on long enough. I'll tell you what. Why don't you two guys and Sam and I get in my car and we'll go have a good time at the Pump Room.'' The Pump Room may have been Chicago's most ritzy restaurant at the time, probably the most expensive. It was on the north side, a long way from where we were in the western suburb of Forest Park.

"You guys go to the Pump Room and we'll go too,'' Maz replied. ''We go wherever you go. Yeah, the Pump Room would be nice, we've never been there.''

Although we had seen the inside of many of Chicago's fanciest restaurants during those days of "Wining and dining on Mo,'' we hadn't yet chosen the Pump Room.

Chuckie English could see that this conversation wasn't leading anywhere. He entered the Armory Lounge. We followed him in, checking to make sure Mo was there. Mo had seated himself at his regular table.

We took seats at the bar about five yards from Mo. Immediately we were surrounded. Tony Tisci, Giancana's son-in-law and the administrative aide to congressman Libonati, was there. Blasi, English, Haircuts, and ten or twelve other pug uglies flanked us on all sides.

"Talk about Russia!'' they yelled at us. ''You guys have no right to do what you're doing to Sam!'' Now I knew why Sam had brought us to his joint. Everybody in the place was one of his guys. We had walked into the lion's den this time, that's for sure.

I looked at Sam. He laughed at me. The tables had turned.

I thought twice about ordering a beer, knowing how bartenders in mob joints spit in beers of people they recognize as cops. But I did. I figured if worse came to worse, I'd have my gun in one hand and a beer bottle in the other.

The mob pressed in on us from all sides. Chuckie English even went inside the bar, keeping an eye on us from that side. Fortunately, it never got to the point where I was concerned for my safety. It just turned into a lot of yelling and obscenities.

It was about nine when we got there. About midnight, the crowd had calmed down. I had had three beers and didn't want any more, as it might be a long night. I looked at Maz and nodded. We had served our purpose, we left, Maz to his car, me to mine.

As I was heading to my car, Chuckie English came running out of the lounge after me. ''Sam wants to give you a message.''

I said, "What's the message?"

"He says if Kennedy wants to talk to him, he knows who to go through," Chuckie told me.

"Sounds like he's talking about Frank Sinatra," I said.

English looked at me. "You said it," he said.

I walked over to Maz's car and told him what Chuckie had told me.

"That's interesting," was Maz's reaction.

Several days later I went down to the FBI office to catch up with "Al," "Mo," "Shade" and "Plumb." As the tape rolled on "Plumb," I found this is what we had picked up:

Frank "Strongy" Ferraro, the underboss to Giancana, had come to Marina City. He'd gone up to Hump's 51st floor apartment, in a great state of agitation.

"So help me God, I'm about to jump out your fucking window," he'd told Hump.

"What's wrong?"

"That fucking Giancana, wait till you hear what he's done now. I tell you those guys are driving him goofy. He's not making good decisions!"

"What happened?" Hump asked.

"Saturday night, Roemer and my friend, Rutland; they're on Giancana. He takes them to the Armory. They get in a fucking shouting match with Roemer and Rutland. Whole bunch of our guys and Roemer and Rutland. When it's all over Giancana sends Charley McCarthy out to see Roemer. As he's driving out of the parking lot. What do you think he told Roemer?"

"What?" Hump asked, apparently perplexed by all of this.

"Charley McCarthy told Roemer that Mo told him to tell Kennedy that if he wants to talk, he's to go through Sinatra!"

"For Christ sakes, that's a cardinal rule!" shouted Humphreys. "You don't give up a legit guy! He tells Roemer that Sinatra is our guy to Kennedy?"

"More or less, for Christ sakes," Ferraro replied. "I'm so fucking mad, I could jump out your fucking window!"

Now that was interesting! A discrepancy—but I wasn't quarrelling with it. English, who Ferraro had called Charley McCarthy because he was Giancana's puppet, had not told me it was Sinatra, although he certainly left me with that impression. *I* guessed he was talking about Sinatra, and he just confirmed it.

What made it especially interesting was the violent reaction of Ferraro—a reaction shared by Humphreys when he heard the story—that Frank Sinatra had been identified by Sam Giancana in such fashion. Obviously, they wanted that kept a closed secret.

Ferraro also told Hump that he had gotten the story from Butch Blasi, another interesting piece of news. Blasi, of course, had been at the Armory during our sojourn there and had been seated at the table with Giancana when we left. For him to tell the underboss about the violation "of the cardinal rule" by the boss was something I would tuck away for future use.

Ferraro and Humphreys then discussed what they should do about this violation of mob rules on the part of Giancana.

"We got to do something about this," Ferraro said. "The 'G' is driving the man goofy. He's not right, he's making mistakes. He don't belong in that spot if the pressure gets to him like this."

Hump couldn't agree more. "I think this has got to be brought to the attention of Joe and Paul. They've got to know the condition of the man's mind."

They agreed. Joe Batters (true name Tony Accardo) and Paul Ricca, the two former bosses of the Chicago family, should be informed that Giancana was being badly affected by "lockstep" and was not making rational decisions.

I readily understood why Humphreys and Ferraro considered that Chuckie violated a "cardinal rule" by identifying Frank Sinatra as a conduit between Giancana and JFK. Sinatra was purported to have a liaison with the President and his father. If what Sinatra indicated to Giancana was true—that he could influence the President to go slow on Giancana and therefore the whole Chicago mob—then Sinatra was extraordinarily valuable. Such an intermediary might never appear again. If Giancana destroyed the confidentiality of that relationship just to settle a personal vendetta, then the "connection guys" of the mob (the leaders of what we called "the corruption squad") were justified in thinking that Giancana was, in fact, going "goofy." No wonder they thought our lockstep tactic of all-out surveillance was having a gross adverse effect against him.

This in fact, seemed to be the situation. So we were very happy as we listened to this conversation. We were keeping Giancana out of the Dominican Republic—what might have been a gold mine for the Chicago mob. This in itself proved the efficacy of lockstep. By bringing the purported relationship of Giancana with Sinatra out of the closet, we were winning some battles. And we could now use Giancana's message to me through English for counterintelligence purposes.

I assume Frankie Strongy and Hump did go "out west" to Accardo and Ricca. They certainly intended to when Ferraro left Hump that afternoon. But the meet must have been in one of the few places which we hadn't covered. We heard no more about it.

However, I think that conversation was the beginning of the end of Giancana's rule. The other mob chiefs were beginning to see that the flamboyant ways of Momo were not in keeping with mob strategy. Capone had gotten into such trouble because he thumbed his nose at the authorities. The mob thereafter tried to keep its lid on. Nitti, Ricca, Accardo were all iron hands in the velvet glove—quiet, unobtrusive, with low profiles. Was it any wonder that the FBI code named its 1946 investigation of the Chicago mob "*Reactivation* of the Capone Mob?" They thought the Chicago mob had dried up and gone away after Capone and had remained inactive under Nitti, Ricca and then Accardo.

"Reactivation?" They had gone no place. They had merely muted the noise.

Now, however, in Giancana we had the reincarnation of Capone. Flashy, he liked displays of fast cars, splashy women, and big money all over the world. He would yell obscenities at a public airport at the FBI. He would surround FBI agents with his thugs and shout more obscenities at them. From the rooftops he proclaimed, "I'm Sam Giancana! I'm the boss! Chicago is *my* town!"

Would he get away with it? He had broken fast in this race against the FBI, but could he stand the pace?

We soon had our answer. Not only could he stand the pace, he was going to step it up!

28 Giancana Beats the FBI

As "lock-step" continued into July we noticed a definite change in Sam. He had been arrogant before, but now he was on the attack! Whenever we came near, which was all the time, around the clock, he pointed it at us—not a gun, but his camera.

Instead of going to nightclubs and restaurants, he went to church and to the grave of his deceased wife. At the gravesite he bowed down and appeared to be praying.

Wherever he went, he took his movie camera and he took movies of us. We thought he was probably taking films to show the entire mob who we were. They'd have more film and photographs of us than we had of them.

Most of the guys would duck down or cover up. They had no desire to be in Sam Giancana's film library. I never backed away an inch. I'd walk right up to his camera and face him down. Screw him. If the mobsters in this town don't know me by now, the hell with them I thought. Pride goeth before a fall!

One Sunday morning he went to Mass at St. Bernadine's, the parish where his wife had worshipped and been buried. Anyone could tell that he rarely went to church. At the Gospel—the part in the Mass where the faithful traces with the thumb a small cross on the forehead, lips, and heart—Sam got stuck. He looked around at the crowd in order to imitate the parishioners. I looked right at him and frowned, as if to say, You dummy, trying to pretend you do this regularly! Soon we learned why the change in tactics.

Pretty soon we realized *we* were being followed. Sam had hired a private detective agency to shadow the FBI! The John T. Lynch Detective Agency assigned Don Ricker, its top operative, to the case. He easily confirmed that we were following Sam and he filed a report to that effect.

Sam had consulted with his son-in-law, his courier, Tony Tisci, who was a member of the Illinois Bar. They in turn decided to consult with a real attorney. Tisci suggested that they see George N. Leighton, one of the top civil rights lawyers in Chicago, a graduate of Harvard Law School.

Leighton advised Giancana to sue us! Go into court with his film, his private detective's reports, and some witnesses like Butch Blasi and Chuckie English and get an injunction stopping this invasion of his privacy.

What a legal coup! Even Capone wouldn't think twice against advice like that. Sue the FBI to keep them from following the boss of the Chicago family of the La Cosa Nostra? If you put that in a movie script—even a comic strip—nobody would believe it!

Sam did it. He followed the lawyer's advice and took us to court. His petition was to enjoin us from harassing him, and from violating his civil rights. Leighton claimed our lockstep policy was a violation of the Constitution.

The case became banner headlines in the Chicago press. All the television stations made it their lead item. GIANCANA TAKES ON THE FBI. GIANCANA TAKES THE FEDS TO COURT! MOB BOSS SAYS FBI "HARASSING" ME!

Marlin Johnson called me in. "Whatever made you run that surveillance out there like that?" he demanded.

I quietly mentioned that although it was more or less my own idea, "everybody from Mr. Hoover on down knew what we were doing." But, of course, we had "embarrassed the Bureau." If identifying Frank Sinatra had been the cardinal sin of Sam Giancana, my cardinal sin had been in "embarrassing the Bureau."

Worse was to come!

Sam brought in his witnesses. His aunt, Rose Flood, testified she was "terrified." Ricker told how close we kept to Giancana, Chuckie English testified that Marshall Rutland and "Fred" Cook (there was no Fred Cook, it was Bob Cook) had ribbed him about a pair of red Bermuda shorts he had worn on the golf course.

Then Giancana himself took the stand. He told the court about my remarks in the park, suggesting that he leave the country. This is when my remarks came back to haunt me. He showed his film in the darkened courtroom.

"That's the north end of Roosevelt Road," he said.

The judge, Richard B. Austin, remarked,, "There is no north end of Roosevelt Road, it runs east and west." Sam pointed me out in the picture. "That's Roemer. Playing right behind us."

Seated in the courtroom, I was still thinking there was a bright side to all this. By getting on the witness stand, Giancana had now opened himself up for cross-examination. Good questions could be put to him such as: "Why were you being kept under surveillance?" "Are you a private citizen, Mr. Giancana?" "What is the nature of your business?" "Did you sanction the killing of Guy Mendola?" "What is the source of your income?" "Do you know the sitting judge here, and what is the nature of your association with him?" "Do you know the chief of detectives of the Chicago Police Department?" "What is the nature of your relationship with him?" "What is the nature of your relationship with John D'Arco?" "Do you know Congressman Libonati?" "What is the nature of your relationship with *him*?" Those and scores of other pertinent questions could have been asked, and I thought they would be.

But the U.S. attorney handling the case had his orders. Bobby Kennedy had instructed that the strategy of the entire proceeding be that Giancana had no jurisdiction, in that the judiciary branch of the federal government had no right to supervise the legitimate activity of the executive branch. So he instructed that no defense be put on. The U.S. attorney took this to mean he was not to cross-examine Giancana, the absolute top boss of the Chicago family of the Mafia! Giancana had taken a large gamble when he stepped up there, but he won.

I could respect Bobby's decision to handle the defense of Giancana's suit in the manner he did. He wanted to show that the judiciary had no jurisdiction to decide how another branch of government—namely the executive—could perform the day-to-day activities in its domain. I respected Bobby and I figured he knew what he was doing. If, after doing the appropriate research, he decided to heed the advice of his subordinates in the Justice Department, that was good enough for me. I never have, and do not now, have any suspicions that John Kennedy went soft on Giancana. But the outcome of RFK's decision was unfortunate. It meant that the prosecution could not pursue any line of questioning about Giancana's actual activities.

When asked the question, "Were you, Sam Giancana, guilty

of breaking any local, state, or federal law that could warrant such FBI surveillance," Sam looked Leighton right in the eye and gave an unequivocal answer: "No!" Even that statement was allowed to go uncontested by our side.

The plaintiff, Giancana, brought Marlin Johnson onto the stand in observance of a subpoena that had been served on him. Marlin was asked, among other things, if he was my boss. Did William Roemer work for him? Was I under his orders?

Mr. Johnson softly answered, "I respectfully decline to answer the questions based on instructions from the U.S. attorney general, order number 260-62." The SAC of the Chicago office of the FBI took the 260-62! The hoods take the Fifth. He took the 260-62. Thirteen times.

That was it. We put on no defense at all. "The court has no jurisdiction" was the sole grounds of our plea.

Judge Austin, in his supreme wisdom, ruled. One foursome must be kept between the FBI and the Giancana foursome! Only one car could be parked near Giancana's home, and that must be kept a block away! Only one car at a time could follow him! Judge Austin lashed out at the FBI. Our surveillance was an "admission of ineptness and a confession of failure to obtain the information sought by methods normally used."

I smiled at that. If only he knew!

But then he really hit us in the face. He cited Marlin Johnson for contempt of court and fined him five hundred dollars!

Wow! We sure got hit over the head with that one. Sam got even—for O'Hare, for the Czech Lodge, for everything—in one fell swoop!

Of course Marlin called me into his office. "You're a very impetuous fellow." That was one of the nicer things he said to me. A scapegoat was needed here. Talk about "embarrassing the Bureau!" I had sure broken all records! I was the guy on the street, responsible for running the lockstep. I had been more or less responsible for thinking it up in the first place. Forget that it had been approved. Forget that Maz had kept everybody advised, practically on an hourly basis. Marlin and everyone in the Bureau back at SOG could say it was never approved to that degree; Roemer and those guys just went out there and did what they wanted.

I kept quiet. But I felt strongly that it had been a good idea. As it turned out, lockstep had delayed Giancana's plans in the

Dominican Republic just long enough. The revolution occurred very soon after, and it completely shut down any further efforts to open a mob operation there. I wasn't smug, but I didn't sulk. I had learned long ago that you win some and you lose some, and some of the things you work for the hardest don't pan out. But you don't quit, you don't give up, *you keep punchin'!*

First thing I did was call Dick Ogilvie. When I told him I thought his men should take over lockstep, he thought that was a capital idea. "Hell, yes, I will," he said. "Let Sam take *me* to court and see if I take 260-62!"

Ogilvie's guys in the sheriff's office took it over, and Ogilvie *dared* Giancana to try that stuff with him! He didn't. After a few days, Giancana threw up his hands and took off. For a while, we didn't know where he had gone.

Then we learned. To Cal-Neva. To Frank Sinatra. To Phyllis McGuire. He ran from the flaming skillet right into the fire.

As I mentioned earlier, the Cal-Neva Lodge is located on the border between California and Nevada, on Lake Tahoe. Part of the lodge is on the California side, and the casino is on the Nevada side. The lodge is perched on a high bluff with the Sierra Nevadas to the north and Lake Tahoe, below, to the south. Down that bluff are chalets, separate lodges for high rollers, away from the simple hotel rooms for the low rollers.

Chalet number 50 was the lodging of Phyllis McGuire. Sinatra had another. The other McGuire Sisters had two others.

As I heard the story, one evening Sam got into an argument with Phyllis. He became quite critical of her. Into the chalet came Victor LaCroix Collins, a manager of the McGuire Sisters.

Victor, as I was to find out later, was wound tight. He was a little guy, but very tough. He had been a Canadian cattle puncher, a rodeo bronc rider, and he was not afraid to come to Phyllis's aid even though he knew who Sam Giancana was and what he stood for. He made Giancana back down by telling him to quit his haranguing of Phyllis.

Sam was somewhat docile up to that point until Sinatra, having heard the commotion from his nearby villa, burst into the room. Then Sam screwed up his courage again. Victor might be wound tight, but now it was two against one. Sam started the fight over again. When Victor made a move, Sinatra jumped on him and held him as tight as he could, while Sam the tough guy punched Victor's lights out.

Though I wasn't there and we had nothing planted there, I got the information a couple of years later from Victor. And that's how I remember him telling me the story.

The fight caused attention—attention that reached the chairman of the Nevada Gaming Control Commission. When Sinatra cursed that man out on the phone it set in motion the loss of his license as casino owner. That was Sinatra's penalty for allowing Giancana to be there.

Sam had himself a busy summer.[1]

29 The Killers

While listening to "Mo" one day in early 1962, I heard Jackie Cerone come in to talk to Sam Giancana.

In 1962 Cerone was considered by us to be an up-and-coming younger guy who bore watching mainly because he was Tony Accardo's constant companion. He was called by the press "Jackie The Lackey" due to being closely identified with the most respected mob leader.

We were to find that he was nobody's lackey. He has a strong personality in his own right and is, in fact, one of the most intellectual guys in the outfit. He even read best-sellers, something I don't think even Humphreys did.

In those days, Accardo made his headquarters at Meo's Norwood House Restaurant in Norwood, a small western suburb. His constant companions were Cerone, his driver, and Paul Ricca, the boss who had preceded Accardo in the 1940s.

It was the daily custom of Cerone to pick up Accardo at his

---

[1](Later, Judge Austin's ruling was overturned on appeal and all restrictions on our surveillances were removed. At the same time, the ruling of contempt against Marlin Johnson was reversed and his fine was therefore never imposed.)

home in River Forest and drive a few blocks away to pick up
Ricca. They would then proceed to Meo's where they were assigned their regular table in an alcove. They had a nice vantage
point from which they could see any strangers in the place but
could not be seen themselves.

Because Accardo and Ricca were called on only for major
policy decisions and had no hand whatsoever in the mob's day-
to-day operations, we hadn't concentrated on Cerone, who
seemed to spend almost all his time with the old guard.

We were about to change that in a hurry! In late January 1962
Cerone appeared at Mo's to talk to Giancana.

"That hit you gave me on Frankie. I'm pretty well all set on
that. I went down to Miami and rented a house that we can work
from and I got in touch with Davey. I've got my crew all lined
up and we're about ready to roll. We'll move into the house on
February first and we can roll from out of there. Here's the
address. In case you're down there at the time, drop in and say
hello."

Obviously Jackie Cerone had been assigned by Giancana to
carry out a killing of somebody named Frankie who must be
down in Miami. He had gotten in touch with Davey Yaras to
somehow facilitate the murder. Yaras was a former partner of
Lenny Patrick in Chicago who had moved to Florida years before and was associated with Henry Susk in a rental car agency.
He had been a prime suspect, with Patrick and a guy named
Willie Block, in the killing of James Ragen in 1946—the incident
that had caused the Chicago FBI to initiate CAPGA. This was
the "reactivation of the Capone gang," the short-lived investigation to determine whether the Capone mob had been "re-
vived" in Chicago.

Ragen ran a race wire service that the mob wanted to muscle
into. They shot him, but did not kill him. They had to finish the
job by poisoning him while he was in the hospital recuperating
from the shotgun wounds.

Obviously, therefore, we knew that Yaras was no virgin when
it came to what I euphemistically call "the ultimate discipline."

We did not think Cerone would be selected by Giancana to
lead such a foray into Florida. But, obviously, we had to believe
our ears.

I put the information into my daily summary airtel and casually explained it. "Cerone is going to Florida shortly to kill somebody named Frankie and has lined up a crew to assist him, including Davey, who is undoubtedly Davey Yaras." It was an unusual piece of information, but not overly dramatic. With all that was coming in from all our bugs, I had no reason to make a particularly big deal out of it.

But the shit hit the fan when that airtel arrived back at the Bureau. "Holy smoke, Chicago, you guys are certainly getting pretty blasé out there. Your information may not be all that important to you, but it is to the Miami office. Those guys haven't seen anything like this. They are all excited over the copy of the airtel you sent them, and the SAC has been on the wire wanting to know what we intend to do."

The long and short of it was that Miami didn't have experienced agents to cope with what obviously was about to descend on them. At least not in 1962. They had no bugs, no informants, and no agents who had gained any background in these techniques. Yet we in Chicago had now found that all three were indispensable in dealing with organized crime.

For this reason, the Bureau organized a "special." They designated Chicago to send two experienced CIP agents and the New York office to send two. It looked like a great opportunity. Spend the last few days of January and the first couple weeks of February in Miami? There were plenty of volunteers.

I was not one of them. I was coaching grade-school basketball and playing in a league of south suburban parishes every Thursday night. We were nearing play-off times for both teams. I always tried to duck out of town assignments during my Bureau days for similar reasons and was usually successful. Most of the other agents loved the change of pace and volunteered for the opportunity to see other cities.

Ralph Hill was still with us in 1962. He and John Roberts were originally from the Miami area. And they met all the qualifications for this caper. Both had been on the squad since the Top Hoodlum Program started, and both had top-flight mobsters assigned to them. You couldn't find more savvy, seasoned guys.

In New York, Warren Donovan and Pat Moynihan were chosen. I did not know either at the time, but I later got to know them both. Moynihan is a good-looking, intelligent guy who had the same kind of background as Hill and Roberts. He had been on the THP from its inception. Donovan, as I got to know him later, was the "Bill Roemer" of the NYO (at least I'd like to think of myself as his counterpart). He was the agent in the NYO who stayed on the street for his thirty years in the Bureau and fought the bad guys pillar to post. His bad guys—or "wise guys" as they call the New York mob—were in Brooklyn. He knew them all, down to the scars on their kneecaps, and they knew and hated him. Warren died in 1988 and is now included in my daily litany of prayers.

Hill, Roberts, Donovan, and Moynihan convened in Miami. Their collective decision was to get out to the address that Cerone had so conveniently given Giancana in front of Mo and plant a bug.

The house was empty. Jackie's lease didn't start until February 1, so he hadn't moved his crew in yet. The installation of the bug was completed quickly and without incident. After the months of work that were required to put in Little Al, Mo, and Shade, this was almost too easy for Hill and Roberts.

As a matter of fact, it was not until February 11 that Jackie moved his crew in. The Miami FBI raiding party found that the crew consisted of two more well-known Chicago hoods, Fiore "Fifi" Buccieri and Jimmy "Turk" Torello—two real bad-asses. Fifi at the time was the capo on the West Side. He led the crew that Torello, his top aide in 1962, would eventually take over. Joe "Negal" Ferriola, who would ascend to become the top boss in Chicago, was also with that crew. Without question, this has been the toughest, most ruthless, most aggressive regime in the history of the Chicago family.

In other words, what we had in the peaceful vacation resort of Miami in that lovely winter of 1961—1962 was an invasion by three of the most dangerous guys in Chicago, who hooked up with an old Chicago killer to eliminate somebody named Frankie.

It was a job for the combined forces of the Chicago, New York, and Miami offices. What Ralph and John told me when they returned to Chicago was that they had decided to show Miami how things were done. From the Bureau in Washington, they had to get carte blanche to investigate the mobsters in Miami. But at that time of the season, there were many. Giancana himself came down along with several New York wise guys. Donovan and Moynihan recognized the wise guys and went after them.

One night, they heard that Giancana was in a nightclub in the Fontainbleau Hotel. The FBI guys set up a surveillance. Hill walked into the club, spotted Giancana's party, then came back outside when Mo's party was getting ready to leave. Hill suggested to the others that they go out to their cars while he took a walkie-talkie and climbed a palm tree outside the entrance to the club. He would signal the others when the Giancana party departed. From his convenient palm tree, he would tell them which cars the hoods were entering. Then he would direct our traffic to tail those cars as they left. All went well, according to Donovan, up to a point. Ralph climbed the tree, all right, and he got in radio contact.

"Here they come now, get ready to follow, oh, a-h-h-h-h!"

The other agents heard a loud crash and went running toward the club to see what had happened to Ralph. It seems that just as Giancana was leaving the club, just as he reached the foot of Ralph's palm tree, Ralph "stuck his big nose out too far." He came tumbling down out of the palm tree, right at the feet of Giancana! I'm sure Giancana felt he couldn't get away from Hill anywhere.

(Which reminds me of a case of mistaken identity on the part of the mob. In New York there was another agent named Bill Roemer. Whereas I am William F. Roemer, Jr., he is William J. Roemer, Jr. This "New York Bill Roemer," who I always call the *good* Bill Roemer, was assigned in the sixties to the CIP. We sent a lead one time to New York to contact an associate of Giancana. Bill Roemer got the assignment. He identified himself to the associate as "Bill Roemer of the FBI." When the word go back to Giancana in Chicago that the associate had been contacted by "Bill Roemer of the FBI," Giancana exploded in front of Mo, "That cocksucker Roemer, he's all over the fucking place!")

In Miami, the agents were unable to find Cerone and his crew until February 11 when Cerone finally moved into the house where the bug had been planted. From the way the agents talked, I knew they had already staked out their victim. It turned out the victim was Frankie "the X" Esposito, an official of the Laborers International Union, a union with close ties to the Chicago mob.

We never have learned why the mob wanted to kill Esposito. The conversation that took place in the house in Miami on

the night of February 11, 1962, is so illuminating that I am going
to include it here in great detail.

The conferees in the conversation are Jackie Cerone, later to
become the absolute boss of the Chicago family of the La Cosa
Nostra; Davey Yaras, the former Chicago mobster and the chief
suspect in the Ragen murder; Fifi Buccieri, the capo of the Chicago family responsible for the West Side of Chicago; and James
"Turk" Torello, Buccieri's top man who was to take his spot
years later (he was present but not heard). Their reference to
D'Arco is to my old friend, Alderman John D'Arco of the First
Ward who also happened to be vacationing in Hollywood, Florida. I smiled at their regard, or lack thereof, for the life of
D'Arco although I don't know why the prospect of taking him
out with Esposito filled them with apparent glee. The reference
to "Skippy" is to Frank Cerone, a cousin of Jackie and a less
important Chicago hood. The official FBI transcription is as
follows:

Cerone: The fuckin' guys lay there and watched, but that cocksucker never left his porch. All he would do all day long is walk
to the fucking front and then walk to the back. He walked three
or four miles every day but that cocksucker never left his porch.

Yaras: I wish for Christ sake we were hitting him now, right
now. We could have hit him the other night when there was just
Philly [Alderisio, another Chicago mobster who had gotten in
the way] and him.

Cerone: Yeah, that would have been a perfect spot to rub him
out. Well, if we don't score by the end of the week . . . then we
got to take a broad and invite him here.

Yaras: Leave it to us. As soon as he walks in the fucking door,
boom! We'll hit him with a fucking ax or something. He won't
get away from us.

Buccieri: Now, if he comes with D'Arco . . . we could do
everybody a favor if this fucking D'Arco went with him.

Cerone: The only thing is he [meaning D'Arco] weighs three
hundred fucking pounds!

[Pause]

Cerone: Get the boat tomorrow.

Yaras: I'll get the boat and everything else.

Cerone: We'll get him on the boat if he takes a walk—then
it's nothing for me to call him.

Yaras: Then you can say, ''Hey, Frank, what are you doing here?'' You know what I figured we could do? Early in the morning we could go there in bathing suits. When we got him in the car, we don't have to do nothing with him in the car.

Cerone: All right. Here's what we do. Monday, we work. We start. Skippy and Davey will work on it. Next morning we go out there and we do it all over again. Even I can go out there one morning. We can take turns. The guy must take a ride. Maybe he won't do it for a week, maybe the tenth or eleventh day, he might take a ride alone. We can pull our car alongside . . . we can all step in . . . even if it's daytime. One guy grabs the wheel, throws him in, let him holler.

Buccieri: Well, we got the knife and he's got to move, with us jabbing him with the knife.

Cerone: We'll put him on the floor and away we go. We can ride around with him. Before we do it.

Buccieri: Well, we got him coldcocked after we get him in. We'll drive slow.

Cerone: Yeah, we can drive around and then we can find a prairie. We can have everything with us, the ax and everything.

Buccieri: We can't let any blood show. We got to keep that guy alive until we're in a good safe spot.

Cerone: No, no, you can't touch the guy until we've got him in the car.

Buccieri: Yeah, we keep him alive until we're ready.

Cerone: Yeah, you can't afford to have a man dead on your hands. I got the contract. Did you know that?

Buccieri: Yeah.

The conversation halted for a while. There was some irrelevant chitchat while the group fixed sandwiches. Then the conversation changed to a different subject—the previous effort of Cerone to kill a mob rival, ''Big Jim'' Martin, a policy-betting kingpin who was being muscled by the Chicago mob. Cerone described this earlier incident in detail.

Cerone: So when I banged the guy, I caught him with a full load . . . but it had to go through a Cadillac. I blasted him twice. Joe says, ''Is the guy dead?'' And I said, ''Sure.'' Because when I nailed him, his head went like that, you know? The next morning, the headlines are in the paper. The guy is still living . . . this double-o [buckshot] was ten years old . . . it wasn't fresh, so the guy lived.

Yaras: That's one thing, when I use that double-o, I got to use fresh ones.

Cerone: The guy [Martin] was a big nigger. He left the country and went to Mexico. That's what we wanted anyway. We would grab up all his policy games. The next day, I'm on the corner where he was shot. I went to the place all dressed up. The police squads and the cars are all around. I'm right there. And everybody is talking and I say, "Oh, that's terrible. But them fucking niggers are always fighting one another, you know."

[Pause]

Cerone: I wasn't known for a long time. I kept away. I kept away. I wasn't seen with nobody, never mixed. I was always hidden, for many years.

[Pause]

Cerone: I remember one time we was on this guy for a week. You know, you get close and you blow it and then you try again. So this one night, we pull up on the guy and he's with his wife. So he says, "What the hell, I'll get him." So I grabbed the wheel and he jumped out and chased the son of a bitch for half a block, but he nailed him. Remember the time you popped that guy and you rolled him over a couple of times and he lived?

Yaras: I didn't do that . . . Oh, yeah, now I remember, I did that with Johnny. I'll tell you a funny story. You know, I think that cocksucker tried to hit me at the same time I hit him. I swear. Because he put a shot right through the windshield.

Buccieri: I remember we had to hit him in the belly, then we had to burn him. We couldn't even get the handcuffs on him.

Cerone: All these fucking years, Davey, why didn't you move in on some of these fucking guys down here?

Yaras: First of all, down here they got the lights on. You hate to be connected. But these New York cocksuckers in Miami. I'll tell you something. You think we got some bad guys? These guys are real assholes. They want to knock their heads around. You don't like to be with them.

Cerone: If I was down here all these years, Davey, I would have moved into those guys.

Yaras: Yeah, but with some of these guys, you couldn't do nothing with them. You should see some of these guys. They won't even let nobody else on the track. You'd have to hit them.

Cerone: Have to hit them all!

* * *

This was a surprising conversation to me. Ralph called me from Miami the morning that he got it transcribed and read me the major portions. In Chicago at the time we had not figured Jackie as the major hit guy he admittedly was. Or Yaras. It seemed like he too had pulled several hits. Obviously, we had missed something.

We had considered that the two major hit guys in Chicago were "Milwaukee Phil" Alderisio and Chuckie Nicoletti. I'm sure they were at the time. But here was Alderisio in Miami, apparently with his friend Frankie—but the two were not being used on this job.

The Chicago police at one time had caught Alderisio and Nicoletti in their "work car," a car with all the equipment needed to hit a victim. The hit was always by shooting, and then the work car was used to escape. It had a souped-up engine, a retractable license plate in the rear, slots for hidden shotguns and rifles, reinforced shocks, armor plating on all sides and bullet-proof windows. I was reminded of that car years later when I saw the classic car exhibition outside the Imperial Palace hotel and casino in Las Vegas. There was Al Capone's old car from the twenties, made up much the same way.

Later in the transcript of this conversation, there are references to "Action" Jackson.

Action Jackson was a juice collector in Chicago. We had tried to turn him into a source of information, but he would not turn. However, he had a friend to whom he told many of his activities, and we turned his friend. Had Jackson been our source, we would have been very careful to use his information judiciously so as not to compromise him. However, since he refused our advances, we were not in that position. I guess some of his activity was handled in such a way that the mob got the idea that he was a stool pigeon for the FBI.

In any event, they suspected Action of squealing and they grabbed him. He was a three-hundred-pound gorilla. They forced him at gunpoint to accompany them to a meat rendering plant on the Southwest Side of Chicago. There they hoisted him a foot off the ground and impaled him on a meat hook through his rectum! They tied him there securely so that he could not wriggle off. With Action in excruciating pain, they questioned him about his relationship with us. He didn't "confess" because he couldn't, having nothing to confess to. They then took a cattle prod—an electrified stick used by cattlemen to entice cattle to move—and applied it to his penis. They plugged it in. This still didn't get the desired result. They then poured water on the cattle prod, increasing the voltage. Still no result. Then they smashed his kneecaps with a hammer. When that didn't produce a confession, they stuck him with ice picks.

Finally they gave up. But they didn't lift him down. They let him hang there for three days until he expired. They then stuffed him in the trunk of his car and parked it under Wacker Drive. When the stench of the deteriorating three-hundred-pound body finally prompted somebody to look inside, the inquisitive person found the decomposing body of Action Jackson.

I saw the dozen or so glossy photographs taken of that body. Enough to make a strong man sick.

In the case of "Frankie The X," Hill, Roberts, Donovan, Moynihan, and the Miami agents didn't want another Action Jackson situation. They put a tight surveillance on Esposito as soon as they arrived. They also warned him: that was why he stayed on his porch, walking miles a day but not coming off it. And they alerted the Dade County sheriff. They made sure that he was not about to be hit.

Soon our heroes became aware of this. They gave up and came back to Chicago.

When Esposito also came back to Chicago, I gave him a call, wanting to make an appointment to see him. I told him who I was and what I wanted to talk to him about. "That's all a bunch of bullshit," he told me. "Those guys wouldn't want to hit me, you guys are full of shit. I have no reason to talk to you." And he hung up. That was the thanks we got! As far as I know he is still alive. If I hadn't heard it myself on the tapes, maybe I would have thought it was all "bullshit," too.

My last contact with Jackie Cerone as of this writing came in May 1989. I was contacted by the veteran "60 Minutes" producer Lowell Bergman. He asked if I would be interviewed on camera for a special "60 Minutes" in the fall. He also asked if I might have the wherewithal to induce one of the "biggest names" in the mob today to submit to an interview. I suggested

Jackie Cerone. He immediately agreed that Cerone would be a real coup if he could be persuaded to submit to such an interview. So I went to Chicago to meet with Jackie's son. I had a most amicable conversation with young Jackie, a Chicago attorney and a chip off the block when it comes to his dad's personality. I received little encouragement but was put in touch with Jackie the father, who is in the Federal Correctional Institution in Balstrup, some forty miles from Austin, Texas. At the age of seventy-five, he is serving the third year of a twenty-three-year sentence and is not in the best of health. He agreed to see me at any time but was adamant that he would not appear on "60 Minutes." He opened our chat by bellowing at me, "What the fuck are you doing now! How come you're bothering my son! Haven't you bothered us all enough for one lifetime, you asshole! You never quit, do you Roemer! Why don't you lay off!" When I angrily began to explain that I didn't intend to bother his son, that it was him I wanted to "bother," he laughed and said, "Calm down, Roemer, I'm just needling you. How are you?" We then had a pleasant talk, but I could not make him change his mind about the "60 Minutes" interview.

30 "Retribution in Kind"

One day in the mid-sixties, one of our top agents came back to the office all beat up. He had a swollen jaw, partly closed eye, and battered ribs.

As he told the story, he had gone out to the Casa Madrid, a nightclub located in Melrose Park. There he intended to interview the owner, Rocky De Grazia. De Grazia was a made guy, but he had fallen from some favor in the outfit because of unproved stories that the Casa Madrid had become a welcome place for drug dealers and their customers. And the Chicago mob is opposed to drugs.

There was a long tunnel extending into the adjacent parking

lot from the Casa Madrid. In the old days, so the story goes, it was used by Al Capone and some of his henchmen as a favorite escape hatch. When tailed by the law or by his rivals, Capone was supposed to have led them to the Casa Madrid, entertained for a short while, and then escaped out the tunnel, leaving his watchers wondering how Capone had disappeared.

When our agent arrived alone, he found the club to be empty. He looked around, found the door to the tunnel open, and looked in. At that point he was grabbed by three men, one of them De Grazia. Despite protesting that he was with the FBI, he was beaten, most likely because he may have stumbled into a drug deal. De Grazia probably panicked because he didn't want to be identified with any drugs in view of the mob's prohibition against them.

Vince Inserra was the supervisor at the time. He called three of us into his office—Johnny Bassett, the former professional light heavyweight contender; Gus Kempff, a tough former Buffalo police officer; and me, the former Marine and Notre Dame boxing champ.

"What are we going to do about this?" Vince asked.

We all quickly agreed that such activity demanded a like response. The Chicago mob had not previously used physical violence against us. It would be a mistake to let something like this pass without swift and sure retaliation.

John, Gus, and I headed out to Melrose Park that same afternoon. When we got there, the place was closed. We barged through the door. No one was inside. We found the tunnel, went down it, and again found no one. (At that time, we were unaware that Rocky lived upstairs in a lavish apartment.) Waiting for some kind of a response from having kicked the door in, we looked around. There was a long bar, tables, and a stage. Not exactly the Chez Paree, but a nice place where the blue-collar crowd from Melrose Park could have a good time.

When no one showed up, we began to feel frustrated, and we decided to break the place up a bit. We took a dozen or so bottles of booze and smashed them against the mirror behind the bar. We broke several chairs and tables. I then took out my business card and placed it carefully on the bar so that there would be no doubt as to who was responsible. We then slowly walked out to the parking lot and drove away.

We expected to hear about our invasion of the Casa Madrid

one way or another, either from the police or the mob. When
we heard nothing, it frustrated us more. What good had it done
to retaliate, if it hadn't caused a ripple? How could we preach a
lesson if no one was listening?

A couple of weeks later, the three of us headed out to Melrose
Park again. It was a Wednesday morning. We went directly to
Rocky's upstairs apartment. Rocky answered on the first knock,
threw the door open, and said, "I'll be ready in a minute." He
was expecting someone to take him to a funeral of a relative.
He didn't realize it might be his own.

We strode through the door.

"Rocky, we're with the FBI," I said. "The other day I think
you met another FBI agent. Do you remember that?"

De Grazia looked at us, suddenly very sorry he had opened
his door.

"Yeah, but that was a big mistake, let me explain," he started.
That was all Gus Kempff needed. Out came his big police special, his standard issue .38, not the snub-nose most of us carried.

Into Rocky's ear went the .38. I grabbed Rocky by the shirt
and pulled him toward me. Gus kept the gun in place. I hissed
in Rocky's face. "This is what happens to punks like you, Rocky,
who mess with FBI agents! You're going to remember this day,"
I said, remembering the words Sam Giancana had yelled at me
at O'Hare.

But at this point, the odor of shit became overpowering. Rocky
had defecated in his pants. He began to tremble.

"Don't kill me, don't kill me. It was a mistake, it wasn't my
fault!" he screamed.

We pushed him around a little. None of us struck him. We
actually never harmed him. But we had put the fear of the Lord
in him. He would think twice about smacking an FBI agent
around again.

John and Gus went back to the FBI office to report to Inserra.
Since it was noonish when we returned to the Loop, I went over
to Morrie Norman's Restaurant in the basement of the Pittsfield
Building. I had another part of the plan to carry out.

I knew I would find one or more of the connection guys at
Morrie Norman's.

I knew, for instance, that it was the daily lunch spot of Ralph
Pierce, who had been Murray Humphreys' partner for decades,

starting with Hump in 1932 when the Chicago Crime Commission designated Hump "Public Enemy Number 1," following the incarceration of Al Capone. Pierce was a most prominent member of the connection guys and, in addition to that, was the mob boss of the South Side. I also knew that Les Kruse, who the newspapers called "Killer Kane," another connection guy, made Morrie Norman's his regular noon meeting place.

When I walked in I immediately spotted Pierce, Kruse, Bill McGuire, and Hy Godfrey. Bill McGuire was a former Chicago police officer who had gone into bookmaking on the South Side and later was to join Joe Ferriola, Donald Angelini, and Dominic Cortina in their gambling operations on the West Side. Godfrey was the runner for the connection guys, their message courier, appointments secretary, you name it.

As I walked up to their table, they all recognized me. I'd had dozens of encounters with Pierce and Kruse, and several with McGuire and Godfrey. I got along with all of them since they were all in the mold of Murray Humphreys—very personable, affable guys who wouldn't tell you anything and didn't expect anything from you. They coexisted on this planet with the worst and the best, and made the most of it.

"Fellas," I said, "we just had an incident out in Melrose Park that I'd like to explain to you. You all know Rocky De Grazia. About two weeks ago, he beat up one of our agents. We don't stand for something like that. We went out and messed up his joint. Today we got ahold of Rocky and put the fear of the Lord in him. What I call 'retribution in kind.'"

I could see that my phrase "retribution in kind" went right over their heads. I explained. "Retribution in kind, Hy, means the way you and I would understand a counterpunch. He throws a shot and we counter. Understand? We took action after he started it."

Hy Godfrey, the old fighter, understood that. I think Bill McGuire and Ralph Pierce and Les Kruse may have generally understood "retribution in kind", but I was taking no chances.

"Now here's what I'd like," I went on, still standing at their table. "I'd like you guys to spread the word. Tell the rest of your people just exactly what happened. Rocky De Grazia beat up one of ours, we retaliated. Remember that phrase if you will—'retribution in kind.' You throw a shot, we'll throw one, too. We've got eight thousand FBI guys in this country, about three hundred of 'em right here in Chicago. Anytime you think about starting something, think about that. Take this back to all your people. We want this clearly understood.''

I felt certain it was clear and I was sure my message would be repeated. I left.

It was several years before I learned exactly what happened after that. (Later developments were revealed to me by a source high up in the mob.) In the meantime, I only knew that word of the De Grazia incident spread through the Chicago underworld; when I would meet a mobster or even a common burglar for the first time he would recognize me by name as "the guy what beat up Rocky de Grazia."

I have never really taken any pride in that. There were three of us against one that day—the same odds Rocky had given our agent—and what we had done hadn't required any particular strength or courage. But sometimes it is the least of your accomplishments that appear to be of significance to others.

The direct result, as I learned later, was this. Ralph Pierce took my message straight out to the boss, Giancana. Giancana, not for the first or last time, blew his stack.

"That fucking cocksucker, Roemer. I've had it with that guy. This is the final straw. I'm setting up a special fund of $100,000. To figure out how to get that fucker. That's it. I've had it.''

The mobster who was to become my source was with Giancana when he made that decision. He decided that Giancana had now gone "goofy"—just as he had when he allowed me to identify Frank Sinatra as the person who should be contacted if the Kennedys wanted to sit down with Giancana. His fixation with Bill Roemer had affected his ability to make decisions.

My source then sent word to Paul Ricca and Tony Accardo—not directly, but through a conduit. That was how Accardo and Ricca, the grand old men of the mob, learned what Giancana had planned.

Giancana then got the word from them.

"No way," he was told. "De Grazia started this fucking thing. Roemer finished it. Now leave it alone. You can't take on the whole fucking FBI, and that's what you'd be doing. Let it die.''

In discussing this incident, let me clarify the mob's general attitude about harming police officers, members of the media, and public officials. The mob occasionally misinterprets the actions of people like us, and they sometimes feel that the public person carried his responsibilities too far, so that he is no longer acting within the realm of his official duties. In these cases, they may take action. And if the public person was on the pad and therefore double-crossed the mobsters, he's in danger. But otherwise, they have a strict hands-off policy.

There are exceptions to this rule, but most cases can be explained rationally. Usually, the mob is eager to let the world know why it resorted to violence against a public person. They killed two police officers in Chicago in the early 1950s. They killed *Chicago Tribune* reporter Jake Lingle. They murdered a politician named Charley Gross in 1952. But these were isolated cases of mob retribution.

Those victims were not necessarily corrupt. But in each case the mobsters felt they had cause to overstep the usual boundaries. They carried their duties ultra vires, as we used to say in law school, beyond the power conferred on them.

As long as the law enforcement officer, newspaper or TV reporter, prosecutor, and judge stays within the bounds of his job, it is the unwritten law of the mob that he is not to be touched. The rule is not there because the mobsters are nice guys. It is there because they know that if any one of these professionals is harmed, the whole weight of the world will come down on them.

If a Bill Roemer is harmed today, the FBI, the Chicago Crime Commission, the U.S. Senate Permanent Subcommittee on Investigations, the Pima County sheriff's office, the Arizona Department of Public Safety, and probably one or two other agencies will turn over every rock to find who harmed him.

A prime example is what happened when Don Bolles was killed in 1976. Bolles had been a veteran reporter for the *Arizona Republic* newspaper in Phoenix. He was a well-known investigative reporter who specialized in organized crime. When Bolles was killed in a parking lot, the press world descended on Phoenix in an effort to learn who was responsible. Reporters were loaned to what came to be called ''The Arizona Project'' by newspapers from all across the country, including Bob Greene and Tom Renner from *Newsday*, the Long Island-based newspaper, who had created an organization called the Investigative Reporters and Editors (IRE) to help other crime-fighting journalists. They published a series of articles in newspapers around the country about organized crime.

The mob learned to be very sorry that Bolles had been hit, but personally I don't believe they had much to do with it. Bolles was working at the time on the connection a New York corporation had with horse and dog racing in Arizona. Though the corporation had been convicted in Las Vegas of hidden ownership, its ties to organized crime were tenuous.[1]

The formation of the Investigative Reporters and Editors is a prime example of what organized crime can expect if they alter their policy and go after individual law enforcement or media representatives. They would be committing suicide.

It is also the reason why organized crime families do not resort to the ultimate discipline as quickly as some people suppose. Tony Accardo, the Chicago consiglieri who must sanction any hit recommended by Chicago, knows that every time there is a gangland slaying it raises a hue and cry. Undesired public attention focuses on the mob. Such hits are thus counterproductive and rarely sanctioned.

Tony Spilotro was buried in an Indiana cornfield in the hope he would not be discovered. One thing the Chicago mob in particular has learned from the bad examples of Al Capone and Sam Giancana is that the glare of klieg lights is not the atmosphere in which mob operations can flourish. When the public gets concerned about what its law enforcement representatives are doing to combat organized crime, the mob operates with least efficiency.

That is the reason congressional investigating committees like the Kefauver Committee, the McClellan Committee, and recent hearings of the Senate Permanent Subcommittee on Investigations under Senator Bill Roth of Delaware are so effective. They alert the public to the problems of organized crime. If the public fails to keep up the pressure and neglects what its public servants are doing, law enforcement becomes complacent. If the law-

---

[1] Perhaps as a result of continued pressure from the press, the Arizona Attorney General, Bob Corbin, announced on February 18, 1989, that he was reopening the investigation of the Bolles killing that occurred in 1976 and that he was reassigning three experienced investigators full time to determine whether there were more conspirators involved, other than Harvey Adamson, who has been convicted.

makers don't care, they don't fund law enforcement adequately
with sufficient manpower and equipment or enforce laws against
the mob.

I am frequently asked whether I am fearful that the mob will
hit me. After all, I still work against them in my defense of
clients who have problems with the mob.

First of all, I have learned not to be afraid. If it were not for
people who stand up against them, this country would be in far
worse shape than it is. We must constantly battle these guys.
And the best way to fight them is to do so intelligently. I believe
that the mob's quick resort to the ultimate discipline—murder,
mayhem, and throwing fear—is enough reason to rein these guys
in. But, apart from their crimes of violence, they can do massive
damage to the public by using the income from their illegal
activities to corrupt our public officials. Just think what it means
for the mob to have a congressman on the Judiciary Committee
of Congress. At least one, Congressman Roland Libonati, was
so brazen that after the Giancana lockstep surveillance, he introduced a bill to prohibit the FBI from any type of physical
surveillance of a mobster!

I realize that Accardo could decide at any time that I am now
ultra vires, and that what I do these days in my "after life" is
beyond the scope of what he might consider tolerable from a
private citizen. Or a new consiglieri might decide Bill Roemer
has overstepped his bounds. Everybody takes chances. A man
doesn't get into the arena without risking harm, whether that
arena is the boxing ring of my youth or the ring of fire from the
mob. It would reduce my own self-esteem if I were to withdraw
because I was afraid.

Having said that, I will also admit that I am not nearly so
courageous as that sounds. The La Cosa Nostra is still populated
by intelligent men. Accardo from Palm Springs, Jackie Cerone
from his prison cell, Angelini, and Cortina, the top guys in
Chicago today are all extremely able mob leaders. They know
much better than I do, from their many years' experience, that
to hit a guy like me would bring down the wrath of law enforcement and the media. Consequently, you might say that my very
activity in fighting and speaking out against them is my body
armor, my insulation from harm. Nonetheless, I never take un-
necessary chances, as when Accardo wanted to meet me in Santa
Monica, and I refused to do so on his terms. In fact, after my

thirty years with the FBI and my nine years of after life, you might say I've grown eyes in the back of my head.

31 Giancana Puts Himself in Jail

In the winter of 1964–1965 we began to devise a new strategy, one that had never been tried before on an organized crime figure. It was the brainchild of the Justice Department. At the time, Nicholas Katzenbach was the attorney general and Bill Hundley was chief of the Organized Crime and Racketeering Section. Henry Peterson and Archibald Cox were key officials in the department. Ed Hanrahan was the United States attorney for the northern district of Illinois (Chicago); Dave Schippers and Sam Betar were his assistants.

The idea was this. A grand jury investigation would show that Giancana, the target of the grand jury, had made a series of three thousand telephone calls across state lines having to do with organized crime. The specific charge to the grand jury was that Giancana, by making these calls, was in violation of the Federal Communications Act. He would be given every opportunity to respond to questions pertaining to those phone calls. He would be questioned about his associates, illegal activities, travels, and about the public officials with whom he was connected.

The theory was that this would put Giancana in a dilemma. Would he answer truthfully, for instance, about his relationship with John D'Arco, Pat Marcy, or Roland Libonati, the congressman? Would he reveal the mob status of Tony Accardo, Paul Ricca, and other Chicago crime figures? Would he talk about the Commission, and La Cosa Nostra itself? Would he tell of the connection between the casinos in Las Vegas and the Chicago mob, and how many millions of dollars the mob skimmed each year?

We felt certain that he would not. He could not be truthful and live up to the oath of *omerta*. Of this we had no doubt.

His alternative to that, we reasoned, would be to take the familiar course of action—invoke the Fifth Amendment and claim his right to refrain from incriminating himself. However, if he took the Fifth, we were prepared to ask the chief judge of the U.S. district court of the northern district of Illinois to grant him immunity!

This was a novel strategy devised by the Justice Department. Such a grant would prohibit any prosecutor on any level—city, county, state, or federal—from trying Giancana for any of the crimes he had committed at any time in his life—even murders for which there is no statute of limitation. All would be swept clean.

This procedure would give Giancana another option. After receiving the grant of immunity, he could go back before the grand jury and answer the questions. If he answered truthfully and accurately, he would violate his oath of *omerta*. If he lied, then he opened himself up to prosecution for perjury. We believed he would never answer truthfully, for to do so would be to involve not only himself but his dozens of associates in the mob and in politics. But if he lied, then it would be up to us to prove that he had done so by supplying legal evidence to that effect.

The Justice Department in that case would turn to the FBI—to Rutland and Roemer in particular—and say, "Okay, guys, you got us into this, you get us out. Prove that he's lying. You guaranteed that if it came down to this you would save our butts. Now let's see if you can make good. The ball is finally in your court, you better stroke it back."

Obviously this strategy was not to be taken lightly. We would be charting virgin territory. Such a strategy had never been used before and was never to be used again under these circumstances. If we succeeded, we'd be heroes. If we lost, we would go down in history as the dumbest law enforcement people of all time.

It was a scary situation to be in. I actually had nothing to do with making the decision. But I furnished my opinion. I said that if we got down to the final option—when Giancana would perjure himself and the burden would then fall heavily on us to prove he was committing perjury—Rutland and I could do just that. The strategy was obviously a calculated risk on the part of the FBI and the department.

The department wanted to see the questions we could prepare before they made up their mind. They also wanted to check out the availability of proof that he was lying. The proof had to be admissible in court. Collecting proof was a task that took months. It was one thing to draw up a list of questions, and quite another to affix to each question the true answer and the statement of evidence that would prove that any other answer was perjurious.

We did all this in addition to our regular monitoring, transcribing, analyzing, and reporting of daily conversations heard over Little Al, Mo, Plumb, and Shade. For six months or so, almost all my work was in the office. It was far less enjoyable than the challenge on the street, but it was a challenge that had to be met.

When we finally completed the compilation, we took it upstairs to Hanrahan, Schippers, and Betar. They perused it closely, then sent it along—possibly with some legal alterations—to Washington for Katzenbach, Hundley, Peterson, and Cox.

The questions that we listed concerned just about every facet of Giancana's life. Had he murdered Teddy Roe? Had he kidnapped Eddy Jones? (Both were policy operators Giancana muscled when he brought the Chicago mob into policy and numbers operations in the South and West sides of Chicago.) What was the nature of his association with Pat Marcy? With John D'Arco? Had he ever received money from Buddy Jacobson? Why? What was its source? (During a surveillance our agents had observed Jacobson delivering an envelope that we believed contained $30,000 to Giancana in an Oak Park restaurant.)

What was the nature of his association with scores of mobsters like Murray Humphreys, Frank Ferraro, Ralph Pierce, Les Kruse, Sam Battaglia, Tony Accardo, Paul Ricca, Frank Nitti, Jackie Cerone? Had he ordered Cerone to go to Miami to kill Frank Esposito? Why? What was his position in La Cosa Nostra? What *is* La Cosa Nostra? What is the Commission?

Had he sanctioned the murder of William "the Saint" Skally? Had he sanctioned the murder of Sam DeStefano? Who had he ordered to kill DeStefano? Did he own a piece of Lorimar, the record company fronted for him by Chuckie English? What was the nature of his association with Frank Sinatra? Did he send the message to FBI agent Roemer that if John or Robert Kennedy wanted to talk to Giancana they should use Sinatra as an intermediary? Did he use the credit card of Phyllis McGuire and her home phone to call Butch Blasi to give him orders? Did Blasi call him at McGuire's home to relay messages? These and hundreds of other such questions were on our list.

We waited for the final decision. If the department were to decide that the questions were not hard-hitting enough or that, more likely, the proof was inadequate to support a conviction for perjury should Giancana lie, then there would be no grand strategy for the grand jury. The investigation would be called off, and the months of office work would have been for naught. We held our breath.

In April the word came. It was a go!

Since we had virtually guaranteed to the department that we could sock it to Giancana if it came to that, we knew we had better produce.

In May 1965 we started serving subpoenas. We intended to bring before this grand jury any Chicago mobster worth his salt. It was a roll call of the high and mighty. If you didn't get an invitation to this party, you didn't belong.

Thanks to all our bugs (and by that time we had had some nineteen in operation), we had a pretty good idea who was in town and who was not.

I served Hump and Gussie. I would have served Frankie Ferraro as well, but he had died of cancer by 1965. I also got Ralph Pierce and Les Kruse, both connection guys, along with three or four others. But the guy I relished putting the paper on most was my old friend John D'Arco. I caught him one evening while he was arriving for dinner at the Beldon-Stratford Hotel.

I also dropped the paper on Pat Marcy and Buddy Jacobson. We were sparing few stars in the galaxy of mobsters and their buddies.

The first guy to appear was a low-level mobster named Americo "Pete" DiPietto. It was the tactic of Schippers, Hanrahan, and Betar to make it appear that they had a real songbird. Pete was in prison in Leavenworth at the time, away from his associates. Schippers and his crew brought him in and kept him before the grand jury for two days. He said nothing of value, but we knew that Giancana realized DiPietto was a made guy. He surely had enough information so that if he took two days to tell it, he could be damaging.

Then the rest of the Chicago mob was brought in one by one: Chuckie English, Giancana's boyhood pal who had ascended the ladder with Giancana and who, with Butch Blasi, was his closest confidant; Butch Blasi himself (what those two guys could tell about Giancana!); English, who was running Lorimar, the record distributing company, as a front for Giancana; Blasi, his appointment secretary, driver, and bodyguard.

Next came Humphreys, the master fixer and leader of the connection guys. Gussie Alex, who later that year upon Hump's demise would take over that spot. Ralph Pierce and Les Kruse, the other two connection guys.

D'Arco, Marcy, and Jacobson were brought in to be questioned about their connections to Giancana and their operation of the Anco Insurance Company.

We called Tony Tisci, the son-in-law of Giancana and aide to Frank Annunzio, another West Side congressman now more powerful than ever in the 102nd Congress.

And others: Sam "Teets" Battaglia, who had been designated to succeed Giancana when and if he went down. Jackie Cerone, one in the line of mobsters who were to succeed Giancana. (Jackie, of course, would be questioned about the killing of Action Jackson and the stalking of Frankie "the X.")

Accardo and Ricca, the predecessors of Giancana.

Dick Cain, the made guy who had successfully infiltrated law enforcement for so long.

Fiore "Fifi" Buccieri, another of the plotters in Miami against the life of Frankie "the X." His brother, Frank, who was to succeed him very briefly as the capo on the West Side. (There's a funny story here. We had amassed a gallery of photos of the mobsters to be shown to each of them when asked if they knew each other. The photo of Frank Buccieri showed him riding a horse that had been given to him by a girlfriend, a Playboy bunny. There was also a photo of the "bunny." When the photos were shown to Fifi, he was asked by Dave Schippers if he knew these individuals. Fifi asked, "Which one?" Schippers responded, "Take your pick." Fifi quickly came back, "I take the Fifth on the horse and the broad!")

None of those questioned did anything but resort to their rights under the Fifth Amendment. None made a positive response to any of the questions. Nor had we expected that they would. We would have been shocked if they had offered evidence. The purpose in calling them was to instill fear into Giancana by making him believe that some of his associates were, in fact, answering the questions truthfully, thereby incriminating him.

We had recommended to the Justice Department that Frank Sinatra be subpoenaed along with others of the Rat Pack such as Sammy Davis, Dean Martin, and Joey Bishop, all entertainers of considerable note in those days. But they were not.

But there was one celebrity whose presence was mandatory for the success of the strategy—Phyllis McGuire. The whole case was based on the use of the telephone by Giancana to make out-of-state calls, presumably in furtherance of his role as the boss of the Chicago family. Many of those calls, we found, were made on her credit card. We had located records for the some three thousand calls made by Giancana from such places as the Armory Lounge, his headquarters, and the Amber Light, a bar in Cicero that he used frequently. We had also tailed him frequently to public phones. After noting the precise time he made a call, we were able to get the records showing the numbers he had dialed. The calls were to Commission members, associates in other cities, and back home to Blasi. The records of those out-of-state calls represented the prosecution's legal ''hook,'' since they constituted a violation of the Federal Communications Act.

Phyllis took the town by storm. She was in her mid-thirties then, very pretty and extremely vibrant. As always upon seeing her I wondered what drew her to Giancana. But one doesn't always make the right decision in affairs of the heart. I suspect that the aura of Sam Giancana was what attracted her to him. I don't think there's much doubt that she actually did love him. She must have, to jeopardize her career and that of her sisters in order to be around him. Phyllis and her sisters have been one of the greatest show business acts in our time. They had more than twenty top hits, starred on two network TV variety series, and performed all over the world. At the time of her appearance before the grand jury they were at the height of their success. Her appearance before the grand jury and the attendant publicity about Phyllis's romantic ties to the pug-ugly Giancana was to throw the McGuire Sisters' act into a steep decline that led, three years later, to their disbanding.

Phyllis arrived on that May day and gave the waiting paparazzi her most dazzling smile. It appeared she would have been happy to display all her charm for the crowd had she not been hustled onto an elevator by her attorney.

Schippers strung out his questions and there were many, because the strategy called for her return the next day.

On the way out, Phyllis played her own game. She cozied up to Dave Schippers and led him to believe that if he would assist her to avoid the press and the crowd downstairs in the lobby, she might be more cooperative the next day. Dave guided her down back elevators and out a side door of the building. She had escaped the crowd. Phyllis then jumped into a taxi, drove around to the front of the building and got out, right in front of the press! Thereupon she held a press conference announcing what a good little girl she had been in answering all the questions of the grand jury. We could only surmise she took this action to gain public attention, although why under these circumstances is puzzling.

The next day was much tougher for Phyllis. Schippers put it to her, asking questions that were difficult to deflect. Answering truthfully was dangerous. When she was finished she was not up to theatrics. She rushed to the elevator, descended into the lobby and took off. No press conferences that day.

Waiting his turn, as Phyllis fled out of the grand jury, was Giancana. He had only to take one look at her to see that all had not gone smoothly. She rushed right by him without a word. I'm sure it did little to settle his nerves as he was escorted into the grand jury.

Most grand juries hear evidence from an assistant United States attorney, several federal agents, and perhaps one or two witnesses before returning an indictment, usually the same day. This grand jury, however, had been going on for weeks. To Sam Giancana, the evidence must have looked voluminous. Now at last the star himself was to be put on the stand. Under these conditions, even the boss of the old Capone mob must have been apprehensive about what was about to happen.

The Justice Department had taken the 250 questions that my fellow agents and I had prepared and, for starters, arranged them in a sequence that would hide the real purpose of the proceed-

ings. The questions seemed to have no order; one did not lead
logically into another. Giancana's attorney was not allowed in
the room to represent him, although according to the rules of
grand jury proceedings Sam could take time out and step into
the corridor to consult with his attorney.

As expected, Giancana took the Fifth in response to all questions. Actually, there was little in that first set of questions that
would have surprised him, although the answers, if truthful,
would have destroyed his oath of *omerta*. Some of the first set
of questions involved his relationship with Keeley Smith, the
singer wife of Louie Prima, the bandleader. He was also questioned about his use of Phyllis McGuire's telephone credit card.
It was hoped that he would realize Phyllis had been asked the
same question. We wanted him to think she responded by de-
tailing the nature of these many calls he had made around the
country.

The government then took its second shot at Giancana. He
was brought before the chief judge of the U.S. district court,
William J. Campbell. This posed a problem for Giancana because Judge Campbell was not one of Pat's guys. Nobody, not
even Pat Marcy, could reach him. He was a stone wall when it
came to resisting corruption.

As part of the strategy, Campbell granted Sam immunity. He
told him that if a police officer, right that minute, was placing a
parking ticket on Sam's car, he was immune. He had a free pass
on anything and everything he had ever done during his life.
Nobody, not the federal government, not any state government,
nor the city of Chicago, could hereafter prosecute Giancana for
anything he had done right up to and including that moment in
May 1965.

Tom Wadden, Giancana's attorney, asked Schippers, "Now,
what do you intend to do?" They sounded like fighting words
rather than a rhetorical question.

But I was not in the courtroom. I was downstairs at that moment, on the phone in Vince Inserra's ninth-floor office. We
were getting the word from Christy Malone, our man upstairs
in Judge Campbell's courtroom and in constant contact with
Schippers, Hanrahan, and Betar. Christy told us, "Just after
Judge Campbell gave him the immunity, Hanrahan turned to me
and said 'This is it. I hope you guys know what you're doing!' "

I looked at Maz. I knew he shared my thought. If there were

to be scapegoats in the event Sam answered the questions and we couldn't prove it as perjury, nobody upstairs and in Washington would look beyond the two of us. We could look forward to Butte, Montana, the field office for people who displeased Mr. Hoover.

When Sam walked back into the grand jury room, he swaggered. He gave every indication of having us by the gonads. He was now going to answer the questions. In fact, Tom Wadden said as much.

I understand the first question put to him was "What is your name?" He didn't take the Fifth. He answered.

The next question was "Where do you live?" He didn't take the Fifth. He answered.

The next question was more pertinent. He took the Fifth on that one—and on every question thereafter. He had no right to the Fifth Amendment, as his grant of immunity robbed him of that right. If he could not be prosecuted for any crime, it was impossible for him to incriminate himself. If he could not be punished, he could not be incriminated. Therefore he had just two recourses: answer and lie, and then try to beat the resultant perjury rap; or answer and tell the truth, and then try to deal with the associates he would thereby incriminate.

Judge Campbell had explained all that to him. Sam understood. Therefore when he took the Fifth he was plunging right into the hurdle, not leaping over it! There would be no scapegoats on the ninth floor that day!

Sam was taken before Judge Campbell again, and again the judge explained to Sam the consequences of his actions. When Sam indicated he fully understood the possible punishment, Judge Campbell ruled: "You are in contempt! This is not an appealable or bondable offense. I hereby remand you to the Cook County jail. You have the key to your own cell. Whenever you decide to obey the lawful order of this court, notify the U.S. marshall and he will bring you before the grand jury."

It had been such a good tactic that the Chicago press predicted it would be used time and again. In fact when Chuckie English, Sam's lifetime companion, was brought in to testify shortly thereafter he came in old clothes and with just a five-spot in his pocket because he was sure he would be rousted the same way. However, it was decided not to overdo a good thing. That would

be counterproductive. This particular grand-jury tactic should
be saved for special occasions.

Meanwhile, Sam was obviously fretting in his cell. But we
learned he was having it somewhat easier than his cellmates.
The best chateaubriand was being catered to him from his favorite restaurants. One-dollar Cuban cigars were available. He
had a refrigerator for his favorite beers, a shelf for his cocktail
mix, a stove to cook his favorite "Italian," and the best silver
with which to eat from his china plates! The guards were even
doing his laundry.

As sheriff, Dick Ogilvie had ultimate command of the Cook
County jail. When a little bird started twirping in his ear, he
was outraged! He put the guards on the lie box. When two of
them admitted catering to Giancana, Ogilvie summarily fired
them. He found that Sam DeStefano had placed a friend in the
jail as a guard; that friend was ensuring the soft treatment of the
mob boss. No more of that! Ogilvie made sure Sam was on his
feet at 5:00 A.M. with the rest of the inmates, had his bowl of
oatmeal, and followed the same routine as the ordinary thief,
rapist, and pickpocket. No more special treatment for Giancana.

Giancana was to remain in the slammer until he used his "key"
(deciding to talk) or when the grand jury term expired, which
was to be on Memorial Day, 1966. In the meantime he put out
another $100,000 contract. This one was a reward offered to
anyone who could come up with a scheme to spring him. Many
of the defense lawyers in Chicago put their heads together, but
none could figure out a way to force the release of a man who
had voluntarily put himself in the pokey.

His attorney filed an appeal. Sam, growing morose in the
county jail with the scum of the earth, hoped against hope. He
had gone from the penthouse to the outhouse. He was used to
worldwide travel with the likes of Phyllis McGuire and Keeley
Smith, to consorting with the likes of Frank Sinatra, to lounging
in the luxury of Las Vegas and Lake Tahoe; to catering from the
world's best maitre d's. Now Sam was penned in. Oatmeal had
replaced caviar. Milk was served instead of Dom Pérignon. He
wore prison grays instead of five-hundred-dollar, custom-made
suits from Celano's Custom Tailors. It was enough to make a
strong man weep.

His appeal was turned down. Even worse trouble loomed on the horizon. That little birdie who flew over Chicago in those days told Sandy Smith, then with the Chicago *Sun-Times*, that the government would repeat the same procedure with Sam upon his release. We would use those questions Schippers had never gotten around to, the other half of the 250, and start all over again. If Giancana was granted immunity and once again took the Fifth, he'd be back inside for the duration of the grand jury.

What a prospect—especially since the life of a grand jury is eighteen months! Sam had been somewhat lucky this time that the grand jury had already been in session six months when he was held in contempt. The next time, it would be eighteen months. After that, who knew when the bastards were going to stop the merry-go-round?

While Sam was in jail, his compadres were having their own troubles. Tony Tisci, his son-in-law, lost his job with the congressman after the press raised a stink about how this "public servant" could spend government time defending his mob-boss father-in-law against the government.

The biggest problem of course was the spotlight. Organized crime operates at its efficient best when nobody is watching and at its worst when the attention of the world is focused on it.

At no time in the history of the fight against the mob was the glare of public attention so bright as during the sixties when Sam Giancana took us to court and then we turned the tables and took him to court. Both cases were unprecedented. Just think of taking the FBI to court to stop them from close surveillance when the plaintiff is the worst hoodlum in the world. Conversely, just think of putting that worst hoodlum in the world in the position of locking himself in the slammer.

The eyes of the world were fixed on Chicago during those early and mid-1960s just as they would continue to be focused on the city during the Days of Rage soon to come.

Sam Giancana, however, would not be around Chicago to experience those days. It was immediately following his release from jail after the expiration of the grand jury in May of 1966 that he voluntarily abdicated his leadership of the Chicago mob and exiled himself from the country as has already been detailed in Chapter 25, where we chronicled the all-in-one-piece story of Dick Cain.

32
A Typical Day in the Life of a Mob Leader

After the demise of Little Al and his brothers in July of 1965 (thanks to Lyndon Johnson), my life changed drastically. I had received several incentive awards, cash awards, and many letters of commendation for my work with the bugs. In fact, when the FBI made a new award available to FBI agents in 1965, I was the first to get one in Chicago. The awards were called "quality raises" and were especially valuable because they stayed with you for the rest of your career. Once an agent got a quality raise, he continued to get the raise for the rest of his career on an annual basis. Obviously this was a very nice form of recognition.

Now, however, I was able to spend more time on the street. Shortly after the bugs were pulled, Hump also departed our lives. Al and the others left in July, Hump died at Thanksgiving.

I was reassigned to Gussie, my old whipping horse. About that time he moved to his present address at 1300 Lake Shore Drive. Divorced from Margaret, he found a new love and remarried. She was a German girl who had come over to this country and become a Playboy bunny. As such, she came under the tutelage of Eddy Vogel's girl, who was a Playboy bunny den mother. Her name was Suzanne Fueger, but Gussie calls her "Shatzie," which means "sweetheart" in German.

We found that Gussie was traveling extensively to and from Switzerland, St. Moritz in particular. That was one of the things that had mortified Margaret. We had tracked them there while she was still married to Gussie and asked Customs to search them when they returned to the United States. They stripsearched them both, which was very embarrassing to Margaret. The search had turned up a body belt that Gussie was wearing to conceal the hundreds of thousands of dollars he was bringing back into the country.

It was obvious to us that Gussie had a Swiss bank account. Although he enjoyed skiing in the Swiss Alps, obviously his purpose in traveling frequently to and from Switzerland was not just to ski. I had SOG contact the state department. They put in motion proceedings so that his travels to Switzerland were thereafter "interdicted," as they called it.

I then began to spend more time watching Gussie. I developed sources at his lakefront apartment building. The doorman and a garage attendant on all three shifts kept me informed of his comings and goings and his visitors.

About three mornings a week, I found that he would drive to the offices of the coin-operated machine distribution business he shared with Eddy Vogel. Eddy spent most of his time with his girlfriend, Ann Fenner, in Encino, California, leaving the operation of the business to Gussie. Payday at the company was on Thursdays, and I always knew I could initiate a surveillance of Gussie on Thursday mornings at 7730 Milwaukee Avenue, where the company was located. Gussie had to be there to sign the payroll checks.

I found that his usual procedure was to return home around noon. He would then have lunch with Shatzie and walk the fifteen blocks or so to the Loop where, often as not, he would visit the law offices of Carl Walsh in Suite 820 at 39 South La Salle Street.

We strongly suspected that Gussie used Carl Walsh's office as a message drop. We decided that he probably met people there for business. As the leader of the connection guys, it was his job to act as the mob's main corrupter. It seemed probable that Pat Marcy and John D'Arco would travel the three blocks or so from their offices on La Salle Street to meet with Gussie—also with labor leaders such as Joey Glimco, Ed Hanley, and Dominic Senese. The law offices were located in a high-rise office building in the heart of the financial district, almost within the shadow of the Chicago Board of Trade—a natural place for such people to visit.

Because of its location, however, it was also a very difficult place to keep under surveillance. To tail any of these people into the building was not all that difficult. But then we had to accompany them onto an elevator to the appropriate floor.

They would ordinarily take the elevator to a higher or lower floor and then take the stairway to the floor of Walsh's offices.

If anyone accompanied them in the stairway there was no way they would exit on Walsh's floor. And even if we had been successful in this, how could we then determine that they met with Gussie inside the law offices? They could always say they had business to do with Attorney Walsh.

The answer, of course, would have been to install a mike in Walsh's offices. We never considered that—not in the offices of a legitimate, highly regarded attorney. Attorneys discuss their clients' defense with them. For a law enforcement agency to eavesdrop or wiretap such conversations is a gross violation of the law, and it would poison the prosecution of any crime so discussed and overheard. There is no way we would have requested authority from J. Edgar Hoover for something like that. We would have been censured for even suggesting it.

Today times have changed. Under the authority that the FBI now has to install court-ordered microphones, the United States District Court of Northern Illinois (in Chicago) has even allowed the Bureau to place a microphone in the chambers of the chief judge of the Cook County Traffic Court, documenting corruption in the "Greylord" investigation, taking bribes from local attorneys to fix traffic tickets. But prior to Title Three authority in this regard, granted the Bureau by law in 1968 and not used extensively in organized crime investigations until somewhat later, the FBI did not seriously consider bugging an attorney.

Carl Walsh is the son of Maurie Walsh, for years a favorite attorney for the mob. When Carl graduated from Notre Dame and then the DePaul Law School in 1965 he joined his father's practice, and when his father died he took it over. His clients include Gussie Alex and Tony Accardo, and he is associated with Art Nasser whose clients included Tony Spilotro. When I wanted to officially interview Gussie, he would arrange it in Carl Walsh's offices. When I was attempting to serve a subpoena on Tony Spilotro in Las Vegas, it was Nasser who finally made the arrangements. There are several attorneys who represent mobsters in Chicago. Among them are Walsh, Joe DiNatale, Jackie Cerone, Jr., Nasser, Frank Oliver, Sam Betar, and Santo Volpe. I have no quarrel with any of them. A man is entitled to proper representation, and these attorneys make sure the mobsters get the best. They fight as hard to defend the hoodlum as we do to incarcerate them. That's the nature of the business, the way the game is played. Many like Nasser, who was an appeals attorney for the IRS in Chicago, and Betar, learned their trade while with the government. It's a fact of life that they have the right to enhance their income after leaving the government by defending the same people they had attempted to prosecute.

The problem comes when an attorney conspires with the mobster to help him break the law. It is highly objectionable when a lawyer plots with the mobster so as to insulate him from future investigation and prosecution. I have always looked down on lawyers who do so, because of their "mentoring" of the hood. Those lawyers teach the hoodlum the methods by which he can break the law and get away with it.[1] Bieber and Brodkin were prime examples.

After Gussie left the offices at 39 South La Salle, he would then take a cab to 400 East Randolph, the Outer Drive East Apartments. John D'Arco lived there. But Gussie did not go to see D'Arco. From a cabana at the Riviera Health Club and Spa Gussie would take his daily swim. Eddy Vogel shared the place with him. They stocked the cabana with the best in whiskey and cocktail mix, had a small TV, and beds for each of them. Also a telephone. Following his swim, Gus would take a late afternoon nap.

At about five o'clock on an ordinary day in the life of the hoodlum, Gussie would take a cab home.

Dinner with Shatzie would follow, occasionally but not often at one of his favorite restaurants like the Whitehall Club, the Pump Room, the Consort Room, or the Cape Cod Room in the lower level of the Drake Hotel. More often than not, Gussie and Shatzie would watch television through the ten o'clock news on Channel 2, the CBS affiliate, knowing that John Drummond, the dean of Chicago TV crime reporters, would have the news Gussie was interested in. They would then turn out the lights

---

[1] I want to make it clear that we never verified our suspicions that Gus Alex may have been using the law offices of Carl Walsh and Art Nasser in any of the activity I suspected. Gussie went there regularly in the early 1970s and continued to do so up until the time I left Chicago in 1978. But we never once authenticated my suspicions. Carl Walsh and Art Nasser are reputable Chicago attorneys, and it is very possible Gussie visited their offices on strictly legitimate legal business only. Had not Gussie gone there so frequently, I wouldn't have had suspicions.

and retire to one of the two bedrooms in their thirty-first-floor
condominium overlooking Lake Michigan.

Gussie bought the apartment for $70,000 in November of
1973 when it went condo, after he had rented for several years.
He still lives there today. Overlooking the lake is their dining
room, living room, and kitchen. From the bedrooms Gussie can
look out over Astor Street, the street of many famous old line
Chicago families. I found that he had a hard time looking down
on Banks Street, so that is where I would wait in my car to tail
him when he left his underground garage.

Gus and Shatzie used to spend their weekends at "Farmville," the farm that brother Sam owned in Cassopolis. Sam is
gone now, and this practice has ceased.

More and more these days Gus spends time at his other home.
This one is located in the Regency Towers South at 3750 Galt
Ocean Mile in Fort Lauderdale, Florida. There the weather is
much more conducive to Gussie's preferred lifestyle. He swims
in the Atlantic Ocean, walks along the beach, and perfects the
dark tan in which he indulges. He spends as much time there as
he can.

But, like his close pal (probably his only close pal now) Tony
Accardo, who prefers to be left alone in Palm Springs, Gussie
can't escape the call of duty. Today he is still, at the age of
seventy-four, the leader of the connection guys. The others are
all gone, including Guzik, Hump, Ralph Pierce, Les Kruse, and
Frankie Ferraro, his boyhood chum. Even Hy Godfrey moved
to San Diego and later died there. It is left up to Gussie Alex to
handle the entire job formerly shared by a handful.

Of course, Gussie still has Pat Marcy. Pat himself is no spring
chicken. He is a guy who likes to get away from Chicago, usually to The Spa in Palm Springs where he can surreptitiously
consult with Accardo. The Spa is about seven miles away from
Accardo's condo along the Indian Wells Country Club fairways,
which hosts the annual Bob Hope Classic golf tourney.

Gussie's routine would apply only to an ordinary day. It would
not include those many days when the former boss of the Loop
would be more heavily engaged in his business—corruption.
Then, of course, his routine would change. But we no longer
were able to follow its twists and turns as we had when Little
Al was in place.

Who were they corrupting? How? For what favorable treatment? Since we could no longer find out from the perpetrators themselves we now had to get that information from informants. It was to be a long while before we got up to speed with that phase of our investigative activity.

Accardo and Gussie are the dinosaurs these days. Joe is in his eighties and Gussie in his seventies. They have ridden the tide of a long, hard life and are now near the shore. Bittersweet it will be for me when they go, just as when Hump departed. The three of them, along with Giancana and Joe Bonanno, gave me great adventure as I tracked them and fought them, and my prayers are with them in spite of everything.

33 Bernie Glickman

It was mid-January in 1965. That particular week-end was as cold as I can recall in Chicago, down to twenty below zero. It was a Friday afternoon, when Vince Inserra came up to my desk.

"Bill, Johnny is coming in with Bernie Glickman," he said. "He just called to say he's got something hot. I'd like you to sit in on it."

Two things came to mind. One, that John Bassett, the former pro fighter, had been attempting to "develop" Bernie Glickman as a source. Bernie was the front for the Chicago mob; he was also the manager of Sonny Liston and Ernie Terrell, the heavy-weight champs, and Virgil Akins, the former welterweight champ. Did John have something for us? Up to this point, Glick-man had been friendly with John, and it would be a real coup if Johnny was bringing Glickman downtown to the office to de-velop some information further.

The second thing on my mind was that I was due to coach in a CYO grade school basketball tournament that night and the rest of the weekend.

As Vinnie left me, I looked out the window. It was a blizzard out there. It was two o'clock, and I would have to leave now if I was going to keep my commitment.

Come on in, John, I thought to myself. I'll see what you've got, suggest to Vinnie what we do, and get out of here.

At about quarter to three John and Bernie Glickman finally arrived. "Lousy weather," Glickman allowed. Yeah, I thought, let's see what we have here and let me get going.

What Bassett and Glickman had was pure and simple extortion. It would blow the lid off the mob's control of boxing all across the country. As soon as I heard it, I knew I was going nowhere but with Glickman and Bassett that night. The basketball team may have counted on me heavily, but they would have to carry on without me that night.

I called Jeannie. Good soldier that she is, she understood. She would have to drive in the blizzard into Chicago with the kids. It was not her idea of a good time, particularly since she has never reconciled herself to driving in blizzards. But she would do it. She had encountered problems like this before. (At least by 1965 she wasn't being contacted by some hoods telling her I was sleeping with somebody else).

I went back to Glickman and Bassett. Glickman was a sharpie. Even if he was a front for the mob in the fight game, some of the profits from the big gates Liston, Terrell, and Akins were bringing in stuck to him before the rest went to the mob.

He told us just enough to whet our appetite, but enough to give us a clue that what he had was dynamite.

What we heard about was the mob's influence in boxing nationwide. They controlled such fight managers as Blinky Palermo in Philadelphia, Charley Black in New York and New Jersey, and Frankie Carbo on the West Coast. Glickman himself, of course, controlled Chicago. There were connections between Ralph Pierce and the International Boxing Club; Jim Norris and Truman Gibson. And there was the inkling of a violation of the Interstate Travel in Aid of Racketeering Act, one of the three acts enacted when Bobby Kennedy became the attorney general in 1962, making interstate travel in furtherance of organized crime a federal violation. This violation of what we referred to as ITAR concerned Glickman's travel to New York with Felix "Milwaukee Phil" Alderisio, the mob hit man, to meet with some New York mobsters.

I left John and Glickman in the complaint room and headed back to Inserra's office.

"Vinnie, this stuff is dynamite. John has done a hell of a job bringing this guy in. If it holds up it'll give us the inside on the mob's control of the fight game, not only here but all over. And if he stands up we'll get the mob guys behind him. He won't give us much now, he wants to make a deal, but he's got 'interstate travel in aid of racketeering.' He met with mob guys here and then with some wise guys in New York. It's interstate, which gives us jurisdiction, and I think it might be extortion. I think John ought to stay with it, but you know I've got a ball game tonight, I've got to go."

Vinnie laughed. "You talked yourself right into this one, Roemer. You're going to go all right. Right with Glickman and Bassett."

I knew I couldn't argue. As much as I wanted to coach that ball game that night, I knew I wanted more to be one of the two guys who would tear the lid off the mob's control of the fight game, a game that was close to my heart.

I said, "Okay, I agree. Here's what I think. We ought to get this guy out of the office, down into the basement on the prisoner elevator so nobody sees him, and take him someplace remote to work out this deal."

That's what we did. We slipped into the office prisoner elevator, went nonstop down into the basement and right into a Bureau car, which another agent brought in. We then headed out the Eisenhower to the Holiday Inn in North Aurora.

We rented a suite and started to talk. But by about seven o'clock, no progress was being made because Bernie Glickman wanted to hammer out our side of the deal first, whereas I wanted to find out what he had to deal with. We went down to the lobby restaurant where a large buffet was laid out.

I was a little fed up with Glickman at this point. He really was a wiseass. Sharp tongued, he knew what he wanted and went right after it. What he wanted was to be named the commissioner of boxing for the United States government. There was no such thing. "All right, not now, but I want you to guarantee that the FBI will organize such a commission and put me in charge," he insisted. "I want to run boxing in this country."

It wasn't even something we could negotiate. The FBI had no power to form any such commission, let alone put him in charge.

It was an unreasonable demand and not even a starting point in our negotiations.

"I'm going to go help myself to the chow," I announced.

"My life is in danger and all this guy can do is think of eating," Glickman hissed.

I went and filled up my plate. John and Glickman then followed my example.

When they returned, I got up to go for a refill at the buffet.

"Wait a minute, for Christ sake," Bernie exploded. "We are not here to eat, we're here to save my life and make a deal. Let's keep that in mind."

"Bernie, I've been hearing that in the FBI office, on the two-hour drive in the goddamn blizzard, and up in the room," I said. "But what I *don't* hear is you telling us anything except what you want. How about giving us something we want for a change!"

I was annoyed. It still bothered me that I had left my wife to drive in this blizzard and left the team without the head coach to start a tournament that we had been shooting for all year. It didn't ease my spirits to have this guy give us his demands before he gave us something to work from.

In spite of my outburst, we got nothing from Glickman during the dinner. We then repaired back up to the room.

"Mr. Glickman, listen to me for just a minute," I said. "We are here to help you. We will do what is best for you. Here's what we'd like. You give us your story. We'll respond to that the best way we can. If you don't like our response, you walk out. We'll drop you off wherever you want and not bother you again. I guarantee you on our honor that we'll all walk away from this if that's what you decide, and whatever you tell us we will forget we ever heard."

My outburst cleared the air. Glickman agreed. He would tell us his story on the agreement. Then if later we couldn't satisfy him, we'd back completely away as if we had never met.

The story came out this way. Glickman was a close friend of Tony Accardo. Every Sunday morning he brought lox and bagels to Accardo's home in River Forest and they breakfasted together. It was a regular routine that had gone on for years. Glickman had ingratiated himself with wealthy mob members by selling them top-grade awnings from his Cool Vent Awning Company for practically nothing. We could spot a hood's house in those days by the awnings on the windows and porches.

Glickman had further ingratiated himself by being a witness and perjuring himself for Accardo during the income tax trial prosecuted by Dick Ogilvie. Glickman, who owned the Hickory House Restaurant in the Rush Street area of Chicago, had testified that he purchased Foxhead 400 beer from Accardo and on occasion would notice Accardo drive up in his Mercedes-Benz in order to sell beer. That testimony had been extremely helpful to Accardo because he was being charged with making false deductions for the use of that car. We had many witnesses who testified they never saw Accardo selling beer, in the car or out. (If the jury had believed Glickman and not our witnesses, Accardo would have been acquitted on his first trial. Instead, he had to sweat out a second trial before he was finally acquitted.)

Independent of his friendship with Accardo, however, Glickman used some of his wealth to invest in prizefighters. Soon he had Sonny Liston, one of the all-time great heavyweight champions. As he had just recently told Sam Giancana in front of Mo, "Liston doesn't trust nobody in the world but me. I've had him since he got out of the can and built him up to where he is today, the world champion."

When Glickman invested in Liston and became his manager, it had nothing to do with Accardo or any other hood. But, because he liked to hang around the hoods, he courted favors from them. They were able to help facilitate his handling of his fighters. Soon, he found that they had declared themselves in with him.

He stated that they just pushed their way in, something that was very common in the fight game. According to Glickman, they used no particular threat; they just declared one day that they now considered Glickman their "partner" in Liston and others in his stable.

He found that the mob had done much the same with those managers across the country whom he mentioned on our first contact in the FBI office—such as Palermo, Carbo, and Black. Bassett was very interested in this because Charley Black had been his manager during his pro career in New York. Glickman was unable to say whether the mob used any force when they moved in on these (and several other) prominent figures in boxing. But he suspected that they had.

He knew that professional boxing was under the strong influence of the mobs across the country, especially in New York, Pennsylvania, Illinois, New Jersey, and California. Glickman recalled that "Soldier" Farr, a prominent Chicago bookmaker who had a suite in the Morrison Hotel in Chicago, was very close to Murray Humphreys, Ralph Pierce, and Gussie Alex. At the same time, he was also close to an official of the Illinois Boxing Commission. Glickman also furnished anecdotal information about fixes that this trio arranged around boxing matches in Chicago. Both Pierce, the boss of the South Side of Chicago, and Alex, the boss of gambling in the Loop, bet heavily on these matches, knowing what the outcome would be.

Then Glickman identified Pierce as being the Chicago mobster responsible for Chicago mobsters' liaison with fight figures, particularly with Norris and Gibson of the International Boxing Club, the IBC, which promoted fights across the country. He told us the IBC was so strong that nearly all managers in the country did its bidding. They set up matches in which the outcomes were often predictable, in order to be able to get fights for their fighters. Through Pierce's closeness to Norris, in particular, he was able to feed on this inside information. Pierce would then utilize this information in making and laying off bets on the fights that were going to be affected by the fixes. Glickman also told us all the bookmakers on the South Side; Gussie's bookmakers in the Loop; Fifi Buccieri's bookmakers on the West Side; Caesar DiVarco's bookmakers on the near North Side; Lenny Patrick's bookmakers on the far North Side; Frankie LaPorte's bookmakers in the southern suburbs; and Les Kruse's bookmakers in the northern suburbs would be let in on the fixes.

In late 1964 Glickman was managing Ernie Terrell, another heavyweight champ. He agreed for Terrell to fight Cassius Clay, aka Muhammad Ali, for the world heavyweight title. The fight was to be held on favorable terms for Glickman and Terrell at the Chicago Amphitheater.

But suddenly Glickman received word—the fight would be held in Madison Square Garden in New York or it would not take place. The word came from a spokesman for the Genovese family in New York. That spokesman was a front for them who owned the pretzel concessions in the New York subway stations.

Glickman disagreed. He was a Chicago guy, and he wanted

the big fight in his town to take place under the good conditions he had negotiated at the amphitheater.

"You want your legs broken, boy?" came back the word.

Glickman was now concerned. The next Sunday morning when he took his lox and bagels to the mansion of Tony Accardo, he brought it up with his friend.

"Joe," he said, calling Accardo what all his close associates and friends call him, Joe Batters, "I got a little problem that you might not want to get involved in. I know you have told me in the past not to bring my fight business with me, as you want nothing to do with it. But let me tell you what has happened and see how you might want to advise me, just as a friend." He then told Accardo about the muscle he was receiving from the New York family.

"Bernie, here's what you do," Accardo said. "I'll give you one of our best guys—Philly. He'll go with you to New York, they know who he is, you won't have to introduce him or explain why he's with you. He'll listen to the problem and help you out."

To Bernie Glickman that was manna from heaven. He knew who Philly was—Felix "Milwaukee Phil" Alderisio, the man in charge of the "heavy work" in Chicago. He was Chicago's hit man, the muscle. If Alderisio went with him to New York, he'd straighten out those wise guys, all right.

Glickman bought the plane tickets. As a matter of fact, he produced them for us later, a salient piece of evidence showing interstate travel.

But when Glickman and Alderisio arrived in New York, they were met by a "heavy" guy from the big city—Frank "Funzi" Tieri, who was just beginning to take over as boss of the Genovese family.

After hearing both sides of the story, Alderisio wound up agreeing with Tieri. They had accommodations with Teddy Brenner, the matchmaker at the Garden. And for certain reasons, which Glickman never would make plain to me, they had a case for having the fight in New York, not Chicago.

Glickman was outraged. I have always thought there was a little more to it than that, that somehow the New York mob demonstrated to Alderisio that they had a piece of Terrell and that Glickman was in danger of losing Terrell completely if he didn't cooperate. In any event, Glickman came back to Chicago in a state of seething anger.

About that time, who should propitiously make contact with him but Johnny Bassett. John dropped by the gym that cold Friday afternoon in January 1965 just to touch base with Glickman and to indulge his curiosity about how Terrell was coming along in training. John's plan worked out into something much better than just gathering information on Terrell.

I knew we had something at this point. But my legal training at Notre Dame and at the FBI academy told me we needed just a little bit more.

"Bernie," I said, using his first name now that he was going along with us. "Fine, we're interested in all of that and it might give us a case. But is there anything else?"

I didn't want to suggest to him what I had in mind. But I wanted him, of his own volition, to recall any part of the story, accurately and truthfully, that would give us extortion.

"On the way back to our hotel right in the elevator that son of a bitch punched me in the stomach, shoved me around, pushed his palm into my face and swore at me," Glickman said.

That's what was needed. But we still had to get a little more. "Bernie, at any time, especially during that trip to New York, did Alderisio or anybody else say anything that made you think they might try to steal your fighter?" I asked.

"Why, absolutely! That was the whole fucking point of it. Absolutely!"

"What did they say, as close to their actual words as you can recall?" I asked.

"They said I got to do what they want because they own a piece of Terrell and they're going to make sure they get it. The best way for that is to have the fight at the Garden where they can cut into the gate. That's the whole point, bring the fight to New York where they got control. Cut me out. That's where that fucking Philly double-crossed me. I think they were going to cut him in if he swung the fight to them, can't you see that, Roemer? I thought you had some knowledge about these things. John, you see that, don't you? You know how these things work, for Christ sake. Am I dealing with some fucking novices here?"

The fucking novices never did understand every nuance of the case. I'm sure Glickman always held back why the New York mob had a right, at least in their opinion, to a piece of what

Glickman had. The truth was, I didn't ever want to push him on that. It might open up a lot of things I didn't want to hear about our witness. On the other hand, if he had ever indicated he might cut loose with that information, we would have been very interested. You never want to be surprised when your main witness takes the stand. But Bernie would never discuss that aspect of the case.

Okay, now we had the story. It was our turn.

It was now about midnight. I was tired and so were John and Bernie. But we plowed on. John gave Bernie a sheet of legal paper on which he began to list his demands. We struggled over the commissioner bit. Finally we resolved it by telling him that J. Edgar Hoover would be advised of his cooperation and of his desire to be named United States Commissioner of Boxing. We said it would be left up to Hoover to do what he could to influence the formation of the commission and Bernie's appointment as chairman.

The other conditions had to do with his safety and the precautions we would undertake to protect his life. He said he would testify as to all he had told us, with the exception of his relationship with Accardo and Accardo's part in the affair.

"Whoa, back up here, Bernie," I coughed. "We want Joe in this. He's in it. He put you with Philly. Philly traveled with you only because he was ordered by Accardo, the consiglieri of the Chicago family of the La Cosa Nostra. He's an integral part of this conspiracy!"

"No way. Joe did what he did as my friend. I made that clear. He had no part in this. He was as double-crossed as I am. Under no circumstances whatsoever am I gonna hand up Joe."

It was now about three. We battled on that particular point for another hour. Finally John and I gave up. If that was the one condition he attached to his testimony—and since that was so important to him—we settled on leaving Joe out. We would start to prepare our report in the morning, but we would leave Accardo out.

Finally, about four we hit the sack. At four-thirty, I heard Glickman yelling at me, pulling me awake.

"My God, Bernie, I just got to sleep. What now?" I asked.

"I forgot one condition. A very important one. I want you to write it down. Number nine."

"Oh Lord, Bernie, not another. We made our deal, now let's sleep on it."

"One more, Roemer, this is a must."

"What the hell is so important, Bernie, I thought we had it all settled," I said.

"A promotion for Johnny Bassett!"

"A promotion for Johnny Bassett," I repeated numbly. "Fine, a promotion for Johnny Bassett."

"You might notice, Bill, no promotion for you," he said.

"No promotion for me," I again mimicked him.

"Johnny Bassett is in this because he's my friend. He wants to help me. You're in it just because it's your fucking job. You just want to put Alderisio and Funzi and the rest in jail, that's all you want, you don't feel for me. My friend here is Johnny Bassett!"

He had me. I learned a lesson from that. You can never develop a source unless you sincerely, and I mean honestly, put yourself in his shoes and develop a bond with the guy. You must actually get to like the guy. You have to know that it is taking a great deal for him to "turn" and come over to your side after a lifetime of being on the other. He is taking his life in his hands, and you better, by God, appreciate it.

Bernie Glickman taught me that. He had sensed that what I was doing was professional, not personal, that I really cared a lot more for the duties and responsibilities of my job than I did for what this might do to him. He sensed that John Bassett was not that way, that John had Bernie's interests more at heart than the interests of his job. That came across to him. If it were not for John Bassett, we never would have gotten Bernie Glickman into this investigation. If I had been alone, we never would have gotten this case out of North Aurora.

As the years went by and I was to find that source development was something I enjoyed, I kept all this in mind. I quickly came to realize that there is little hope in developing a source unless there is some kind of a chemistry involved. If you really don't like the guy—and it is obvious that most hoods are not likable—then there is little hope of bringing him over. Then it is strictly a case of money or leverage. You can use money to bribe him, or the leverage of offering a deal so he won't have to pay for his crimes. Those situations I always found difficult.

My forte, I was to find, was to hook up with those few hoodlums I could feel very comfortable with, whose company I enjoyed. When I found those kinds of guys—and they were out there—I discovered I could achieve considerable success in luring them over. If they liked me, trusted me, put their faith in me, and began to see my side of the situation (and, after all, it *was* the right side), then the battle was won. I was to find, however, that it was extremely difficult to successfully encourage a man who has been a hoodlum all his life to continue to engage in his illegal activity but to do so as a source for me, thereby endangering his life. The attitude had to be completely altered for him to put his life in my hands. And it was a tremendous responsibility for me to have a man do that.

I was to learn many of my lessons in source development in the next several months with Bernie Glickman.

Once Bernie went to sleep, around six in the morning, we couldn't get him up. I called home. Jeannie told me we had won our game and that our team would be playing again in Chicago at St. Florian's at one o'clock that afternoon. We let Bernie sleep, feeling that he needed all he could get at this point. I finally had to call Jeannie and tell her that she and the team would have to do without me again. She quietly informed me that she had gone out to try to start our old Pontiac, standing out in the twenty-below weather (since we had no garage), and couldn't get it started. I suggested that she call one of the other parents and see if they would drive the players. Great wife and mother that she is, she handled it.

Finally, Bernie rose. He seemed much more relaxed. We went down and had lunch, and in the early afternoon we started again. Bernie now had many reservations, mainly about what he would do with his life, should he have one, after he testified against Alderisio and Tieri, the two mob capos. He was beginning to realize that he wasn't going to be named United States Commissioner of Boxing. His idea that he could somehow get even with his mob oppressors by ruling such a commission was fading. Fast.

So now the entire focus of his attention was: How could we protect him and set him up for a new life after he exposed himself by testifying in open court?

At this point (1965) we had almost no experience in witness

protection, surprising as that may sound. I had had none and neither had Johnny Bassett. We were unsure how much we could guarantee him. I left the room, called Vinnie and asked him to call the Bureau. It was a Saturday, and for one reason or another we never were able to get any definitive answer to our problem. The suggestion was made that we "finesse it." Big help. I sure didn't want to mislead Bernie at this point by promising him something that we would not be able to live with in the future. Or more to the point, that he would not be able to live with.

All that we could say was that we "probably" could help him change his identity and could "probably" assist him in moving to another community. (In Chicago, we knew he would un-doubtedly be recognized sooner or later.) Bernie's children were grown and living away, so that was no problem. In fact, his son Joel was to become one of Chicago's leading bookmakers. But Bernie did have a loving wife with whom he lived. What about her part in all this?

It wasn't easy. We spent the entire day on that one problem. Obviously, it was the key. Without his satisfaction on this issue, there would be no deal. When we retired that night we had pretty well satisfied Bernie that, although we would make no guaran-tees, all we knew about the FBI convinced us that he would not be left twisting in the wind. The federal government would see that we gave him as much protection as we could.

It was not nearly as definite as we would have liked and cer-tainly not as much a commitment as he wanted. Knowing that the final agreement on this point was "iffy," I realized Bernie must feel that he was between the proverbial rock and a hard place as we carried on further negotiations.

I had no idea then that it would be up to me alone, in another pact with the mob, to ensure Bernie's life.

The next day we finally got down to preparing the interview report form. We agreed that whatever was in the report we would expect Bernie to testify to, nothing more and nothing less. It was therefore important to us that we include as much in it as we could. It was important to Bernie that the report contain no mention of Tony Accardo. That was our agreement. We had Alderisio, Tieri, the Madison Square Garden matchmaker, the pretzel guy who was the front for the New York mob in the subways, and two other less important figures in the extortion. We had the threats that Alderisio had made to Glickman when he punched Glickman in the elevator in New York, and the plane tickets as exhibits. Altogether, we had everything I felt we needed for a major case, not only because it implicated two of the major mobsters in the country but because it exposed the mob's influence in the fight racket.

About six that evening we left Aurora. Bernie wanted to go home and explain the entire situation to his wife. We agreed, mainly because we felt that he was in no danger yet. He had done nothing to cause suspicion except miss his regular Sunday breakfast with Accardo, something that could be excused because of the horrendous weather. But also, because we had no place to put him.

While I handled the paperwork, John handled Bernie. About ten days went by. One night, just as John was arriving at Bernie's house, he saw Alderisio rushing out. John hurried into the house to find Bernie, battered and bleeding. Alderisio, of course, had done the job.

John called me at home, then brought Bernie downtown to the FBI office. I hustled down and we took photos of Bernie in his bruised condition. John, of course, would testify that he had seen Alderisio leaving and had found Bernie like that. We were sorry that Bernie had to go through a beating, but it served to tighten the noose against Alderisio and his coconspirators.

 34 **The Midnight Walk**

The night Bernie came to us all battered and bruised, we put him in a Loop hotel. The next day, John and I headed out to Fort Sheridan, the army base located about twenty-five miles north of the Loop. We talked to the commander and made an agreement with him to house Bernie. It was decided that Bernie would pose as a retired army colonel. We felt he would be safe there and somewhat comfortable.

All was well until we got a call about three weeks later. Bernie was too much. He not only posed as an army colonel, but he acted like one. He gave orders to everyone on the base below the rank of colonel. Repeated warnings by the commander failed to do any good. He would have to go.

Before we went out to pick up Bernie, we hastened to the fifteenth floor. We had been firmly informed that by the rules of procedure, Bernie was now a witness of the Justice Department and that they, not the FBI, now had jurisdiction over him. Ed Hanrahan, United States attorney for the northern district of Illinois, was the man now responsible for the care and safe-keeping of Bernie Glickman, rather than John Bassett and Bill Roemer or anybody else in the FBI. He firmly reminded us of this. We were to step out of the case. Bernie was his responsibility from then on through the trial.

We went back downstairs and into Marlin Johnson's office. We told him of Hanrahan's attitude and his orders to us to step out of the case. We told him we felt responsible for Bernie, and that he would not have agreed to cooperate had it not been for John and later me. We told him that even if we didn't have a clear legal responsibility, we felt a moral obligation.

Marlin called SOG. The long and short of it, as Marlin soon explained to us, was that Hanrahan was right—we had no right to interfere with his witness. We were told to keep our hands off and walk away.

We headed out to Fort Sheridan. At least we could say good-bye to Bernie and explain what had happened. As you can imagine, this was a bad day for him. And it was a bad situation for John and me. We strongly disagreed with our orders. There was little we could do, however, other than let Bernie know our hearts were with him, whatever consolation that was.

The U.S. marshals soon arrived. Under Hanrahan's orders they took Bernie to St. Louis. And threw him in the county jail!

What a way to treat a friend! When we learned what had happened, we were shocked. But, again, what could we do? It was out of our hands.

As the weeks went by and Hanrahan prepared for a federal grand jury hearing leading to indictments of the conspirators, Bernie's mental, physical, and emotional condition deteriorated in the county jail. He was not as strong in any respect as he had been when he came to us. He was fading fast.

The grand jury was to hear the evidence on a Monday. On the

Friday before, we heard that Hanrahan was bringing Bernie back to Chicago to work with him on his testimony. We contacted the marshals and learned that they would be bringing him into O'Hare from St. Louis that morning. John and I hustled out to the airport to greet our friend. When Bernie arrived, we approached him.

"Back off," the marshal told us. "We have orders from Hanrahan that you guys are not to talk to Mr. Glickman!"

We soon learned why. The Chicago newspapers had been full of the news that week that Bernie Glickman was talking about mob influence in the fight game and that he was soon to testify before the grand jury. Then, that morning, Sandy Smith broke a bombshell in his paper. He had actually found out, weeks before, that Bernie was being kept at Fort Sheridan. Bernie had called him from there, told him he wanted to write a book with Sandy, and had invited him out to Fort Sheridan. With Bernie's connivance as a "colonel," Sandy had been passed through the guarded gates and got Bernie's whole story. The one condition was that he not report it in the paper but hold it for a book.

But then Art Petacque, the ace investigative reporter for the *Chicago Sun-Times*, who was Sandy's chief rival, scooped Sandy and broke the story. This caused Sandy, without consulting us, to feel that he was freed of his commitment to Bernie to hold the story for the book and was morally free to break the story in his paper. He did.

The story made the front page with a photo of Bernie. The story jumped into the back pages with photos of Alderisio and sidebars about the mob's influence in boxing. Bernie had become the A-number-one topic in Chicago. The next day, there was to be a story about a mob contract out on the life of Bernie Glickman. The mob was out to kill him, so the story said, before he could bring them down with his testimony.

Hanrahan blamed us for bringing Sandy Smith together with Bernie Glickman at Fort Sheridan. He had issued orders to the marshals not to allow Bernie to confer with us until after Hanrahan had a chance to talk to Bernie and get to the bottom of the story.

Only after Bernie told Hanrahan that we were not involved in his meeting with Sandy—and that he had done it all on his own—were John and I allowed into the lock-up in the marshal's office to meet our friend.

We were shocked. Bernie was a shell of the man we had known. His condition had badly deteriorated. He mumbled, he kept his gaze directed toward the floor. He hardly seemed enthused about seeing us again, but after we sat with him for a while, he seemed to perk up. I think he realized that he had no friends left anywhere in the world, and that John and I were the closest things to it.

We spent time with him again on Saturday and Sunday. By Monday, he seemed to be much sharper mentally and emotionally. One last time, we went over terms of the agreement we had finalized that Sunday afternoon at the Holiday Inn. Hanrahan was with us and I pointedly said, "Remember, Ed, there is nothing about Tony Accardo in here." Hanrahan agreed.

Johnny Bassett and I waited in Hanrahan's private office while he took Bernie into the federal grand jury room. An hour went by. Hanrahan and Bernie rushed into the office. "Here, I'm writing out a check for witness fees for seventy dollars. Take this son of a bitch and get rid of him. It's all over!" Hanrahan screamed at us.

"My God, Ed, what happened?" John and I yelled in unison.

What had happened was that Hanrahan had taken Bernie right down the list. Alderisio, Tieri, the matchmaker, the pretzel guy from the subways of New York. All had gone well. Bernie had testified fully and completely, a fine witness to that point.

Then Hanrahan, apparently forgetting or misunderstanding our agreement with Glickman, questioned him about what role Accardo may have played in the conspiracy.

At that point Bernie, knowing what the agreement was, lied. He perjured himself by saying that Accardo was in no way implicated in this conspiracy. Hanrahan realized Glickman was thereby discredited, that he had impeached himself and so was of no further value as a witness even against Alderisio, Tieri, and the rest.

I did not see the grand jury minutes, nor of course was I there. But that was what Bernie told us had happened. He felt bitterly betrayed. I have no reason at all to doubt Bernie's account.

Hanrahan repeated his order. "Take this man out of my office. He's no longer a federal witness, I wash my hands of him. Put him out on the street!"

Put him out on the street? He might get two blocks! The mob

would kill him immediately. His life on the streets of Chicago wasn't worth a plugged nickel.

We told Bernie to stay right where he was. Obviously, this made Hanrahan furious. John and I hustled down to the ninth floor and straight into Marlin Johnson's office. We told him what had happened. Marlin picked up the phone and called Hanrahan. He held the phone so that we could hear Hanrahan's screaming. "You get Roemer and Bassett back up here right now to pick this man up or I'll have your job!"

I'll say this for Marlin Johnson. He replied in kind. "You'll have my job?" he yelled back. "There is no way a man like you can take my job. I don't work for you and neither do Roemer and Bassett. They work for me and I'm keeping them down here!"

Marlin then called SOG. We knew what that was going to mean. As we suspected, the orders we got were to leave Bernie right where he was. He was the responsibility of the Justice Department as a federal witness, not of the FBI.

It was a dilemma. Bernie was our friend. We had put him in this spot. Could we now desert him and let Hanrahan throw him on the street, to almost certain doom? But how could we do otherwise? We were under the orders of our superiors from Marlin Johnson all the way up to J. Edgar Hoover. To disobey would certainly mean our jobs. There were no two ways about it.

I had an idea. I went to Vinnie Inserra, my supervisor, and spelled it out. He agreed.

First I called Bill Duffy, the deputy superintendent of the Chicago Police Department. I explained the entire situation to him. He was fully aware of who Bernie Glickman was and how he had been expected to testify. I asked Bill, as a personal favor to me, if he would send two of his men immediately to Ed Hanrahan's office, pick up Bernie, take him to a hotel, and guard him until I could make other arrangements. Bill agreed.

They housed Bernie under tight guard at the Pick Congress Hotel.

Then I hustled over to Morrie Norman's, the restaurant in the Pittsfield Building basement where the connection guys had lunch. It was too late. Morrie told me that Ralph Pierce had been there but had left.

"Morrie," I said, "this is a matter of life and death. I'm

deadly serious. I have to find Ralph or Les or one of those guys and I have to do it now." He was unable to help me.

I rushed to the parking lot at Wabash and Van Buren, behind Old St. Mary's Chapel where I worshipped almost daily. Thank God, Ralph's car was still there. That meant he was still somewhere in the Loop. I knew he regularly met with his bookmakers at Pixley and Ehlers, the cafeteria located on Van Buren, but I couldn't find him there either.

I went back to the parking lot and sat on his car. About three o'clock he showed up.

"Ralph," I explained to him. "I need to see Accardo immediately. It's a matter of life and death, it really is. I think if I can properly explain everything to him, we can save a life here— a life that I think Joe will feel should be saved if he knows the whole story. It's Bernie Glickman's. I want you to set it up."

"Bill," he said. "I can do that. But there can't be any tricks. If there are, if you're pulling something here, I'm fucked. I have to trust you on this."

"You have my word, Ralph. I'll come alone, anyplace, anytime you say. He can have all the guys he wants with him and if I don't keep my word that it's for our mutual interest, then I'm fair game. Tell him that. I think you guys know I'm good for what I say. Trust me."

He did. I told him I would wait in the FBI office for a message from him. He didn't have to identify himself, as I would recognize his voice. "Just call 431-1333 as soon as you can, and give me a time and a place, I'll know what that means."

About six he called. "In the Sears Parking lot at North and Harlem at midnight," was the terse message.

I drove out to the Sears, Roebuck store on the far West Side of Chicago, arriving there just before midnight. I was unarmed and alone, as I had promised Ralph Pierce I would be. At precisely midnight, Pierce stepped out of the shadows. He obviously had beaten me there and observed the scene as I had arrived, waiting ten minutes or so to ensure I had kept my promise to come alone.

"Walk west for a couple of blocks," he said and then walked away.

I did as I was told. At midnight the homes in the neighborhood were completely dark and it was quiet except for a barking dog as I walked west on a side street north of North Avenue into

Elmwood Park. After I had gone about two or three blocks, Joe
Batters, aka Tony Accardo, stepped out from behind a tree. I
recognized him immediately. I said, "Joe, I have to search you.
What I want to talk about might tend to compromise me, and I
want to make sure you're not wired."

With that, I took off his hat. Immediately, six guys jumped
out of two cars in the vicinity and came running. I thought I
recognized Jackie Cerone as the lead runner. Right away, however, Accardo waved them back. "Hold on, I think it's okay."

The six bodyguards of the mob consiglieri stopped in their
tracks. I completed a pat-down of Accardo and was satisfied he
was not wired.

"This is a switch," he said. "I trust you and you don't trust
me. I'm the guy should be afraid you are wired."

"Yeah, you're right. I shouldn't have been suspicious. How
do you want to handle this, you want to go someplace?" I asked.

"No, let's just take a walk here," he replied.

We walked north on a street in Elmwood Park about two
blocks west of Harlem Avenue, a very quiet, residential street.
We'd walk about two blocks north and then turn around and
retrace our steps. One car preceded us and one car followed.
When we turned around they would just back up and keep us
sandwiched. Backing up posed no problem since there was no
traffic on that side street at that hour.

"Here's what I want to talk to you about, Joe," I began. "You
know Bernie Glickman testified today before the grand jury. Our
agreement with him was that he would testify about Philly and
the New York people including Funzi. But not about you. His
deal from the very beginning was that he wouldn't bring you
into it. As you can imagine, we wanted you in it badly and so
did Hanrahan. But he wouldn't budge from that agreement.
Today he goes before the grand jury. He tells all about how
Philly double-crossed him. I think you know he did, Joe. From
what I understand of the whole situation, Philly didn't do what
you ordered him to do, he double-crossed you, too. So I'd want
to talk to Philly Alderisio pretty carefully, Joe. But that's not
why I'm here.

"I'm here to tell you that after Bernie had completely implicated Philly and Funz and the rest, a very good catch for us, he
was then asked in front of the grand jury about you. He lied to
protect you. He said he never came to you, you were no part

of all this. When he did, he destroyed his credibility about all
the rest. Hanrahan has no more use for him. He's thrown him
out. The case against everyone is out, kaput. Finished!"

"Where is he now?" Accardo asked.

"I'm not going to tell you that, but he's in a safe place," I
replied.

"What is it that you want of me?" Accardo asked.

"What I want from you is your word that Bernie will not be
harmed. Call off the contract."

"You believe what you read in the fuckin' papers, huh, Roemer. Is there a contract?" Accardo asked.

"We won't debate that, Joe. I don't expect you to acknowledge any contract. What I'm asking is for you to give me your
word, which I can then pass on to Bernie, that your people will
not hurt him. Listen, Joe, he's in bad shape. We had him in a
comfortable spot but then he went and screwed it up and we had
to put him in a county jail. It really got to him. He needs a lot
of help. He not only needs peace of mind to restore his sanity,
he needs a lot of medical attention and rest."

I will remember Accardo's words forever. "Roemer, I thought
we was supposed to be the bad guys. It seems to me here you
are the fuckin' bad guys!"

He had me there. This whole situation had gotten so far out
of hand that I surely wished we had never heard of Bernie Glickman. Not that it was his fault. It was ours, meaning the whole
federal government: the Justice Department and the FBI.

We walked on in silence. Then I said, "Joe, this guy is in
such bad shape, he's just about to snap. And he is in that position
because of what we did, I admit it. But the primary reason he
is in that condition is because of his overriding loyalty to you.
If he had testified, instead of lying about it, that he came to you
and you gave him Philly, then he'd be sitting pretty somewhere,
in good health, protected and cared for for the rest of his life. It
was his loyalty to you that got him where he is tonight. That's
what I want you to understand. He's your friend, your people.
If it wasn't for that gunsel, Philly, who beat the hell out of him
and double-crossed him and you, too, he never would have come
to us in the first place. It was Philly who made him come over
to us, and then it was his loyalty to you that put him in the no-
man's land he's in today."

I think that outburst finally got to him. We walked again in silence for a while.

"Okay, he won't get hurt," he said at last.

"I've got your word on that?" I asked.

"You got my word."

"That's good enough for me. And I'm sure it will be for him," I said. Accardo paused for another couple of seconds and then said, "Tell me what you're talking about with Philly."

"Why I say he double-crossed you and Bernie both?" I asked. He nodded.

"Because you sent him to New York with Bernie to be on his side. To straighten out those New York wise guys. And he did just the opposite. He took their side and beat the hell out of Bernie. There may be an explanation for that, but if there is, I don't see it. If I were you, I'd call Alderisio in and find out what his side is. And I'd talk to Bernie about it. If you call off the contract on him, I would imagine he'd be glad to give you his whole side of the story."

We talked casually for a few minutes after that. I asked him how Ross, his oldest son, was and told him to give him my regards. I had met Anthony Ross Accardo when he operated the Plan-It Travel Agency in Chicago with Nick Nitti. He was a well-mannered young man who Joe could be proud of.

Then he reached out his hand, shook mine, and was off, jumping into the lead car. I walked back to the Sears parking lot and drove back to the FBI office. I signed out. Then I walked to the I.C. station at Michigan and Van Buren, took the train to 147th Street, walked to the manufacturing plant where I kept my car about three blocks away and drove the three miles or so home, arriving home about four in the morning. Jeannie woke long enough to ask, "Have a nice day, Honey?" I allowed it had been an interesting one.

That morning I reported my contact with Accardo to Vinnie and John. We told no one else. I then called Bill Duffy, asked him where he had Bernie, and told him that John Bassett and I would be there very shortly. He should alert his guys to our arrival.

When we got to the Pick Congress Hotel, we suggested to the Chicago police officers that they could go and thanked them. We then filled in Bernie on my midnight chat with Accardo. It was like a ten-ton truck had been lifted off his back.

"Joe said it was all right?" he asked incredulously.

"He said you won't be hurt," I answered. "And I suggested to him that he will want to talk to you about Alderisio. Tell him about that back stabber," I suggested. "If I were you, I'd go right to River Forest right now. You know Clarise. Even if Joe's not home you can wait there for him."

Later I was to learn that when Bernie met with Accardo, Accardo gave him a hug, just what Bernie needed, and told him not to worry. Then he took him to Presbyterian-St. Luke's Hospital and had his doctor hospitalize him for a couple of weeks. I understand Accardo picked up the entire doctor and hospital bill. Bernie then moved to southern California and resumed his life.

Though John heard from him periodically, I never did. After all, he was John's friend, not mine. In 1986, Ben Bentley, the highly regarded Chicago television personality, Park District official, and man about town who was a friend of Bernie's during his days as a fight promoter, told me that Bernie had died on the coast from natural causes. I pray for his soul daily.

I never did hear what Bernie may have told Accardo about Milwaukee Phil Alderisio. Not from either of them. But Alderisio was to let me know a couple of years later that he was no fan of mine.

35 We Get Them But They Get Ours

By the mid-sixties, the Chicago office of the FBI was enjoying outstanding success prosecuting the bosses of the Chicago mob. We put away each of the four successive top bosses. First it was Giancana who was incarcerated in the Cook County jail for a year from May 1965 to the end of May 1966. When he was released, he feared a repetition of the grand jury ordeal, so he abdicated as boss of Chicago's mob and fled the country to operate with Dick Cain, as detailed earlier in this book.

Giancana was succeeded by Sam "Teets" Battaglia, who had been a member of the old "42 Gang." This gang of punks had grown up with each other in the Patch. Its members, like Giancana, had graduated to bigger and better things in the Chicago crime syndicate. "Teets," who lived in Oak Park, had become a capo on the West Side, replacing Giancana as boss. His reign was to be of very short duration, however—about a year or so. He was hit with a tax rap by the IRS, convicted, and sent to federal prison. Released for medical reasons, he died at home a short time later.

Battaglia was succeeded by Felix "Milwaukee Phil" Alderisio, Bernie Glickman's old antagonist. "Philly" was the toughest of the tough. He had "made his bones" by being the number-one hit man of the outfit for years. Because of the way he'd beaten up Bernie Glickman, I felt the same regard for Philly that I did for Giancana. I considered him a real animal.

Thanks to our efforts, Alderisio's reign was just about as short as Battaglia's. Johnny Bassett, Denny Shanahan, and I arrested Philly one Sunday morning in his home in Riverside. We got Philly on a twenty-one-count indictment for defrauding the Parkway Bank in Harwood Heights of some $80,000, a violation of the Federal Reserve Act. He and his coconspirators had set up fake collateral for loans. One of his coconspirators would not live to stand trial. His body was found in handcuffs in his car in Skokie. He had been shot.

As we were driving Philly to the FBI office in the Loop and then to the Chicago Police Department lockup to house him overnight, Alderisio turned to me, and said, "Roemer, you been bad mouthing me all over Chicago. Calling me an animal, telling Joe Batters I double-crossed him, and talking about how many people I killed. That's not right."

I looked this hit man in the eye and said, "Philly, if you weren't what I say you are, I wouldn't be telling people those things. But where you're going, you'll have more to worry about than what Roemer says about you."

He glared at me and then shut up.

Like his predecessor, Battaglia, Alderisio would never return to cause us any more problems. He was to die in prison.

The next in line was Jackie Cerone, Accardo's protégé, who

had been in charge of the hit of Frankie the X in Miami. Jackie was far from a "lackey," his media nickname. Tough and intelligent, he was a deadly combination of muscle and brains. I have had several meetings with Cerone and I have come away with respect for the man. We have always gotten along. My respect, of course, would be much greater if it weren't for the Miami tapes. It is difficult to respect a man who would do the things he bragged about. But in his dealing with me, Cerone always kept his word.

One of the reasons he was straight with me may have been because of a man-to-man conversation I had with his son. Before he had risen to the top, his son Jackie passed the Illinois Bar examination and began practicing law in Chicago. When I heard that, I placed a phone call to young Jackie.

"Jackie," I said, "my name is Bill Roemer. I'm a senior agent on the organized crime squad of the FBI here in Chicago. I'm calling to congratulate you on passing the Bar. I know what it takes. And I want to say this to you. If anybody gives you a hard time just for the reason that you are your father's son, give me a call. Remember my name, Bill Roemer. If you have problems solely for the reason that you are named Jackie Cerone, Jr., let me know. I'll do what I can."

Cerone's daily routine was as regular as Gussie Alex's. Up every morning early for a jog in his Elmwood Park neighborhood, he spent the morning at his headquarters, a restaurant-bar named Rocky's on North Avenue in Melrose Park. Rocky's was to him what the Armory Lounge had been to Giancana—the place where he met with his subordinates and settled the problems confronting the mob. He would remain at Rocky's until midafternoon or so, then travel to the Regency Health Club in the Hyatt Regency O'Hare. Here he would do headstands and lift weights.

Cerone looks like a weight lifter, with powerful chest and arms. Whenever I needed to intercept him for an interview or to initiate a tail, it would be as he arrived at the Hyatt. After his workout he would have a cocktail or two in the hotel and then head home to Clara for dinner. Occasionally he would meet an associate for dinner, usually right there in the restaurant.

Cerone took over after we arrested Alderisio on July 29, 1969. But his days at the very top of the Chicago mob were to be as short-lived as had been Battaglia's and Alderisio's.

Paul Frankfurt was to be Jackie's downfall. Paul was one of the more experienced agents on C-1. Frankfurt was getting to know Lou Bombacino, who worked under Joe Ferriola, Donald Angelini, and Dominic Cortina, rising stars in the mob at that time. Of course, he hoped Bombacino would come over to our side.

Luck played into Paul's hands. While Frankfurt was talking to Bombacino, Lou had a falling-out with his superiors. The dispute was taken all the way to Cerone. He arbitrated it and decided against Bombacino. Lou was angry, of course, and that put him right into Paul Frankfurt's hands. Frankfurt asked a lot of questions, and Bombacino gave good answers. Based on Bombacino's information, we initiated an Interstate Travel in Aid of Racketeering-Gambling (ITAR-Gambling) case against the whole bunch, from Cerone on down.

In order to question Lou further, we took him to a farm near Elgin, a town about forty miles from the Loop. We worked four to a shift, guarding and debriefing him.

It was a fun time. The farm was located on a lake, and we worked twenty-four hours on and twenty-four off. When there, I would run around the lake to stay in shape. The fresh air was great!

But the best time was dinnertime. Lou turned out to be a great Italian cook. Every day we would take a list of the grocery items Lou needed back to an Italian grocery store in Chicago where Lou knew the best ingredients could be bought. Then Lou would spend the day cooking and simmering. That evening we would all sit around the table enjoying Lou's dinner. Chicken cacciatore was our favorite. We had a different dinner every night, but always Italian food. Elaine Bassett still has Lou's recipes.

We all pitched in; everybody had a task. Mine was to wash the dishes, which is about all I am good for in a kitchen. The one time they gave me a cooking job, they told me to make toast. I placed the toaster on the plastic seat of a dining room chair. How was I to know that the toaster would start a fire? After that, I was restricted to clean-up.

We got to know and enjoy Lou's company. After a couple of weeks, he was ready to testify against Cerone and many of his top lieutenants.

Once the trial had begun, I stopped in from time to time to see how it was going. On my fourth or fifth visit, Jackie Cerone noticed that I had entered the courtroom and taken a seat. Sitting at the defense table, in full view of the jury, judge, and prosecutors, he motioned to a henchman in the courtroom. When the guy came over to him, Jackie whispered something in his ear. The guy hurried from the courtroom. About twenty minutes later a young man came in and went up to Cerone at the defense table. Cerone pointed me out, and the young man then came over and sat down next to me on the bench.

"Mr. Roemer," he said, "I'm Jackie Cerone, Jr. I have never thanked you for what you said when I passed the Bar. My dad told me you were here and wants me to express my thanks to you. I really appreciated it at the time but I didn't know what to say. Thank you."

He got up and left. Jackie Sr. looked over and nodded to me.

At the next recess, the agents in the courtroom and the prosecutors came over to me. "What the hell was that all about?" they inquired. They shook their heads in amazement when I explained.

Lou Bombacino's testimony sunk Cerone and his crew. They went away to federal prison.

This time we had a little more experience with the protection of our witnesses. The Bureau had gone to school on the Bernie Glickman episode and wisely decided that that was not the way to handle such situations. They were surprised Bernie was still alive. (They did not know about my midnight walk with Tony Accardo.)

This time we got in touch with Walt Peters, a former Chicago agent who had transferred to Phoenix. Peters had a close contact in Casa Grande, a town south of Phoenix, off Interstate 10. Peters' friend said he would give Lou a job in his business. We assisted Louie in changing his name, and two agents drove him out to Casa Grande.

Everything went well. We brought Lou back to Chicago a few times to talk to him about other matters pertaining to the mob. I remember one time Johnny B and I had him at the Holiday Inn in Lansing, a southern suburb of Chicago. Lou insisted we all go to a bath house he knew of on the West Side and get a colonic. "What the hell is a colonic?" I asked. When he explained that it was a hosing up the rectum to clean out your colon, I quickly thought up an excuse not to go. I said it was too dangerous to go on the West Side, his old stomping grounds, for a colonic or anything else. I'm glad he didn't know of a place to get a colonic out near Lansing.

A couple of years went by and Lou, we thought, was doing well.

But unknown to us, he got into a problem in Casa Grande. He was accused of theft by his employer. The case was dropped, but Lou rashly decided to sue the arresting sheriff for false arrest. He used his real name, Lou Bombacino, in bringing the suit. It was a mistake. When one of the several transplanted Chicago hoods in Arizona picked up on that, the word got back to Chicago. They had their little birdies, too.

Lou was then living in Mesa, a Phoenix suburb in Maricopa County.

One day in 1974 he came out, turned on the ignition in his Cadillac and, boom, that was the end of our good friend Lou. It was a very sad day for all of us—not only because Lou Bombacino was a really nice guy and our pal but also because of the deterrent factor. Obviously, it is very tough to develop sources and witnesses when they find out what happened to guys like Lou Bombacino.

The Chicago mob eventually turned to a triumvirate to run the organization. They began to rule by committee. After the example of the last four absolute bosses, they decided to compartmentalize the operations. (I'm sure they didn't use words like "committee" and "compartmentalize" but that was, in effect, how they were set up.)

They brought Tony Accardo back. He would now have to assume more active control, with more day-to-day, hands-on responsibility.

They did something else they'd never before done. They made a non-Italian one of their trio of top leaders. In fact, his nationality was Greek. And he was an old pal, Gussie Alex. With Gussie on their side, they had a more active connection group to fight our prosecutions of their leaders.

The third boss, the guy who would actually be in charge of the street activity on a constant basis, was Joey Aiuppa, the guy they call "O'Brien." He's even less Irish than I am. The mob leadership was now "Triple A."

When I learned of this new triumvirate running the mob, I could readily admit that Accardo and Alex were capable leaders.

But not the other "A," Aiuppa. I remembered a conversation from Little Al, when Sam Giancana had informed Frankie Ferraro that Aiuppa was likely "to come running to you." He told Ferraro that Aiuppa was broke, "and he wants us to pull his chestnuts out of the fire. I told him to go fuck himself, we can't be responsible if he can't make a go of Cicero. That's a good territory; if he can't make a living in Cicero he must be a real dumb ass."

Ferraro responded that if Aiuppa came to him begging, he would send him on his way. How times change; now Aiuppa was a top boss, Giancana was in exile, and Strongy Ferraro was dead.

36 Head Busting, in More Ways Than One

The Top Hoodlum Program was launched in 1957; by 1974 the Bureau had come a long way. We had sent 238 organized crime figures to prison, including many of the top leaders from just about every major city. Raymond Patriarca from New England was in jail. Carlo Gambino was in New York awaiting prosecution, as was our old friend Funzi Tieri. Sam DeCavalcante, in New Jersey, had been convicted. Angelo Bruno, the boss in Philadelphia, was dying of cancer—he was to be murdered before he could die of natural causes. The boss in St. Louis, Tony Giardano, had been convicted. Nick Civella, the boss in Kansas City, was awaiting trial. Carlos Marcello, the top man in New Orleans, had been in prison for slugging Pat Collins, an FBI agent friend of mine. In Denver, one of the Smaldone family that ran the Mile High City, was behind bars.

In Chicago, of course, we had put away the four consecutive absolute bosses, the supreme accomplishment of any office. In Los Angeles, Nick LaCata, one of the bosses, had been convicted. The big news from Philadelphia was that the blacks had gone into the Italian area in South Philly and were muscling into the mob gambling operations. That would never happen in Chicago, not with the guns Chicago had in its arsenal.

There were twenty-seven Mafia families in the United States in 1974; there are now twenty-four. Several of these, however, like the ones in Rockford and Springfield, Illinois, are very small, almost insignificant families. All of those west of Chicago are dominated by Chicago. In 1974 there were 3,000 members of the La Cosa Nostra, but we had made absolute identifications of just 1,800.

The national commission of the LCN was then at nine members. But with the demise of our bugs, the FBI was unable to definitely identify the members of the commission. We knew, however, that there were probably five from New York, and that either Tony Accardo or Joey Aiuppa represented Chicago.

The Top Hoodlum Program went through two name changes between 1957 and 1974. When Bobby Kennedy became the attorney general, the Top Hoodlum Program was renamed the Criminal Intelligence Program. After J. Edgar Hoover died in May of 1972, it finally achieved its lasting designation, the Organized Crime Program.

By 1974 the Organized Crime Program had 1,100 agents around the country. We had found that the Detroit, New York, and Newark families were heavily involved in narcotics, while Chicago, Boston, and Cleveland were not. In Philadelphia, if an LCN member got caught being involved in narcotics, the family would not raise a finger to help him; he was on his own.

In Chicago, where the mob has ruled that narcotics is forbidden, you were not only on your own with narcotics—you were killed. Chris Cardi found that out. He was convicted of dealing in narcotics and sent to prison. Almost immediately after he was released, he was murdered gangland style.

As I have emphasized throughout this book, the Chicago mob, because of its far-flung reach, depends more than any other family on protection from public officials, including judges and law enforcement officers. If these public officials believed that the Chicago mob controlled narcotics—considered the most heinous of crimes—they would be much more reluctant to patronize them. If these public servants can rationalize to themselves that gambling is the major source of Chicago's income and that the mob "only kills its own," then they are much easier to corrupt. From my investigations up through 1990 and in talking to my

old colleagues around the country, I believe that the prohibition
against narcotics is still the rule in Chicago.

I am concerned that, with guys like John "No Nose" Di-
Fronzo and Sam "Wings" Carlisi taking over for the old guard
of Ferriola and Accardo, the prohibition against narcotics in
Chicago could wither also. The DiFronzos and the Carlisis may
not be able to withstand the temptation of the millions of dollars
that narcotics trafficking could bring to the Chicago mob.

I had one other active interest in the early and mid-seventies:
boxing. In 1972 I turned 46, but I was in the best shape of my
life. I was working out daily, skipping my lunch three times a
week to work out more than the hour three times a week that
Mr. Hoover had set as a standard for FBI agents.

In the seventies, I had made a contact at the University of
Illinois Chicago Circle Campus and was allowed to use their
facilities. I got to know Bill Fudala, a University of Illinois
coach. Bill had been a star linebacker in the 1960s and was then
their linebacker coach and boxing instructor. We began sparring, and soon it was a regular event.

Each Friday morning for several years, Bill and I would go
three rounds. We had one rule. Each of us could hit as hard as
we could with the twelve-ounce gloves, but when one of us got
hurt, the other was to back off. Hit the other guy but don't kill
him.

During our sessions Bill broke three of my ribs, putting me
on sick leave for the last time in my Bureau career. That was
about twelve years before my retirement. I broke his jaw once.

The only other damage was one brief case of amnesia. One
day, just as we were about to finish our third and final round, Big
Bill got me with a tremendous right hook. Three hours later, I
found myself standing in line at the Civic Center in the Loop,
about seven miles or so from the University of Illinois campus,
waiting to get a swine flu shot! I have no idea how I wound up
there. Bill told me later that we had finished the fight, went upstairs to play some one-on-one basketball, and showered. I said
good-bye and drove off, leaving him totally unaware that I was in
any way messed up. But I can't remember any of that!

Bill Fudala and I continued our Friday morning fights until I
transferred from Chicago in 1978. On my last physical at Great
Lakes, it was discovered that I was in danger of a detached

retina, obviously from too many blows to the eye. It was rec-
ommended that I cease and desist boxing. But I continued for
several more months until the transfer ended it. When I got to
Tucson, I continued to shadowbox, as I do every day now, but
I didn't look for a new sparring partner. At the age of fifty-two
I gave it up.

During the 1970s, however, I was looking for every opportunity to extend my youth. At one point I found out that Muhammad Ali, the world heavyweight champ, was training for a
fight at the Navy Pier in Chicago. Ben Bentley, the bon vivant
fight promoter, was in charge of Ali's workouts. I was a good
friend of Ben's from the earlier days when he was the public
relations guy with the Chicago Bulls pro basketball team, and
knew he could get almost anything done in Chicago.

I asked Ben if he could arrange for me to spar with the champ,
Ali. He said he would try. I told him to keep it quiet, because
if it leaked back to Marlin Johnson, the SAC, I'd be in hot water
again. (Ali was very controversial at the time, having just
emerged from the period when he had evaded the draft.) Johnny
Bassett warned me to be careful. He told me that Ali had no
love for the U.S. government at the time and would love to make
mincemeat of an FBI agent. I waited around in the Fireman's
Gym for several days, but Ali was never able to find time in his
schedule to fit me into his sparring routine.

Failing that, I got another idea. During the sixties and early
seventies I had been invited to referee the Bengal Bouts, which
were still being put on at Notre Dame by my old boxing coach
Dominic "Nappy" Napolitano. On one occasion, I refereed the
heavyweight championship fight, which was won by Mike Mc-
Coy, the All-American football tackle. (He would later go on to
become an All-Pro tackle for the Green Bay Packers.) In 1972,
McCoy was in the early prime of his football career. I wrote
him a letter and asked if he would return with me to fight an
exhibition at the Bengal Bouts on St. Patrick's Day of that year.
He wrote back and said he'd be glad to fight me.

It would be a good gate attraction—the four-time champ, Roemer, against the recent champ, McCoy (who had the additional
cachet of being well known to all Notre Dame fans.)

I wrote to Nappy and told him my idea. He wrote back and
okay'd it, agreeing that it would be a real gate attraction. We

would put on a three-round match during intermission at the finals.

I'll leave the story to Bob Wiedrich, the columnist of the famous "Tower Ticker," the column that ran for decades in the *Chicago Tribune*. This is his column in the *Trib* for February 11, 1972:

It's Saturday, March 18. The scene is the University of Notre Dame's Bengal Bouts, the school's annual championship boxing matches.

In this corner is muscular Mike McCoy, defensive tackle for the Green Bay Packers. He's a former All-American from Notre Dame who dabbled sufficiently in the art of fisticuffs during his collegiate days to achieve championship status in that sport, too.

At 23 years old, Mike qualifies as somewhat of a behemoth. He weighs in at nearly 300 pounds, stands 6-feet, 5-inches tall, and wears shirts with 19½-inch collars and 52 long suits.

Right now, he's standing there nonchalantly hitching up his boxing britches. He's got a date with his wife tonight and wishes this exhibition were over.

Now, over in the other corner is bouncing Bill Roemer, all-time boxing champ of Notre Dame. He's no Tiny Tim, either, weighing 200 pounds, standing 6-feet, 1-inch tall, and wearing 16½-inch collars and 44 long suits. Usually, Bill also packs a gun, for he is an FBI agent of considerable stature.

But today he stands there just in his skivvies and with two hefty dukes as his only weapons.

The 10-second buzzer sounds, signaling the start of what Jack Dempsey used to call the loneliest moment in a fighter's life.

"Did I do the right thing or didn't I?" Roemer asks himself. "What am I doing here?"

McCoy was graduated from the university in 1970. He is in the peak of condition, a finely tuned professional athlete.

Roemer is 45 years old, a veteran of FBI battles with the Mafia. When gangster Salvatore [Momo] Giancana used to see Roemer loom around a corner, he'd head the other way. Eventually, he ran all the way to Mexico.

The seconds tick off.

Roemer's momentary doubts are needless. He's been training for this bout ever since he first suggested the idea to Notre Dame athletic officials two years ago. He's a good rapper with a sneaky left hook.

"But don't forget, old boy," Roemer cautions himself. "That McCoy's got a helluva Sunday punch."

Roemer thinks back to his Golden Gloves days and the coups he counted there. He recalls the years he walloped his way through a Marine Corps hitch. He wishes J. Edgar Hoover were here today.

The gong rings. The fighters move out into the ring.

"Ladies and gentlemen," the announcer bellows to the crowd, including bus loads of FBI rooters from Chicago in the audience. "You are about to witness the battle of the generation—gap, that is!"

Well, that's how things may well be come March 18.

McCoy has expressed willingness to partake of the exhibition match. And *Roemer's raring to go*.

But were McCoy to bail out at the last minute for some unforeseen reason, Chicago fight promoter and publicist Ben Bentley has another ace up his sleeve, fearsome Fred Houpe, the 21-year-old heavyweight champion of the 1969 Golden Gloves.

A mere sprite of a lad, Houpe stands only 6-feet, 2-inches tall and weighs but 205 pounds.

Heck, Roemer, if this comes to pass, he'll already have been cut down to size!

I'll let Bob Wiedrich finish the story with an item in his column of February 21, ten days later: "Notre Dame athletic director Ed "Moose" Krause has turned thumbs down on a planned boxing exhibition match March 18 between Mike McCoy of the Green Bay Packers and Chicago FBI agent Bill Roemer. Although both are Notre Dame graduates, Krause says he doesn't want outsiders doing battle during the annual student championship boxing matches. The fact that McCoy is 24 years old and outweighs the 45-year-old Roemer by 100 pounds had nothing to do with his decision, Krause reports."

Obviously, I was thwarted again. Who knows, maybe Ali or McCoy would have landed a lucky punch and made me sorry. Maybe it was for the best.

37 My Friends

Of course, I wasn't spending *all* my time in Chicago gyms. In fact, I was getting a lot of work done. Probably the best testament to that were the words of Jackie Cerone, who was to call me "the nemesis of Chicago organized crime." In a motion he filed in the Circuit Court of Cook County in 1981, Cerone attested that "this famous former FBI agent dogged the footsteps of Sam Giancana, John Cerone, and others for years—round the clock in a tireless effort." I'm glad Cerone and his associates in the mob believed I was putting in a "tireless effort," because there were those like Vince Inserra who would smirk at that. I think the adage "you are known by your enemies" applies here. Of all the scores of commendations I was to receive from the FBI, perhaps that one from Jackie Cerone is the one I regard most highly.

In the 1970s I was spending most of my time (and in 1975, full time) developing sources within the mob. I was now developing about 75 percent of those contacts myself, and the rest I was supervising. I was in charge of seeing that all were handled properly by the other agents on C-1 and C-10. Eventually, I was to have great success as a full-time developer of inside sources.

Two of my top sources accounted for a lot of my time.

"Sporting Goods" (I can't reveal his real name) was high up in the Chicago mob. He was what we call a "street boss"—the boss of a territory for the outfit. Sporting Goods's information was vital to us for more than a decade. He kept us informed as to who was who in the outfit, what they did, who they did it with and to. For instance, if the police captain in his territory was corrupted, either by him or by the connection guys, he told me. We could then put the "little birdie" in flight and put the word in the ear of Joe Morris or Bill Duffy so that this captain could be transferred to an innocuous spot where he couldn't help the mob.

If a politician took graft from bookmakers in order to allow them to operate (commanders in the Chicago PD were not placed in the ward of any alderman who objected), then we gave that information to the little birdie so that he could sing to Dick Ogilvie. Then Dick would see what he could do to isolate the politician. Or the information would be given to Art Petacque of the Chicago *Sun-Times* or Ron Koziol or John O'Brien of the *Chicago Tribune*, knowing that these ace crime reporters would find a way to work that data into one of their many penetrating stories on the Chicago outfit.

Sporting Goods and I had a routine. Every Friday night I'd drive to Barthel's Supper Club. The Supper Club was in Dolton, just across Cottage Grove Avenue from South Holland. I'd get there at six-thirty in the evening, sit in my car across from the supper club, and watch. When Sporting Goods arrived, he would drive past the club three or four blocks. I would watch to see if he had been followed, either by law enforcement or by his own people. (In this situation, both were enemies.) I didn't want us identified by another police agency who might conclude that I was on the pad. Sporting Goods would die in more ways than one should he be identified as my source.

As Sporting Goods drove past the club a second time, he looked for my signal. If he was "clean," I was to do nothing. If I was suspicious that he was being followed, I blinked my headlights as he went past. (I never did, because he never was.)

Then I entered a side door of the club. We picked that particular club because it had very dim lighting. Unless you sat right next to someone, you couldn't see him well enough to identify him. I would walk around the club, observing the other patrons as well as I could. If I saw no one familiar, I went to the side entrance. By now, Sporting Goods was parked in the parking lot. When he saw me come to the door, he knew the place was safe, at least in my opinion. He would then enter by the front door and case the place himself. If he saw nothing that looked suspicious to him, he sat down in a remote booth far from the dance floor. (We had reserved this booth under the name of "Mr. Blue" for every Friday night.) Sporting Goods would order his usual steak sandwich, and I would order fish (since it was Friday), and we would watch the floor show while we talked. After two or three hours—depending on how much he had to tell me—we would depart as we had entered. It wasn't foolproof; it would have been safer to sit in a darkened car. But he enjoyed the night out and so did I.

Sporting Goods used to call me at home, and when I wasn't there he would talk to Jeannie. Jeannie knew who he was and soon they developed a friendship. Occasionally, Jeannie would join us at the supper club.

I remember one time our dog Moose, a huge boxer, got sick with a brain tumor. The vet told us about a new experimental drug being developed by a drug company, not yet available to the public. One day Sporting Goods called my home in my absence. When he asked Jeannie how she was doing, she broke down a little and when he asked what was wrong, she told him about Moose. She also told him that the only chance to save Moose was with an experimental drug not yet authorized for public distribution. Sporting Goods commiserated with Jeannie and hung up. A couple of days later, again in my absence, he showed up at the house and handed Jeannie a package. Our vet couldn't get the drug yet because it hadn't been approved for sale. Sporting Goods hadn't let such legal niceties stop him. He and his bodyguard went to the drug manufacturer and got a "sample." When I asked him that Friday night whether it took muscle or "cumshaw" (money) to obtain that sample, he hushed me up. "You don't want to know," was all he would tell me.

One Saturday some time later, Jeannie answered the phone to hear a woman on the other end. "This sounds silly, I know, but I'm just doing what my husband asked me to do," the woman said. "This is Mrs. Sporting Goods calling for Sporting Goods. Do you make any sense out of that?" Jeannie, of course, made good sense of it. She called me to the phone. The caller repeated what she had told Jeannie.

Then she said, "My husband has had a bad heart attack. He is in the intensive care ward," and she named the hospital. "He wants you to come immediately. He is dying and knows it. He says he wants to talk to you before he passes on. But there is no way you can get in to see him. They won't even let me in the intensive care ward. I'm calling you just to tell you he would have wanted to see you before he died. But there is nothing you can do."

I was in a quandary. I could, perhaps, get into the intensive care ward if I identified myself as an FBI agent and obtained the physician's approval. Even that was problematic. No good doctor would jeopardize a dying man's life, especially when it might excite him to be contacted by the FBI. But I remembered Johnny Bassett's adage: "When in doubt, just go place your body. You never know what serendipitously might just happen." So I drove into Chicago to the hospital.

When I got there I was told that the intensive care ward was on the second floor. I started to walk up. By chance there was a doctor's gown hanging on a post on the stairway. An idea came to me. I took the gown, put it on, and strode into the intensive care ward.

Have you ever noticed that if you look like you own the joint— that if you act like you belong right where you are—nobody questions you? It's true. I sternly asked the nurses in the ward where my friend was. They pointed to his bed. I strode over to it as if I was one of his doctors. I picked up his wrist as if I was checking his pulse. The nurses lost interest.

Sporting Goods was asleep or in a coma. Would I endanger him by shaking him awake? Or could I chance standing there for perhaps hours before the nurses caught on or his real doctor appeared? I shook him gently. He opened his eyes.

"Hi, pal," he said softly. He recognized me.

"Hi, pal," I whispered back. "I'm here. What can I do for you?"

"Nothing you can do," he haltingly got out. "I'm gone, I know that. And it's okay, I'm ready. Too much pain to go on. But the reason I had my wife call you . . . she's gonna have a lot more money than she needs. I've got enough left over for you to be comfortable for the rest of your life. How about it?"

"Jesus," I said in one of the rare times I evoked the Deity outside of prayer. "No, pal, I can't. But I will always remember your offer. You're one hell of a pal. You'll always be in my prayers." And he is, every day.

The strange thing is he didn't pass on right away. He lingered. Every day I would call his wife to determine his condition. I also knew that Sporting Goods had a lifelong mistress. He loved her along with his wife. But the mistress had no way of learning how Sporting Goods was doing. She couldn't call the wife, that's for sure.

On the next visit of "Dr. Roemer" to my friend, he asked me to contact his mistress and let her know his condition. I was to be the only conduit between Sporting Goods and his mistress in his dying days.

But there was a problem. I couldn't let his mistress know who I was. Sporting Goods was so secretive that he didn't want to be identified with me even after he was gone. So I would call the mistress after talking to Mrs. Sporting Goods and pose as "Dr. George." She was to learn of her lover's condition daily from Dr. George. I felt funny, using the wife to keep the mistress advised, but I knew that is the way my pal wanted it.

He died after about three weeks. I sure miss the guy, especially those Friday nights at the supper club.

I had another source who was high up in the ranks of the Chicago mob. As I was leaving Chicago I suggested to him that he continue to work with the FBI but he refused, saying that it was me that he trusted, no one else.

After I left, he got a lot of pressure from my successor, who was the coordinator of source development. When I left, a tremendous gap opened up in the ranks of our sources. The Bureau was upset. They put a lot of pressure on the office to bring the number and caliber of our sources up to the level where it had been before I left. That was virtually impossible because it takes years, even decades, to entice a made guy, no less a capo, to cooperate by furnishing information about the mob. An agent cannot just go out and snap his fingers and obtain the full co-operation of a hard-core mobster. It takes scores and scores of hours over many years to do so. After I left, all the sources I had developed would not cooperate with other agents.

As a result of Bureau pressure, the Chicago office tried to hold on to the mobsters I had developed as sources. They re-fused to continue the relationship with other agents. When con-tacted, some even denied they had ever known me, and all denied that they had ever cooperated with me. What else were they to do, if they had decided to no longer cooperate? Many of them, in fact, had no idea I was reporting what they told me.

I never went out and said, "Tell me all you know about Tony Accardo or Jackie Cerone." My plan of action was always to invite a potential source to lunch or dinner. Then, over a cocktail or a beer or two, I would guide them to the subject in which I was officially interested.

For instance, when Dominic DiBella, the capo on the North Side of Chicago, died, we weren't able to ascertain who his successor was. I went to my source, the made guy who was in the same position as DiBella, and after a few drinks and well into our dinner I said, "We hear that Caesar DiVarco is going to get DiBella's spot as capo on the North Side." My source (not Sporting Goods) came back. "You guys don't have it right. It's Vince Solano."

When I pretended that such information was faulty, he nailed it down for me. "I've already sat down with him. You can take it to the bank. It's Vince Solano."

If I had come straight out and asked my source, "Who is replacing Dominic DiBella as the capo up north?" he very well might have clammed up. He didn't want to be quoted as the source who identified Solano. But when finessed, he did. So when the new coordinator sent agents out to see this guy, he sincerely told them he had never been a source for the FBI.

But the FBI, after I left, put tremendous pressure on this par-ticular source to reinstate his status. When he refused to talk to the new agents, his life for all intents and purposes was ruined.

Except for me, he would have been just another highly placed Chicago mobster. Because of me, the FBI zeroed in on him with every resource available both to the FBI and the Justice Department. They tried to "leverage" him to furnish information and thereby beef up the FBI statistics. This time there was no way I could go to Tony Accardo to intercede. I had to let my friend suffer without help from me.

It's a cruel world out there. I was to think again of the words Tony Accardo spoke to me during our midnight walk: "We're supposed to be the bad guys. I think it's you who are the real bad guys." When a man becomes uncooperative, as my friend did, the FBI can be at least as hard as the mob. The methods differ, but sometimes the outcomes are just as tough.

Although I enjoyed my contacts with the mobsters who I targeted for source development, and although I had great success with them, I knew at all times I was playing with dynamite. Sometimes it exploded.

38 Bye-Bye to Momo

Sam Giancana apparently enjoyed Christmas in Santa Monica with his new love. Then, as Dick Cain had told us, he spent New Year's on the beach at Waikiki.

By the time he returned to his castle in Cuernavaca, things were going very well for him. Although he had needed Cain in the early years of his self-exile, he was now doing well without him. Giancana ruled the gambling empire that Hy "Red" Larner was operating so efficiently, and he was very comfortable at home where Jorge Castillo was keeping the Mexican government at bay. Mo hadn't been granted permanent resident alien status, but after eight years of *temporary* resident alien status, what difference did it make?

On July 18, 1974, Giancana got up around nine, as was his custom. Still in his pajamas, he wondered out into his luxuriant garden, enjoying the bougainvillea and other flowering plants. The air was fresh, the rising sun warm. All was peaceful in Sam Giancana's world. Millions were pouring in from his gaming casinos, both on land and sea. He was in love. His health was good. What more could any man sixty-two years old want in life? It was all his.

But it was about to change. Two men jumped out from behind two large trees. They grabbed Sam. Before he knew what hit him, he was handcuffed and thrown into a car. At first Sam thought they were rivals in the mob, kidnapping him just as he had kidnapped Theodore Roe, the black policy king in Chicago, so many years before. But these men were Mexican and the car they bundled him into was marked "Immigration."

Sam was taken into detention. He was told to take off his pajamas. He was given a blue work shirt and a pair of blue work pants, four sizes too large, without a belt to hold them up.

"I want to call my attorney," Giancana yelled to his captors.

"Fine, go right ahead," one of the officers responded, winking at the other.

Jorge Castillo was nowhere to be found. The Mexican official who had been glad to take Sam's "drop" had been elevated out of his post. He was no longer interested in Sam Giancana. Moreover, the Mexican government was receiving constant inquiries from the United States embassy as to why Giancana was allowed to retain his temporary resident alien status after eight years. These inquiries were beginning to embarrass the Mexicans. Relations between the two neighboring countries were being strained. It was getting a little too "hot," and with Sam's patron no longer taking his drop, the immigration department began to do its work. When that happened, Sam was out of luck. Castillo found he could do nothing. He conveniently left the country when he learned that Sam was to be deported.

And deported he was. In the blue work clothes and the pants much too large, Sam was put on a plane to San Antonio. There, our agents served him with a subpoena. He was then put on a plane to Chicago where the subpoena commanded that he appear before another one of those infernal grand juries.

I was out on the street that morning when my car radio squawked: "Car forty-two, call the office immediately."

Vince Inserra wanted to talk to me. "Bill, your buddy has been thrown out of Mexico," he said. "He's on flight twenty-four coming into O'Hare on American Airlines at eleven-thirty. Thought you might want to be there to greet him."

Ho, ho, ho, it's Mo again, I thought. And in the same con-

course of American Airlines as twelve years ago! This time I'll
be alone, with nobody to hold me back. We'll see what happens
this time if he takes me on. I'd overheard enough of Mo, telling
his guys that I wasn't enough of a man to stand up to him.
This time I decided, if he gave me cause I wasn't going to
hold back.

With that attitude I headed for O'Hare.

Sure enough, here he came. I almost didn't recognize him.
Dick had told me about the white beard, but I still wasn't prepared. He had aged tremendously. And he looked ridiculous in
the work shirt and big pants. He had no baggage—fortunately—
because he needed both hands to hold up his pants. He was
undoubtedly the wealthiest person on that plane, but he looked
like some Italian immigrant landing at Ellis Island, destitute and
frail. Who would ever recognize this man as the successor to Al
Capone?

I stood in his way. He stopped in front of me. "Roemer," he
said very softly, "I should have known you're behind all this."

I started to shake my head, to tell him I had nothing to do
with it. But he continued, "Now look, I'm back here but I don't
want to be. You know all about that, I'm sure. I'm not gonna be
involved in anything anymore. You'll soon find out that I have
nothin' goin' for me here, I'm out of it. So, please, just leave
me alone. Nothin' personal like it was between us before. If it
takes an apology, then this is it. Let's just forget what has been
before."

That sure took the wind out of me. This was an entirely different guy than the Sam Giancana I knew—the swaggering, arrogant mobster.

My entire experience with Giancana flashed before me—all
of our encounters when he had been a bitter, able foe. I recol-
lected all the great satisfaction I'd had over the years, working
"in a tireless effort" to hamper his reign as the proud successor
to Al Capone, as the great Chicago don.

I think at that moment I realized I had won. It had been a
long, hard struggle to neutralize this mob boss—arguably the
most powerful in the country during his heyday in the early and
mid-sixties—but with the help of some great partners and fellow
agents I had mastered the game and truly had become his nemesis. This shell of a man before me now was but a shadow of
the great godfather.

Could I take the credit for bringing him down? Some, but not all. I had hounded him much longer than any other lawman in his history. I had been there almost from the very first day of his reign as the boss in 1957. And I was there to see him, today, in his ignominy. Could this emaciated-looking wreck of a man at one time have been the great Momo?

At that point, Sergeant Jerry Gladden of the Intelligence Unit of the Chicago PD, now the able chief investigator for the Chicago Crime Commission, came up with one of his men. They wanted to question Giancana about the murder of Dick Cain some seven months before, and they wanted him to come downtown to be interviewed.

Giancana turned to me. "Should I go?" he asked.

Should I go! What a change this was! The last time I had seen him, he would have turned on Gladden and said, "You got no paper? Then go fuck yourself!" He would then have turned to me and shouted, "And up *your* ass too!"

I almost felt sorry for the guy. I told him he'd better go, although I knew full well there was no way they could force him since they had no warrant or subpoena. He went.

As we were walking down the concourse to the parking ramp, Gus Kempff arrived with his trusty camera. He had been sent by Inserra to take photos of Giancana. In the old days, Giancana would have hurled insults to any photographer. This day, he looked meekly into the camera and merely frowned.

I was never to see Sam again. I was then developing Sporting Goods as a source, and he confirmed to me that Sam, although physically back in Chicago, was inactive in the mob. The mob wanted no more to do with him, and he was content to leave it that way.

What Sporting Goods also told me, however, was that the mob badly wanted the gambling empire Giancana had put together with Dick Cain, Hy Larner, and Lou Lederer in the Caribbean, Central America, and Iran. Sam took the position that this operation was entirely his, to be shared very sparingly with the mob. That share was represented by his payments to Butch Blasi and Gus Alex, who apparently had offered some assistance. Gussie may have used some of his contacts as leader of the connection guys, and Butch may have lent physical support to his closest associate in the mob. Other than those small payouts, Sam refused to cut the rest of the mob in on this personal conquest. In his opinion, the offshore operation was something he had accomplished when he was no longer with the family.

We left Sam alone. In early 1975, I switched over to C-10 and spent all my time developing sources. Bill Thurman, a young agent on C-1, took over the assignment on Giancana.

He found that Giancana was not often at his residence in Oak Park. I learned from Sporting Goods that Sam was spending a great deal of time in Santa Monica visiting his lady friend, the former actress roommate of Lauren Bacall.

Butch Blasi, his confidant, had switched his mob duties to Joey Aiuppa now that Aiuppa was one of the "Triple A's" who formed the triumvirate running the Chicago family. Blasi was now the appointment secretary-driver-bodyguard of Aiuppa, just as he had been for Giancana when Sam was the boss. However, notwithstanding his official responsibilities to Aiuppa, Blasi still devoted some time to Sam.

In late 1974, Giancana had answered the subpoena served by our agents in San Antonio. He must have been concerned we were going to offer him immunity again and go through the same process, eventually finding him in contempt of court. We had no further interest, however; Sam was now more or less passé in the eyes of the FBI and the Justice Department.

The U.S. Senate Foreign Relations Committee, chaired by Senator Frank Church, was interested in Sam, however, because of his involvement in the CIA-Castro caper. Now that Sam was back, a subpoena was served on him and he was scheduled to testify. First, however, the committee heard from another one of the three mob participants. Johnny Roselli testified at some length.

I didn't think the mob would hold his testimony against him, although any testimony before a congressional committee is frowned upon. Lou Lederer told me that Johnny was broke and had come to Lou for a loan, which Lou gave him. Lou then told me the same thing Dick Cain had said, which was that Johnny was living with his sister in Fort Lauderdale.

One day John Roselli left his sister's home. When he did not return, she notified the police. His body was later recovered from Biscayne Bay. It had been dismembered with a chain saw and stuffed into an oil drum. When the body released its gases as it decomposed, it caused the drum to float even though it had been weighted down.

In May of 1975, Sam was out in Santa Monica with his lady when he became very ill. It was diagnosed as a gallbladder problem. Dr. Michael DeBakey in Houston was recognized as the top surgeon for such problems, and Sam insisted on the best. He was flown to Houston and Dr. DeBakey performed a cholecystectomy.

When he was well enough, Sam returned to Oak Park. There he was attended by his youngest daughter, Francine, her husband Jerry DePalma and by Butch Blasi whenever Butch could divorce himself from his duties with Aiuppa. Daughter Toni was persona non grata with Sam, and Bonnie was living in Arizona. Soon Sam had a relapse. He again insisted on being treated by Dr. DeBakey and was flown back to Houston. After a week or so when his health improved, he sneaked out of the hospital, using the delivery entrance to evade both the Houston PD and the press (which had been tipped off to his presence in Methodist Hospital). He was flown back to Oak Park.

DePalma accompanied Sam on the plane from Houston and the ever-faithful Butch Blasi met him at O'Hare. They took him to the Oak Park home he had clung to all these years, at 1147 South Wenonah, and they helped him into the lavish basement apartment he had furnished for himself. From the upstairs where they lived, Joe DePersio and his wife Ann came down to attend Giancana. (Joe, an old employee of a mob gambling operation, had become Giancana's caretaker years before.)

After Sam took a nap, Jerry and Francine arrived. So did Blasi and Chuckie English, Giancana's other pal from his youth. They had a quiet party, celebrating Sam's return to health and to Chicago.

At about ten, the party broke up. Francine had brought Sam the makings for his favorite meal, one that he could once again enjoy after his gallbladder had been removed—Italian sausage, escarole, and ceci beans. He began to cook it on the stove in his basement apartment.

A squad of the Intelligence Unit of the Chicago PD was watching the house that evening. But their detail was actually focused on the residences of the more active members of the Chicago family who lived in the general area—Spilotro in Berwyn, English and Accardo in River Forest, Aiuppa in Oak

Brook, Cerone in Elmwood Park. They casually noted when Blasi and English left, then lost interest in the Giancana house and went on to bigger things.

After Francine and Jerry left, they discovered that Francine had left her purse at Sam's house. They returned at about ten-fifteen to retrieve it. As they left for the second time, they noticed that Butch Blasi was also returning. At the time, Blasi's return didn't mean anything. They continued on their way.

At ten-thirty Joe DePersio yelled down the stairs to Giancana, asking him if there was anything he wanted. Joe said he was going to watch Johnny Carson. Giancana said no, he was going to cook up his sausage and ceci beans, have that late night snack and then to go sleep.

Whoever was there with him must have been trusted. Sam must have felt comfortable with him. First of all he admitted him into the basement, and then he continued to cook his "Italian." The standard weapon of the mob when a hit can be done at close range is a High-Standard Duromatic with a silencer—a small-caliber, lightweight .22. The killer used seven of the ten bullets in the gun, all at point-blank range, all to the head—in the mouth, under the chin, to the brain. Sam didn't have a chance. He had never given his own victims a chance, so why should he be treated any differently?

The body was discovered by Joe DePersio. He called down just before drifting off to sleep. When he got no response, he went down to Sam's quarters. He found the body, probably just minutes after the deed was done, and turned off the stove so the food wouldn't burn.

There are law enforcement people who believe it must have been Butch. After all, he was seen returning to the scene just minutes before Sam was killed. Sam would have been comfortable with him and would have freely admitted him.

Another reason for suspecting Blasi is that the .22 was subsequently found and, through ballistic tests, identified as the murder weapon. It was discovered on Thatcher Road, on the way from Oak Park to River Forest where Butch resided. It was reconstructed that at the precise time the killer had been headed north on Thatcher, a squad car with siren screaming was headed south on Thatcher. It may have caused the killer to panic, thinking the squad was after him, and to throw the gun into the weeds along the road where it was later found.

I personally don't think it was Butch. I had gotten to know him well. He had once been implicated in a burglary scheme, a petty crime that was far below his mob stature. I talked at length to the witness against him, and even though I didn't believe what the witness was telling us, the case went forward. It was presented to the grand jury, and both Butch and I testified.

We sat together on the bench outside the grand jury room while other evidence was being presented. I told him that after we both had testified, I wanted to stay with him because I had been assigned with Johnny Bassett to arrest him when the true bill had been handed down and the indictment received. I told him that if he wanted to make it hard for us to find him, okay, but we would get him eventually and our investigation would embarrass him in his neighborhood and with his family. When he went in to testify, I told him to wait for me. I said as soon as I finished giving testimony, John and I would stick with him until later in the afternoon, at which point we would arrest him.

I then went in and told the grand jury about my problems with the witness's credibility. Butch waited for me as I had requested, then John and I accompanied him to his home in River Forest to await word that he had been indicted. We would then handcuff him, Mirandize him and bring him back downtown to the Federal Building.

We waited in the guest house by his pool while he served us a nice Italian meal. Inserra, knowing our arrangements, then called me late in the afternoon. The witness had been discredited by my testimony and a no-bill was voted. Butch was not indicted. He was grateful. He understood that I had not wanted to do him any particular favor, but because I had been honest and truthful he had been able to walk. Whenever I saw Butch thereafter we were friendly. Very friendly. I got to know him well as the years went by. Very well.

A big investigation was mounted by local authorities in an attempt to determine the identity of the killer(s) of Sam Giancana. The FBI participated minimally, having no jurisdiction in local murders unless there was some attendant situation, such as obstruction of justice or the killing of a witness called to a grand jury. When John Jones kills Sam Smith, the FBI is not officially involved. So, although we talked to our informants in an attempt to discover information that could be disseminated to the local police, we conducted no active investigation to solve Sam's murder.

It was a gangland slaying, but only one of a thousand recorded by the Chicago Crime Commission after they began keeping statistics (1919). We had no official interest.

But I was interested because the finger of suspicion pointed at Butch. Most of my colleagues and most of the local authorities believed Butch was there—that he either set Giancana up by introducing the killer(s) into the Giancana basement or that he had fired the shots himself. Since I had a reasonable relationship with Butch—for decades, I had been the case agent on his investigation—I went out and talked to him.

It was a cordial conversation, but Butch said to me almost from the beginning, "Mr. Roemer, I have nothing to say to you about it. I won't insult your intelligence by telling you I wasn't there before it happened. But I won't talk to you about it. If you have a warrant or a subpoena, serve me. But if you don't, I say to you in all respect, I'm not going to discuss it with you or with anybody else."

I left it at that.

A subpoena was served on Butch. He was hauled before the Cook County grand jury set up to investigate the case but took the Fifth Amendment and no indictment was ever forthcoming. Several years later, a federal grand jury designed to hear evidence about organized crime was convened and Butch was summoned before this grand jury. When he again invoked the Fifth, immunity was granted to him, just as it had been fifteen years before to the man he was accused of killing. When he followed the pattern of his mentor and, in spite of the grant of immunity, refused to answer the questions of Doug Roller, the federal Strike Force attorney handling the investigation, he was held in contempt of the grand jury. He was sent to the Metropolitan Correctional Center on Clark Street on the far South Side of the Loop. There he spent over a year, but never talked. He is out now. I attempted to reach Butch in the spring of 1989 but was told by his loving wife of many years, Connie, that he has an advanced case of Alzheimer's disease and is no longer lucid enough to know even her. God bless him, he's another guy I pray for daily.

Needless to say, I did not have any remorse for Giancana. Unlike Humphreys, who had died an able adversary and had earned my grudging respect, I had no respect for Giancana. I felt sorry that his life ended the way it had; nobody is gleeful even when a Giancana is disposed of in such a manner. But there was no void in my life, such as there was after Hump's death. As far as I can see, Giancana never brought a bit of good to the world, and it is a far better place without him.

I know Phyllis McGuire feels otherwise, and I give her credit; she had the guts to be seen at his funeral. His then current lady didn't show nor did any of his dozens of other old girls. Neither did the mob. Only Butch and Chuckie showed up. The man left the world just about as he came. Almost nobody cared.

Insofar as is known, his daughters, who were his sole heirs, were left very little. The mob must have finally obtained what they wanted with his murder—his gambling ventures in the Caribbean, Central America, and Iran. Obviously, they didn't hold on to the casino in Teheran very long. They would have needed an Ollie North to handle that.

39 Good-Bye Chicago FBI

The 1970s brought a great deal of change in my personal and professional life. The decade began with the boys leaving home, and it ended with Jeannie and me pulling up stakes and moving to Tucson. This was also the decade in which I had to say ''good-bye forever'' to one of my supervisors and to two of my closest friends.

My son Bill started at Notre Dame, then transferred to the University of Arizona in Tucson. Upon graduation, he took a broadcasting job, and by 1975 he was sports director and sports anchorman at CBS affiliate KOLD-TV in Tucson.

Son Bob was drafted out of high school by the Atlanta Braves, but he decided to go to Notre Dame, where he had an outstanding athletic career in baseball and football. After college, he signed with the Pittsburgh Pirates, and he played for a while in their farm system. Then he left pro ball to become marketing director of an insurance company in Arizona, Colonial.

On a visit to see Bill in Arizona, Jeannie and I got the idea that we'd like to move out there. But it was some time before that happened.

When Bill took the job in Tucson in television, Jeannie and I drove out to see him in 1975. While staying in his home the phone rang one day. It was Vince Inserra.

"Bill," he said, "Peggy Rutland wanted me to call. Maz has suffered a relapse of his leukemia and is in a coma. He may hang on for a while, but they don't expect him to make it."

Maz, just forty-five, was then a unit chief in the Special Investigative Division, responsible for supervision of our organized crime program back in Washington. I had last seen him in November of 1974 when I attended In-Service Training at Quantico and he picked me up on arrival at National Airport. I spent the night at his house.

On December 13, Maz passed away. Since it was logistically difficult to get to Washington for the funeral, I climbed Tucson Mountain at the hour it was being held. Scaling to the top I sat for an hour, saying good-bye to my old partner and pal.

Ralph Hill and Johnny Bassett were both in Washington attending the funeral. John was on temporary assignment as a counselor for a national academy class. Ralph was then a Bureau supervisor, overseeing the organized crime programs of several field offices.

By 1976, however, Ralph had moved to become the assistant special agent in charge (ASAC) in Milwaukee. One night he suffered a massive heart attack. He could barely get to the phone. But he managed to call an emergency number. When the ambulance arrived, he was just about gone.

When I heard the news, I wanted to rush to Milwaukee but was informed by the SAC that Ralph was in intensive care and could not be visited. I decided not to try my "Dr. George" bit, but to wait until he was well enough to be moved to a private room before visiting him. Fortunately after five or six days he was moved, and I hustled up to Milwaukee to visit him in St. Joseph Hospital.

When I walked into the room, Ralph opened his eyes. "Hey, Zip, good to see you." I told him it was greater for me to see *him*. He then picked up the bedside phone and called the office.

An agent came to the phone. "This is Hill," he said. "Would you go out and get me four martinis and bring them to the hospital?"

"Hey, Ralph, I can't drink four martinis, you remember that!" I shouted.

"*You're* not going to drink four martinis, Zipper," he shot back.

When the agent arrived with the martinis, Ralph quickly gulped the first one down. I protested that he had just escaped death—now he was flirting with fortune! He hid the drinks when the nurse came in to give him his heart medicine. Waiting until she left, he gulped down the pill with the second martini. Not all that smart but vintage Ralph Hill.

Ralph was to beat the heart problem, but he later developed Hodgkin's disease. By then, he had remarried and was living in retirement in a condo development in San Jose. Jeannie and I visited him there.

It was the last time I was to see Ralph. After much chemotherapy he had beaten his Hodgkin's disease, but all those treatments took the fight out of him. One night soon after our get-together, Betty rolled over in bed to find Ralph had died quietly in his sleep. The greatest of agents and the greatest of guys—gone. He was fifty-seven. Another devastating personal loss.

John Bassett moved up. He left Chicago with former SAC Dick Held, who became the associate director of the FBI, the number-two position in the Bureau. John became his administrative assistant. That was 1976. Back in Chicago, I missed my old partners; Ralph, Maz, and John were now gone.

Vince Inserra retired and went with the Kemper Insurance Company as the director of security, a job he still holds.

Of the old hands from the days of lockstep—to say nothing about the guys who worked on the bugs—none were left.

I transferred back to C-1 when Vinnie retired. It soon became obvious to me that I was the dinosaur, the old-timer. I could lick any of them, I could outrun almost all of them, but the replacements on C-1 were fifteen to twenty years younger. I really didn't have the old rapport with them that I'd had twenty years before with my old partners.

There is no doubt that I missed the camaraderie. The type of person who can be found in the FBI is very special. It was truly a pleasure to work the long, sometimes hard, but always pleasurable hours I did, because I was working with the greatest bunch of guys I could ever hope to be associated with.

Few of us really "fit the mold" of the public conception of FBI agents. Ralph Hill, for instance, was unique. He had gotten his early training in the Bureau as a member of the pussy posse, the squad investigating white slave traffic, which was officially the nomenclature for prostitution. I remember one night with Ralph when we had a surveillance scheduled on Tony Accardo in River Forest. Since Ralph lived in Melrose Park near River Forest, he invited me to dinner at his house before instituting the tail. I thereupon met his first wife, Billie. I immediately blurted out, "Lord, Ralph, with a beautiful wife like this, why do you spend so much time on Rush Street?" (Rush Street is the nightclub area of Chicago.)

Forever after, Ralph would complain to me that Billie taunted him with my words. Ralph made a point of enjoying whatever he did. But Ralph loved the nightlife, the wine and roses, the fast lane, the bright lights. He loved to discover who was the new girlfriend of Giancana, or Caifano, or Alderisio, and then spend hours and days attempting to develop those girlfriends as informants.

Ralph wasn't a particularly good-looking guy or particularly well built. I don't think he ever exercised a day in his life. But he could attract the ladies. As a result of his activity, he and Billie eventually divorced, and it wasn't until years later when he was the ASAC in Milwaukee that he met Betty and married her.

Another partner who didn't fit the mold was Maz Rutland. Big, strong, handsome, with prematurely gray hair, he was a man the ladies loved and chased. He was a cross between Ralph and me: he loved the nightlife like Ralph, but like me he devoted hours to physical conditioning. He was a better handball player than I was, and we partnered three times a week against John Roberts and Denny Shanahan, two of the other great C-1 agents.

The third partner of my days in Chicago was Johnny B., John Bassett. Nobody ever would accuse him of fitting the mold. In his teens, he had run away from home in Burlington, Vermont, to become a prizefighter in New York City. His manager was a front for the mob. Johnny B. came to the attention of a priest, who encouraged the bright teenager to get his high school diploma. He then joined Jack Dempsey, the old heavyweight champ, in the Coast Guard.

Johnny's savior, the priest, had him enroll at Seton Hall; he worked in the East Orange, New Jersey, Police Department while going to college. There he came to the attention of the resident FBI agent who recognized his abilities and encouraged him to apply for the Bureau. He was accepted and in the early 1960s joined C-1 when Bobby Kennedy influenced Mr. Hoover to intensify the Top Hoodlum Program.

Ralph, Maz, and I quickly recognized Johnny as "our kind of guy." He joined up on many of our escapades, whether on a tail, an interview of a mobster, an installation of a bug, a night with Jim Saine on Rush Street, or a moment of "wining and dining on Mo" with Angelo Girabaldi.

Ralph left me in 1963, Maz in 1966, and John in 1976. I was as lucky as could be to have such great partners. But had fate decreed otherwise, I'm sure that I could have partnered with almost any of the other sixty-five or so agents on C-1. The FBI is unique in picking fine guys.

Perhaps of equal importance are the wives. It is the nature of our jobs to be transferred routinely in our early years, and we work crazy hours. The wives support each other. Emily Liston, Joyce Tyson, and Mary Hazen were all wives of first-office agents like myself in Baltimore when I was working long hours; without their company and moral support, Jeannie's life would have been almost unbearable. The same was true in New Haven. There, Alfreda Sims, Jeannie, and Lola Price kept each other company while their husbands burned the midnight oil. In Levittown, Jeannie had Mary Staples, who was a godsend, particularly since we did not have a car and the shopping center and church were a couple miles away. In Hammond, Indiana, where we lived for a short time while I commuted to Chicago's Loop, Woodie Coffey and Jeannie watched out for each other. And, of course, Peggy Rutland and Elaine Bassett were close friends throughout the Chicago years.

To this day our best friends remain fellow former Bureau employees. John and Elaine Bassett visit us twice a year from their home in Panama City Beach, Florida, and I'm sure the Hills and Rutlands would be as close as ever had Ralph and Maz survived. Wherever I travel on business—and I have made some 240 business trips all over the country since 1980—I get in touch with old pals from the Bureau. The Bureau encourages the Society of Former Agents of the FBI, with over 10,000 active members all over the United States. I make sure I get to the monthly luncheons when I'm in New York, Los Angeles, Chicago, or Las Vegas. "Moose" Nelson and Frank Mellott, stalwart former C-1 squad members, are members of our local chapter in Tucson. Moose was a soundman, a technician, and Frank was the guy who rescued Sandy Smith's cameraman at the Screwy Moore funeral.

There is no way FBI work could be accomplished so well and so pleasurably if it were not for the harmonious relationships we form. Two o'clock in the morning on a stakeout would be a bear if not for the companionship and support of a close pal. I loved almost every minute of my career.

In December 1977, Jeannie and I traveled out to Tucson for the sixth time to visit Bill. Every time we went, we got to love the desert country more. And each time we left, we felt a stronger tug to return. On this occasion, we arrived home a couple of days before Christmas. The contrast in the weather was cataclysmic.

January and February of 1978 in Chicago were two of the worst months of all time. It was even colder and more blizzardy than usual.

I was assigned to be the night supervisor in January from midnight to eight in the morning. Driving in at eleven-fifteen one of those nights, the engine in our 1972 Olds froze up while on the Dan Ryan Expressway. It was seventeen-below that night and snowing. In February I had the same duty again, this time on the four-to-midnight shift. Again, I encountered the hassle of driving home after midnight in the freezing cold.

Thank God I was still enjoying the work. With Bill and Bob

both gone, Jeannie and I had more time with each other, but we still had Tucson on our minds.

Then a guy named Freddie Kane came on the squad. He transferred from Phoenix, but he had worked in Tucson. He told me that the Tucson resident agency was about to start a major investigation of Joe Bonanno, the charter member of the Commission and New York boss of his own family who had taken up residence in the "Old Pueblo."

I thought to myself, if I could have the challenge of going against the famous Joe Bonanno, along with the enjoyment of the lifestyle in Tucson, that would be like heaven.

There were two major obstacles, however. I was over fifty, the minimum retirement age for an FBI agent. (That was why most of my peers were gone—they had retired to start second careers.) There is a rule in the Bureau that once an agent reaches fifty he cannot get an office-of-preference transfer. Also, for me it would be the second office-of-preference transfer, since I had already been granted one when I left New York for Chicago. That was therefore against me.

The other obstacle was a separate rule preventing an agent from transferring directly to a resident agency (RA). You must transfer to the division headquarters and then wait in line to be transferred to an RA.

But I decided to give it a try. John Otto had just been transferred in from Minneapolis as SAC. (Later he was the number-two man in the Bureau.) He didn't know me then, but I gambled he would know my reputation. I went into his office and told him what I had in mind.

He raised his eyebrows. Obviously, an agent over fifty who had already had one o.p. transfer and who was asking for a transfer to a resident agency was asking more than just a bit much. But he promised he would look into it.

Three weeks later as I was working late one night, the new C-1 supervisor called my home in my absence and asked Jeannie, "Are you all packed, ready to move to Tucson?"

Jeannie replied, "I'm not that optimistic."

"Well," he said, "you better be, it just came through!"

"Direct to Tucson?" Jeannie asked, incredulously.

"Chicago to Tucson, direct!" he replied.

We were on our way. I remember, the next night, watching a television special that Jack Brickhouse did on WGN, narrating an anniversary of the Cubs. (Jack is another close pal of mine, as is his wife Pat. He narrated big plays of Gabby Hartnett, Big Bill Lee, Lou Novikoff, Andy Pafko, Ken Hubbs, Gene Baker, Ron Santo, Ernie Banks, Billy Williams, and the other Cub stars down through the ages.) All the way through Barbra Streisand sang "The Way We Were." It was quite nostalgic, which is how I felt. Watching Jack that night, I realized that packing up and moving on after twenty-four years in Chicago was not going to be so easy.

I had to say good-bye to a lot of guys, not only in the office but all over Chicago. I had lunch every working day for three weeks with my closest friends. I sat down with my score of mobster friends who were furnishing me with valuable information and explained the situation. I stopped by Morrie Norman's and said good-bye to the gang. I said good-bye to Bill Fudala and Tommy Russo and the other coaches at Circle Campus.

The office put together a gathering for me, kept small at my request. Since a couple hundred of my best pals had already preceded me, I wanted the party kept to a minimum size. I had already picked out my own going-away present from the other agents. There was a painting I had admired, a view of the Chicago skyline looking from Soldier Field to the Hancock Building. It hangs in our living room today.

But there was another party that I was to find I enjoyed the most. Some other people wanted to say farewell and good riddance—my longtime adversaries in the mob.

40 Good-Bye Chicago Mob

A couple of weeks after my transfer to Tucson had been approved, while I was winding up my work and good-byes, I dropped into Morrie Norman's Restaurant. Ralph Pierce and Les Kruse, the two connection guys, had died,

Ralph in 1975 and Les a year later. Hy Godfrey had moved to San Diego. The restaurant was no longer the prime meeting place, especially since 1974, when Morrie himself had passed away.

On this day, Bill McGuire was there. Bill was the former Chicago police officer who had left the department and had become involved in gambling activities with Pierce, Kruse, Chuckie English, Turk Torello, Joe Ferriola, Donald Angelini, and Dominic Cortina. His activities were entirely benign, insofar as any of the rough stuff was concerned. He was not a made guy, just a gambler who was very popular with everyone who knew him, including me.

When I walked in, Bill came up to me. "I've been waiting for you to show up here one of these days," he said. "Have lunch with me, I want to discuss something with you."

After a few amenities, he said, "Bill, it's a small world. You have met my daughter, although I don't think you put two and two together and figured out who she is. You met her at your son's apartment in South Bend. Her fiancé played pro ball with your son."

No, I hadn't put two and two together. I remember being introduced to a girl at Bob's apartment, but I hadn't known she was McGuire's daughter. Now I recalled a lovely girl who had been at the apartment with her fiancé, a very close friend of Bob's.

"Look," Bill McGuire continued, "you know they are getting married in a couple of weeks and your son is in the wedding party. We'd like you and your wife to come also."

"That's very nice of you, Bill," I said. "Sure, we'd love to come."

"Hold on a minute though, until you know all the facts. There will be a lot of guys there."

"You mean guys I know?"

"Guys you know, guys you have put in jail, guys you'd like to put in jail, guys you have followed, guys you have listened to, all kinds of guys. A lot of them," Bill said.

"Won't that screw up your wedding?" I asked. "How would they feel if I showed up? I'd think that would put a real damper on things. And they might think I was there working rather than just for pleasure."

"Bill," he said, "I've talked to the big guys who are com-

ing—the ones who count. They have thought about it. They
know you are leaving after all these years. They have respect for
you. They remember you were the guy who set up the deal to
keep the families out of it. Some of them were even on your side
with Giancana. A lot of them, like us, never liked that guy, as
you know. They also know why you did what you did with
DeGrazia. All in all, they like the idea of your coming. They're
glad to see you go, but they'd just kinda like to say good-bye.
What do you think?''

"I like the idea, Bill," I replied. "If that is their attitude, I'd
like to respond in kind. I'd like to say good-bye after all these
years as well. But let me talk to Jeannie. She may not be all that
comfortable with it. I'll get back to you.''

When I talked to Jeannie, I found her to be enthusiastic.

"Sure, let's go, it will be fun," she said. "We like the couple.
Bob is going to be an usher, and it sounds like it'll be a good
time.''

So we decided to go. In April of 1978, we went first to the
wedding in a church, and then for a short private reception at
Bill's house.

Donald Angelini and Dominic Cortina were there. Today,
both are capos in the Chicago family. I had arrested Donald
twice, had known him since the late 1950s and had encountered
him many times over the years. He and Cortina, who is called
"Large," grew up together and have remained closest friends
ever since. I spent about fifteen or twenty minutes with them at
Bill's house. Now that it was all over and I was no longer going
to be the Chicago mob's nemesis—at least in my own mind—
we relaxed in each other's company and had a pleasant chat. I
introduced Jeannie and they introduced their wives. I had met
Donald's wife when I had arrested him in their home in the Lou
Bombacino case and knew her to be an attractive and very pleasant lady.

Cortina, although not as polished and articulate as Angelini,
is of the same stripe. Not your Giancana, Alderisio, DeStefano,
or Spilotro. I have no reason to believe that Donald ever participated in any "heavy" stuff. He made his bones in the outfit by
the weight of his intelligence and his unique expertise in gambling. They call him the "Wizard of Odds." I don't know
whether his partner, "Large," is Donald's equal, but I suspect
that he is.

I can only hope that these current mob leaders have the nerve and muscle to continue to enforce the Chicago family edict against narcotics. I can see how, if the current leadership loses control, things could deteriorate. If the Chicago mob were to branch out into narcotics—as some families in the East have done—as far as I'm concerned, their members would become the very dregs of society.

Following the private reception at Bill and Marilyn's home we moved to the country club where the public celebration was held. Sure enough, there were thirty or thirty-five guys I immediately recognized, guys I had confronted many times during my twenty-one years on the organized crime squads of the Chicago FBI. Some I had arrested, many I had tailed. A couple I had monitored during the days of the bugs. Many came over, shook my hand and said the same thing. "Good luck, but I can't say I'm sorry to see you go."

One guy who came up to me said that Butch Blasi was keeping a low profile in view of the investigations swirling around his alleged involvement in the Giancana murder. Though he would not be there that evening, he asked that I be thanked one last time for not "framing" him. I assumed he was referring to the burglary case where I had testified to my doubts as to the credibility of the witness against Blasi.

Bill McGuire brought a guy over. "Bill," he said, "I don't think you've ever met this fella, at least not personally. I think you ought to talk."

It was Joe Ferriola. They call him Joe Negal and Joe Nick in the outfit. He was then a capo, at least for all practical purposes. Fifi Buccieri had died of throat cancer and his successor Turk Torello was also terminally ill. Ferriola was running the West Side faction of the mob in 1978. Moreover, he had taken over all gambling operations in the entire Chicago area. Donald Angelini and Dominic Cortina were his two key aides at the time.

I later found out that Ferriola ruled with an iron hand. Al Pilloto, the capo in the southern suburbs, was shot on a golf course shortly after Ferriola took over. The theory was that he was shot either because he resisted the inroads of Ferriola, Angelini, and Cortina into his territory or because he didn't, and his own men took him out. In any event, the Ferriola Westsiders soon took over the whole Chicago area for gambling, the life-blood of organized crime.

At the wedding, Ferriola and I just chatted for fifteen minutes or so. I quickly recognized the inner power of the man. He may not have had the quiet power of Tony Accardo or the fierce arrogance of Sam Giancana, but I recognized in him the kind of steel that was a cross between Murray Humphreys and Accardo. Diplomacy and statesmanship first, but the iron fist close behind.

Events were to bear out my estimation of the man. When Ferriola took over as absolute boss in January of 1986, several recalcitrants were killed in quick order. The victims included Tony Spilotro, the mob's man in Las Vegas, who had gotten too big for his britches. The mob soon learned that the new man at the top, Ferriola, was nobody's patsy.

That April evening as I stood at the country club talking with Ferriola, I said to myself, "Kid, if you were going to stay here, this is the guy you would focus on. This is the guy you would devote most of your attention to." He had the charm of Hump, the brains of Accardo, and the strength of Giancana at his prime. He was not someone to be dealt with casually.

As a matter of fact, one of the last things I said to agents at the office before I left Chicago, was, "Keep an eye on Joe Negal, I betcha he will be the top man here soon." How right I was.

The evening was most enjoyable. Jeannie enjoyed it almost as much as I did. I would whisper to her, "See that guy with the blonde in the green dress? That's Georgie Colucci—used to be with Ralph Pierce. You've heard me talk about him."

Many of the people she had seen on television or in the newspapers or heard me talk about, she now saw in person. And it was truly a lovely wedding. I don't use that word "lovely" much, but that's what this was. The bride was gorgeous, the groom was the handsome athlete-intellectual, and no expense was spared to make it a truly memorable occasion.

I was to consider that my farewell party from the Chicago mob. They were glad that they were getting rid of their self-acclaimed nemesis, but they were saying good-bye with class. But even without that it would have been a wedding of all weddings.

Jeannie, Bill, Bob, and I have kept in touch with the couple. They are doing well, raising Bill and Marilyn's grandsons and rising high in the business world.

In late 1987, seven years after I had retired from the FBI, I was to call Donald Angelini. A client in San Francisco was having a major problem with two made guys in Chicago who were attempting to muscle into his business. I thought it could be handled by my talking to someone higher up in the mob who could straighten those two bozos out. I called Donald at his home in the western suburbs. I told him vaguely what I wanted to come see him about. He agreed to see me at any time. Then he told me, "Your friend, Bill, is dying of a brain tumor. It's just a matter of time. You might want to call him."

When I did, Bill was his usual gracious, winning self. When I think of hoods, I don't think of Bill McGuire. He associated with them, but he was not one of them. He was a gambler, not a mobster. It didn't seem like he was dying, although he told me of his illness. I told him I'd be in touch on my next trip to Chicago—one that I make several times a year either for the Chicago Crime Commission or for private clients having problems with organized crime figures.

Two weeks later, I got a call. Marilyn wanted me to know that Bill McGuire had passed on. I was extremely sorry. Another old friend had joined my daily litany.

41
Hello Tucson; Hello Bonanno

I drove to Tucson from South Holland by myself, a twenty-seven-hour drive, door to door. The next day, May 25, 1978, I reported to the Tucson resident agency and met my new boss, Tom McGorray. He told me he was very happy to have me, but not for the reason I expected. He was a fine handball player, and there was no one else in the office who could give him a game.

Within a matter of a couple hours we were on our way to the Old Pueblo Club to test each other out. I discovered that he was a fierce competitor, a very poor loser. He was someone I would not beat very often.

I was very pleasantly surprised by the high level of professional talent among the agents. I found them to be top drawer. On the orders of "Bud" Gaskill, the SAC in Phoenix—the headquarters city to which Tucson reported—I was assigned to work organized crime exclusively. In Tucson there were two major mobsters—first and foremost, Joe Bonanno, but also Pete Licavoli, the Detroit capo. Bonanno had brought two of his aides from New York City with him—Charlie "Bats" Battaglia and Pete Notaro. There were a dozen or so other organized crime figures in Tucson, but none of these began to approach the three hundred made guys in Chicago.

At first I moved in with my son Bill. Later, Jeannie and her mom followed me out and we found a home in the Tucson Mountain foothills.

Soon after I arrived in the RA, I got a call from Jack Smythe, the supervisor of the Organized Crime Program in Phoenix. The program in Tucson was under his direction. He told me he wanted me to take over the investigation of Bonanno. It was to be an intensive investigation, not a lockstep but an all-out effort to discover all we could about the mobster. Once and for all, we wanted to know whether this leader of a New York family was in violation of any federal statute or, as he claimed, whether he had merely retired to Arizona.

I took Smythe's call at my desk. When he told me what he wanted, I immediately said I did not feel it was in the best interests of the investigation that I be put in charge. I had decided, as soon as I received my transfer, that I would not come into Arizona as a self-acclaimed heavy, a cigar smoker, and throw my weight around. I wouldn't assume that I knew it all or that I was in any way superior to my new fellow agents.

I had already met the other three agents assigned exclusively to organized crime investigations in Tucson. These included Bill Christensen, who was the case agent on Bonanno; Donn Sickles, who had been a Bureau supervisor back at SOG; and Louis "Skip" George, who had the ticket on Licavoli. I was greatly impressed with all three of them.

When I told Smythe that I didn't think the case should be taken from Christensen—who had been working on Bonanno for years—he seemed very surprised. Gruffly, Smythe hung up.

I looked over my shoulder. Who had been listening to every word of my conversation but Bill Christensen. He obviously had been warned that Smythe was calling me and that he would be offering me the ticket on Bonanno. He smiled at me. I felt good that I had refused the offer.

It was at that moment that I felt that I had been accepted into the Tucson RA and become one of the guys. Christensen, Sickles, George, and I worked closely together from then on.

We started our work on Joe Bonanno. Bonanno was one of the dinosaurs of organized crime. Only Tony Accardo could match his tenure as a mob leader, and it had taken Accardo much longer to climb to the top of his family.

Joe Bonanno's autobiography, *A Man of Honor*, provides a good account of his exploits. He was a product of the Castellammarese Wars in New York. When those wars between the rival mobs in New York were settled, Joe was selected to be the boss of one of the five families that was to rule organized crime in New York City. At a meeting in New York in 1931, Joe was named a charter member of the Commission, the ruling body of all the families across the country. Law enforcement discovered that Commission when Little Al gave us the Accardo-Giancana conversation in September 1959.

Bonanno continued to rule his family of the La Cosa Nostra until 1964. At that time, I had had an oblique hand in his fortune. He had been in Canada in the summer of 1964; as we knew from Little Al, he had been in trouble with his fellow Commission members. We had learned that Giancana had problems with Bonanno and disliked him greatly. Later, we were to learn from Bonanno's scribblings in his home that at one Commission meeting, Albert Anastasia, a New York boss equal to Bonanno, had told Giancana to shut up or he would put "his big finger up his *culo*," (his rear end) and send him back to Chicago, *"arreso,"* (crying uncle). Giancana obviously had endeared himself to his colleagues on the Commission about as much as he had to me. What we didn't find out, however, was how Giancana had reacted to Anastasia's threat. Knowing Giancana, I'm sure he got his revenge in some form.

When we learned that Bonanno was flying from Canada through O'Hare and then to New York, the New York office of the FBI obtained a subpoena for Bonanno, calling for his appearance before a federal grand jury. The Bureau sent the subpoena to Chicago and asked Maz Rutland, Christy Malone, and me to serve it on Bonanno at the airport. We did. Then we spent about an hour that afternoon interviewing Bonanno in the presence of his son, Salvatore (who is called "Bill") and his attorney, Al Creiger. I had gotten to know Bonanno slightly, therefore, before I arrived in Tucson.

Bill Christensen, Donn Sickles, "Skip" George, and I soon had a conference with the agents of the Arizona Drug Control Agency. This law enforcement unit had originally been set up by Senator Dennis DeConcini when DeConcini was the county attorney. It was the host agency of the Rocky Mountain Strike Force, also called the Rocky Mountain Information Network, a grouping of five states—Nevada, Utah, Colorado, New Mexico, and Arizona—that had banded together to fight organized crime and narcotics activity.

At the conference I learned that for some years the FBI and the drug agents were engaged in a surreptitious activity that had given them considerable evidence of Bonanno's involvement in organized crime. What they were doing was picking up Bonanno's garbage twice a week.

Now, we had never done that in Chicago. But we didn't have a mobster who wrote notes to remind himself of his agenda for each day and then tore them into four pieces and threw them in his garbage! For instance, one of the notes Bonanno had written to himself—as I was shown at the conference—appeared to implicate him in the murder of Frank Bompensiero. "Bomp" had been a capo of the Los Angeles family in San Diego, and he had also been a great source for the FBI. Bomp had been uncovered and murdered as he left a phone booth in San Diego. As in the killing of Sam Giancana, the weapon was a .22. One of Bonanno's notes indicated he had something to do with Bomp's murder.

At that conference we began to develop a further strategy for the investigation of Bonanno. The purpose of the grand jury was to look into organized crime activity in southern Arizona, Tucson in particular. Bonanno, being the most prominent LCN member in the area, was a prime target. We did not intend to employ the same immunity strategy that we used against Giancana, but we did want Bonanno to appear before the grand jury. We decided that I was the one who would serve a subpoena calling for Bonanno's appearance before the investigative grand jury.

I caught up with Joe at the post office, walked up to him, identified myself, and served him the paper.

I then said to him, "Joe, you probably don't remember me but I am one of the FBI agents who served the subpoena on you at O'Hare in Chicago."

"Bill, you were a young, handsome man in those days!" Bonanno announced in his heavily accented voice.

Hey, thanks a lot. I hadn't noticed I had ever been handsome, but I also hadn't realized that I changed all that much in the past fourteen years. Bonanno knew just how to hurt a guy.

We chatted for a while about mutual friends in Chicago—Ricca, Accardo, Humphreys, and Giancana. He told me he had respected Hump. I gained the impression (reinforcing my view) that Bonanno hadn't cared much for my old adversary Sam and that Accardo was not his favorite, either. I then mentioned that I was a friend of an old adversary of his, Warren Donovan, a tough New York agent. He recalled the time years before when another family member of the LCN had beaten up FBI agent Pat Foley. The FBI in New York had entered the church, interrupting the funeral of a mobster until the gun taken from Foley was given back. All this was like reminiscing with an old friend. And my only job at that point was to serve a subpoena.

But I saw a lot of Bonanno most of the time I was in Tucson.

According to the plan we devised, I was assigned to be in charge of the street surveillances of Joe. I guess I had done that once or twice before! Our plan was to follow Joe (surreptitiously, of course) and to learn the location of the many phones in Tucson that he was using. He, like any other self-respecting hood, would never use his home phone. Instead, he moved around the city using public phone booths. We wanted to learn what he was saying and who he was saying it to.

We code named Bonanno "Lone Ranger" for car-radio purposes. We called his gray Cadillac "Silver" and we called his home "the nest." (He lives at 255 East Sierra Vista Drive, near the posh Arizona Inn.)

After three weeks or so of full-time tailing, we turned up seven locations where Bonanno used the phone more than once. They were at the post office at Plumer and Speedway where I had served him; at Himmel Park, a city park; at St. Mary's Hospital in the third-floor reception area; at the Woods Memorial Library, inside the lobby; at the Thomas-Davis Medical Clinic, inside the lobby; at the Walgreen's Drugstore at Speedway and Campbell; at a public phone in the Stone-Grant Shopping Plaza; and at a gasoline station at Speedway and Tucson Boulevard.

We found that he was regularly picked up by either of his two underlings, Pete Notaro or Tony Cacioppo. We code named Notaro "Junk Man" and Cacioppo "Shorty."

At that point, Bill and Donn prepared an affidavit requesting court authority to eavesdrop on Bonanno's conversations. They had to be specific as to the location of the phones: that was the purpose of the tails.

The authority, called "Title III authority," was granted by the courts in Tucson. This approval, named after the title in the Omnibus Crime Control and Safe Streets Act of 1968, grants law enforcement agencies the right to wiretap phones and eavesdrop through microphones, but only after approval by a court. The intelligence developed through these methods is, unlike Little Al's, now admissible in court.

Our technique was for me to lead several agents, some of whom were sent down from Phoenix to bolster our manpower, on the tail of "Lone Ranger." When he approached one of the seven phones for which we had Title III authority (and *only* then because we listened to nobody else's calls on those phones), I would radio Skip as to which phone Bonanno was about to use, and he would then activate the tap on that phone and record Bonanno's conversation.

We discovered that Joe was orchestrating the strategy to be used by his two sons, Salvatore (Bill) and Joe junior, in a federal case in which they were defendants in San Jose, California. The evidence clearly showed that Joe senior was attempting to obstruct the proceedings of the grand jury by coaching the witnesses before they appeared. This was a federal crime.

On St. Patrick's Day we struck. A combined band of FBI agents and drug control agents armed with a search warrant raided Bonanno's residence. When he refused to come to the door when we knocked, I was the first one over his fence. I went around back—braving the snarls and barks of his large doberman "Greasy"—and through his side door. We charged into the house to find Bonanno in his bedroom, on the phone, attempting to call Notaro or Cacioppo or perhaps his attorneys.

I showed him the search warrant. It was my job to stay with Bonanno and prohibit him from impeding the search in any way. Up until that time, Joe and I had been somewhat friendly.

But now he was really miffed. At that point, we were not up against a strong physical adversary. Joe Bonanno was seventy-three in 1979; physically he was nowhere near his peak. Furthermore, he had few of his henchmen at his command. Giancana could quickly summon a Butch Blasi with his machine gun as he had threatened to do at O'Hare, or DeStefano and Spilotro with their guns—or any number of the other three hundred made guys in Chicago. But Bonanno had less than a handful of his New York wise guys. We did not feel threatened. After what I had gone through in the crucible that was Chicago, this was like taking candy from a baby.

The search lasted most of the day. Joe has a basement office in his home that contained what he calls his "buco," a safe. He also had a concealed safe in the cement floor of a closet in his bedroom. Christensen, Sickles, and George, along with drug control agents, conducted the search. I detained Bonanno in the living room. Fortunately his wife had left prior to our arrival and was not to return until after we left. She was visiting her son, Joe junior, in Safford, a correction facility.

As soon as we arrived, Joe felt sick. I therefore called his personal physician, Dr. Kohl, who came immediately. We took Joe into one of his bedrooms, where he became nauseated and threw up. Dr. Kohl gave him some medicine and we attempted to get him to lie down, which would have made the whole procedure much easier. But he remained on his feet, attempting to go to his basement to see what the agents were finding. He finally called one of his three sets of attorneys, a young Tucson lawyer named Steve Hoffman, who brought his assistant with him. I patiently explained to them what we were doing and exhibited the search warrant, which they agreed was all above-board. There was nothing they could do to prevent the ongoing search of the house.

I never had to restrain Joe physically. But several times I placed myself in a position between him and the door to the basement office, blocking his way. He implored Hoffman to tell me I had no right to prevent him from going anywhere he wanted in his own house. Hoffman repeatedly asked me, as did Joe, what I would do if Joe tried to physically push me aside. I merely replied, "I hope you won't try. I don't want it to come to that." Frankly, I didn't intend to physically restrain the old man, and I would not have if he had disobeyed my wishes. However, he never did.

I have seen what I have previously described as the "Mob illness" before. Some organized-crime fighters have noted that mobsters feign illness on many occasions to evade congressional hearings and court appearances.

Bonanno, in my opinion, tried a similar type of evasion when he feigned a kidnapping in 1964 in New York City. That was to evade further grand jury appearances in response to the subpoena I had served on him at O'Hare. (He claims that the kidnapping was genuine, but I have serious doubts about that. He remained away from the demands of the grand jury for eighteen months, and it was only after his attorney realized the government had lost interest in his appearance that he showed up again.)

And I may have been wrong when I interpreted Joe's illness, that St. Patrick's Day in 1979, as being feigned. I assumed from Bonanno's background, as an active participant in the Castel-lammarese Wars, as a charter member of the Commission and as an active leader of his own family of the La Cosa Nostra from 1931 until at least 1964, that he was a tough mobster. However, from my observance of him in 1964 and again during this period in 1978 and 1979, when he was an old man in his seventies, he had lost whatever courage and fight he had had in his glory years. To me, he was a constant whiner.

I had seen it happen also to Giancana, although to be fair

Giancana quietly gave up the fight. He took the medicine dished out to him. Bonanno did not. He complained, he cried, he got sick—anything to gain sympathy. I'm sure some of it was physical. But he did not live up to the "tradition" he speaks about so much in his book, at least not in the days that I knew him.

Most of his old confederates came to violent ends. Those who didn't faded away with their self-proclaimed "honor" intact. The Joe Bonanno I know is a far cry from the other dinosaur I know, Tony Accardo. Both are relatively the same age and in the same health. But one is spending his last years as a crybaby, while the other is still the grizzly bear.

Perhaps, in view of the recent episode in Santa Monica, I should wish that the bear would lose his claws and "do a Bonanno!" I have no respect for or fear of the whiner who lives just several miles from me. But as for the bear who lives hundreds of miles away, I have grudging respect for him. And, yes, perhaps I should have a little fear of someone like Accardo.

42 Good-Bye to the FBI But Not to the Mob

Based on the evidence we had developed by searching through the trash, and conducting the Title III telephone taps and the St. Patrick's day search, we were ready to indict Joe Bonanno for obstruction of the federal grand jury, which was hearing evidence against his sons in San Jose.

When it came time for his arrest, Joe quite typically took the easy way out. His attorneys made an arrangement with the United States attorney's office to surrender him to us in the FBI office in Tucson. I greeted him when they arrived, took him through the fingerprinting and mug shot photo procedures, and then escorted him to the U.S. marshal's office.

Soon after that, I found there was little left for me in the FBI. The challenge had been met. In Chicago I felt I had left the Organized Crime Program in great shape. In Tucson the "big guy" Bonanno had been indicted and was on his way to conviction and prison, and the number-two menace Pete Licavoli was down with a terminal illness.

For a couple of months I worked on the "Joe Punks" who were left in Tucson. I also worked hard to get myself into good physical shape. Tommy McGorray transferred to Sacramento. When he left, I pretty much gave up handball but I got heavily involved in weight lifting and road racing, entering all the 10-kilometer and 15-kilometer road races I could find. Jeannie joined me, not only in the daily training runs but also in the races.

The lifestyle in Tucson was just as we had expected. We still consider it as we did when we first came out in 1975, as our "vacation spot." When I'm at home, which these days in my "after life" is every other week, I get up before the sun and watch it come up over the Rincon Mountains. I tend our grapefruit, orange, fig, lemon, lime, peach, and apricot trees. I hike in the desert with Jeannie and with our dogs Rex and Salty each morning. I lift weights every other day and do my calisthenics and shadowboxing. I play tennis with Bill and golf at the El Rio golf course near our home. Life has been very good to us.

But the challenge of my work seemed to fade after the indictment of Joe Bonanno in 1980. At fifty-three, I was just a year and a half from forced retirement at the age of fifty-five.

Then the offer came. The Rocky Mountain Strike Force, aka The Rocky Mountain Information Network, decided that I would be the man to head their organized crime division. It seemed to me to be the perfect solution to my malaise. The Arizona Drug Control Agency with which I had worked on the Bonanno case was the host agency for the Rocky Mountain agency. Their headquarters were in Tucson. I could continue to live the lifestyle I loved, and I could work just ten minutes away.

Just as important, I would be able once again to match wits with the Chicago mob. An integral part of the job would be focused in Las Vegas, and I would frequently travel to Las Vegas, Denver, Salt Lake City, Albuquerque, Santa Fe, Reno, Lake Tahoe, Colorado Springs, and Phoenix. I negotiated to be allowed to take Jeannie with me whenever she wanted to go—

in the private airplane owned by the network. With my pension amounting to some $45,000 a year now, my income would substantially exceed what I was making in the FBI in 1980. I enthusiastically accepted the job.

But fate reared its pretty head. After I had accepted the job but before I put my papers in, I got a call from a guy I had known of but had never met. His name was Clarence Newton and he had been a firearms instructor at the FBI academy in Quantico. He had retired from the Bureau several years before and had become director of security for Ronald Reagan when Reagan was the governor of California. He was now a private investigator in Sacramento.

"Newt" told me that he was the investigator for the defense team representing the *Sacramento Bee*, a newspaper in Sacramento. The paper and its ace crime reporter Denny Walsh were being sued for an article Walsh had written and the *Sacramento Bee* had published about organized crime in Palm Springs. Sinatra, who had been described in the article as being number one on a list of organized crime subjects and associates who reside in eastern Riverside County—the Palm Springs area, as maintained by the Riverside County sheriff's office—threatened through his attorney to sue for libel. The suit, however, was never brought after his attorney, Mickey Rudin, talked to the sheriff and confirmed that indeed there was such a list and that indeed Sinatra's name was right on top. Shortly thereafter a member of Sinatra's entourage, a Palm Springs car dealer, did bring a suit over the same article with Rudin representing him.

Newton asked if he could come to Tucson to see me. He had been introduced to me over the phone by Skip George, and I quickly agreed to talk to him. I had been the case agent in Chicago when there were allegations linking the Palm Springs car dealer to Gussie Alex through the dealer's partner in a Skokie auto agency, Henry Susk. There were alleged to be other links to Les Kruse, who used the agency as an office, and to Pat Marcy. We had monitored conversations at least once between the dealer and Marcy at Shade. When he learned that I was retiring, Newt asked me if there was any way I could join up with him and help him investigate the case. He would pay me twenty-five dollars per hour—which in those days I considered pretty good—and all expenses to travel first class with him to Chicago, Palm Springs, Sacramento, and Las Vegas to conduct the investigation.

Eager to take on the case, I worked out a postponement of my timetable for reporting to the Rocky Mountain job.

On the day of my retirement from the FBI—February 29, 1980— the Tucson RA, with Donn Sickles in charge, threw a real wing-ding of a retirement party for me. It was held at the Arizona Inn, the luxurious Tucson resort. Some old pals from Chicago showed up to pay their respects, and many of my fellow agents made short farewell talks.

They presented me with the actual credentials I had carried for almost thirty years mounted on a wooden plaque, including the FBI shield and my three service awards. There was also another plaque "in appreciation for a career of dedicated service," which listed the field offices I had served in. Still a third plaque "To The Rock—From the Tucson RA" was signed by each of the guys and gals in Tucson. Finally, a shield with a pair of boxing gloves attached was inscribed "William F. Roemer, Jr.—Keep Punchin'—From Your Associates, Tucson, Arizona, February 29, 1980." ("Keep Punchin' " is a regular salutation I give my friends and contacts.)

It was a great send-off. I had spent the week previous to my retirement working on a murder case on the Fort Huachuca army base in Sierra Vista, about thirty miles from Tucson. I was to realize immediately that I was no longer a member of the FBI when, at about eleven o'clock that night as we were lingering over our farewells, the call came that a badly wanted federal fugitive had been located, holed up in Tucson. All my fellow agents, or at least those who had been my fellow agents up to that moment, piled out to participate in the thrill of the capture. I was abruptly left behind. It was no longer any concern of mine, at least not officially. That's when it hit me. After thirty years, I was no longer an FBI agent!

There is a Latin maxim: *Persona est homo cum statu quodam consideratus*. A person is a man considered with reference to a certain status. The status I had lived with for three decades had been lifted from me. It was a strange feeling. There are, of course, loftier positions in this world than that of an FBI agent. But for me it was the perfect niche. As I look back, I see it was the ideal job for me, one I always reveled in.

The FBI motto puts it succinctly: Fidelity, Bravery, Integrity. I tried to be all of that at all times. Even though we have had a handful of agents who have not fit the mold, have slipped through the intensive background investigation, or who changed once they became FBI agents, I consider FBI agents, no matter what their color or gender, to be the greatest. I was so proud for so many years to be a part of that outstanding organization—along with Notre Dame and the Marine Corps, two other great institutions I have been a part of.

Now it was all about to change. I had identified myself in my thoughts as an FBI agent, from the age of twenty-four. Now, at fifty-three, I had just thrown off the mantle. How would I react to that?

Thanks to my after life, the second career that closely mirrors my first, the adjustment has been easier to bear. I still fight against the mob, though now privately. I still visit the Tucson RA where many of the people I worked with remain; and I get into Chicago four or five times a year and visit the FBI office there. I work with ex-agents in Chicago, Las Vegas, Los Angeles, San Diego, San Francisco, and New York.

Almost all ex-agents belong to the Society of Former Special Agents of the FBI, and we have annual conventions and quarterly regional meetings. Each area has an active chapter, and I therefore have lunch monthly with the twenty-five or so members of the Tucson chapter and the couple hundred in Chicago, when I happen to be there during one of their monthly luncheons.

So the umbilical cord hasn't really been severed. Mr. Hoover was once said to have announced that "there is no such thing as an ex-FBI agent." Once in, never out, it seems. Thomas Wolfe said you can never go home again. In some ways that is true—times and places change. But I still get that special feeling when I'm with an old colleague, or when I enter the Chicago or Tucson office. I miss the banter and the needling, the shared dangers of a bug installation or an active extortion case, the long hours on tails and bugs.

My solution has been to throw myself completely into my second career. The Monday following my Friday retirement I was on my way with Newt to Chicago to start work on the libel case brought by that car dealer from Palm Springs.

For a couple of weeks we contacted old friends in law enforcement who knew the score. We also reviewed the records of the business relationship between the auto dealer and his partner Henry Susk, the close pal of Gussie Alex.

Then I got hold of Bill McGuire. (That was in 1980; Bill died in 1987.) We had lunch at Crane's, a restaurant then near the corner of Washington and Michigan Avenues, across the street from the Chicago Public Library. I explained to Bill what I was doing.

"Here's what I'd like you to do, Bill," I said. "I'd like you to get word to Gussie and to Tony Accardo that we fully intend to bring them into this case. We have developed sufficient evidence to show that both have had such a close relationship with the auto dealer that we will be able to get a subpoena from the judge in Palm Springs ordering their depositions. I think they will realize that I know enough to assemble some very interesting questions for them. They will either answer, which will help our side, or they will take the Fifth, which will badly hurt their case and prove most interesting to a jury."

"I don't have direct access to Accardo and Alex," said Bill. "But I'll talk to the people I'm close to, and you can rest assured that Accardo and Alex will get the word pronto." Three weeks later, the auto dealer withdrew his suit.

"That was good work, Roemer," said Newt. "Say, look, I've got another libel case—this one in Fresno. Do you think you could push your job back another month or two with that Rocky Mountain bunch and come to Fresno and work with me on this one?"

"What do I know about Fresno?" I replied. "I've never been there, and in fact hardly know where it is."

"It's in the San Joaquin Valley, at the foot of Yosemite," he said. "You'll like it. We'll contact the hoods there and put the pressure on them like you did on Accardo and Alex."

We did just that. We even went to the ranch of Joe Sica, reputedly the organized crime boss of Fresno. It was not quite as quick as in the case brought by the car dealer, but eventually the Fresno case was settled and we won that one, as well.

Now Jack Barron approached me. Barron was another ex-FBI agent, the former supervisor of the "OC" squad in Los Angeles. The owners of La Costa, the posh resort north of San Diego, were suing *Penthouse* magazine. One of the plaintiffs was Moe Dalitz, the godfather of Las Vegas, the old associate of Accardo,

Humphreys, Ricca, and Giancana. Would I help Barron on that case against Dalitz?

I decided that this work was just as interesting as the work with the Rocky Mountain people would be. In addition, it had two advantages. One, my fees were escalating considerably from the twenty-five-dollar-per-hour plus expenses that I had taken on the Palm Springs libel case. Secondly, I was able to schedule my travel so that I would be on the road one week and home all the next.

I went to Gene Ehmann at the Rocky Mountain Information Network. He understood my position. We agreed that I could back out of my commitment to them. It turned out for the best, because a couple years later the Arizona Drug Control Agency had some internal problems and was disbanded. Since that was the host agency for the Rocky Mountain agency, I would have had to move from Tucson in order to stay with the Rocky Mountain group.

Instead, I opened my own private investigative consulting agency, called Roemer Enterprises, Inc. I continue to live in Tucson. Between 1980 and mid-1990, I made some 240 business trips around the country and to London, Hawaii, and San Juan. Most of my work is in Las Vegas, where I have had six cases, and in Chicago. In 1983, working as a special consultant on organized crime for the Chicago Crime Commission, I testified before the U.S. Senate Permanent Subcommittee on Investigations, offering a history of organized crime particularly in Chicago (which you'll recall from Chapter 4).

I have also worked extensively in New York City, where I am under retainer from a prominent New York law firm to handle their organized crime work from Chicago to the West Coast, including San Francisco, Los Angeles, Reno-Tahoe, and many other places. This work involves almost anything clients need when they are having problems with mob figures.

All in all, I have found the past ten years to be as challenging as my Bureau career. And much more lucrative.

With much of my recent business in Las Vegas, and with all the knowledge I acquired working the Chicago family (the dominant mob in Vegas) for more than twenty years, I am now most comfortable in Vegas and consider it my second city in terms of opportunities to be a gangbuster. I don't yet consider myself the arch foe of the Las Vegas bad guys, as I was in Chicago. But I don't feel out of place as I stroll the Strip or Glitter Gulch holding my head high, knowing I understand where the bodies are buried.

The question I am often asked by talk show hosts and callers to those shows is, "Aren't you afraid, now that you are no longer in the FBI, that the mob will come after you?"

My stock answer to that is that I really don't think about it. I would be most concerned if I felt that Jeannie, Bill, and Bob or the grandkids, Chris, Matt and Tim, were in any danger. But they are not; the "family pact" still holds and I don't do anything in my after life to violate it. As for myself, I guess I'm fair game. But I have gotten calloused after thirty-nine years in this business, officially and privately. If I were to worry about things like that, I would forget the challenge and the competition. I'd "retire retire."

As of this writing, the Chicago mob is in a state of flux. On March 11, 1989, Joe Ferriola died of kidney failure after battling cancer and heart problems. He died in Methodist Hospital in Houston, where he had been treated by the renowned Dr. Michael DeBakey, who has also treated Sam Giancana. The stress and tensions of being a mob boss exact a heavy price. There's always the fear of crossing somebody else within the outfit, as well as the threat of prosecution.

But even with the death of its leader, Chicago's family of the LCN carries on. In fact, it is the FBI's official position that out of the twenty-four families in the country, only two are carrying on their long tradition of strength—and one of them is Chicago. My sources inside the mob and inside law enforcement in Chicago tell me that as the mob realized that Ferriola was waning, it made the appropriate arrangements for succession. Accardo, the old bear who is now in his mid-eighties, has been seen once again meeting with other mob leaders in Chicago. In recent years, he's mostly stayed in his Palm Springs home, particularly during the winter. Even though Accardo might be playing his eighteenth hole, he remains the strong consiglieri at a time when his capability and experience is needed the most.

In Chicago, Accardo stays in the guest quarters of his daughter's home in the Barrington area. In the spring of 1989 he was seen consulting Sam Carlisi and John Di-Fronzo, leading most investigators to believe that those two would be assuming Ferriola's mantle. "Wings" Carlisi is the former driver-bodyguard of Joey Aiuppa, now in federal prison in Minnesota after conviction in "The Strawman Case" in Kansas City. "No Nose" DiFronzo, whose base of operations in Elmwood Park brought him to the attention of Jackie Cerone, was just a common burglar when I worked in the Windy City, and his ascension is a surprise to me (although I did mention him in 1983 in my testimony before the Senate). Cerone is in federal prison in Texas after conviction in the Strawman case. (The Strawman case led to the conviction of nine mobsters from cities as diverse as Chicago, Cleveland, Milwaukee, and Kansas City for skimming gambling profits at the Tropicana in Vegas.)

I was told by a mob source in the spring of 1989 that Cerone continues to exert a strong influence on organized crime in Chicago, being consulted regularly in prison by people who bring his orders back to Chicago.

This pattern resembles what Paul Ricca did while he was in prison in Terre Haute in the mid-1940s as Accardo was taking over from him. Accardo himself would visit Paul, posing as Joseph Imburgio Bulger, a Chicago attorney, who was on Ricca's visitation list. In the 1930s, Lucky Luciano, the New York boss, ran his operations from Sing Sing, while Capone did so from Atlanta until those tactics caused his transfer to Alcatraz. Cerone, although in his mid-seventies, is a vital physical and mental specimen; even behind bars he is a force to be reckoned with.

I'm told that Rocky Infelice, Vince Solano, Dominic Cortina, and Donald Angelini remain powerful figures in Chicago. My friend inside the mob tells me that Donald is Chicago's man in Las Vegas and the rest of Nevada. But my friends in law enforcement in Chicago and Las Vegas have not caught him out there yet, although he has been tailed in California and other western states. In Las Vegas law enforcement has reason to suspect that the Buffalo family is making inroads, and agents there are watching them.

In May 1989, Jim Brosnahan, an outstanding attorney with Morrison and Foerster in San Francisco, called me. He had been retained as the defense attorney for a multimillionaire former cabinet member in Jerry Brown's California gubernatorial administration who had just been indicted in a money-laundering case investigated by the FBI in San Diego. Would I work with

him as the chief investigative attorney? I told him I was pleased
to be solicited, but my first thought was not to work against my
old colleagues in the FBI. He sent me the indictment and other
papers pertaining to the case, however, hoping I could see fit to
change my mind. I immediately noted that Chris Petti, a code-
fendant and a man known to me as the Chicago mob's representative in San Diego, had been seen by the FBI meeting with
Donald Angelini in San Diego on three occasions in recent
months. That helped me conclude that I wanted no part of that
defense team, as lucrative as it would be. It also confirmed, as I
suspected a year before, that Angelini was the Chicago mobster
now responsible for their West Coast operations, having taken
over for Tony Spilotro when Spilotro was murdered gangland
style in June 1986. Petti had been Spilotro's man responsible for
San Diego. Now he was Angelini's man, Angelini being responsible for such territories as Las Vegas, San Diego, Los Angeles,
and Arizona with old Spilotro lieutenants such as Petti, Joey
Hanson in Los Angeles (Marina del Rey), and Paulie Shiro in
Phoenix (Scottsdale) as his main underlings. Angelini, whom I
have arrested twice and confronted dozens of times, would now
appear to be one of the kingpins in the Chicago mob hierarchy.

Gus Alex, Pat Marcy, and John D'Arco remain in place. The
connection guys continue to work their trade in Chicago's halls
of justice. Chuckie English, who brought me the message that
Sinatra would be the man to set up any meeting between Giancana and the Kennedys, has been murdered by his own people.
My sources say Chuckie was murdered for continuing to bad
mouth the successors to his buddy, Giancana, even after repeated warnings.

Allen Dorfman was murdered by the Chicago mob after conviction in the Pendorf case, due to the mob's concern that he
wasn't strong enough to withstand a long prison sentence without talking of his association with the Teamsters Union. The
Teamsters Central States Pension Fund is no longer available to
the LCN, and the government has won a major settlement in the
RICO case it brought against the Teamsters in March 1989. In
that settlement, the Teamsters agreed to a three-man board of
overseers and agreed to let their membership hold secret elections.

In the spring of 1989, the Chicago office of the FBI felt they
were close to solving a string of gangland murders in Chicago—

a major investigation headed by my old pal, Gerry Buten, who had the unprecedented assistance not only of a squad of agents but of five Chicago PD detectives and three state policemen, assigned full time, with desks in the Chicago FBI office in the Dirksen Federal Building. This was an obvious indication that the FBI now has reason to trust the Chicago Police Department and the Illinois State Police. Frankie LaPorte would be astounded.

The FBI itself continues to battle hard in the fight against the mob. The five different mob street crews in Chicago are covered by five separate squads, and FBIHQ exercises constant pressure on them to do the job. Oliver "Buck" Revell, another old Chicago pro, is now the executive assistant director in charge of investigations for the Bureau. One of the other two EAD's is John Otto, who helped me get my transfer to Tucson in spite of the difficulties involved. They make sure organized crime investigation remains a top FBI priority. In fact, I was told by a highly placed FBI supervisor in the spring of 1989 that within a year there will be arrests in Chicago that will "bring the Chicago mob to its knees."

Although Chicago papers were speculating that the Chicago outfit was easing its absolute restriction against narcotics trafficking and, in fact, under Ferriola had become so involved, there seems to be no real evidence of that. My contacts inside the mob insist that the prohibition against drug dealing remains as hard and fast as ever, and one tells me that as long as Tony Accardo has anything to say about it any made member caught "dirty" with narcotics will be dealt with as usual: "clipped." And, Accardo still has the ultimate vote. My sources inside the FBI confirm that they find no evidence that the Chicago mob is involved in narcotics.

I'm told that a few individuals with tenuous connections to the mob have been convicted of narcotics dealing. One or two collectors of the street tax—the fee leveled by the mob on people involved in activities such as pornography—have been involved, but no hardcore or made member has been. I'm aware that Rocky Infelice, the underboss under Ferriola, has a conviction for narcotics, but that was long before he became involved with the LCN and long before he was made. In fact, in the early eighties, a couple years before he was murdered, Chuckie English came out to Arizona to see me in order to check out Infelice's possible involvement in narcotics. When I told Chuckie I knew nothing of it, that the Drug Enforcement Administration had arrested Infelice, he seemed relieved and felt that if Infelice had been involved in narcotics to any significant extent that I would have known about it. Shortly after he went back to Chicago, Infelice was named the underboss. I always felt that perhaps I should have adopted a different slant on his background for Chuckie's sake and that it might have prevented Infelice's ascension. But he has been no worse than others who might have filled the slot.

So the beat goes on. The long battle of law enforcement against the Chicago mob continues unabated. The long, hard road with its many potholes that we have traveled, with all its hills and valleys keeps on awinding, as the song goes. I have been proud to be a part of it, the "Rock," the nemesis (at least in the eyes of some), and proud that able agents like Art Pfizenmayer, Gerry Buten and Pete Wacks—who is probably the foremost street agent in the FBI today—are still in place to fight the battle. And I am proud that I am able to consult with them from time to time, still an ex-officio member of the crew. I'm also currently active again as the special consultant on organized crime for the Chicago Crime Commission, that fine group of private citizens formed in 1919 to fight organized crime, political corruption, and inefficiency in government in Chicago. They do a great job for the Chicago citizenry, keeping the searchlight on the mob. John Jemilo, the executive director and a former deputy superintendent of the Chicago Police Department, is its very capable leader—in the mold of his predecessors Virgil Peterson and Pat Healy, two past giants in the field. I am proud to assist in the commission's work.

So, I'm still able to "fight the good fight" against the mob.

As long as I remain as physically, emotionally, and mentally fit as I feel I am now, I will continue the fight. It is what I thrive on. When I was fifteen I looked for the challenge of the boxing ring. Now nearly fifty years later, I still need the stimulation of competition. It comes from my inner conviction that I am still the mob nemesis. My desire to beat those guys continues to consume me. One day we will win or they will win or I will wither away. Until then, I "keep punchin' " and I "keep the faith."

EPILOGUE

Updating the status of the mob in Chicago into the 1990's, it is noted that Tony "Joe Batters" Accardo remains the *consiglieri* in Chicago, the guy who calls the major shots. He continues to reside along the Indian Wells Country Club fairways in the Palm Springs area but comes into Chicago frequently where he stays with his daughter and her husband in their guest house in the Barrington Hills area.

The major recent change involves Donald Angelini, the "Wizard of Odds." He was convicted, with his fellow capo, Dominic "Large" Cortina, of an Interstate Transportation in Aid of Racketeering-Gambling charge in late 1989, and at present both are in federal prisons. In addition, both were indicted on October 26, 1989 on federal charges of using a suburban Baltimore, Maryland bingo parlor to launder cash from their gambling ventures. They were also charged in the indictment filed in the U.S. District Court in Baltimore with conspiracy to burn down a competing bingo hall called the Bingo Palace. They will be tried in Baltimore after they complete their sentences for the ITAR-Gambling conviction.

Obviously, therefore, Angelini no longer represents the Chicago mob in Las Vegas.

Otherwise, Gussie Alex continues to lead the "connection guys" in Chicago; Rocky Infelice, John "No Nose" DiFronzo, and Sam "Wings" Carlisi are the other top leaders there. Sal DeLaurentis and Lou Marino, other upper echelon leaders, are incarcerated along with Infelice in the MCC, the Metropolitan Correctional Center, in Chicago after being indicted for a RICO violation and while awaiting the trial which has been set for September, 1990 in the U.S. District Court.

Pat Marcy and John D'Arco, Sr., continue as functionaries of the Regular Democratic Organization of the First Ward of Chicago. However, they are believed to be targets of Operation Kaffe Klatch, the FBI investigation into corruption in Chicago—the investigation which included the installation of the video camera in Counsellor's Row Restaurant as described herein.

There have also been some humorous developments since this book was first published, most of which occurred during the book tour while I was promoting this book. While in Las Vegas, I appeared on Don Jaye's "Talk Back" radio program on KLAV, broadcast from the Landmark Hotel. After I detailed the history of mob involvement in the casinos, Jaye took a break for a commercial with the announcement that "Mr. Roemer has now given us the history of the mob in Las Vegas. When we come back, he will tell us about current mobbed-up casinos here." Within a minute all power to the Landmark Hotel went down. Jaye joked. "Must be the ghost of Bugsy Siegel." When the power stayed off, however, for three more hours, well after the talk show was scheduled, the talk became more ominous. Especially since it was only the power to the Landmark that went off, not to the Riviera, the Hilton, or the Convention Center across the street. Now it became "Somebody doesn't want the public to know."

During a reunion of my law class at Notre Dame in June, 1989, I was assigned a room on campus with a fellow graduate of the class of 1950. After unloading my bags in the room, I journeyed to the famous Grotto to make a visit. When I returned, the registration clerk informed me that my roommate had moved out. He had read this book, and upon learning that I was to be his roommate, asked to be reassigned. When I caught up with him later he told me: "Roemer, the mob will get you one of these days; I don't want to be there when they do!"

"Hard Copy," the nationally syndicated television program, asked me to be on their show in the fall of 1989. They requested that I take them to Chicago and narrate scenes from my "exploits" and from the history of the mob in Chicago. As part of the show, I took them to the current mob meeting place, a restaurant in Norridge, a northwestern suburb. While we were filming outside, the car hiker went inside to alert the mob of our presence. After the filming, I went inside alone to say hello. Inside I was greeted by Don Angelini. After a few pleasantries, I asked him if he had read this book. He replied that he had. I asked him how he liked it. He merely scowled, flipped his fingers under his chin, and glared at me.

Actually, Angelini possesses more social graces than almost any of his mob associates, although Accardo, Alex, Cerone, and Cortina are in about the same class. He is intelligent, well-read, a gentleman, and a fine family man. He gained his position as a capo, a captain, in the mob as a result of his expertise in the lifeblood of any mob, gambling, and not as a killer, as did so many of his colleagues.

I was curious to learn how many of the mobsters read this book and what their reaction was to it. When I addressed this query to a couple of the informants inside the outfit whom I had developed while with the FBI in Chicago for over two decades and with whom I still maintain contact, I found that almost without exception all of the 300 Chicago "made" guys have at least skimmed it—depending on their literacy. All were interested in seeing how I depicted them. None enjoyed the book. However, none had any particular complaints about its accuracy.

Of the fifty or so book reviews this book received, only one could be deemed unfavorable. That one criticized me for being hypocritical when I wrote that I pray for some of the hoodlums I came up against. I feel sorry for the mind-set of the reviewer if he has problems believing that.

Outside Chicago, Joe Bonanno continues to reside just several miles from the author, in midtown Tucson, Arizona. He is relatively inactive, however, in the affairs of the Bonanno family of La Cosa Nostra, headquartered today in Brooklyn.

This author continues his crusade against the mob. I continue to "keep punchin' and keep the faith!" In this regard, I authored a follow-up book to this one, *War of the Godfathers*. Within three weeks of its being published in November of 1990, it climbed high on the *Chicago Tribune* bestseller list based on actual sales in the Chicago area.

Glossary

AIRTEL	An internal communication between FBI field offices and/or FBIHQ which mandates priority attention. It derives its name from the fact that the leads contained therein are to be covered as expeditiously as those set out in a teletype, but instead of being teletyped it is sent airmail (even in the days when other FBI mail was mailed by ground transportation).
APALACHIN	The watershed meeting of scores of prominent members and leaders of La Cosa Nostra in 1957 in the village of Apalachin, New York. It was discovered and broken up by the New York State Police, which led to the formation of the Top Hoodlum Program by J. Edgar Hoover, bringing the FBI into investigation of organized crime per se for the first time in its history.
ASAC	Assistant Special Agent in Charge of an FBI field office.
AUSA	Assistant United States Attorney.
THE BUREAU	Used to identify the FBI. Also used internally in the FBI to signify FBIHQ in Washington, D.C.
THE BLACK BOOK	The official list, promulgated by the Nevada Gaming Commission, of persons excluded from Nevada hotels and casinos, mostly mobsters.
BOOK	A bookmaking establishment.
BUG	A microphone placed in a premise; differentiated from a tap (on a phone).

C-I	Criminal Squad Number One in the Chicago FBI Office; assigned the investigation of organized crime. Formerly handled all major criminal cases.
CAPO	A captain in the La Cosa Nostra; short for caporegima (captain of a regime) or capodecima (captain of ten). Crew can be any number. A high level position in organized crime, just below the boss, underboss and consiglieri.
CASTELLAMMARESSE WARS	The internecine wars in New York between mob families. Its conclusion resulted in the formation of the five New York families as they are constituted today and of the "Commission," the national ruling body of organized crime.
CASINO CONTROL COMMISSION	The agency designed to police the gaming industry in Atlantic City; the Division of Gaming Enforcement is its investigative arm.
CENTRAL STATES PENSION FUND	The Central States, Southeast and Southwest Areas Pension Fund of the International Brotherhood of Teamsters Union. For many years used as the "bank" of the Chicago family of the LCN and, to a lesser extent, by other families. Used to finance high risk ventures by loans to associates of the LCN, frequently in Las Vegas.
CHICAGO CRIME COMMISSION	A privately financed group of concerned citizens, interested in good government in Chicago. Organized in 1919 to spotlight organized crime and corruption in Chicago. Offices at 79 West Monroe.
CIA "ASSET"	A source or informant of the Central Intelligence Agency.
CIA "CUTOUT"	A non-employee of the CIA used by the agency for a special mission, sometimes to contact third parties and thereby insulate the agency.
CIP	The Criminal Intelligence Program of the FBI. The nomenclature used by the FBI from the early 1960s to the early 1970s for its program of organized crime investigation. Formerly known as the Top Hoodlum Program and now known as the Organized Crime Program.

CIRCUS GANG	A group of hoodlums, mainly on the West Side of Chicago in the 1920s. Spawned the likes of Tony Accardo and others who were assimilated into the Capone mob and became hard core members of organized crime in Chicago.
"CLIP"	To murder in gangland style.
"CON"	Deception; duplicity. As in "con game" and "confidence man."
CONSIGLIERI	The highly respected advisor or counselor in an organized crime family. Ordinarily a senior member with considerable accomplishments therein. Tony Accardo has been the consiglieri in Chicago ever since he voluntarily stepped down as absolute boss in 1957, surrendering his position to Sam Giancana.
COUNTER SURVEILLANCE	Measures to ensure against a surveillance; usually by using third persons and cars.
CONSULIERI	Used interchangeably with consiglieri.
THE COMMISSION	The national ruling body of the LCN. Consists of nine to twelve members who are the bosses of families of the LCN in Chicago, New York (five), Detroit, New England, New Jersey, Philadelphia, and sometimes Pittsburgh, Cleveland and Buffalo.
"COMP"	Term used in gaming industry to signify complimentary services given to "high rollers" and other V.I.P.'s, such as free rooms and meals.
"CONNECTION GUYS"	A group of very important members of a LCN family responsible for corruption of public officials, members of the judiciary, law enforcement officers, labor leaders, or anyone else in position to provide favorable treatment to the family. Called "the corruption squad" by FBI agents in Chicago. A prime investigative interest of the author.
"DISNEYLAND"	Name given to headquarters of the Intelligence Unit of the Chicago Police Department in the 1960s by police officers and adopted by the mob.
DIVISION OF GAMING ENFORCEMENT	The regulatory agency designed by the State of New Jersey to police the gaming industry in Atlantic City. A division of the Casino Control Commission which conducts investigations of license applications and other matters.

"DRY CLEAN"	To take evasive and precautionary action to preclude a physical surveillance.
"ELSUR"	An electronic surveillance; a "bug."
"FAMILY"	A branch of the LCN; located in 24 cities across the country. Named for its boss in the early 1960s, such as the "Giancana Family" or the "Gambino Family."
FBIHQ	FBI headquarters in the Hoover Building at 9th and Pennsylvania Ave., Washington D.C.
FBIRA	The FBI Recreation Association with a chapter in each field office.
FIVE POINTS GANG	A gang of hoodlums in Brooklyn, N.Y. Spawned Johnny Torrio, later to become Al Capone's mentor in Chicago.
"FISUR"	A physical surveillance.
FORTY-TWO GANG	The gang of young thieves and burglars who grew up in the Patch, that area of Chicago centered at Taylor and Halsted Streets on the near southwest side that spawned several hoodlums who later became top leaders of the Chicago LCN, such as Sam Giancana and Sam Battaglia.
"THE G"	Term used by mobsters to refer to government agents, particularly FBI agents.
"GHOST JOB"	A job with a municipal or state agency provided by a city official for a favored beneficiary, which usually does not require the job holder to report for work or perform any services. Sometimes features "kickbacks" to the patron but is almost always a reward for some service other than the designated work or for a beneficiary who is favored by a third party having influence over the city official—for instance, a relative of a mobster who has influence over the official. Sometimes used interchangeably with the term "payroll job."
GLITTER GULCH	Downtown Las Vegas; primarily Fremont Street.
"GRIND JOINT"	A casino which thrives on "grinding" patrons in and out quickly, the intent being to win money quickly.

"THE GREYLORD CASE" Investigation of the Chicago FBI Office and the United States Attorney's office for the Northern District of Illinois (Chicago) of corruption in Cook County, Illinois courts, particularly the traffic courts. Has resulted in over eighty convictions of judges, lawyers, police officers, and bailiffs during the mid to late 1980s.

"THE HOLLYWOOD EX-TORTION CASE" Infamous case wherein the Chicago mob under Frank Nitti and Paul Ricca extorted almost $2,000,000 from all Hollywood film studios in 1930s through labor unions they controlled. Resulted in major scandal in Truman administration when convicted mobsters received early paroles. Nitti committed suicide upon indictment.

"HIGH ROLLER" A gambler in a casino who wagers high amounts of money and is given preferential treatment by casino management. A "V.I.P."

ITWI; ITAR AND ITWP The anti-gambling statutes passed in 1961 giving the FBI jurisdiction for the first time in this area. The most important of these statutes is Interstate Travel in Aid of Racketeering, which is the statute used to convict Jackie Cerone and his top aides when Cerone was the mob boss in Chicago in the early 1970s. Interstate Transportation of Wagering Information also has been used to convict interstate gambling kingpins; however Interstate Transportation of Wagering Paraphernalia is a little-used act.

INCENTIVE AWARD A cash award given to FBI agents by FBIHQ for particularly meritorious accomplishment.

"JUICE" Loan sharking; shylocking. Loaning of money, almost always to high risk borrowers, at usurious rates of interest, usually "six for five." (a commitment to pay back six dollars for every five borrowed). A commitment made with knowledge that physical violence will be used if necessary to recover the amount of the loan and the usurious interest.

KEFAUVER COMMITTEE A committee chaired by Senator Estes Kefauver (D-Tennessee) which held hearings on organized crime in the United States in the early 1950s.

LETTER OF COMMENDATION	A letter, generally from the FBI director, to any employee worthy of special recognition for services well performed.
LA COSA NOSTRA (LCN)	Traditional organized crime in the United States. Italian for "our thing." The term given organized crime by its leadership when it was formed. Used extensively in the east but almost never by its members in Chicago.
"THE LOOP"	The downtown area of Chicago.
"MADE GUY"	An actual member of the Chicago family of La Cosa Nostra; an initiated member. In New York a "wise guy."
"M.O."	Modus Operandi. The method of operation of a law enforcement agency to conduct routine investigation or of a mob to conduct its ordinary activity.
MAFIA	Strictly speaking, the Sicilian group of organized crime. Used herein, however, interchangeably with the La Cosa Nostra, the mob, the outfit, organized crime. However, the Sicilian mafia and the LCN are two separate and distinct organizations. For instance, the "Pizza Connection" case prosecuted in the late 1980s in Manhattan concerned the Sicilian Mafia and had little connection with the LCN.
"MARKER"	In gaming industry parlance, an I.O.U. The paper manifestation that a debt is owed to a casino or sports book.
THE MAGNIFICENT MILE	That stretch of Michigan Avenue on the near North Side of Chicago from the Chicago River and the Wrigley Building to the Outer Drive and the Drake Hotel. An area of luxury shops corresponding to New York's Fifth Avenue or Beverly Hills' Rodeo Drive.
"THE MAYFIELD ROAD GANG"	A group of organized crime figures in the 1930s and 1940s in Cleveland, mainly involved in gambling in northern Ohio and in northern Kentucky. Headed by "Moe" Dalitz. Top figures therein moved the base of their operations to Las Vegas in late 1940s where they allegedly fronted for the New York and Chicago mobs in hotel-casinos.

THE MCCLELLAN COMMITTEE	A select committee of the U.S. Senate chaired by Senator John L. McClellan (D-Arkansas) which conducted hearings on organized crime around the country in the late 1950s and early 1960s. A predecessor of the U.S. Senate Permanent Subcommittee on Investigations before which the author testified in 1983.
"MUSTACHE"	Reference to an old line, old time mob figure; usually an aging Sicilian or Italian. Also: "Mustache Pete."
NEVADA GAMING BOARD; NEVADA GAMING COMMISSION	The Commission is the regulatory agency legislated by the state of Nevada to police its gaming industry and, among other things, to restrict licensing to reputable applicants. The Board is its investigative arm.
NHO	The New Haven field office of the FBI.
NYO	The New York field office of the FBI.
ORGANIZED CRIME PROGRAM	Formerly called the Top Hoodlum Program and then the Criminal Intelligence Program, the OCP is the FBI's program mandated to investigate organized crime.
"OFFICE"	A bookmaking establishment.
OMERTA	The oath of secrecy taken by "made" members of the La Cosa Nostra and the Mafia not to reveal the secrets of the organization or to inform on its members and associates.
"ON THE ARM"	To muscle, to intimidate, to extort.
"ON THE PAD"	On the payroll of a mobster; usually refers to a police officer who is accepting graft from the mob in return for favorable treatment.
"THE OUTFIT"	A popular name, even among its members, for the Chicago mob. Frequently used to refer to the Chicago mob by Chicago newspapers, radio and television. Also by law enforcement.
"TO PACK"	To carry a gun; to be armed.
"PAYROLL JOB"	See "ghost job." Used almost interchangeably.
"THE PENDORF CASE"	Investigation of the Chicago FBI and the Justice Department Strike Force in Chicago which resulted in convictions of Allen Dorfman, of the Central States Pension Fund of the Teamsters, Roy Williams, president of the Teamsters, and Joey "The Clown" Lombardo, a Chicago capo. A major accomplishment of the FBI and the Justice Department.

"PINEAPPLE"

A small bomb, a favorite of the Chicago mob under Capone and Nitti. Also the type of microphone planted by the author and his associates in the FBI in mob headquarters in Chicago in the late 1950s through the mid-1960s.

QUALITY RAISE

A particularly unusual raise given to a handful of FBI agents annually in a field office for exceptional service during the previous year. Whereas a letter of commendation or an incentive award (other rewards for meritorious service) generally are for a specific instance of accomplishment, a quality raise is generally for exceptional service over a long term on many assignments and is renewed on an annual basis for the rest of the employee's career. The highest award for a street agent.

RACE WIRE

The wire system used in the 1930s and 1940s to speed the results of horse races to bookmakers throughout the country; necessary for bookmakers in order that patrons became immediately aware at the conclusion of a race as to the results so that they could place additional wagers.

RED BOOK

A confidential listing by Metro, the Las Vegas local law enforcement agency, of persons having organized crime associations. For use by Metro personnel for intelligence purposes only. Not available to the public; not to be confused with the Black Book.

RESIDENT AGENT

An agent assigned to a resident agency of the FBI, a smaller office which reports to a headquarters city (for instance, Rockford to Chicago, Tucson to Phoenix). A SAC in the headquarters city has the responsibility for that city plus the "R.A.s" which report to him, up to four or five.

RICO

The Racketeer Influenced and Corrupt Organizations law, passed in 1970, making it a federal crime to conduct the affairs of an enterprise through a "pattern of racketeering." A pattern is said to exist when members of such an enterprise have committed at least two acts of racketeering within 10 years of each other. These acts include murder, robbery, gambling, securities fraud, and using the telephone or the mail for illegal purposes. Can be applied criminally or civilly and can result in confiscation of the ill-gotten goods. In a civil RICO case, plaintiffs may collect triple the amount that they claim they were damaged. Drafted by G. Robert Blakey.

RUSH STREET

The nightclub area of Chicago on the near North Side.

S-1

Security Squad Number One of the Chicago field office of the FBI. Investigated underground Communist Party members when the author was a member in the mid-1950s.

SAC

The Special Agent in Charge of a FBI field office. The top job in a field office except in New York, where an assistant director is in charge.

SAINT VALENTINE'S DAY MASSACRE

The killing of seven members of the Bugs Moran mob in Chicago by members of the Al Capone mob including Tony Accardo, the current consiglieri and former absolute boss of the Chicago family of the LCN. On Valentine's Day, 1929.

"SCAM"

A scheme designed to defraud the victim; almost but not always illegal.

"SIT DOWN"

A conference or meeting between mob members with each other or with outsiders.

"SKIM"

The art of diverting money and chips from the tables and slots of gaming casinos before they can be officially counted and recorded. The prime motivation for the mob to be involved in legal casinos. It is estimated that "skim" has resulted in billions of dollars flowing to the coffers of mobs across the country since the late 1940s.

"THE STRAWMAN CASE"   Investigation of the Kansas City FBI and the Kansas City Strike Force into skimming activity of Las Vegas casinos by mobs in Chicago, Cleveland, Milwaukee, and Kansas City. This double-phased investigation resulted in the conviction of the top leadership of the mobs in Chicago, Milwaukee and Kansas City.

SOCIETY OF FORMER SPECIAL AGENTS OF THE FBI, INC.   The organization to which nearly all former agents of the FBI belong. It organizes monthly luncheons in its scores of chapters in cities across the country, has regional conventions and an annual convention (Orlando in 1989).

"SOLDIER"   The lowest rung of membership in a family of the LCN.

SOG   The Seat of Government. Used to designate the headquarters of the FBI under J. Edgar Hoover. Now called FBIHQ.

THE STRIP   Las Vegas Boulevard in Las Vegas; the location of most of the most luxurious hotel-casinos in Las Vegas.

STRIP JOINT   A burlesque theater featuring nude or almost nude female entertainers. Now somewhat passe, formerly controlled by the mob in Chicago.

STREET CREW   A faction of the Chicago family of the LCN under the control of the leadership, Chicago being a monolithic organization under tight discipline.

STREET TAX   The fee imposed by the Chicago mob on marginally legitimate and illegal operations as a license to operate in Chicago. Entirely different than the graft such operations may pay to corrupt law enforcement officers. The street tax is imposed by the mob on burglars, thieves, pornographers, prostitutes, pimps and X-rated movie houses and is becoming more and more a prime source of income to the Chicago outfit.

STREET AGENT   The FBI's front line of combat against lawbreakers. The Special Agent who carries out the task of the FBI in field offices: investigation, arrests, surveillances, undercover work and counter intelligence work. Also called the action agent or in official FBI parlance, the field agent.

STING
An investigative technique. A setup. Used by law enforcement to provide a situation convenient for criminals already committed to criminal conduct. A prime example is the situation whereby a law enforcement agency provides a setting where thieves can fence their stolen goods. Care is taken in proper sting situations not to cause entrapment, whereby the seed to commit the crime is planted in the perpetrator's mind.

TAIL
A physical surveillance; to follow.

TAP
As in wiretapping; to monitor telephone calls, as differentiated from "bugging," placing a microphone in a premise.

"THROW SOME FEAR"
The practice of mobsters to intimidate a victim short of killing him. Many times by breaking legs, kneecapping, or beating; but in some cases short of that by luring a victim into a situation of risk and causing physical fear without actually inflicting physical harm. Used ordinarily to deter conduct deemed a threat to the mob or to induce a course of conduct desired by the mob.

THP
The Top Hoodlum Program.

TRADECRAFT
The art of police work; usually used to define the trade of espionage and counter espionage agents. Used more by CIA than FBI agents.

"TOMMY GUN"
The Thompson sub machine gun, the weapon of choice of the Chicago mob under Capone and Nitti.

TOP TEN PROGRAM
A listing of the ten most wanted FBI fugitives, given widespread attention in the media. Designed to make the public aware of the most wanted fugitives.

"VEGMON"
The official FBI designation for its nationwide investigation of the receipt of "skim" by mob bosses around the country as couriers delivered it to Chicago, Miami, New York, Cleveland and Milwaukee from Las Vegas.

VIG
Vigorish. The rate at which bets on sporting events is made. Usually 11 for 10. At a Las Vegas sports book it takes $11 to win $10.

WANTED POSTER
Officially called an Identification Order by the FBI. A cardboard poster publicly displayed, such as in a post office, identifying a sought-after fugitive.

WEST SIDE BLOC — Group of Chicago politicians and public officials generally regarded to be subject to influence by the Chicago mob. Mainly but not exclusively from wards and legislative districts in the Loop and on the West Side of Chicago.

WFO — The Washington, D.C. field office of the FBI.

"WHACK" — To maim or kill.

WISE GUY — Ordinarily used to describe an actual member of a mob on the east coast. One who has undergone the initiation ritual of La Cosa Nostra. Hardly ever used in Chicago or west of Chicago where the nomenclature is "made guy." "A good fellow."

"WORK CAR" — A specially souped-up car, reinforced, to be used by burglars and thieves to perpetrate a crime and to escape therefrom.

UNDERBOSS — The number two man in a family of La Cosa Nostra. In the east sometimes called the "sottocapo."

USA — United States Attorney, the chief federal prosecutor in a federal judicial district.

Index